THE WILD, WILD EAST:

Adventures in Business
From the Cold War to the War on Terrorism

Thomas E. Meurer

A Topographical Map of Yemen.

THE WILD, WILD EAST:

Adventures in Business
From the Cold War to the War on Terrorism

Thomas E. Meurer

Academica Press
Washington~London

Library of Congress Cataloging-in-Publication Data

Names: Meurer, Thomas E. (author)
Title: The wild, wild east : adventures in business from the cold war to the war
on terrorism | Thomas E. Meurer
Description: Washington : Academica Press, 2022. | Includes references.
Identifiers: LCCN 2022949448 | ISBN 9781680537048 (hardcover) |
9781680537055 (paperback) | 9781680537062 (e-book)

CONTENTS

This book is dedicated to my family.

It took me nearly four years to write and complete this book. My wife, Sharon, spent hours going over each draft of the manuscript for grammar mistakes and clarity. Our daughter, Tanya, a writer and former English teacher who lives in Quebec, enriched it with written corrections and suggestions. Our granddaughter, Amanda Norman, a skilled artist and digital designer who designed and worked with Soumyadev Bose on the book cover. I could not have done it without their help.

I also want to thank my copy editor, Irina du Quenoy, who was of great help in finalizing the manuscript. She is a master of her craft.

This has been a labor of love. Fortunately, I kept pocket journals of my many travels. My trip reports, letters, memos, and later emails were great sources for accuracy, as were press clippings and relevant books that referenced some of my activities. Much of the POW portion came from a private two-volume book that I wrote and edited about H. Ross Perot's POW activities in 1975, called *United We Stand*.

INTRODUCTION

This is a book that I am writing for my daughter, Tanya, my grandkids, Nick and Amanda, and any future family member who may have an interest in it. The idea came to me when my granddaughter, Amanda Norman, brought her boyfriend to dinner one night and, while introducing me, asked what I did back when I was working.

Further, today, many people are subscribing to "saliva test" companies providing them with a DNA history. Sharon and I did this, and the returned diagnosis indicated that I am four percent Neanderthal. Knowing that this is a recent technology, I am sure it will be refined and may, at some point, define the person, location, and general diet of those particular ancestors. (As is, the results were no surprise to Sharon, as she has always figured that I have some Neanderthal in me).

Still, I reasoned that while advances in DNA technology may provide our descendants with a lot of information about our specific characteristics, it will not convey to them the stories and events in an ancestor's life. Thus, this book is also written for those descendants of Tanya, Nick, and Amanda who may be alive hundreds of years from now. Essentially, this a window into a period of time when I was allowed to grace this earth.

This tome is about my life and adventures through more than fifty-seven years of a military, government, and business career in the United States of America from the mid-twentieth century to the early twenty-first. I have also included some life lessons that I have learned along the way.

Over these fifty-seven years, I have had the opportunity to be on the edge, or the sidelines, of history. During this period, I interacted, bumped into, or participated in: the Cold War (1963 to 1992); the Vietnam War (1963 to 1975); the Yemen Civil War (1994); the terrorist attack on America (2001); the long Iraqi and Afghan Wars starting in 2001; the collapse of the USSR and the troubled rebirth of Russia, and the incredible economic rebirth of China. Throughout, I did business in countries that were breaking apart; watched tribalism emerge from the vacuum left in the passing of the Cold War; saw democracy come to much of Latin America; and observed realignment, and in many cases, restructuring after the fall of the failed ideology of communism.

Ironically, as I write this in 2022, a small group of Americans still believe that the socialist government-controlled system is best for achieving an egalitarian society. They don't understand that political leaders mostly strive for power and many of the societies that have tried this system have ended up being run by a "strong man" or a small group of the favored few. Most often, the leader does not want to leave office and jury-rigs an election or constitution so that he can stay in power. Countries that are ruled this way today include Russia, China, Iran, Syria, Venezuela, Cuba, Nicaragua, North Korea, Kazakhstan, Belarus, Laos, and many countries in Africa.

Then there was the revolution in information technology heralded by the entry of personal computers (Microsoft and Apple), software advances that grew almost geometrically in speed and storage capacity, and the internet. By the late 1990s, this began to be the way people communicated and engaged in commerce. I witnessed some of this while working in the software business at EDS. Later, in the 1990s, we were investing in many new "dot com" companies through our internal company, Hunt Equities, Inc.

The interesting thing for me was to see how the microchips (transistors) got smaller as their capacity increased. Computer hardware began changing dramatically. Personal computers, watches, calculators, and mobile phones eventually became substantially more powerful, with many more functions than the nearly room-size IBMN 360/40 computer in 1968, on which I learned to program.

What was also interesting was the impact Moore's Law (which essentially says the number of transistors on a microchip doubles every two years, while the cost is halved) had on the development of these new incredible companies. Once the speed and storage capacity were there, bright young entrepreneurs invented ways to harness this power for commercial purposes. Netscape, Apple, Google, Yahoo, eBay, Angie's List, Amazon, and Facebook all testify to this.

I have done business in one form or another in over fifty countries during my career. (Additionally, Sharon and I have traveled to some fifty-nine countries and counting.) During this time, I have dealt with presidents, prime ministers, foreign ministers, finance ministers, oil ministers, senior military officers, sheiks, tribal headmen, governors, senators, congressmen, CEOs, actors, and people of questionable character.

I have witnessed many changes in the world's political structures, especially the slow and steady wave of change from socialism and communism to capitalism and socialized capitalism of the 1980s and 1990s (China and Vietnam). I was in many of these countries during the changes and saw much of it firsthand since I was dealing with government offices in some of them.

In the late 1980s, I dealt with officials of the USSR on a deal in South Yemen. Soon afterward, when I went back to the "USSR," I returned to a smaller country with the old name of Russia.

I also learned that it is not easy for a country to change from a totalitarian system to a form of democracy. A second or third generation accustomed to the inefficiencies of the socialist system still found it difficult to adopt the newly allowed "freedoms." Democracy meant that you now had to be responsible for many things that the government had taken care of, even though you did not get proper food, job, and medical care from the inefficient economy and the propagandizing, power-hungry people at the top. However, through the control of the press and only allowing people to watch government TV, these regimes managed to persuade people that the whole world was like them for food and basic necessities and that they were better off ruled this way.

These systems evoked, for me, Jean-Francois Millet's painting the *Man with the Hoe* and Edwin Markham's poem of the same title (which you should see and read). Although they were painted and written in a different century as a protest on behalf of the peasants, I think the principle still applies, if you think about the ways in which the socialist system stunts individual initiatives.

As the Soviet Union changed, so too did Yemen and, in 1990, that country merged with communist South Yemen (People's Democratic Republic of Yemen). It should be noted that during the Cold War, most countries that selected communism—whether forcibly by intimidation and deception (Eastern Europe) or revolution (China, Cuba, Vietnam, Laos, Cambodia, etc.)—decided to let the world think the people voted them in. Thus, the change of the name of the country to reflect this, e.g., People's Republic of China (PRC), People's Democratic Republic of Yemen, German Democratic Republic, Democratic Republic of the Congo, Islamic Republic of Iran, etc.

I was doing business in Yemen continually from 1981 to 2009. My first trip to China was in 1979 and my business there continued through 2014. In both cases, I witnessed the profound changes these societies underwent. I will comment extensively on both later, but for now, it suffices to say that countries with a sound culture and strong institutions can adapt better to political changes.

It was an exciting time to be in many of these countries and see the changes going on around me. I started working with officials in some communist countries that then rejected communism (Albania and some of the countries in Eastern Europe). Others remained communist but became somewhat more liberal economically, like China and Vietnam (socialistic capitalism).

Of the eight countries that were made into separate nations as a result of the Cold War (North and South Vietnam, East and West Germany, North and South Yemen, and North and South Korea), I did business in all but North Korea. As of 2022, the Koreas are the only ones in the list that have not united. Vietnam has remained communist, while Yemen and Germany are democracies (although Yemen is in the midst of a civil war caused by Iran's expansive policy in the Middle East).

Communication changes during this period altered the way business was done. When I started doing business overseas (1969), we used the telex (I used it also in Yemen in 1981), wherein messages were sent and received on a teletype. It was very expensive, and they charged by the word, so messages were structured like you text on your smartphone. The process took time because you generally had to wait in line to get to the clerk, after which you would compose the message and the clerk would send it. Then there'd be the receiving end process and, finally, the message would be delivered to the addressee by hand or mail.

Often, telephone calls from Third World countries took longer to make than they would have been within the United States; they were expensive, too. Sometimes I would call the hotel operator to arrange a time to make a call, and at times, it could be twenty-four hours before my turn came up. There were few overseas lines in the poorer countries.

In the developed countries at first-class hotels, it was faster, but, more often than not, there would be a short wait before the operator gave you a line. But here again, it was expensive and it was not unusual for me to spend several hundred dollars at a time calling my office. Consequently, I did not call home very often and would have my secretary relay a message to Sharon.

Communications began to advance rapidly in the 1980s. By the time we discovered oil in Yemen and put in our infrastructure for producing and exporting it, we had built a microwave communication station (in 1985). Now I could call a manager in the capital city of Sanaa or one of the production field offices and the refinery in the eastern desert or the export facility on the Red Sea by pushing an automatic call button on my phone in Dallas.

The introduction of satellite phones really made a difference. By the early 1990s, they came in a suitcase with a dish you could assemble. Our geologists in the jungles of Laos could dial in and talk to Dallas and send in seismic sections that could be interpreted by a team of geophysicists. Then the interpretation would be sent back to the geologists. This was remarkable as we had instant communications, yet it would take up to two days for the food and supplies to reach the geologists in their jungle camp by ox cart. By 1994, we could carry the phone and dish in a briefcase. (We tried to smuggle one into Yemen that year during their civil war, a story I will relate later).

One day in the early 1980s, our mailroom manager came in to ask me a question about some business mailing we were doing. She explained that a new technology called a fax could transmit letters over a phone line and that this was considerably cheaper than mailing them. We, of course, decided to go that route. (Later, I called my broker to see who made these machines. He said Canon and Xerox. I immediately bought shares of Xerox and made some good money on the stock's appreciation).

In the early 1990s, the internet was introduced to business. (Vice President Al Gore once claimed that he invented it, which became a joke. Still, even though he did not invent it, as a U.S. senator he was instrumental in getting it moved into the public domain).

By then, we had personal computers and could email messages. I was setting up an office in Argentina and dealing with the typical paperwork. The manager in Buenos Aires suggested he just PDF the legal documents to me. Up to this time, our method of sending documents would be to fax them to the office, after which a secretary would make copies and use office mail or hand-deliver them to the legal department. Now, he argued that he could simultaneously forward the documents attached to an email to all the different parties concerned.

When I saw the PDF come in, it was a "Eureka" moment. I now realize I had witnessed productivity take a quantum leap before my eyes, because we eliminated copying the faxes and then delivering them. Further, I realized we were entering a new paradigm in the way communications would be done in the future. This led us into the "Dotcom Bubble" and the growth in private equity in the 1990s (I will comment on this later).

Seeing how the internet has affected our country (let alone the world) and the people, especially the young, has been an eye opener, as was the impact of Moore's Law on computer design. Today our cars are basically a computer on four wheels and a shell body.

Again, this is a tale about my career and I am doing this because of Amanda's question, "what did I do when I worked." With my family as the primary audience, it will include where I grew up and the influences on my life in the early years. It will briefly touch on college and my four-plus years as an officer in the United States Air Force. It will then talk about my joining EDS and later Hunt Oil Company. It will cover the many things I did as an assistant to H. Ross Perot, which includes working in a presidential campaign and later with the White House and then on the release of American POWs during the Vietnam War. It will cover my forty-year career with Hunt Oil Company and the many adventures I had being part of a team to build a multi-billion-dollar company, one of the larger private companies in the United States.

This is not to be a chronology, but rather tales in a career that was formed by doing what was fun, working with smart people with similar values, and always striving to be on the learning curve in the fields of energy, real estate, ranching, and information technology. And taking the forks in the road when my instinct told me to.

I was not trained in the disciplines in which I engaged or headed (other than leadership, which I learned in the Air Force training and as an active military officer).

I learned by asking questions and reading a lot of books, journals, and data related to the job I was doing at the time. More importantly, I always saddled up to or hired people who were smarter than I was and made sure I gave them credit and recognition. But the biggest thing I learned was that people are 95 percent of the business and that the key to success is learning to deal with people and ensuring they know they can fully trust you.

I married the most wonderful woman in the world, who has been my partner in life and shared many of the adventures described here. We had two wonderful children and great times and adventures during their formative years. I had an enjoyable time in the military and even dabbled in politics ... and I had an exciting business career being associated with two great, outstanding, and successful Americans, Ray L. Hunt and H. Ross Perot. Also, because of these associations, I came to know and work with many fine and famous people and participate in activities, events, and adventures that few individuals ever have a chance to experience.

CHAPTER ONE

THE VALLEY OF THE FERN ROOTS

In the northwest part of the State of Washington lies a beautiful valley traversed by a scenic river. Located in Whatcom County, the river and valley, both named Nooksack, are the key features for the major communities in the area.

They are framed to the east by the beautiful Cascade Mountains and to the west by Puget Sound, the vast inland sea bordering Canada to the north and west. Here reside the communities of Deming, Everson, Bellingham, Blaine, Meridian, Sumas, Concrete, and my hometown of Lynden.

During my childhood, the primary industry here included dairy farming, truck gardening (strawberries, raspberries and string beans), and a paper mill in Bellingham.

This was fortunate as there was a lot of work available in the summer for local students and migrant workers from Canada and Texas. It was harvest time … strawberries in June, raspberries in July, and string beans in August.

I started working in the fields in the summer after finishing first grade and I did it every summer into high school. Initially, I worked as a picker, then later as a laborer, and finally in my senior year, as a half-owner of a bean farm with my friend Johnny Clark. (We rented our farmland from his dad, then contracted with the cannery for a loan to buy the seed, wire, poles, and gunny sacks). It was a great learning experience for both of us. Fortunately, we had a good harvest and reasonable prices and the profit helped me with my early college expenses at the University of Washington.

Now, the meaning of the word Nooksack had first been told to me at age ten by my fishing idol, Vern Hawley, a legendary old fisherman on the Nooksack River. He informed me that, in the local Lummi language, Nooksack meant "fern roots."

The Lummi were a native people whose reservation was located around the mouth of the Nooksack River where it flowed into Puget Sound. In the 1950s, the reservation was run-down because of improper management by the then-Bureau of Indian Affairs. Fortunately, today it is a proud nation and I'm pleased to sometimes read how the Lummi are now among the leaders in defending Native American rights.

As a kid, I thought it was neat that we had the Lummi reservation in our county. However, there is a story that I have to tell you about your grandfather, Granny Meurer, who was an original environmentalist when being one was not popular. In 1968 there was a court ruling in the State of Washington that the treaties signed in the 1800s were not being honored and that the Lummi and other tribes along the state's coast should be allowed to harvest all the salmon they wanted in accordance with the stipulations of the original treaties.

To my eighty-eight-year-old dad, this did not allow for the technological advancements made in the fishing industry in the last hundred years. The ruling did not favor the salmon entering the Nooksack to begin their tortuous journey up the river.

These, like all pacific salmon, returned after four years at sea and struggled scores, if not hundreds, of miles up the river to the creek bed where they were born so they could reproduce and then die; that way, their bodies could provide nutrition to the newly hatched salmon coming down the river for the next cycle. My dad, knowing this, reasoned that the now improved and powered Indian nets strung across the mouth of the river would impede the salmon's efforts to spawn. To him, this was not considered when the judge signed the order.

His solution was to repeatedly load the bed of his pick-up with sticks, leaves, logs, and other troublesome flotsam and dump them from the bridge above the mouth of the river so that the flotsam would float down the river and get caught in the nets, which would have to be raised and cleaned while some salmon got through to spawn. He did this until he died in his ninetieth year. I do not know how effective his tactics were, but his heart was in the right place when it came to the fish.

In any case, my parents were part of a group of schoolteachers that bought a line of beach lots from the Lummi on Puget Sound in the late 1950s. They built a beach house on their acre, which became our summer retreat until Dad sold it in the early 1980s.

I was born in the port town of Bellingham. It is, in my opinion, the most beautiful city in the United States, as it sits on the eastern edge of the great inland sea, Puget Sound, and has the beautiful Cascade Mountains and the magnificent Mount Baker to its back. The town slopes to the west facing the Sound and many islands. It has fantastic sunsets year-round. It is a community with a fine university, wonderful year-round climate, and mixed industry and services. If our later roots and investments were not so tied to Texas, we might have retired there.

My uncle Phil Rosser (my mom's brother) was the local executive manager of Puget Power and Light (one of the larger local employers). He was a leader in the community and an inspiration for me to follow a business career. He was a World War II veteran who fought the Japanese and brought back an officer's sword, which he gave to my dad. I have it hanging in my library.

My grandfather and grandmother (Frederick Hermann Meurer and Hannah Endarht Meurer, known as Fritz and Lizzy) homesteaded in Lynden, Washington, in the 1880s and raised nine children there. My uncle Frederick Jr. was killed at age twenty-one in a motorcycle accident. My uncle Bill was a businessman who traveled the Pacific selling timber. He would regale me with his tales of Asia that sparked my interest in that part of the world. My aunts—Helen, Emily, Hannah, Jean, Louise, and Elise—were my village and had some influence on my development. I would spend time in July with some of them in the raspberry fields when they would come up to help Louise (who was married to Ray Shumway) harvest the raspberries on the Shumway farm. Em, Elsie, and Louise were the most influential of the aunts. I would spend some holidays and family visits with all of them, except Jean, who lived a hundred miles away. I had relatively little contact with Jean, who never married and died in her nineties of cancer. However, I do recall that she had grit, because up to a week before she died, she was hand-mowing lawns in her trailer court for whiskey money.

All of the Meurer family were practical jokers, and at our gatherings, each guest would try to outdo the other. This is where I learned my love for practical jokes. I also at a young age appreciated the jokes and would laugh excessively at the good ones. My relatives appreciated this.

The aunts also hovered over their baby brother (Dad was the youngest kid and lost his mother and dad growing up) and nurtured him to be smart-witted and comfortable around older women with humor.

Fritz Meurer and his brother migrated from Germany in the 1870s when, as I was told by Aunt Louise (the oldest of the kids), Prussia was drafting young men. She told me they were from a wealthy family, but their mother told them that if they left Germany, they would be cut off from their inheritance. (I guess they were, since none of the family in the United States ever saw any of it).

While Fritz's brother stayed in Minnesota, Fritz, who had attended the University of Heidelberg, joined the railroad as an accountant and managed to earn enough money to buy land.

I wish he had not sold the land he bought in Wyoming and later in Los Angeles. Both properties would be very valuable today. Eventually, Fritz and his family ended up in Whatcom County in Washington State. I tried to buy their 160-acre homestead from the farmer who later owned it, but he would not sell.

Fritz's brother stayed in Minnesota (we think). Apparently, there are a lot of Meurers in the Midwest. Whether he was a relation or not, I do not know, but when I applied to graduate school at St. Mary's University in San Antonio, the president asked me to visit his office. I realized in the conversation that he recognized the name Meurer, which was an important family in the area. He thought I was one of those Meurers and wanted to "butter me up." When he found out that I was not related to them, I never heard from him again.

My dad, Elbert Hermann Meurer (Granny), was the youngest of the kids, born in 1904, just after his dad, Fritz, was killed by a horse kick to the head while shoeing the animal.

I was told by my Aunt Louise that there was another brother who became a World War I U-boat captain and later an admiral, and that he surrendered a part of the German Fleet to Admiral Beatty of the British Navy after the armistice. During the surrender negotiations, the fleet was scuttled by the "communist crew" on the Isle of Skye in Scotland, which today is an outstanding snorkeling area because of the cold clear water. One of my German colleagues obtained this ancestor's military record and picture, including a painting of the surrender. Admiral Hugo Meurer looks just like my dad, as you will see when you see the picture in the files.

My dad was an intelligent man. He played sports in high school and semiprofessional baseball until he permanently damaged his elbow while trying out for the St. Louis Browns (I heard this story one thousand times).

He wanted me to play baseball, so from age seven to twelve, we would play catch and pepper (where he would teach me how to catch grounders). I think he was pleased that I did well in sports, especially baseball.

Dad worked as a salesman and equipment implementer for the Whatcom County Co-op and was good at his job. I learned a lot from him, especially persistence in sports, dealing with people, and how to survive in the wild.

My maternal grandparents were E. A. and Stella Gants Rosser. Unlike my paternal grandparents, whom I never met, I remember E. A., although he died when I was four. He owned and operated a general merchandise store in Stanwood, Washington. Ironically, when Sharon and I brought our parents (hers were Howard and Lois Frissell) together to meet each other, we found that her Grandfather Frissell owned the general merchandise store on Camano Island, which was about twenty miles from Stanwood. Further, her dad went to Stanwood High School with my mother, although a couple of years apart.

My grandmother Stella was a really strong woman and, up through my college days, we would take the three-hour drive to Stanwood to gather with relatives at her house for Christmas Eve. I remember that, as a small boy, I would help her catch a chicken and then see her chop the head off and scald off the feathers in a boiling vat (this is where I learned the phrase "like a chicken running around with its head cut off").

My mom, Dorothy Rosser Meurer, was wonderful and my idol. I was like an only child since my sister, Connie, was nine years older than me and went off to college when I was eight or nine.

Connie was important to me as a big sister and I listened to her. To this day, I still do. For example, she was the one who advised me to retire. Even though I loved working and told her so, when I turned seventy-two, she asked me when I was going to retire. She said, "You better think about it, buddy, because if you want to do things in your life, you should consider it, as you're not getting any younger." That statement stayed with me for three months and in the end I took her advice.

Her husband, Walter (Woody) Wood, is also an inspiration. He was a successful dentist, now retired, a USAF fighter pilot (which made me want to go into the USAF), and a scratch golfer and tennis player who I have had trouble beating.

My mother was a seventh-grade teacher and very well-educated and always learning. She was also the school's librarian and a part-time librarian at the city library; thus, I spent a lot of evenings with her at the library when I was young. She would provide me with her selection of books to read and I think this is where I developed my love of books. My grandmother Stella was also a librarian, and on my rare, extended visits to her, I would spend time at the library where she worked.

Mother had a sister, Marg Gregory, with whom she was very close. They would travel the world together during the summers as I got older.

I was told I was a very challenging kid in my early years, which may have been the result of some form of ADD. Still, my mother knew how to handle me, although a neighbor told me she went back to teaching to get away from me "for part of the day."

Mom was born in London, Ontario, and later became a naturalized US citizen. She was a great teacher and, one year, won a national Eisenhower Award as one of the top teachers in Washington State.

I can also proudly say that I am the son and grandson of immigrants. Meurer and Endarht are the grandparents from Germany.

We have relatives in British Columbia named Mackenzie, descended from E. A. Rosser's sister, Bertha.

On the Gants' (Stella) side, we have a family tree that includes the poet John Greenleaf Whittier and Noah Webster of dictionary fame. Probably a lot of horse thieves and scam artists, too. Mom traces one of her soldier ancestors back to the Revolutionary War and so she qualifies as a "Daughter of the American Revolution."

I was raised in Lynden, Washington. The town was founded in 1871, on the site of Nooksack Indian Village. To this day, Lynden stands on a rise above the meandering Nooksack River.

Our house was on a hill above the river and we had a great view of the river valley and the 10,440-foot Mount Baker from our kitchen window.

During my childhood, Lynden's population comprised, among others, original homesteader descendants, Dutch immigrants from the Netherlands fleeing the Germans, and people from Missouri who came out to farm the area.

Lynden proudly boasts a legacy of Dutch history. There are a number of Dutch Reform churches of different degrees in town, a separate private school called Lynden Christian, and a separate Dutch cemetery at the entrance to the town.

This was a great environment in which to be raised. It was a small town where everyone knew each other.

Many years later, I was honored to be designated as an outstanding alumnus of Lynden High School and flew to Lynden to accept the award. I was asked to speak to the student body as a "worldly" businessman.

My message was that being raised in a small town was a great advantage for me and that the students, too, should be grateful that they are from a small-town high school because

1. When you walk down the street, you need to make sure you say hi to people, because if you don't, they may call your mom and she will comment on it when you get home. You develop the skill of saying "Hi" to people and making small talk.

2. You have the opportunity to participate in many more school activities with a high school of three hundred than you would in a school of three thousand. This is good for self-esteem and builds confidence.

3. You learn to get along and communicate because you know almost everyone in the school. It is difficult to walk away from people you run into without saying something.

Life growing up in a rural area was wonderful. I learned how to hunt and fish with my dad. During the summers, I played baseball at night and worked on the farm during the day. As I've already mentioned, during my last summer in high school, Johnny Clark and I rented land from his dad and grew string beans and got exposed to the ins and outs of running a business.

In the fall of 1959, I entered the University of Washington as a freshman. It was a big jump to go from a school of three hundred students to a school of twenty-five thousand students in the state's largest city. However, with the people skills I had learned in Lynden, I had no problem adapting.

I joined the Phi Gamma Delta (FIJI) fraternity and dove into studies, activities, and sports. I played and started my freshman year in baseball. However, since it took so much time in late winter and spring and I knew I was not good enough to play professional ball, I concluded that it would be better to spend my time where my real strengths and interests were.

I knew I had to go into the military after college because of the draft so I decided to join AFROTC and became an USAF officer when I graduated. I did well and graduated as a RDMG (top 10 percent and Regular Distinguished Military Graduate).

I was also active in school activities and was the 1962 homecoming chairman. I had to speak to sixty-five thousand people in the stands. (I had about eight lines and sweated the talk all week.)

My favorite courses were economic geography, Far Eastern history and studies, physical geography, and geology. In order to graduate in four years and meet my military obligation, we cobbled all my courses and came up with a degree in Far East Geography. Since I was going into the military and war was brewing, I thought it would be good to know about Russia and China. Little did I know how this major would affect my future.

I really enjoyed my years at UW. I made a lot of friends, learned a lot about dealing with people and, most important of all, met the love of my life, Sharon Frissell.

She was a Kappa Alpha Theta, which was the sorority next door. We were set up on a blind date in the spring of my sophomore year (her freshman) and I was smitten thereafter. She was smart, beautiful, concerned about people, and a natural leader. She became president of her sorority her senior year.

We dated through college and did a lot of fun things together. She was a year behind me, and, thus, during her senior year, I was stationed in Loring AFB, Maine. I wrote to her every day and called her weekly (there was a pay phone in the bachelor officer's quarters and it would take a bag full of quarters to make an hour call).

We got married in Spokane, Washington, on June 20, 1964. I bummed a ride with two fellow officers who were going to Iowa and then Minneapolis, where I boarded a Northern Pacific train to Spokane. The car only stopped for gas and pit stops on the entire trip. We took turns sleeping and driving and ate nothing but K-rations. (These were military meals for soldiers in the field that were opened with a built-in key and consisted of a mystery meat, mashed vegetables, crackers with cheese, and a surprise dessert. There was variety in the meat and the vegetables and it was very nutritious.) The food service officer was a good friend and supplied us with rations for the road.

We honeymooned for four days in New York City (with hardly any money) and then flew to northern Maine. Sharon set up house in Wherry Housing (officers' quarters) and soon got a job teaching first grade on the base.

My only regret on our wedding day was that Sharon talked me out of wearing military dress (officer tux) … She later agreed it was a mistake as I was proud to be a military officer who was prepared to give his life for his country if need be.

CHAPTER TWO

UNITED STATES AIR FORCE ...
1963 TO 1968

In the 1960s, the military draft was in effect whereby any male over eighteen was eligible to be drafted for two years for military service to his country. You could be exempt for certain reasons. Additionally, you could get a deferment if you were in college, but then you were subject to a call up after you had graduated. However, the bulk of the young men had a draft card number (mine was 45-21-41-267) and were on a list to match a quota from their local draft boards.

As mentioned I opted to join the United States Air Force through AFROTC at the University of Washington and received my officer training along with my college education. I was "gung-ho" and wanted to become a flashy fighter pilot. The training primarily focused on science, military history, and leadership and included a summer boot camp at Fairchild Airforce Base in Spokane. This latter included a couple of days of map and survival training.

We were individually dropped off in the remote forest of northwest Washington State and instructed to find a given location by the following day. We were given a knife, topographical map, and a fishing line and hooks. Actually, I found this to be really fun. I was alone and could regain some of the sleep I had lost during bootcamp. I had grown up hunting and fishing in the mountains with my dad. I loved topographical maps, so this environment felt quite natural.

Thus, I easily determined where I needed to be the next afternoon and found a nice meadow next to a creek that had wild strawberries. Here I settled in and made a comfortable bed out of the long grass and cedar boughs, fished, ate berries, and cooked trout. I then wandered into the coordinated location the next afternoon for a big meal of beef cooked in a pit (even though I kind of wished I had an extra day to wander around on my own).

I was commissioned a Second Lieutenant in the United States Air Force, and, later in the Congressional Record, on June 13, 1963, I was referenced as being commissioned and referred to as "an officer and a gentleman" (this was a proud moment for me when I read it). I was ordered to report to Loring Airforce Base in far northern Maine. The only other time my name was in the US Congressional Record involved my testimony before a Senate committee in 1992 concerning American POWs and MIAs.

When I enrolled in AFROTC, I wanted to be a fighter pilot and shoot communists. That was my category until my physical in my junior year. One had to have 20/20 vision to become a pilot. Unfortunately, my vision deteriorated while I was in college and so by the time I graduated, my job had been changed to Air Force personnel officer. I was disappointed but had no other choice. (I always regretted that they didn't have contact lenses in those days.)

I was to report to Loring AFB on a certain date and was given a travel allowance. Another new officer was driving to his new base in Ohio and offered me a lift, which was a fun adventure. It was very educational driving across a cross-section of the country and seeing how the geography changed as we moved east. We also listened to Yankee baseball and the duel between Mickey Mantle and Roger Maris chasing Babe Ruth's home run records for a season.

Once in Dayton, Ohio, I grabbed a flight to Maine and reported for duty. (My first time in a commercial jet.) Within a month, I was ordered to go to a personnel officer training school in Greenville, Mississippi. So, another friend and I drove to Mississippi from Maine for five weeks of training. This also gave me a feel of the geography from north to south.

The ugly racial segregation in Mississippi in 1963 was a real eye-opener for me. I had grown up without witnessing real racism and had not been exposed to what was happening in other parts of the country. The institution of racism was so bad in the South that there was an USAF regulation that a Black officer and a white officer could not ride in the same car together in Mississippi. Also, there was a regulation against interracial dating.

In Greenville, there were signs designating segregated areas for whites and colored. You could see this on drinking fountains and in other public areas. In the movie theaters, Blacks had to use a different entry and sit up in the balcony. Also, there were big billboards along the roads that read "KO the Kennedys" and "Impeach Earl Warren."

This is where I got into my one and only bar fight. A couple of my officer friends (two were over 6'3") and I went into a local bar for a beer. While drinking, I commented on how stupid the people of Mississippi were to put up with racial segregation. The remark was overheard by some locals who apparently took umbrage. As military officers, we were all in good shape so it did not take long, but I did tear the sleeve in my new thirty-dollar seersucker sports coat.

I was glad to get back to Loring so I could sink my teeth into my new job of Chief of the Professional Development Division, although northern Maine was a shock to my system as the winters were long, cold, and snow laden. We could get up to 130 inches of snow each winter. Snowplows would pile the snow up along the roads so you would have to extend your car radio aerial and tie a red rag on it for other cars to be able to see you at certain intersections on base. (Most cars had an external radio antenna on the right side of the window. They were telescopic so you could extend them up to five feet in order to get better reception on your car radio if need be).

I did love my job, however. As a green Second Lieutenant, I was put in charge of a personnel division for a base of five thousand persons. Sixty airmen and five noncommissioned officers reported to me (later, there was an officer, too). This was heady stuff for a twenty-two-year-old college graduate. I fell back on my officer training and realized I needed to earn the trust and respect of these men and women, despite my higher rank.

In 1963 the protocol of the USAF was that the enlisted and officers did not fraternize, but I felt I needed to know my senior people better, so I broke this rule. After Sharon and I married, we had an apartment on base and would invite the NCOs and senior airmen and their spouses to our home around holiday events. (Since the Air Force would not pay for it, we had to stretch the budget to cover the costs).

In the office, I would not act like I knew everything (which I did not) but seek their counsel and then make a decision. I learned three lessons from managing in the Air Force:

1. Listen to your men and women, as they collectively often know more than you do.

2. Give your people credit when credit is due and reflect it on their evaluation reports.

3. Know that the Air Force is always transferring people, so learn to take a new person assigned to your division and work to develop and motivate them to be a productive member of the team.

The latter is the most important lesson I learned since I did not have the choice to select the people for my team. I had to accept whomever the Air Force gave me and basically could not fire, replace, or demote them. Thus, I developed the skill to identify weaknesses and strengths in a person and then work on their strengths to make them a contributing member of the team. (This skill really helped me later in business).

I believe most people have strengths and a manager needs to identify them and then identify what motivates that person. Knowing this allows a manager, in most cases, to effectively build his or her team.

I loved the Air Force but realized that, since I could not become a pilot, my chances for exciting commands and for becoming a general officer were not that high. Therefore, I decided to put in my time, do my duty, and pursue a career outside of the military.

I did develop confidence in leading men and women, an invaluable lesson.

By 1965 the conflict in Vietnam was expanding. Unfortunately, in my opinion, incompetent leadership in Washington by President Johnson, Secretary McNamara, and a close-knit group of advisers caused the United States to head full force into an Asian land war that was not winnable under their rules. I concluded this as a student of Asia and a lecturer teaching "real-time what was going on in the war" to future officers at the USAF officer training school between 1966 and 1968.

Unfortunately, none of the above-mentioned policy makers had any training or knowledge of Vietnam. They made decisions in a vacuum and kept a lot of information from the press and American people.

Initially, this was done because President Johnson was more concerned with his domestic legislation. He treated the conflict in Vietnam as a sideshow and reasoned that he could apply a flexible response to North Vietnamese aggression by hitting them a little harder each time so that they would eventually stop supporting the Viet Cong guerillas and reluctantly agree for South Vietnam to remain an independent country. He did not listen to or trust his generals (although a few of them exhibited equally poor judgment). Johnson thought that if he could get to Ho Chi Minh, he could put his arm around him and work out a deal as he had done many times with a recalcitrant senator.

On the other hand, the North Vietnamese leadership had one goal, to unite all of Vietnam. This made them effective in warfighting, while Johnson made one mistake after the next. Crucially, Johnson's generals argued that the use of massive military force would get Ho's attention, but the president was unwilling to commit on such a scale. (Nixon did it four years later and got an agreement).

Thus crept on a war that I did not think needed to happen, although it would have taken a lot of strategic bombing of dikes and early mining of Haiphong Harbor and other targets that Johnson refused to hit to get the North Vietnamese to agree to US terms. I think, personally, that the use of quick overwhelming force would have done it. (I don't believe there was a risk of Chinese interference, because they were into the Red Guard Revolution at the time; as a case in point, when the Chinese did, later, go to war with Vietnam, they ended up with a bloody nose.).

Secretary McNamara did want to use it as his "whiz kids" felt the gradual pressure on the North would eventually bring them to serious negotiations. They went to the table, but they were not serious. It was just a tactic to make the United States look bad and slow down the war.

This build up in 1965 affected me in that the United States was gearing up to move hundreds of thousands of American troops to Southeast Asia. Additionally, they were calling for the training of more officers at USAF officer training school at Lackland AFB in San Antonio, Texas. I saw this as an opportunity to do something else, applied, and was accepted as a training officer (TAC Officer), a position in which I would have a flight of trainees (college graduates, lawyers, and doctors), many of whom essentially decided to apply for the Air Force Training School to avoid being drafted by the Army. A flight consisted of thirty officer trainees and the course spanned ninety days of drilling and classes.

I taught one class and was then asked to join the teaching staff as a mass lecturer because of my background in Asian Studies. I was given the block on International Affairs, War, and Vietnam (this was one of the most enjoyable jobs I ever had).

I was initially sent to a teaching school to learn how to teach the Air Force way. It was a week-long course and there were about twenty other officers in the class with me. On the final day, you had to select a subject and give a talk to the group for your final grade.

I chose poisonous snakes of Texas and prepared an excellent talk. I was graded down, however, because of a disruption.

You see, the day before a large rattlesnake had been run over directly in front of our class building, which everyone present witnessed. Now, the basic teaching formula in the military is:

1. Get the audience's attention.

2. Tell them what you are going to tell them.

3. Tell them.

4. Tell them what you told them.

I did 2, 3, and 4 very well.

However, for my introduction, I stood up in front of the class and commented on the big rattlesnake that they all had seen yesterday. I then told them that I had wired that big snake to under one of the chairs in the classroom. (I hadn't, of course.) Virtually every officer jumped out of their chair. The instructor believed the snake was there, too. It took several minutes for everyone to settle down and stop laughing.

The instructor felt my introduction was too disruptive and marked me down. Maybe so, but everyone remembered my presentation on the Poisonous Snakes of Texas.

I now moved into the mass lecture department at the officer training school (OTS) and was addressed as Captain Meurer. I would teach sixteen platform hours of lectures each quarter. Because I had to update the lectures weekly, my days would be spent reading major newspapers, journals, magazines, intelligence reports from government agencies, and any other source from which I could get information on current affairs. What was neat was that my supervisors did not have a lesson plan to follow since my lectures were, essentially, current working papers.

The officer trainees had a hectic schedule and many were tired when they came into my class and welcomed the comfortable seat in cool air-conditioning. They were ready to wind down, which presented a challenge in terms of keeping their attention. Thus, I would use audio/visual aids a lot.

My lecture on nuclear war in particular got their attention. The students would file in and take their seats. I would then cause the lights to be turned off. There would be no sound for ten seconds, and then, in the dark, sounds would erupt as if of a jet flying through the auditorium. Then, again, there was silence for five seconds and then the big screen would light up with the growing mushroom cloud of a nuclear bomb.

For my lecture on Russia, I would use the music track from the Russian Army Choir. (I loved the "Song of the Volga Boatmen"). For each lecture, I would do something unique related to the topic. These too would be updated sometimes to current events.

The lecture I recall where I had the most fun and took the most time to prepare was on von Clausewitz's Principles of War. This was in the summer of 1967 and Israel had just defeated three Arab armies (Jordan, Egypt, and Syria) in six days. These events became known as the "Six Day War." The hero of the war was an Israeli general, Moshe Dayan, a brilliant strategist who had lost an eye in war, wore a black eye patch, and spoke English with an accent. As I analyzed the war and battle plan, I realized how many of Clausewitz's principles the Israelis had followed. Thus, I decided to use the Israeli war plan to teach the students about Clausewitz.

For my lecture, I dressed up as General Dayan in a general's military uniform with an eye patch. And I added a little accent to the speech in which I explained how the principles were applied in the Israeli victory. (The accent took a while to perfect and here I had fun while my students learned).

It was a fun tour and Sharon and I loved our time in the Air Force. Also, because I was a regular officer, it would have been a comfortable life long-term. I had an incredible job where I could express myself. However, the war would not last forever and I could not do this for an entire career.

One thing that made my job especially interesting was that the USAF Headquarters sent a Manpower Department Team to OTS to do a "time and motion study" (the Manpower Department in 1967 was an Air Force section of the Personnel Command that quantified jobs through time and motion study and then assigned them to standard organizational charts in the USAF job listings that were common throughout the USAF manning structure for all bases and groups. The periodic reviews were to determine if they needed to add or remove defined jobs in various categories).

Anyway, they spent a day with me monitoring everything I did, which was essentially reading current papers, journals, etc., and, if necessary, updating and giving lectures to one thousand student officer trainees.

I did not know the team's conclusion until I joined EDS. One of the officers on the team was Jim McFarland, who later joined EDS himself. When he saw me in the SED program, he came up to me and told me that my job was the most unusual job they had seen at OTS. They reported to their higher ups that this officer (me) just sat at his desk and read relevant periodical, newspaper, and intelligence reports and then updated his lectures, which he gave for only sixteen platform hours every ninety days. Jim said they all talked about this unusual job, trying to figure out how I had it so easy.

In reality, of course, I had the additional duty of being the junior officer on the OTS selection committee that had the final say on who got into OTS. It was a three-man committee and I spent some of my time using my vote to offset a racially biased colonel, who among other things hated Ivy League graduates.

I was also spending three hours a day in Physical Training, which according to the PT manual included golf as long as it counted over three hours of walking. This is where I learned to play golf. It was a tough life.

It was a great job and I really liked my colleagues Bob Fuller, Bob Palmquist, Bob Lord, Norm Gissell, Doug Collins, and many others. The analogous civilian job was that of college instructor.

The job gave me the latitude to experiment with my lectures and I learned a lot in the process. I also lectured to a lot of "to become famous" trainees who came through the program. One I found out later was Bob Gates, former director of the CIA and secretary of defense under Presidents G. W. Bush and Barack Obama. I got to know him through Ray Hunt while Gates was with the CIA and we were in Yemen.

Once retired and before he went back into government, Bob was a candidate for the job of president of Texas A&M University. He came through Dallas to give a speech and called me to see if he could meet with Ray to ask for Ray's recommendation. Ray agreed and suggested we meet him for dinner at the Palm Restaurant in Dallas.

The plan was that Sharon and I would pick him up at the hotel and Ray and Nancy would take him back. I found out at dinner that he had gone to OTS and had attended my lectures. I was thrilled to learn this, but I also learned he did not like his experience at OTS.

It was an interesting night because when we picked him up at the Anatole Hotel, the sky was dark gray, with darker, pillowy clouds. I explained to Bob while looking at the clouds that it looks like we were going to have a "frog strangler" (a Texas rain that it is so hard it drowns frogs). We went on to the Palms restaurant and had a wonderful dinner and conversation. During dinner, the violent rains had poured out of the sky but were over by the time we left the restaurant. Ray and Nancy now drove Bob back to the hotel. When they entered the access road off the freeway, the water was so high that the car floated on the road. So, Bob and Ray got out and began pushing the floating vehicle while Nancy was behind the wheel steering the front wheels like a rudder. They soon were in a shallow area in a parking lot where the car settled. By then a large road grader came by and Ray ran out and commandeered the driver to take Bob Gates, shoeless and pants rolled-up, to the hotel.

The next day, in his speech, Bob commented on personally knowing what a "Texas frog strangler" was.

Bob became a good friend and, as Ray's guest, we fished in Mexico and hunted elk in Utah with him. Bob Gates is a great American.

One of the great things he did for me is related to my Uncle Phil. When he retired from the CIA, Bob settled near Mount Vernon, Washington, which is not far from where I was raised. Uncle Phil was president of the Bellingham Rotary Club, which is about twenty miles north of Mt. Vernon. The CIA director living in the area was not a secret, so Phil contacted him and asked him to speak at one of the club's meetings. Somehow, Hunt Oil's name came up (maybe it came up in relation to Yemen in the speech) and after, Phil mentioned my name to Bob and told that I was his nephew. According to Phil, Bob had some nice things to say about me; whether they were true or not, it meant a lot to me

Now, however, since I could not become a pilot, I knew I could not make the Air Force a career because I could not easily rise to the rank of general without being rated. Thus, I decided to resign my commission and enroll at the Thunderbird School in Arizona to get an advanced degree in international banking. I flew out there to check it out, apply, and look at housing. I was excited about doing something new. Sharon was pregnant with Tanya, but we had set aside money for this purpose.

CHAPTER THREE

EDS AND ROSS PEROT

As I mentioned, I was considering an international banking career upon leaving the Air Force. However, in November 1967, a recruiter named Jim Just came to San Antonio. My good friend Doug Collins had told him that I was resigning my commission and might be a good candidate for a small software computer company in Dallas called Electronic Data Systems (EDS). Further, unbeknown to me, Doug brought a copy of my resume to Dallas when he went to interview for a job with EDS in September.

Jim called me and explained who he was and about the company. He wanted to meet with me. I invited him to our house the next evening, where he told us about this new exciting, cutting-edge company started by a creative entrepreneur, Ross Perot. Sharon and I were fascinated, and two evening visits later, Jim asked me to fill out some forms and take a test. The information requested was about my life starting from the age of six ... to include all my honors and achievements, even my current bank account. (I liked doing it, but, today, 80 percent of the questions would be illegal because of progressive policies since the 1960s.) When the results came back, Jim invited me to come to Dallas.

I had already committed to the Thunderbird School in Arizona but had not deposited any money yet. Further, I had never been to Dallas and they were paying for it. Why not check it out?

I flew to Dallas. Once there, I met the EDS representative beneath the famed Ranger Statue at Love Field and we drove to the EDS office in Exchange Park.

In the lobby, a short man with a crew cut came on the elevator and the recruiter introduced me to Ross Perot. He was not famous at the time so I shook his hand and said, "Nice to meet you." Once he found I was interviewing with the company, he peppered me with incredible questions as we rose through thirteen floors in the slow elevator. By the time we reached the thirteenth floor, I instinctively knew this was the man to whom I wanted to attach "my star." He was inspiring and in control of the questions. I realized later that my answer that I was a lecturer in international affairs stuck in his mind and may have been the reason I would become his choice for addressing Nixonian politics and POW activities.

My final interview that day was with the president of EDS, Mitch Hart (Ross did not interview the new trainees). I was also very impressed with Mitch and his infectious can-do attitude. At the end of the interview, Mitch offered me a job as a system engineer trainee.

I told him I had to talk to Sharon first before I could give him an answer. He said I had to decide now as it was policy that the offer was only good for the day. Still, when I told him I would call him on Sunday (the next day) with the answer, he agreed and gave me his home number.

Sharon had no problem with my taking the job so I called Mitch and confirmed that I wished to join EDS. I was very excited as I knew it was a company that shared my values and was on the cutting edge of an exciting new industry, computer software. And I was going to be trained into this new field.

I eventually recognized that the genius of Ross Perot was that he saw the future and built an incredible company to meet the needs of the corporate world. In time, I really bonded with him and never doubted that first instinct I had when we met in the elevator: this was the man I wanted to work for.

I canceled my plans for Thunderbird and submitted papers resigning my commission and leaving the Air Force after four and a half years. Sharon was pregnant with Tanya (whom I called George Washington Swartz since, in those days, you did not know the sex of the baby until it was born). Fortunately, we had saved the $700 cost for the pregnancy and birth, as EDS's health plan did not cover a precondition.

On January 13, 1968, we left San Antonio for Dallas driving two cars ... a '66 Ford Mustang Convertible and a '61 bug-eyed Sprite, both red. We arrived in Dallas, found an apartment in Richardson and arranged to have our household goods moved later. I was not to report to EDS until the twenty-third, so we decided to join Sharon's parents, Howard and Lois, on a week trip to Hawaii and stay in their condo on Kauai. Howard's firm, Metropolitan Mortgage, owned a hotel and condominiums on the island.

It was a wonderful week and, somehow, I impressed the hotel manager as he offered me a job to join their management team. I declined as I knew my future was with EDS and Ross Perot. How life would have been different had I taken the offer!

Once back in Dallas, I reported to EDS and was put into the new Systems Engineering Program (SED) and met our manager, David Behne.

David was hired away from NASA, where he had been a manager on the Apollo Project. He was extremely smart and fun to be around. It was Perot's philosophy to take your most talented employees and have them teach the bright trainees, and so David became the training director.

Although he may not admit it, he taught me a lot (although being a liberal arts major, I had much more to learn in the world of bits and bytes and binary numbers than most of his other trainees).

My first day I was put in the second week of a three-week assembler language class. Behne suggested I should attend because I could learn some things.

It was the most frustrating series of classes for me. I think this was because I was one of the first to report to the new SED program and they were still setting up the course, basing it on individual knowledge. All I know is that I spent a lot of time asking Frank Bezadeski what he thought were stupid questions. However, I came to really like and respect Frank. He was the rare programmer who could sit in a chair, seemingly in a trance, do a complicated program in his mind, and then perk up and write out the code.

In that first month, others would join the SED program ... Jeff Heller, a UT grad, star swimmer and Marine pilot in Vietnam; and Les Alberthal, another UT grad and CPA (both Les and Jeff would go on to become CEOs of EDS after Ross sold it to General Motors in 1967). Stuart Reeves came over from AT&T and was a little more advanced than some of us. He, too, went on to become a top officer of EDS. (His son, Eric, married Ross's daughter Katherine). Two others were Vern Olson, an ex-helicopter pilot and John Ehrlichman's aide during the Nixon campaign, and John Assan, who became an assistant to Campaign Manager John Mitchell during the same campaign.

In this early period, there were many other very bright and accomplished former military officers who went through the program and became senior officers as EDS expanded into a large international company. Some later left for other opportunities or were terminated because they violated the EDS code of conduct. (Essentially, Ross said that if your wife could not trust you, then the company could not and you were out).

We were a tight-knit group, since few had families or former friends in Dallas. The initial SEDs were mostly made up of ex-military officers who were hired out of the military and, thus, were not from Dallas. Accordingly, we would socialize together a lot. Sharon and I really enjoyed this, as many of us came from varied backgrounds and had interesting experiences for our young age.

The first four months in the program was nothing like I had ever encountered. I was used to working long hours under great pressure at Loring AFB. But nothing was like waiting until 3 a.m. to get some computer time to test my program, knowing that if I made an error, I would have to come back the next night to correct it.

In the 1960s, we used the IBM 360/40 computer. It took a third of a room to hold it and all of its appendages. It had the memory and power of a two-dollar watch today in 2020. Back then, time and space were important when programming, as computer time was expensive. The 360 had a light on it called a wait light. When it was on, this meant the computer was not running code. Our objective was to make your program so efficient that there would be little or no wait light on. The faster and more efficient your program was, the more money you could make.

We quickly moved to COBOL (Common Ordinary Business Language). It was an easier language that was taught by programmed learning. Here we would sit at a desk and learn by reading a manual, progressing on to the next portion if you gave the right answers.

During the first two weeks, I would arrive at the office for an 8 a.m. class and remain there until 2 or 3 a.m., leaving for home after getting some time to test a program that I had learned from the book during the day. After about three weeks, I decided I was not cut out to be a programmer. I was dragging and it was not fun.

However, one day the light came on: I saw how things fit together and became energized. Behne saw my new attitude and gave me an assignment to write a payroll program. He said he could crash it (meaning the code was such that, if it were not perfect, an unknown instruction could cause it to crash rather than run). I was so confident now that I bet him a steak dinner that he could not dump it.

Here, I learned humility as I spent a number of nights testing my new program after company business was done and the computer was freed up. I tested and tested, so it was running perfectly. The real test, however, came one morning when Behne walked in, hit a special character on the keyboard which I did not plan on, and the program dumped. (From this, I learned to be careful before accepting things people said). It was crushing, but it helped me realize that my value to EDS was not as another programmer. I now understood how the computers worked and what they could do for business, but I knew I was not a dedicated programmer who wanted to converse with a "three-year-old idiot" all day to design a sophisticated application.

From this point on, however, things started to go easier in the SED program, as we now had to learn EDS sales and recruiting. The reason was that the sales and engineering team had to sell new system contracts. Our human resources were such that once we sold a system, we needed more system engineers to help design and implement the new contract.

After the system was up and running, we needed to sell more contracts and those systems engineers who could sell were put in a sales team to close another deal.

Once that was done, we needed more technical people to get the new project completed, which required recruiting. As the company grew, it eventually expanded to include a sales and recruiting department.

The thing to remember is that this company was started by a man with a vision and a wife who loaned him one thousand dollars from her teacher's earnings.

Ross spent four years in the Navy, and by happenstance, met an IBM executive who was touring the ship. The executive was so impressed with Ross that he invited him to call him about a job when he got out of the Navy. Ross did and was hired by IBM immediately. He became a salesman in the nascent sector of computer hardware for the corporation.

By 1962 IBM had changed their quota/bonus system and, that year, Ross made his quota in January and had maxed out. He had the foresight to recognize that the many corporate executives who purchased computer hardware (many units of which he had sold) did not have the personnel to design and operate it, as there were few trained system engineers (programmers and system designers) in the country.

Ross saw the need and decided to set up a company that would become the data processing department of a corporation ... meaning that it was to be outsourced to another specialized company but designed as if it was part of the company.

To do this, he had to convince older conservative executives and board members of a target company that his young systems engineers were qualified and were there to assist and not be a threat to either their company or their confidential information.

Ross did this with corporate camouflage ... he insisted on a dark blue or black suit with a long white sleeve dress shirt and a nonflashy tie. Black wingtip shoes with knee length black socks. Also, short hair, no facial hair, and no gaudy jewelry.

Thus, while EDS people were giving a sales pitch, there would be nothing on the body to distract the potential clients. Further, the clean-cut conservative look helped allay any fears about turning over the corporate records to these young computer experts.

The story of Ross Perot is on the record in books, movies, articles, and other forms of media. I will not recap this other than briefly tell you how he started his company in 1962.

As I said, he was recruited by an IBM executive in a brief encounter on a ship. After spending several years with IBM as a salesman, he was so successful that he met his quota in January of 1962, which affected his incentive bonuses. He began thinking about forming his own business. He knew IBM sold a lot of computers to companies, but there were not enough trained personnel to design the software and operate the systems.

And so Ross formed EDS, on June 27, 1962 (his birthday). Initially, he would rent computer time at night from companies that didn't operate at night and run applications for his first corporate clients. He then began to grow and hired some associates he had worked with at IBM—Tom Marquez, Mitch Hart, Tom Walter—and slowly began to hire others. He took pride in the fact that he would always have two years of a person's salary in the bank as he grew. This new company, Electronic Data Systems, pioneered the concept of taking over the data processing of a company, hiring its people and assuming the computer leases, operating the existing software, and then designing and tailoring the new applications for the corporate client.

In 1967 they hit the motherlode when the Medicare bill was passed by Congress: the men and women of EDS were in place with the technology and skills to meet the needs of this bursting government program.

EDS went public in 1968 and Ross became a billionaire based on the market value of the stock. With new capital, EDS began spectacular growth and rolled out a Medicare healthcare system that major healthcare providers did not have. For a while, it became a turnkey business, picking up some of the biggest Blue Crosses across the United States as customers.

As the business grew, the SED program began to expand, because the new business needed people for implementation and customer services. After a brief training period, SEDs were assigned to projects across the states.

Because ex-military officers were a good source for the SED program, I approached Ross one day and told him that many officers in Vietnam would take their R&R in Hawaii and meet their wives there. I suggested we put an ad in *Time* and *Newsweek* (the most popular news magazines) to set up meetings in a Honolulu hotel with our recruiters for those who are resigning from the military or thinking about it. The ad would include a number for them to call.

Ross liked the idea and told me to get with Mitch. I contacted Mitch Hart (EDS president), and he told me to contact an ad agency and get some designs and proposals.

We met with some executives of Glen Advertising (the largest agency in Dallas). They came out to learn and understand what EDS was and how they could promote us. They then went back and worked up a marketing plan and we set up a time for their presentation. Ross was invited.

In the meeting, the Glen executives presented a beautiful, sophisticated storyboard of ads that depicted soldiers going through the jungle with copy that was long and verbose, but attractive. At the end of the presentation, Ross interrupted and said, "Cripes, Betty Taylor [his secretary] and I could write ads that would get more responses." Mitch, a born battler, responded that he could not. Thus, a bet was set up where the loser would pay for the ads.

A couple of months later, two ads ran for a month on alternating weeks in *Time* and *Newsweek* (Ross's being a full page with black letters on a white background that simply stated "Military officer … leaving service … looking for a job … call our recruiter at hotel number"). Ross's ads had three times the responses the Glen ads did. Mitch wrote a check to Ross, who framed it. If he ever cashed it, I was going to owe half.

Then, one day in March, I was told to go up to Mr. Perot's office. This meeting would be life-changing.

CHAPTER FOUR

RICHARD NIXON CAMPAIGN AND THE WHITE HOUSE YEARS

During a meeting in New York with his old friend Don Kendall (the CEO of Pepsi Cola), Richard Nixon mentioned that he wanted to use computers in the 1968 presidential campaign. Kendall responded that he had a friend in Dallas who was an expert in computers and that he'd ask him to come to the East Coast and talk to Nixon. Pepsi Cola was one of the first clients of EDS and the person Kendall was referring to was Ross Perot. This invitation prompted our meeting with Ross I just mentioned, at which he asked Tony Weinand and me to draft a report on how computers could be used in the 1968 campaign. We went to the Dallas Library, as it was a quiet place to work, and, after a few days, came back with a report for Ross. Since computers in those days were primarily used for sorting and bulldozing massive information and creating useful applications, it was an easy report to write. The key was the software applications as they applied to the campaign's needs for reliable data. And EDS had the manpower to do that.

Ross liked the report and went to New York to brief Kendall and Nixon. Nixon also liked it and asked Ross for some support. Ross said he could give money, but it would be better if he handpicked some of his computer people and lent them to the campaign. (In 1968, it was legal for companies to make contributions to the candidates.) He would pay the salaries and expenses. Nixon liked the idea. Over the course of the campaign, there were several SEDs and recruiters working part time on various parts of the Nixon campaign, but only three of us in the SED were assigned full time ... Vern Olson, John Assan and myself. Vern was the assistant to John Ehrlichman, the campaign tour director, and John was an assistant to John Mitchell, the campaign director. As for me, I was about to do the most interesting, pressure-intense, and fulfilling job I have ever done. But first, let me go back one month.

When we arrived from San Antonio, Sharon and I rented an apartment in Richardson, a suburb of Dallas. One day a man showed up at the door and said he was in a neighboring apartment and had gotten our mail by mistake. His name was Ron Walker. The next Sunday, we met him and his wife, Ann, by the pool. Ron told me that he was a salesman for Hudson Pharmaceuticals but was resigning to become an advance man for Richard Nixon's 1968 campaign.

I was fascinated (and this was before my report for Ross). I asked Ron what an advance man did, and he explained that they went out ahead of the candidates to set up all the campaign activities for a particular event or string of events. You would show up in a town a week before the campaign stop and meet with local Republican officials, raise money for the events (which could include campaign rallies, dinners, speeches, or dedications), and organize volunteers to pull them off. In addition to this, the advance man would arrange food and lodging for the candidate, extensive staff, press, or all of the above. Essentially, the political advance man was responsible for putting it all together on the front line and coordinating it with the Secret Service (which was provided to presidential candidates after Bobby Kennedy was assassinated in June 1968).

I should also say Ron became a lifelong friend and went on to great heights in the Republican Party. He would become a key executive in the White House, director of the US Park Service, organizer of many major Republican events, and a top executive for Korn Ferry, the top corporate recruiting company in the United States.

As Bob Haldeman would say, the advance man's job was to create a set for the three national TV networks. You may have twenty to forty thousand people at an event, but the TV cameras broadcast it to millions.

Running ahead, I should say being an advance man was a highly stressful job (which I loved) since it meant operating in a short time frame, tight on cash, relying on untested volunteers to carry out crucial functions, and fielding politicians who wanted the limelight and would use every method to get it. It was like throwing a "pop-up," high-security wedding for a celebrity, week after week, using volunteers.

Three weeks later, Ross called me into his office and asked, how would I like to work for Nixon. I told him I was a Reagan man but would support Nixon and would love the opportunity. He said fine and indicated that a man named John Ehrlichman was coming into Dallas on Wednesday to interview a good number of SEDs for some work on the campaign.

On Wednesday, I had my interview with John. Interestingly, he was from Seattle. I told him that I went to UW. He told me he was a real estate lawyer and I asked him if he knew my fraternity brother's father, a big developer in Bellevue named Kemper Freeman. He said he did a lot of work for him. We kind of bonded after that.

John informed me he was interviewing for campaign staff and wanted to know my background. I told I came out of the US Air Force, where I had lectured at the USAF officer training school on Foreign Affairs and Vietnam. He wanted to know about my college days and I told him that I was a distinguished military graduate in AFROTC, played some college baseball, was in the FIJI fraternity (Phi Gamma Delta), and had been active in student activities. The latter got his interest. When I told him I was homecoming chairman, he showed real interest in this and asked a lot of questions. I told him I worked on it for six months, built up the organization, and selected the chairman of twelve events that varied from

Homecoming Queen pageant, the famous sign contest on Greek Row, a Saturday night dance with a major music group, the Beach Boys, a half-time ceremony, alumni relations, etc. What I did not know at the time was that he saw this as perfect training for a political advance man. He then thanked me and said no more.

The next day Ross called and told me that Ehrlichman wanted me and two others and, specifically, wanted me for a Nixon advance man and would I like to do it. I said yes, I would, and was instructed to report to John Neidecker at the Dallas Statler Hilton Hotel the following Wednesday. I was to be a trainee, together with another guy from Dallas.

On Wednesday, I showed up and walked into the room and realized the other person from Dallas was my neighbor, Ron Walker. I do not know who was more surprised. To this day, I think that Ron thought I lobbied for the job after our conversation around the pool a month earlier.

Here, also, I met our trainer and lead advance man, John Neidecker. Known as Rally John, he was in his late fifties or early sixties and a legend in the field of political advance men, the Republicans' answer to the Democrats' Dick Tuck, a famous Kennedy advance man. Over the next few months, John taught me a lot and I really came to like and respect him. In between the campaigns, John was in charge of promotions for a major oil company.

This also was the first time I met Richard Nixon, as he was in town for an airport rally at Love Field, which was to be set up under John's leadership. Nixon came into the room and sat on the sofa. Ron and I were introduced, and found the candidate cordial but not talkative.

John mentioned we would need a lot of business cards signed by Nixon so Ron and I could hand them out to local supporters and dignitaries at the airport rally. (This was very early in the campaign and there was no budget for the cuff links, pens, and tie clasps we would hand out after he was nominated in July.) Nixon agreed and John handed me a big stack that I took over to the couch and sat beside Nixon while he hand-signed each one, one at a time with a felt pen on the book on his lap. I just handed and then collected them … no real conversation because I, the verbose one, who would talk to a signpost, was in awe of the man next to me and he was not one to make small talk to someone he had just met. (Wish I had not handed out all of those signed cards, as they were originals and would be worth something today).

The event at Love Field went off very well and we had a big crowd (which I helped raise by running through the terminal yelling that Richard Nixon was down at Terminal A and would be giving a speech in fifteen minutes). This was a technique that I learned from Rally John, which we perfected later during the presidential campaign. I was reminded by Bob Haldeman that the crowd you built was just a prop, as was everything else at the rally. The key was to position the crowd for the network cameras, so that the TV audience noticed huge crowds.

The plan now was for me to attach to the advance travel team and do campaign stops throughout the United States. Two unfortunate things happened that changed this and the assignments Erlichman would give me. First was the April assassination of Dr. Martin Luther King, one of the greatest Americans of his day, which caused the campaigning to be curtailed out of respect for him. This was followed by the assassination of Senator Bobby Kennedy on June 5, with similar results. We began actively campaigning again in late July.

Meanwhile, in June 1968 I was assigned to Washington, DC, by the campaign to work on the organization Citizens for Nixon, headed by Bud Wilkerson, the former coach of the Oklahoma Sooners, which was working in support of Nixon's election.

I was given an apartment at the Alban Towers and our offices were in a building about two blocks from the White House. This was real heady stuff for me. I worked with a lot of people who became key in the administration, like Lamar Alexander, who later became a US senator, and many others who had key jobs in the Nixon administration and went on to become elected or appointed officials later in their careers.

I really came to know and like Bud. I would spend two weeks at a time in Washington, DC, and then come home for the weekend. Bud would invite me to his house with his family on alternate weekends for Saturday dinners. During the week, I would fly somewhere to meet with Republican delegates to try to convince them to vote for Nixon at the convention in Miami. I really loved this and felt I was good at it. Bud gave me all the data I needed on Nixon's strong points to make me a believer and enthusiastic seller of Nixon for president.

I flew to Dallas for Tanya's birth on July 2 and spent a few weeks home and then was told to fly to Miami in mid-July to prepare for the Republican Convention, which would start on August 4th. There is a good family story as to what happened when I came home for Tanya's birth. (Of course, Sharon has a more descriptive story, but here is my side for the record).

Our apartment was directly across from the Richardson Hospital. Only the busy Spring Valley Road separated the two. Sharon was ready, but we did not know when we should go. So, I thought I should go to the office and she would call me when the baby was "moving."

I was in the office that morning and decided to go over to the YMCA for a handball game at noon. While there, I got the call that she was ready to go to the hospital. I immediately ran to my car (the 1953 bug-eyed Sprite) and headed home … when I got to Walnut Hill Lane (halfway home), the car stopped. I could not get it started so I walked to a gas station for help … a mechanic drove me back and helped me get the car started from the vapor locks that had caused the breakdown (I became an expert on sports car vapor locks after that).

I now began the journey home. However, by the time I got there, Sharon had given up on me and had fought the traffic crossing Spring Valley Road, very pregnant and carrying a burdensome suitcase to the hospital. When I arrived, she was in a room and waiting for more labor pains. I sat next to her from 2 to 8 p.m. and nothing was happening, so I said I was going to run across the street to our apartment to cook a microwave dinner. Sharon agreed and off I went. After eating, I sat down on the couch and fell asleep. At about 7:30 a.m., the phone woke me up and the doctor informed me we had a beautiful baby girl. I immediately tore across the street at warp speed to see my beautiful daughter, Tanya, and Sharon. There is a little more to the story, but it has grown into an ever-legendary account such that even I do not recognize it now.

Two weeks later, I flew to Miami to work for Nixon at the Republican Convention. I advanced the events of the convention, which included an elephant, but I was then pulled off to be Mrs. Nixon's assistant at the main event. This was a position I did not want, as I was missing the action; however, my job was to be in the suite and attend to her needs, so I carried it out without complaint. This only lasted a couple of days but required me to watch the convention from the Nixon suite instead of being on the floor. The sad thing is I had been advancing in Miami for a couple of weeks when Ross called John Ehrlichman and said he felt I should be doing a more important job. (Ross was always calling me and asking what I was doing and what was going on). Later, Ehrlichman called Ross back and said he would assign me as Mrs. Nixon's aide during the convention and campaign. I did not want this and it was quickly settled after the convention when John Davies, an old friend of hers, filled that role. Also, Ross did not appreciate until later what a great skill building job the position of an advance man was.

As a side note, I got to know and like John Ehrlichman as an individual and as someone I worked with. He had a dry sense of humor and was a decisive person. It was sad he got caught up in the Watergate mess and spent eighteen months in jail for perjury. I think he was just trying to protect the presidency and follow Nixon's orders.

I did not know Haldeman as well, but he treated me well and gave me opportunities that advanced my career. In contrast to the affable Ehrlichman, Haldeman was very serious. It was unfortunate that both went to jail for trying to protect Nixon.

The Miami Republican convention of 1968 was a great event and an experience that I will always remember as one of the "greatest shows on earth." I got to rub shoulders with famous politicians, Hollywood stars, and professional athletes. One person was Wilt Chamberlain, a famous NBA player. He was there to lend his name as a supporter of Nixon and the campaign took care of his hotel expenses. I remember when it was over, he had charged thousands of dollars for clothing, food, and other items in the gift store … and the campaign had to pay the bill.

Once Nixon was nominated, the real work began. I got on a campaign plane and flew to Mission Bay in San Diego, California, together with Roger Ailes, who had also been considered as a "man maid" for Mrs. Nixon. Neither of us wanted the position and he was going on to do TV work for the campaign (he later became president of Fox Television) and I was going to advance and set up Mission Bay for Campaign School.

I was made for the job at Mission Bay, as this was a week where the senior managers and politicians to be involved in the campaign were to be gathered to train and prepare Nixon and Agnew for the campaign. Economists and specialists were flown in and out to meet and brief the candidates. My job was to make sure the schedules were on time and that the meals were good. This is where the top official leaders in the Republican Party gathered if they were going to have a role in the campaign. I, personally, made sure that I was in the limo to pick up Arthur Burns and Milton Friedman. As an economics major in grad school, Friedman, particularly, was my idol and to have nearly two hours to and from the airport with him in the car was a dream. He was brilliant, funny, and very down-to-earth. He was also the greatest economist of the twentieth century.

One day, Ehrlichman jokingly chided me on the meals, saying they were very good, but too bad we were not on the East Coast as we could have lobster one night. That evening, I called Boston and arranged to have live lobster flown to San Diego, so we had it the next night … that move really impressed Ehrlichman and helped me bond with him. It was actually a risk (I feel you can't get ahead with or without taking some risks), as the logistics to move fresh food were not sophisticated enough back in 1968 to ensure the live crustaceans would get there as ordered, but I decided to go for it and had steaks as a backup if it did not work out.

It was fun to interact with politicians even though my role was one of organization. One I really got a kick out of was my Texas senator, John Tower. He was a party animal and really enjoyed dressing up in a loud sports coat and going out on the town. Also, I remember specialists spent a lot of time with Spiro Agnew (the VP candidate), as he was inexperienced and needed the time to get up to speed, since he would be campaigning separately from Nixon. Later I did an advance for him in Jacksonville, Florida.

Once the training school was over, we advance men were sent to New York to attend an advance man training school for three days. It gave us a chance to meet and bond with newly hired advance men, since we would, on occasion, be working together. We learned our reporting procedures and were given our initial assignments and trained to work with our scheduler, Ken Cole, in the New York campaign headquarters. (This was for the lead advance man on a drill).

Ken reported to Ehrlichman, who reported to Haldeman, but they both traveled and reported to John Mitchell, the campaign manager, and my interaction with him was in certain stops like Mission Bay or when I would visit the New York office. The interactions were limited, however, to exchanged greetings or him chiding me for something. John Assan and Vern Olson were two of my SED associates assigned by Ross to the campaign. Ross wanted top jobs for them, so Assan became an aide to John Mitchell and Olson to Ehrlichman. (You can see the pattern, as Ross had wanted me to be an aide to Mrs. Nixon).

Another advance man out of the EDS New York office was Dan Gilchrist. Dan basically worked out of New York, as did a lot of the surrogates (prominent individuals who would go on the campaign circuit to campaign for Nixon). George H. W. Bush was one of those, and Dan became assigned to him. Thus, he got to know Bush and, eventually, left EDS and went to Houston to work with Bush. They became good lifelong friends and Dan worked on his political campaigns. After Bush lost a Senate race in 1970, Dan went to work at Paine Webber (a brokerage firm) and became an expert in municipal bonds. At that time, he became my bond broker and moved to Santa Fe. Dan made me a lot of money and became a lifelong friend.

Here I want to clarify why I wanted to be an advance man. The job was this: to act as a part of a small team that goes into a location ahead of the candidate (or the president, as it became in my case later) handling all the logistics and, to some degree, the politics on the ground in preparation for a visit. It was a job that was 50 percent creative and 50 percent problem solving.

Ironically, other than the four and a half years I spent as a military officer, the three and a half years I spent as an advance man for the campaign and White House provided the extensive experience that allowed me to develop the confidence, instincts (to be able to detect the BS factor in people), personal skills, and decisiveness to be a good business executive. Being a lead advance man, which I became in time, was the best possible training one could have. In that position, I was in charge at the local level of a campaign or presidential stop. When given an assignment from Cole or Walker in the White House, I would fly into a town to meet the team, which included a couple other advance men, Secret Service, and the White House communications team as well as the local Republicans and government officials.

Even though I was reporting to the campaign advance office on the campaign and later in the White House, I was, as the lead advance man, essentially in charge initially on the ground, since it was a fluid environment.

I would get my instructions, but once the planning and movement started, the only good information was on the ground and often I would just make a needed decision rather than check with somebody. Things happened fast and my people needed sound, immediate decisions in many cases. This is where I learned to be decisive and built my confidence. It became clear that I could be trusted to make a good decision if I had all the facts available. Also, once it was determined that I was sensible and was not afraid of taking the initiative, I began to receive even more responsibility as an advance man.

One case in point was my first campaign stop after Mission Bay. In August 1968 I was with a team of advance men whose responsibility was San Francisco, which was to be the second candidate stop for Nixon after the initial stop in Chicago. We were to have a number of events and an overnight with a large contingent of campaign staff. Thus, we had to plan for a ticker tape parade, motorcades, hotels, rooms, dinners, meetings, campaign stops, and the traveling press corps, who came on a separate plane.

I was assigned the Chinatown segment, which was to be a motorcade through the narrow and packed streets of San Francisco's Chinatown on Grant Street. At age twenty-six, I had to deal with a number of senior officials and convince them I knew what I was doing. Initially, I had to learn about Chinatown and its layout in order to come up with a recommended pathway. Our local volunteers teamed me up with a Bank of America executive, whose name I have forgotten, who was an American Chinese from Chinatown. He was a great help to me as an interpreter (where one was needed as I spoke no Mandarin or Cantonese and did not know how many Chinese locals spoke English or even would have done so if they did). He also introduced me to the protocol of that world. He knew many of the leaders, so it was of great help to have friendly meetings.

The back streets of Chinatown were nothing like I imagined. We left the tourist part, heading to meet the town leaders to introduce me and explain what we were hoping we could do with a motorcade driving through their territory.

We went into a seemingly run-down building, climbed five flights of stairs, and crossed a catwalk right over to the top of a nondescript building across Grant Street. We entered a large room, exquisitely decorated. There were several elderly men sitting around a magnificent round table, carved out an elegant wood. Who would think such a beautiful room could be found in this plain building?

I was immediately introduced to the group of elders and asked to take a seat. I was instructed to relate what we wanted to do in Chinatown with the candidate and to offer a suggested area. We continued talking while servers brought out all kinds of good plates and placed them on a large two-layer Lazy Suzan. I did not eat a lot, but the gentleman next to me took delight in piling some of every dish on my plate.

When we finished, a very elderly man with a wispy beard spoke and said that they would agree to the path of our motorcade and the buses that followed it ... but Nixon needed to stop and go into a designated building along the way to give a campaign talk. I told them that was not possible because the schedule would not allow it. Only so much time was allowed that day for Chinatown, as there were other events, including a ticker tape parade in the financial area. I received a firm response that there would be no support if he did not agree to speak at the hall. I told them I would check and see.

Later, I called Ken Cole and told him of my conversation and he said no way could they stop and maybe they would just have to cancel Chinatown. I told him I would work it out.

It took several hours of discussions with the association leaders. I did not discuss it with Cole but worked out a solution where we had a rig trailer set up along the route with a microphone and speakers where Nixon could get out of the car, climb onto the trailer, and say a few words to the motorcade crowd. Thanks to this simple solution, the Chinatown event was a great success. And Nixon was very happy with it, as evidenced by a telegram he sent me, which hangs in my study.

One additional thing I did was to control the making of a lot of hand-made signs that were printed in Chinese about Nixon .... "Nixon's the One," "Vote for Dick," "My granddaughter wants me to vote for Nixon," etc. Control was necessary, because during the 1960 campaign when Nixon ran against John Kennedy, a Kennedy advance man had made signs in Chinese that were all derogatory toward Nixon. Unfortunately, there was no one to read them who knew Chinese until it was too late. As you can imagine, this spoiled the event. I wanted to make sure that did not happen again, so I had two people designated for that purpose. We also had sign-painting parties for younger voters that gave us lots of random hand-made signs to hand out. I also had fortune cookies made up with positive sayings about the future of Nixon for the press bus and to hand out to the crowd.

From August to November, it was just one continuous campaign stop after another: Santa Barbara (where I also had to raise money, fifty thousand dollars, to help finance it), Yorba Linda (where Nixon was born), El Paso, and Jacksonville, Florida (where I did an Agnew advance and scouted the democratic candidate, Hubert Humphrey). Also, Grand Rapids (where we designed an old-time whistle stop on a train across Michigan). It was canceled at the last minute because the campaign felt it ate up too much time for the number of people reached, which really bummed me out because I had put in a lot of creative planning into it.

There were other stops, but the most memorable was Orlando, Florida, where Disney was starting to build Disney World. We had an airport rally there, and the Florida governor, Claude Kirk, was going to introduce Nixon once he arrived. We had about twelve thousand people in the crowd when I was notified the plane was going to be about forty minutes late. I was concerned that the crowd would begin to drift away and the press would get bored, too.

One of the VIP guests was an old movie star, Johnny Weissmuller, who played the original Tarzan in the 1930s and in the 1960s was still a well-known star. (I used to love his Tarzan movies). I needed to do something with the governor to entertain the crowd and Weissmuller was famous for his Tarzan yell. So, I gathered the governor, Johnny, and our MC together and informed them that Nixon was late and asked if we could do a little clowning around to warm up and save the crowd by having the governor and Weissmuller do a Tarzan yell contest. They agreed. It went over perfectly and the crowd, for thirty minutes, went wild voting over who was the best. Nixon landed and went up on the stage to a "well warmed up crowd." In fact, they went wild. He was delighted and responded with one of his most enthusiastic campaign speeches.

As I said, Haldeman had drilled into us that the crowd on the campaign stop was just a prop and the upward to a million viewers who saw the event on TV were the real target, so each campaign event was set up like a TV stage; the cameras and the press were aligned (this was before small, handheld cameras) at an angle off the right side facing the stage, so they were forced to pick up the view such that it would be Nixon's left side, which was his best. We also skewed the crowd in such a way that it would appear larger than it actually was and had other props around that would reflect well on the candidate.

The election was in November. Sharon and I stayed at the historic Waldorf-Astoria Hotel to watch the returns. It was a very close election and Nixon barely beat Hubert Humphrey. We went to bed not knowing who won and woke up to learn the man I had been campaigning so hard for was now going to be the next president of the United States.

At 10 a.m. the next day, the campaign coordinator called, telling us to report to a hotel conference room. Nixon came to tell us what a fine job we had done and to thank us for our hard work. I really felt good about the job I had done and realized that, because it was such a close election, I could have influenced something on those many stops that may have impacted the vote count. It was heady thinking for a twenty-seven-year-old. However, I felt sad to have been away from Sharon and Tanya for most of July, August, September, and October, although there was some comfort in knowing they had spent some of this time in Spokane with Sharon's parents.

People began talking about jobs and I was told to think about what I would like to do in the administration. I went back to Dallas, returning to the SED program. Shortly, I was called by Ehrlichman to see if I would like to work for the newly selected national security director, Dr. Henry Kissinger. I did not say yes, but I guess I did not make the cut anyway, being from a West Coast university (but in 1986 we hired Kissinger Associates to help us in Yemen).

I did not know who Kissinger was and really did not have any interest in the offer and found out later that it was good I did not pursue it, as he favored Ivy Leaguers on his staff and was a very demanding boss. I would probably have told him off if I ever felt I may have known more about a subject than he did, which might have taken a while or never.

I did spend time with him in the late '80s and early '90s and found him to be one of the brightest, most perceptive men I knew and kept some contact with him.

Subsequently, I was offered a job by Haldeman to join his staff as a deputy assistant, which would have been a White House Commission. I thought about it and realized that I had already spent four and a half years in government (USAF) and that if I spent four years in the White House, my career path would be that of government, lobbying, or campaign consulting. Further, Ross Perot had wanted me to call him every night while on campaign to report what was going on, and because of this I developed a good relationship with him during this period. EDS had gone public and became the darling of Wall Street. Ross was now a billionaire and I got some stock options.

I concluded that we had just had a new baby, and my future was with Perot and EDS. So, I turned Haldeman down. Later, Larry Higbee, his aide, told me that I was the only one he ever knew to have turned down a White House Commission in the Nixon White House.

I now went back to EDS and into the SED program and was assigned with Roger Bacon to market "Earl Spraker's Personal Response Terminal." Earl was an EDS engineer who invented a device that could connect with an audio response machine (IBM, ARM) by phone. It would respond with a voice audio that had a cradle in the center in which you could put a telephone handset and then push a button that activated an automatic dialing module that connected to the ARM in Dallas. It had a speaker on it so one could hear the response. The automatic dialing module was proprietary then.

We were in the early stage of developing a barcode reader that could be used for inventory. My job was to go forth and try to market it and see if there was a demand for it. This was in the days when touch-tone phones were just coming out in the marketplace. There was no Wi-Fi and everyone had landlines (no portable phones you could carry around and definitely no smart phones). Earl's device was cutting edge but also a little bit ahead of its time.

This also was the beginning of audio response (robots talking to you on the phone). The audio response machine used recordings rather than digital and had 143 spoken words in its memory. I would program it to speak in response to questions using a keypad on the device. The dialing modules would automatically connect the device with the IBM ARM in Dallas. It had great application for life insurance, because an agent could carry it into the home of a client and let a computer suggest what type of policy they should have.

I spent about three months trying to market it and made some conditional sales to a large aerospace company in California, but in the end, we felt EDS was really not in the computer hardware market and sold it to a company that did use it to assist their agents.

Now I did this for a few months, but in the summer of 1969, Ehrlichman called Perot to see if I could come to the White House to work on a project on the future. Nixon was to give a State of the Union speech in six months (January 1970) and they wanted to set up a team to identify the national goals as applied to the future. Somehow, they thought I would be a good resource for this project and I was. It took about two months and I really enjoyed it. Essentially, we set up the National Goals research staff, headed by Leonard Garment, which initially served as a resource for Nixon policy speeches and the State of the Union Address. I worked with one of the brightest men I had ever met, Daniel P. Moynihan, domestic advisor to Nixon. (He later went on to become a US senator from New York). He was smart, very witty, and always had me laughing. After the project, I got a letter from him that I have always cherished, saying how much he enjoyed working with me.

That fall, Ehrlichman again called Perot to see if I was available to do some White House advancing. Apparently, most of the trained and lead advance men had taken jobs in the various departments of government, so there was a shortage of them. Perot said yes, so in September 1969, I became a White House advance man and stayed in that capacity for the next couple of years, until July of 1971.

By that time, I told Ross that it was not really worth doing that job any longer since the White House was becoming paranoid about political enemies and the upcoming election in '72. I sensed something bad was going to happen. Their Committee to Reelect the President (CREEP) had a number of arrogant individuals running it, with too much money to spend. (For instance, Jeb Magruder cornered me one day and warned me that if Perot didn't give more money to the campaign, he would not be invited to any more White House dinners.) Further, I was now getting calls from staffers I did not know asking me to head somewhere in the United States. Thus, I felt it was time to leave this line of work. (Later, I briefly came back into it, doing one for Reagan in the 1980 campaign in Tyler, Texas, at which time I showed the Reagan people how an old Nixon advance man could pack a field house with ten thousand people. At the time I overheard Lyn Nofziger, a Reagan aide, tell an associate that this advance man really took a risk to get ten thousand people in a small east Texas town into that arena at noon on a weekday.)

During my time as a Nixon advance man, I would live in Dallas and do assistant to the chairman jobs on Ross's staff and then do a presidential advance once every two months on average. Again, they were fun, and being a lead advance man for the White House was heady stuff ... you came into town as a representative of the president (even though you were far removed from any real influence in the White House, locals did not know that).

I did advances both in the United States and overseas. Three memorable events come to mind as great stories to repeat.

KANSAS STATE UNIVERSITY ... NATIONAL
SPEECH TO THE NATION, OCTOBER 1969

Nineteen sixty-nine and 1970 were high watermarks for the Vietnam war protests. Every week there seemed to be a protest somewhere. In response, Nixon decided to give a major speech to the nation, and since it was to be nationally televised, we needed a place where the student politics were not a problem (minimum of protestors).

Kansas State University was such a place. So, on the occasion of an Al Smith Award (named for former governor and presidential candidate), Nixon would use this as a forum and basis of his speech. I was selected as the lead advance man and went to Manhattan, Kansas, to meet with the team of White House Communication advance men and Secret Service, local politicians, and university officers. We spent about eight days setting it up.

Little did I know that just a short drive down the highway was the University of Kansas, known as the Harvard of the Midwest and a hotbed for protestors. Once

I got the lay of the land and met all of the players and principals, we set up our plan and schedule in coordination with the White House, Dwight Chapin, and Ron Walker.

The drill was to have Nixon fly in by helicopter and then I would walk him and Pat into the stadium from the practice field next it and into the fifteen thousand-capacity field house, where he would be speaking. We picked the field house because we could control who could go in and keep out people who might be disruptive. We issued special tickets for entry and you had to be a student of KSU or faculty to get them (except for VIPs, who also got special tickets).

Each evening, I would have a meeting with all the staff, Secret Service, and local security officials (as protestors were one of the biggest concerns). Interestingly enough, we had a local state intelligence officer who would brief us on the status of the protestors. He even had some pictures of the leaders. We had set up a number of actions that would slow down the protestors, although we knew Nixon and national TV would attract them. It actually became a war between them and us, although they did not know the extent to which we knew their plans.

First, we would practice our drill as if Nixon would land in the practice field and Governor Docking's helicopter would land in the football stadium nearby. The day before, we falsely let the word get out that the Secret Service had reversed that plan to fool protestors and now Nixon would land in the stadium. Meanwhile, we found out that several busloads of protestors from KU were planning to show up.

Third, I was in my twenties back then and looked like a grad student. The night before the speech, I went into the field house to check everything, especially the sound system. While there, I happened to see five students. There was no reason for them to be there. I recognized three of them as KU protest leaders from our intelligence photographs.

Acting like I was a sound expert, I wandered by them and asked if they were looking forward to the president's speech tomorrow. They said yes, so I volunteered that the best seats in the house were in an area I pointed to and stated that from an acoustic point of view, sound traveled best in that area, implying that you could hear and be heard best from there.

None of that was true. (I knew squat about sound projection). However, I assumed that they had some rogue tickets and so would be at the speech. I wanted to trick them into a special sound spot where they could be heard by the audience but because of the way we set up the camera platform for the press, could not be picked up by the TV cameras. During the 1970s, there were three channels (NBC, ABC, and CBS). Each TV camera was huge and on a stand that had a limited range on the circular compass, so that at most they may have had a 90-degree span. We compensated for this by giving them a camera platform from which they could record and film on the campaigns. Everything worked to perfection.

The White House helicopter now landed in the practice field as planned and

I led the president and Mrs. Nixon into the field house. (Apparently my bright, sixteen-month-old daughter recognized me on TV and told her Mama so).

The several hundred protestors were in the football stadium, having been fooled that Nixon was to land there. It was a real surprise for Governor Docking when he landed there instead. He had trouble getting out of the chopper. Meanwhile, the State Patrol delayed the buses so additional UK protestors never made it to the stadium on time.

And the protest leaders I recognized from the night before in the stadium managed to get ten or twelve of their number into the field house. Better yet, they went exactly to where I had suggested they sit, never making it on camera. The event was perfect. Nixon did not really see those few protestors because of the lack of a line of sight from the podium. During the speech, they yelled their lungs out, but the TV cameras could not swing the degrees on their tripods to pick them up. Further, every time they yelled, they made much of the crowd in the field house mad and embarrassed. It got to the point where the frustrated crowd would even react with applause to a comment Nixon made in his speech. To the nation watching it on TV, it appeared to be a roaring crowd supporting their president. Nixon and Haldeman were very happy with the event. I was really happy and learned an important lesson in how to combat the protestors.

What was really beautiful was that the press never caught on (or at least reported) about our tactics to make it appear that there were only a handful of rude protestors there. That is a perfect advance and I was so proud of our team. If it were a corporate event, I would have given everyone a bonus, but this was the White House.

PERU

A massive earthquake killed upward of seventy thousand people in 1970 ... Our government wanted to respond. Mrs. Nixon went down with millions of dollars in relief supplies. And I was lead advance man.

On the Sunday afternoon of May 31, 1970, a massive 7.9 earthquake struck twenty-two miles off the coast of Peru and affected an area on shore larger than Belgium and Holland combined. Further, it caused the tallest mountain in the Peruvian Andes, called Huascaran, to break off and create an avalanche of ice, snow, and mud moving at a speed of 120 mph and advancing to the town of Yungay, eleven miles away. By this time, it was estimated to consist of eighty million cubic meters of hot mud. It buried Yungay and the neighboring town, Ronrioca, snuffing out the life of the majority of the inhabitants. About 90 percent of Yungay was covered with thirty to ninety feet of hot mud (now it is considered a National Cemetery).

Other cities in the Peruvian valleys were devastated by the quake, including Chimbote on the coast. The toll was later calculated at eighty thousand deaths, 26,500 missing and 143,000 injured, and more than one million left homeless.

It was decided that Mrs. Nixon would personally bring in relief supplies to show US support for Peru. I was selected to lead the advance team and organize the visit. She was to be there from June 28 to June 30 and I went in four days earlier, on June 24. This was real short notice, as normally an advance like this would take eight days to prepare. We had a special KC 135 jet cargo plane that flew our team of about forty and the supplies to Lima. It was a tremendous group with representatives of the State Department, Kissinger staff, Peace Corps, Secret Service, Army One helicopter pilots, WACA, Mrs. Nixon's press secretary, press coordinator, military aides, and me, the lead advance man, who was the coordinator with the White House.

I flew into Washington on the 23rd. I was thoroughly briefed by White House, State Department, and CIA briefers, given my shots (this was really interesting as the same guy who was my doctor when I was at Loring AFB in 1963 was now the White House doctor and gave me my shots for Peru), and handed basic instructions. This was not to be a "rah-rah" trip, but a solemn, subdued occasion and our team was not to be seen sight-seeing … only working. Also, we were not to get in the way of the rescue workers. Further, do nothing that would upset our fragile relationship with the Peruvians.

When we approached Lima, I told the pilots to bring us into a hangar and we would come out in small numbers so as not to draw attention. I also asked everyone not to come back on the plane loaded with souvenirs, but only what they could put in their luggage. We did not want to give the impression that we were down there as tourists, which the communists would have exploited in their papers.

We had rooms in the Bolivar Hotel and I set up our office in one of the suites. This was nice, as we would all meet there to coordinate our relative responsibilities.

The first meeting we had was in the afternoon after we landed. It was with Ambassador Taylor Belcher. He acted like he was in charge and I was to take his orders. I realized I had to put him in his place really quickly or I would lose control and the respect of the State and NSC reps who accompanied me (I felt that they were probably already wondering what this guy from Ross Perot was doing leading a government team … I had already worked with the Secret Service and WACA, so they knew how our team worked and that I would go to Haldeman if I felt I needed to).

Thus, I got the ambassador over in the corner and told him under no uncertain terms that I was totally in charge and had done this stuff one thousand times, and if it was screwed up, it was my fault and no one else's. Further, if he disagreed, here was a White House number to call to voice his opinion, although I added that the relationship between State and the White House was not too healthy at this time.

He reluctantly pulled back but would test me throughout the trip. I did not help his career when I wrote my trip report and commented that the US ambassador should have been up in the valley of the disaster, directing US embassy support, rather than sitting in Lima. He still had not been up there when we arrived three weeks after the quake.

In the initial meeting, he wanted us to go to the northern coast to Chimbote and deliver goods there. It was accessible and less of a logistic and security problem because of the rubble. He also wanted Mrs. Nixon to come to the embassy and visit with staff. I told him we would not have time to do that, and, further, our purpose was disaster relief and we needed to be seen in that mode. I told him that there may be time for her visit to the embassy after everything, but not until then. He was not happy.

The next morning, we met with the Peruvian officials who were responsible for the event on their side—Colonel Ibanez, aide to President Velasco, and General Graham, chairman of the presidential advisors. They also recommended we go to the coast rather than the valley. They said the valley had high winds because of altitude and lots of rubble. Later I learned that the valley was mostly Indian residents and the coast was non-Indian and this was where most of the aid was going. This kind of thing was unfortunately a common theme in most countries in the 1970s ... even in the United States). Later that day, we met with Col. Ibanez and the foreign minister. They had a plan for the visit that was contrary to ours. It was a tough meeting and the foreign minister was a know-it-all and would not listen to reason. We concluded by giving him most of his points, but also we got what we wanted. We were to take the first ladies to the mountain and have two aides with Mrs. Nixon and the press accompany the motorcade (this was crucial and non-negotiable for me).

The next day we flew to the coast (Casa and Chimbote), where there was much destruction. Because of the time pressure—it was Friday and Mrs. Nixon was to arrive on Sunday—I asked Arnie Nachmanoff (Kissinger staff) and Chuck McGuire (State Department) to advance the Lima events. For this purpose, I made them honorary White House advance men and I would handle the other event on the coast. We then flew into the mountains to the valley and checked out Anta (landing area for our C-130) and Yungay and Huaras.

I then got a helicopter pilot to fly me and our White House photographer around the upper valley. In Yungay, I walked on the alluvial mud that buried the city. The stench of the rotting bodies and the dust eliminated it as a place to go. We then flew up to where the mountain broke and followed the mud flow for fifteen miles, seeing the destruction. We next flew to Huaras and found that what once was a beautiful mountain tourist town was a pile of rubble. But this could be where we did the motorcade if we could bulldoze a path through it. It was a visual of how bad the quake was; also the Peace Corps and Red Cross were active up there.

It was too late to fly back to Lima, so we overnighted in Anta with the US Army Helicopter Squadron. I slept on the ground and ate K-rations with a beer. The mosquitos were horrible. I spent most of the evening on a radio phone, coordinating activities with Lima and Chapin in Washington.

We had a couple of incidents that had to be handled gingerly. One involved the senior Peruvian general in charge of the valley where we were to take the first ladies. No one had told him about Mrs. Nixon coming and a motorcade and he was not going to let that happen. I soon found an interpreter and asked if we could meet privately. I then met with him in a tent, apologizing profusely and telling him when I found out who was responsible for the gaffe, I would remove him from our party. Then we drank some of his booze and had a nice conversation. I asked him whether, since he was the senior officer in charge, he would consider riding in the helicopter with Mrs. Nixon and Mrs. Velasco (the Peruvian president's wife). He said yes and that solved my problem. My next challenge was to sell the Secret Service and Chapin on this plan, which I did.

The other issue was that we flew in Army One (the presidential helicopter) and secured it at the Lima airport. The colonel in charge of the airport was curious and wanted to see it, but our guards would not let him near it. This almost became an international incident, but we settled him down by suggesting we board and then offered for him to sit in Nixon's seat and have a photographer take a picture with the promise we would send it to him. (But this is one incident the ambassador would later try to use against me).

I again flew to Anta, but this time in a C-130 with a large bulldozer in it, which was to be used to clear our motorcade route. I had four Secret Services agents, who were to go with me, but when the operations officer commented that he would not ride in the C-130 with that big dozer, everyone became more pensive. I had to go and one of the agents needed to go with me, so Dennis McCarthy and I climbed aboard. I suggested to the others that there was no need to overload it and they could come up after Dennis and I set up the route. (I had all the respect in the world for Dennis.) It was a fun ride. I sat in the seat of the tied-down dozer, and it was thrilling flying over the fourteen-thousand-foot ridge to get into the valley.

Again, Saturday night, I stayed in Anta and flew back early the next morning and got briefed by the team. We were ready to go. Mrs. Nixon arrived at 5:15 p.m. We had an informal dinner.

The next morning, I flew back to the valley to set up all of the events that were to happen there. Mrs. Nixon followed her schedule in Lima with Mrs. Velasco and then was scheduled to fly up to the valley. We moved her to the C-130 and flew the Army One helicopter ahead of her.

We were ready for them when she landed. This was the most difficult advance I ever had, as I had to coordinate eighty people moving into a disaster area, using two helicopters for forty of them and three helicopters for thirty of the others (Peruvian and American press), and Army One for Mrs. Nixon and Mrs. Velasco, their immediate staff, and the general in charge of the area. The event turned out perfectly and it got great press coverage.

That evening we had a formal dinner in the palace and it was a real thrill for me to sit with the leaders of Peru, especially someone like Colonel Ibanez, whom I got to know well.

Mrs. Nixon visited a hospital with the injured from the quake the next morning and departed back to Washington on Air Force One that afternoon.

We wrapped up all the administrative things, worked on thank you lists, went out for a great dinner, and then flew back to Washington the next day.

I came away from this experience with some impressions.

1. The indelible sight of what an earthquake can do to people and property. Most of the population of Yungay was killed. There were a number of survivors, mostly orphans, whom we put on our plane when we flew back to Lima. There were Indians who had never been in an airplane or seen a big city. It was amazing for me to see the expression on their faces when looking out of the window or getting off the plane in Lima.

2. The fantastic dinner for Mrs. Nixon hosted by the Velascos. She did a great job in building a relationship with Peru. The press coverage was great and I received a very nice letter from Pat Nixon afterward.

3. Peruvian officials' mentality and how much time they waste in a meeting. And the lack of knowing simple organizational principles. This had totally changed when I went back to Peru in 2005 when Hunt was investing in a world-class liquid natural gas project.

4. The power of an earthquake. My first night in Lima, an aftershock hit and totally moved me off my bed and onto the floor.

5. Later, I got a call from Arnie Nachmanoff, who told me that he was promoted to head the Latin American area in Kissinger's NSC and he felt that his Peru adventure was a significant factor in the promotion, as Kissinger was pleased with the results. Arnie became a good friend and got us into Oxford Analytica, a great intellectual news report that I used as a resource for our many international investments.

Best of all was an editorial in the *Washington Post* (one of the top newspapers in the country) written on July 3, 1970, which I have included here. It confirms, in my opinion, that the decision I made (and was opposed by many as too rough and dangerous) to go up in the mountains where the affected people and destruction were, was the correct one.

"A stark and terrifying act of nature on May 31 brought countless deaths and vast destruction and suffering to the countryside of Peru. Almost from the moment the earthquake struck, it was evident (1) enormous quantities of relief supplies and funds would be required, (2) the United States would want (and have) to play a large part in any relief effort and (3) the way to doing it was so likely to be fraught with political complications and difficulties. The latter included not just this country's sensitivities with the Peruvian government, but also our relationship to the relationship, as it were, that exists between Peru and Cuba, which has been putting on a relief campaign of its own. Finally, there has been the usual confusion and competition among relief agencies and/or agents in this country.

It is our impression that Mrs. Richard Nixon has threaded her way among all of these political sources of trouble admirably and with skill, keeping paramount in her own mind and in her pronouncements and her activities the brutal fate that overtook the earthquake victims and the simple human response that is required from others at such a time. A few days ago, Mrs. Nixon left for Peru with two plane loads of relief supplies and, on her initiative, she undertook to tour the more rugged and desolate places where the earthquake had struck. She appears to have conveyed to the Peruvians she met a genuine desire to help and have done so with great tact, for all of which she deserves much."

THE "BIG SHOOTOUT"

Texas was to play Arkansas in Fayetteville on Saturday, December 6, 1969. Nixon was to attend and, since both teams were rated at the top, he would present a trophy as national champion in college football to the winner. This was before the BCS and there were just polls that rated the best team, and not all agreed. The president of the United States crowning the winner made a difference; moreover, this was also the hundredth anniversary of football as a team sport. This was a very big deal nationwide and, thirty-five years later, a documentary movie was about it and I was in it.

I was called by Ron Walker, my swimming pool friend and now head of the White House Advance. He asked if I would like to advance this game. I jumped at it. I did not realize until later what a big deal it was and what impact it would have on the State of Texas.

I flew into Fayetteville on December 3 and met Ron. We walked around trying to determine what the drill should be ("drill" is an advance man term that means all the activities of the president and his party). Ron and I came up with a rough agenda, which he agreed to and left me to carry it out.

A funny incident happened when we wandered into the Arkansas locker room, as we wanted to get a locker room layout to see how we would have RN present the trophy. While we were in there, a security man with only four lower and six upper teeth was yelling as he approached us from a distance, "Hey boy ... you all football players?" He yelled this about three times, adding, "Only football players are allowed in here." Ron and I explained who we were, but I do not think he knew Nixon was coming, or, if he did know, thought football was more important. Consequently, we apologized and begged our leave. However, to this day, when Ron and I see each other, the first thing we say is, "Hey boy ... you a football player?"

Ron then went back to Washington and I set off with a staff of volunteers, and our White House Secret Service agents, press advance, and WACA began to form the team.

My first meeting was with the president of the university to tell him our rough plan and to get his buy-in ... and to get twenty-five prime tickets for the presidential party and room in the press box for some senior staff. He was most cooperative and assigned the head of PR as my liaison. He had already acquired the tickets on the fifty-yard line.

Our major actions in this event were getting the president to Fayetteville from Fort Smith, Arkansas, where Air Force One (the presidential plane, a Boeing 707) would land. Then, using two large helicopters or several limousines (both contingencies in case of weather), transport him to the university. From there, a walk into the stadium from the practice field landing to see the game; a bathroom stop at halftime; a halftime interview with Chris Schenkel (a noted sportscaster); a visit to the winners' locker room to present the trophy; a visit to the losers' locker room, and back on the helicopters.

This was actually supposed to be an easy drill. Our big concern was protesters, as this was in 1969 and they were everywhere. The Secret Service was there to protect the president. We had a lot of other security provided by the university, who would be all around if there was a major problem.

In the end, there was no real protesting in the stands and there was an open hill-like area at the end of the stadium where some protestors were sitting, but it was a small number and their signs were hard to see. Also, it was an exciting game and the true fans ignored the disruptive things around them.

Come Saturday and game time, we had everything set up and ready to go. Each member of the team had their assignments. We had a greeting committee of dignitaries to be at the steps of the helicopter to say hi and shake Nixon's hand ... we had people at points in the path who would lead the party down a narrow route beneath the stands and up into the stands on the fifty-yard line.

Bud Wilkerson, the former Oklahoma coach I worked for during the Citizens for Nixon campaign in June and July in 1968, was now the sports commentator for ABC and they were broadcasting the game nationally. I contacted Bud when he got into town to let him know I was the advance man, and I would keep in touch with him as to the president's movement.

Saturday, and just before game time, the stadium was packed. Unfortunately, it was a misty day, so initially I got word that the presidential party would drive up instead of fly. We had another plan and location for the limousines and all the guests moved to that location.

I called Bud and told him that the presidential party was driving so they would be late. He said they would hold up the game, which he did for about twenty minutes, until I called him and told him we lost radio contact and suggested he should start the game.

Within a few minutes, however, an agent came over and told me they decided to use the choppers after all, because Nixon did not want to hold up the game. All of a sudden, I saw the helicopter coming out of the mist and landing in the practice field. The steps came down and Nixon gets off. It was just me and a few agents there. I walked up to him and said, "Mr. President, I am Tom Meurer, your advance man, if you will follow me, I will take you into the stands." The game had been on for about five minutes, and as we began to walk, the stadium broke out into a huge roar and the president turned to me and asked what that was and I responded that they saw you land and it must be a welcome.

I then led him and the party through the prescribed circuitous route to the seats in the stands. As we broke into the area where you could view the field, the crowd did another roar as Arkansas kicked their point after touchdown. Nixon looked at me like "you idiot," as he realized the first roar we heard by the helicopter was for the Arkansas touchdown. They had made it in the first few minutes of the game and, coincidentally, right after he landed.

The game was covered on ABC and my leading Nixon and the party into their seating area was nationally televised. Sharon was watching it and did not see me until Tanya, who was eighteen months old, again pointed out, "There is Daddy." She was very bright even then.

Now, the presidential party consisted of Governor Rockefeller, Senator Fulbright, and elected officials from Arkansas and Texas (including George Bush, who was a congressman at the time). Also included were staff, including Ron Walker and the president's close aide, Steve Bull, who always led him. Steve and I worked together on the campaign and were good friends.

Like everyone at the game, the president needs a bathroom break and we had planned for this. At halftime, Nixon was to go to the top floor of the press box for an interview with Chris Schenkel. On the way up, there was a single restroom on the first floor of the press box. I assigned the PR director to control that bathroom at the beginning of halftime for Nixon, which he did.

At halftime, Nixon began to move. Steve Bull was leading him and I was about fifteen feet in front of Steve, following me. We were both on our radios (with wrist speakers and ear plugs, so we had good communications). As we went up, I told Steve the restroom was ready for him, assuming we would stop there. As we approached, Steve says, "Keep going … he does not need to go." So, we moved up for the interview.

When the interview was over, Steve was taking the president back to his seat. All of a sudden, Steve asks me where is the restroom … he has to go. I tell him it is down a flight and as we get there, I realize the PR director hadn't thought about holding the restroom after the interview. Just as Nixon approaches, a short little man goes in and locks the door. I now tell Steve that Nixon will just have to wait. Nixon now positions himself about twelve feet in front of the door and there was not a lot of room around it but one end was a little open so Nixon was talking with a couple people. The little man had been in there a while, but he finally opens the door and comes out. He is about 5'4" tall and comes straight out walking toward the president with his head down and concentrating on getting his fly up. He stops in front of Nixon and looks up into the face of the president of the United States. He was shocked and speechless and quickly moved out of the way while Nixon just went into the toilet.

I often think of that guy and the story he must tell on how he ran into Nixon.

It was a great game and, by the early fourth quarter, I assumed Arkansas would win. So we set up the Arkansas locker room for the ceremony, which included an area in the locker room where Nixon could give a small talk and present the trophy.

Unfortunately, Texas won in the last minutes and now we had to change locker rooms … and they were not close together. By the time I brought the trophy over to the Texas locker room, the players and Nixon were in there and he was ready to present it. I wore glasses in those days, and as I left the cold outdoors and went into the steamy locker room, my glasses fogged up, and for a second, I stumbled around trying to find the president with the trophy in hand.

This was a great game, which has gone down in the annals of football. In 2009 a producer by the name of Mike Looney produced a film called the *Great Shootout*. He called me when he found out I was the advance man and interviewed me (and Ron), which made it into the film. Later during the promotion, I was asked to attend a panel with some of the players to tell some stories. We have a copy in our library.

I had many other advances with stories worth telling, but I need to get on to the next chapter of these memoirs. I do want to say that I had one advance in 1970 in Dallas that changed my life. George H. W. Bush was running for the Senate against Lloyd Benson. I was asked to do the White House advance on this. Ray Hunt was the local chairman for Bush. Jim Oberwetter was Bush's congressional aide and the three of us worked together and got to know each other and became lifelong friends. Four years later, Ray would hire Jim and, one year later, he hired me.

CHAPTER FIVE

BACK TO EDS ... NONBUSINESS ACTIVITIES FOR PEROT

Having turned the White House Commission down, I returned to EDS. As I said, I came to know Ross very well during the campaign because I would call him each evening while I was on the road to give him a report on the campaign.

He became a very famous person in the fall after taking EDS public for an unheard of multiple where the stock went from $16 to $161 in a year. He became known as the "Fastest, Richest Texan Ever" (as written up by *Fortune* magazine and in many other articles in 1969 and 1970). Interestingly, this publicity got the attention of my friends in the White House and the Republicans I had met on the campaign who were now ensconced in Washington, in and around the administration.

I think they saw me as a direct line to Perot (which was true). This became a real advantage in the upcoming years, as often politicians and government people would call me if they wanted to get to this very rich, well-known person. This was not my role, but, because of circumstances, it often fell upon me ... and as an assistant to the man himself, I had a direct line. This was a real advantage for Ross in the upcoming activities.

Don't get me wrong, he now could pick up the phone and call anyone, including Nixon, and they would return his calls. This is very effective if used prudently and if there was a deal of some kind that benefitted both parties. Ross was a master at this and I learned so much from the opportunity to be around him during these important years when he became one of the more famous people in America and decided to use the millions of dollars he had to do good things for the nation.

Ross was raised in Texarkana, Texas, by two loving parents who instilled important values in him and his sister, Betty. His dad, Gabe, died in his fifties while Ross was at the Naval Academy, but from what I have been told, he was an incredibly smart man and a successful cotton trader who passed on to his son how to read people, calculate odds, and make a good, fair deal.

I knew his mother, Lulu May, and had many opportunities to spend time with her. She was a very wise and loving person who would always inspire me with her sage comments, knowing that I was working for her son. She was a joy to be around and it was a sad day when we lost her.

Now here was a man sitting on hundreds of millions of dollars of his own money, able to buy anything he wanted, and educated in public schools and one of the finest universities in the country, the United States Naval Academy. It was more selective in the 1950s than Harvard or Yale. To his position of power, he brought his values of "I am an officer and gentleman and will act accordingly" and the code of conduct according to which he "will not lie, cheat or steal, or tolerate those who do." And as a good Christian, he valued the teachings of the Bible. This was someone in his late thirties, with love of country, Christian values, a can-do attitude, and a very creative brain.

As a result of his growing wealth and strong convictions, Ross set off on a course to do great things for his country. EDS was now a public company with shareholders, but Ross controlled the majority of the stock and made sure that whatever he did reflected well upon the company and employees.

In September 1969, Ross was interviewed by Murphy Martin, a nationally known broadcaster, who had just returned to Dallas to work for the ABC affiliate. Along with broadcasting the news, Murphy also had a weekly show interviewing celebrities. While waiting to go on, Perot met another guest, Joy Jeffries, and her five-year-old son. Joy was the wife of Bob Jeffries, a POW in North Vietnam. Ross found out that Bob had never seen his son. This really got to Ross and he began to think about what could be done to change it.

Further investigation revealed that our government, until recently, had been keeping secrets about the POW situation from the public. I believe the reason for this was that President Johnson tried to play down the Vietnam War so that it would not interfere with his major legislative push, which was a sweeping civil rights bill.

Consequently, there was no information on exactly how many pilots had been captured, although the number of killed, captured, or missing was several thousand. (Later we would assume there were approximately sixteen hundred POWs held in Hanoi).

We did know they were being neglected and tortured from men who had been released and the press from those groups and countries that were sympathetic or supported Communist Vietnamese who were allowed into Hanoi to take pictures and, later, publish them. (I think the North Vietnamese leaders later regretted allowing these photos to be taken, since we used them in our "Exhibit A" to show how our men were being tortured by their captors).

Also in the fall of 1969, Bob Haldeman (the White House chief of staff) contacted Ross and asked if he would support a movement to "Support the Office of the President." Nixon was going to give a major speech on November 9 to the nation on the Vietnam War and they wanted a marketing campaign that would stress American support for the office of the president.

Ross agreed and set out to interview some New York advertising and PR companies. Their written response was that there was not enough time to do a marketing plan, design the ads and TV spots, print and produce the product, select and deliver them to 117 major US newspapers and 69 TV stations throughout the country.

This frustrated Ross so he decided to do it himself with the help of full-time and part-time EDS members, most of whom came out of the training program.

In late October, I received a call on a Saturday morning to come into Ross's office. There were about five of us there. Ross explained that he was setting up an organization called United We Stand. Its purpose was to support the Office of the President of the United State of America.

Initially, it would launch an ad campaign to call on millions of Americans to let the world know that we stood squarely behind our elected president in his efforts to secure a just and lasting peace in Vietnam. The full-page ads would have two "coupons" that an individual could cut from the newspaper, sign, and send in to United We Stand, PO Box 100000, Dallas, Texas. The ad ran in nineteen major cities in the United States.

In addition to signing the "coupons," the responders were asked to make some additional copies for their friends to sign, send in, and also make a contribution to help defray the expenses in the campaign.

This was a blitz campaign executed in less than two weeks, directed by Merv Stauffer (the EDS manager in Pennsylvania whom Ross pulled down to head it up) and thirty-three part-time EDS personnel.

There were two major full-page ads. The first focused on showing the North Vietnamese that they could not divide the solidarity of Americans on the war. Up to 1969 they had been effectively timing many of their attacks on American troops so that the reporting press could send their stories and film clips back to the United States so the networks could broadcast them while people were eating dinner on TV trays in front of their television sets.

Additionally, the North Vietnamese had been catering to the American peace movement by letting the US peace protesters visit Hanoi and the field for propaganda purposes. They also befriended leftist governments who disliked the United States and courted their presses. (My personal opinion is that one of these early US peace delegations to Hanoi explained to North Vietnam the US networks' news cycle, which involved flying fresh news video tapes from Saigon to the United States so they would hit New York international time for the dinner news, and this helped the North Vietnamese develop their strategy).

This made a great deal of sense, of course. The North Vietnamese (along with their Viet Cong guerillas) wanted to be seen by the world as nice and compassionate, as a small country being attacked by the big, bad USA.

Essentially, these first ads were just the beginning of a major campaign, where Ross set in motion a program by which to "Try the North Vietnamese in the Court of World Opinion" over the next three years.

The initial campaign to create the full-page ads and the thirty-minute TV specials took a mere two weeks and was phenomenally successful. The blitz focused on supporting the president and highlighting the plight of American POWs in Hanoi. Stauffer set up a matrix where EDS personnel individually flew finished print-ready ads directly to the 117 newspapers and film canisters to the 69 TV stations. Many of our people flew to multiple cities, two days in a row, with the ads before they returned to Dallas (starting on November 6). Several did this twice in the course of the night. EDS employees (from our local offices) or contractors would meet the courier at the airport to get the ads or tapes delivered. The courier would then catch the next plane and fly on to the next drop.

The thousands of signed coupons from the ads, together with the TV special starring the astronaut Frank Borman, brought a lot of support to United We Stand. In December, Ross hired Murphy Martin, the nationally known newscaster who had drawn Ross's initial attention to the plight of the POWs, to become president of United We Stand. Jay Holman, Sally Miller, and I were assigned as permanent employees. Merv Stauffer and Tom Marquez were attached, but not employees. Others would be brought in when needed.

We began by setting up United We Stand as an organization that would have local chapters across the country, with the purpose of informing the public on the plight of the POWs. We developed a system and printed an instruction booklet on how to organize, create publicity, and put pressure on officials who could possibly get better treatment for the POWs. Once local campaigns took off, we would provide them with support and advice, acting as a clearinghouse for these initiatives. UWS grew and fostered other organizations with similar goals all over the country, often in areas where we had a concentration of air or naval bases. Since most of the POWs were Air Force or Navy pilots and many POW/MIA families lived on these bases, there was a natural constituency for support of our mission.

One group later came up with the idea of selling metal bracelets featuring the name of a POW or missing man. Others collected thousands of letters that they delivered to Congress or overseas embassies of the North Vietnamese. By 1972 the whole country was aware of the POWs' plight. It was satisfying to know that this broad surge of overwhelming publicity and concern was created initially by the incredible efforts and resources of Ross Perot and United We Stand. There is an incredible story here, and one day, Tanya may write it, as over several years she worked with Ross and archived the thousands of files associated with this remarkable event.

As I said, back in the fall of 1969 it was apparent that the plight of POWs was not known by the American public; nor was the media particularly interested in them. Further, Nixon's new plan of "Vietnamization" meant the war would last longer, and Ross felt it was important in these circumstances for the mental health of the imprisoned men that they knew their country was aware of their plight. They needed hope.

Thanks to Ross's efforts, the US public now knew that the North Vietnamese were withholding names of the captured POWs and men missing in action (MIAs), and that the POWs were being maltreated. It was important that the North Vietnamese leaders know that the American public would not stand for that … and neither would Ross Perot.

Thus, Ross embarked on a new course on the POW issue and this is where my life got real fun and interesting.

CHAPTER SIX

TRYING THE NORTH VIETNAMESE IN THE COURT OF WORLD OPINION

Ross was delighted with United We Stand, but it was the wider, expanded organization that could bring awareness of the POW/MIA issue to the broadest audience. There needed to be more than just the ads and TV specials to sustain the issue with the American public. While the organizational portion of United We Stand was moving forward, becoming viral throughout the United States, Ross planned to move the campaign to the next level.

Murphy Martin had just escorted some Dallas wives to Paris to try to call on the North Vietnamese embassy to get information about their husbands. Before Ross met him in the fall of 1969 for the interview, Martin's trip had received a little publicity. A few subsequent wives' trips became known because word was getting out on these types of trips.

In December 1969, I, along with Bill Cevera (a prominent Dallas newsman who would record the trip) escorted Dotty Hughes and Mitch Jones to Vientiane, Laos. Our mission was to help them meet with the North Vietnamese, Pathet Lao, and NLF (Viet Cong) embassy officials to see if they could get information on their husbands and also deliver some letters and goods to them. It was a long trip and generated a little publicity, but unsuccessful otherwise. The NVN ambassador would not meet with them, as this would recognize their plight too much, so they met on a couple of occasions with a low-level official. There was some good publicity for the women and the North Vietnamese were not pleased that these women were calling on their embassies.

As an interesting aside, this flight to Laos had an indelible effect on me and my future in international air travel.

It was my first time flying across the Pacific Ocean. The part I remember most was the legs from San Francisco to Hong Kong (the whole flight from Dallas included stops in San Francisco, Hawaii, Guam, the Philippines, Hong Kong, Thailand, Laos ... over twenty-seven hours in the air).

In San Francisco, the airline gave me a middle seat in coach from San Francisco to Hong Kong, as we were to overnight in Hong Kong in order to talk to the press (after spending nineteen hours in the air).

When I boarded the plane, I was directed to seat 26B. When I got to it, I realized it was a middle seat in coach, and already sitting in 26A and 26C were two extremely large women from Bombay (now Mumbai) who would become my travel mates. As politely as I could, I wedged myself into the middle seat, where fleshy arms and shoulders pressed me on both sides. I could not really move in this soft wedge.

Now, these were two very fine but size 20-plus ladies. Further, they spoke a high-pitched language called Hindi that was unfamiliar to my ear (and unhelpful if I wished to sleep). On top of that, their meal in San Francisco, before boarding, must have included large amounts of garlic and food familiar neither to me nor my olfactory glands.

My nineteen hours wedged between these two women prevented me from a window view of the mighty Pacific and the islands and atolls I may have seen. Further, it exposed me to smells emitting from the exhaling of their conversational breaths. Finally, it drowned out my ability to concentrate and think or sleep because of the unaccustomed sound of a strange Eastern language.

No real sleep or thinking time on that flight.

When I returned, I went to see Ross and told him I would fly anywhere he wanted me to in the world, but I would not fly coach again on any international flights. After I told him the story, he agreed. From then on, while working for him, I only flew first class.

Back to the POW/MIA story. Ross knew he had to capture more attention and Christmas was coming up. He would do some publicity over the holidays as a hook to capture the attention of the American people on the plight of the men. This time, he would use existing media, his newfound celebrity status, and his own money to do so.

The plan was to organize a trip wherein fifty-eight wives and ninety-four children of POWs and MIAs would be flown from New York to Paris to call on Vietnamese diplomats stationed there. The trip, under the leadership of Merv Stauffer, was a huge success, garnering tremendous publicity. The wives asked the North Vietnamese diplomats point blank to please tell them if they were the wives or widows (a powerful question and message, especially on Christmas Eve). The effort and subsequent pressure became instrumental in getting the NVN to gradually roll out information on the men. Ross Perot and UWS were now starting to be seen by the established POW/MIA wives' community and the US military as a real organization dedicated to helping the POWs.

At the same time Ross sent the planeload of wives and children to Paris, he decided to send one large plane (Boeing 707C) loaded with Christmas dinners and essential items, such as clothing, vitamins, books, Bibles, etc. (thirty tons), to Hanoi for the POWs for Christmas. Initially, the plane would fly to Vientiane, Laos, to meet with the North Vietnamese embassy. Then, once permission was granted to go to Hanoi, an additional 707C loaded with more supplies and parked in Los Angeles Airport (LAX) awaiting instructions would get the signal to lift off. (The planes were rented from Braniff Airlines. They could not get insurance for Laos and Hanoi so Ross self-insured the planes).

I received a call while I was in Laos informing me that a plane was coming in and instructing me to stay in Laos to organize events and set up a meeting for Ross with the North Vietnamese. (Here my advance work came in handy). I was getting subsequent information by telex on the particulars and began to work on it. It was here I parted from Mitch, Dotty, and Bill—it was their last day in Laos as they were returning to the States and stopping in some cities to hold press conferences on the way back.

That same day, US ambassador to Laos G. McMurtrie Godley called me to invite the four of us to the ambassador's residence for dinner that night. I thought it was a nice farewell gesture for the wives. Little did I know there was another objective on the ambassador's agenda.

We had a nice dinner with pleasant conversation and the wives told those at the table about their husbands and our meetings. Later, the ambassador asked me if I could come into his study so he could show me something.

Once in the study, he shut the door. I noticed there was another man in there, who I later found out to be with embassy security. Suddenly Godley looked at me and angrily said, "What in the hell do you think you are doing bringing a plane load of gifts and press into Laos?" He was quite angry.

He had caught me off guard and I had to think fast, while my heart was racing. No one in Dallas had warned me we did not have permission to fly into Vientiane. I decided to bluff and pulled out my White House identification pass (which I carried because of White House advance work), showed it to him, and asked if he had not been notified by Kissinger's office that we would be bringing a plane initially to Vientiane, and then, hopefully going onto Hanoi.

Knowing that he did not report to Kissinger (and that the State Department did not have good relations with the national security advisor), I figured he would not check and would further assume that we had White House permission. It must have worked, because he settled down.

I told him I would bring him up to speed and keep him informed from my end as the plans materialized. I also knew I would need him if I was going to be able to get that plane in and out of Laos and be able to move around freely in Vientiane with a large party of twenty-five.

I was busy for the next couple of days, securing vehicles, hotel rooms, clearances, meetings, and supplies that we would need. I was now in telex communication with Dallas and began to get everything organized.

Ross kicked off this Christmas trip with a press conference in New York explaining the purpose of all three planes, and especially the two destined for Hanoi with sixty tons of supplies for the POWs. He had the press conference as the planes were being loaded. Each day, we got more press. As the first supply plane with Ross and staff flew toward Asia, Ross would have press conferences in the cities where they refueled, thus giving the trip even more publicity, even in Hong Kong, which was only a short flight from Bangkok. However, Hong Kong was important because it was a city for the world press offices in those days. By the time they arrived in Bangkok, the world was watching. Here was a Texas billionaire, flying in a private plane into a "war zone," trying to deliver Christmas gifts to American POWs in Hanoi. It made great copy and the press reports became more sensational as the trip progressed.

On December 23, the plane named *Peace on Earth* landed in Bangkok. It was a 707C we leased from Braniff Airlines. We also had Braniff VP Harry McKillop, who accompanied the plane and helped me with clearances, etc. Harry became a close friend and partook in many adventures in future years with Ross (particularly in Russia and China after the Cold War).

My biggest challenge on the twenty-third was to get the North Vietnamese embassy to grant Perot a meeting. After two days, they had not responded to me, so I finally wrote a long, inoffensive letter that said the plane and Mr. Perot would be coming with gifts for the POWs and accompanied by representatives of the press. I think the idea of the press may have done something, because I got permission for my meeting the very next day, December 24.

Ross and Murphy flew in the night before on a CIA contractor flight that I had rented. It was an eventful flight, as halfway between Bangkok and Vientiane, the door next to Ross came loose and flew off. Ross, figuring that going to Vientiane was just as far as turning around and returning to Bangkok, told the pilot to keep going. He was focused on his meeting with the NVA.

This 707C is a large four engine plane, and the outer two engines were aligned with the edge of the narrow runway at the Vientiane airport. Once it landed, there was a question whether we could take off (but its thirty-ton load of gifts had been temporarily unloaded in Bangkok to be picked up on the way to Hanoi). Still, people at the airport were betting on whether it could take off or not.

The next morning, Ross had meetings with the North Vietnamese and Sot Petrosi, the top Pathet Lao official (the Pathet Lao, or Communist Lao, were similar to the Viet Cong but in Laos and not as effective).

Meanwhile, Ambassador Godley had arranged for us to tour a POW camp of North Vietnamese and Pathet Lao prisoners who were being held outside of Vientiane. We wanted to have clear evidence that the NVN POWs were being treated well (I had visited it earlier to check it out and make sure it was perfect for the press).

The visit was very interesting, as they were indeed treated very well and gave us some letters that we told them we would deliver to their families. I felt honoring this promise would be dangerous because, in the North Vietnamese military, it was considered shameful to be captured. You were either to fight to the death or escape so you could fight elsewhere. (Fortunately, the letters were never delivered and should be in the UWS files and archives that Tanya Meurer set up for Ross to ensure there was an organized record of everything that Ross Perot did on the POW/MIA issue).

That evening I got a call from the US embassy's political officer, Jim Murphy. (As an aside, I came to know a number of people at the embassy, the airport, Air America, CIA, the Laotian military, a Catholic priest, Matt Menger, and USAID personnel, Dr. Jiggs Weldon and Pop Buell. Many of these people would be important to me later when I visited Laos over the next few years looking for information on POWs and MIAs).

Anyway, Jim told me to bring Ross over at about 2:00 a.m. to the embassy— he wanted to show us something. When Ross, Murphy, Tom Marquez, and I arrived, we were escorted into a room where the CIA station chief and a couple of other folks had a map on the table. They told us that there were some caves in the northeastern Laos area of Sam Neua, near the Vietnamese border. There had been reported sightings of twenty-seven Caucasians working in the caves. They cautioned us they did not know whether they were American, Russians, or even French from the 1950s. It is interesting to note that this same number was never accounted for from Laos when the POWs were released. Years later, in 1992, I was called to testify on this before a Senate committee (Senator John McCain and Senator John Kerry, co-chairs). I will talk more about this when I get into the secret activities we did on POWs.

This 2:00 a.m. meeting at the embassy made quite an impression on us. Ross never stopped believing there could be more Americans left in Laos and this, I think, became a catalyst for his running for president in 1992.

That evening we had a Christmas party and invited everyone we had been dealing with in Vientiane, which included embassy people, CIA people, airport officials, USAID personnel, etc.

The next morning, Ross had another meeting with the North Vietnamese, who gave him an official written response that there was a procedure to receive gifts in Hanoi for the POWs and that he needed to deliver them to Moscow before December 31.

Once we got this info, I went over to the Russian embassy in Vientiane, explained the situation, and asked for permission for our plane to land in Moscow. They told me to check with their embassy when we got to Bangkok. Actually, this action by the Russians and North Vietnamese played into Ross's hand, since the timeline made it all the more interesting for the world press.

We now headed out to board the plane to fly back to Bangkok, pick up the supplies, and organize the flight plan for Moscow.

As I mentioned, our huge plane dwarfed the runway and many thought it would not get off. We did take off, however, and when we landed in Bangkok, Jim Murphy from our embassy in Vientiane called me at our hotel. He told me that, as we embarked on our trip to Thailand, the area around the airport in Laos was packed with people and staff, particularly from all the embassies in town. Many had brought picnic spreads to watch the event. He said that as the plane moved down the runway, its outer engines kicked up a dust cloud that, once airborne, rose like a nuclear cloud that was spectacular to see. Everyone, including the North Vietnamese, clapped. He said that it was the best thing to happen to US-Laotian relations since the end of World War II. I regret we did not get a good picture, as other friends who were there told a similar story. (Somewhere in some family album or embassy file dated from 1969, there is a picture).

When we arrived in Bangkok, Tom Marquez and I immediately went over to the Russian embassy to obtain permission to go to Moscow. We were told to go to the Russian embassy in Copenhagen and they would give us permission there.

Now Harry McKillop, our Braniff rep, worked out the flight plan for departure at 8:00 a.m. the next day that would take us over Burma and India. The plan was to stop briefly at the Vatican (to call on the Pope, which only Harry could arrange) and then on to Denmark. We all went to bed, rose early the next morning, arrived at the airport, and boarded the plane, expecting an interesting journey. We just did not know how interesting it would be.

All of a sudden, our flight permission was withdrawn from India and Burma. (We suspected that it may have been at the instigation of our White House, as they were becoming uncomfortable since they were unable to control Perot. Colonel Haig, a Kissinger assistant, who was later to become secretary of state, called Ross in Bangkok and told him he had done a great job of raising publicity but had best return to the US … the Russians probably did not want the publicity surrounding our flight to Moscow either. I think either our government or the Russians put pressure on India and Burma to pull back over the flight rights).

It was maddening, because we had come so far. However, as we were sitting in the private lounge in the airport feeling dejected, the famous US newsman Bernard Kalb, who was now following us, came up to Ross and said, "You need to get to Denmark." He produced a Braniff brochure that showed a route over water so there was no country that could possibly deny us overflight. We would fly to Alaska (which was in the United States and they would not dare deny us landing here) and then onto Copenhagen, Denmark, over the North Pole.

Ross turned to Harry and asked if we could do it. Harry said yes, but we would need to refuel in Japan. We had permission to take off and the tanks were full. So, within the hour, we were airborne heading north over the vast Pacific.

As we approached Tokyo, Braniff headquarters came on the sideband radio with instructions to Harry to not go into Tokyo without diplomatic or military clearance. They repeated this a number of times and Harry just hit the screech button and kept saying, "I can't hear you," and then shut it off. We flew into Tokyo, refueled, and had a press conference with no problems.

We then took off for Anchorage, Alaska. In Vientiane, the North Vietnamese had informed us that we must have the supplies repacked into boxes that were 3 kilograms (6.6 pounds in size). Therefore, we now figured we would stop in Anchorage and repack.

As we were flying, I called a major local radio station in Anchorage on the sideband radio and told them who we were and when we would arrive. I asked if they could help us get some volunteers to repackage the gifts into 6.6 lb. boxes. Of course, they had heard about the plane's plight by now and said they would see what they could do.

This was one of the remarkable things about this trip. By the time we landed, there was a special hanger arranged and scores of volunteers waiting for us, ranging from the Boy Scouts of America to the Anchorage Committee against War and in between. They were great.

We quickly bought large cardboard boxes that we could cut into boxes that would fit 6.6 lbs. of items. We acquired tape, magic markers, box cutters, and scales. We set up assembly lines that could cut the required boxes out of the cardboard, put items in the boxes, weigh the boxes, seal the boxes, and address the boxes. It was all done in six hours and reloaded. We left a real mess in the hanger, which I am grateful the volunteers cleaned up. Those people of Anchorage really extended the trip on to Copenhagen, by helping us meet the North Vietnamese requirement of 3-kilo boxes. We will always be thankful for their spirit and selfless devotion.

On to Copenhagen …

Now we were airborne flying over the Pole and I was in the cockpit watching a compass go crazy … (before GPS), approaching our destination, Copenhagen at 2:00 a.m. on the morning of the thirty-first of December 1969.

We had to meet with the Russians and get their permission to fly to Moscow that same day in order to meet the requirements by the North Vietnamese to arrive in Moscow by December 31.

To prepare the Russians for our arrival and meeting, Ross asked Karen Freitag, a Braniff flight attendant assigned to the crew who spoke five languages (but no Russian) to call various Russian embassies as we were traveling from Tokyo to Copenhagen (London, Stockholm, Bonn, and Rome), since we could not get the Russians to respond to us in Copenhagen. Interestingly, Karen had a nice voice and would call the Russian embassy in the language of the country where the embassy was located. She would ask for an official and, when he would answer, she would start off the conversation with pleasantries and engage in conversation. Whenever she would bring up the trip and Ross Perot, the Russian official would fall back to Russian and indicate he could not understand her.

When we arrived in Copenhagen, we went to our hotel, the Royal Copenhagen. From there, Ross wanted to call the Russians and set up a meeting. He and Murphy came to my room and Murphy called but could not get the embassy to answer the phone, even though we knew they knew we had arrived. Ross became perturbed and asked me who was the head of the USSR. I told him

Brezhnev was party chairman and Kosygin was president.

He told Murphy to place a call to Kosygin. Murphy called the overseas operator and asked her to place a call to President Kosygin at the Kremlin in Moscow, Mr. Ross Perot calling. The Kremlin answered and when Murphy spoke, a woman answered in English. Murphy said Mr. Ross Perot would like to speak to the president (remember this was about 5:00 a.m. in Moscow). The woman said the president was at his dacha and Murphy asked to be transferred there. She did and an aide picked up the phone and Murphy went through the same request. The aide responded that the president was asleep and he could not wake him, but he would have him call back in the morning.

Murphy hung up and, within five minutes, the phone rang in our room and a voice told Murphy … Be at the Russian Embassy at 8:00 a.m. and you will have a meeting … but please do not call the president again.

Promptly at 8:00 a.m., Ross, Murphy and I were at the gate of the embassy. (I remember how dark it was because Denmark was far north and it was December 31, 1969.)

The Russian ambassador and his staff were most gracious and implied that there were just a few requirements Moscow needed and, if we could supply them, then we could be granted clearances. Such data was passengers' information, items in packages, specs on the 707C plane and (the one that got me and made me realize it was just a game) … the weight of the paint on the airplane. There were many more ridiculous requests.

We went back to the hotel and McKillop and the Braniff crew worked on that plane data while we worked on the people and goods data. By midmorning, we had the data and delivered it to the Russians. Then we waited … and waited … and waited.

Ross then got a call from the American ambassador that the Russians had refused permission. Typical Ross, rather than let a defeat get to him, saw this as a PR victory in again trying the North Vietnamese in the "court of world opinion." He called a press conference—recall that by now the world press had been following this plane, named the *Peace on Earth*. It was a great press conference and Ross was at his finest, implying that both the Russians and North Vietnamese denied this humanitarian mission. And then said we were going back to Dallas.

I remember we had two New Year's toasts with champagne (Ross used water) on our return because of going through the time zones. We arrived in Dallas as the Cotton Bowl was being played on January 1 and we flew over it to a cheering crowd of seventy thousand people before we landed.

It was so great to get back to Tanya and Sharon.

A NEW DIRECTION AFTER THE CHRISTMAS TRIPS

By January, Ross had become a household name because of the cause he promoted. He was invited to be on a number of national news and talk shows. He became a sought-out guest on every TV show in the United States. One of them was *Issues and Answers* (a Sunday show with millions of viewers). It was a great interview, in which Ross went through the plight of the POWs and what the average American could do to help. He was then asked if he would pay a ransom of $100 million for the men. Ross said that he could pay $100 million but would not. However, he would consider trading that value in medicines for their release.

That news went worldwide via the four major news outlets (ABC, CBS, NBC, and BBC), except in a totally perverted way. Basic headlines were: "Billionaire Offers $100 Million for Captives of Communists" and "Perot Offers to Buy POWs."

Suddenly, in our UWS offices, we were receiving scores of letters a day from people who could "help get the POWs out … for a fee."

We analyzed these and determined most were bogus, based on the faulty data or lack of data that they presented. But there were some of interest, so Ross sent Tom Marquez and me to Asia to check them out. We did and eliminated many. There was one promising one, however, in Singapore. So, we followed the leads, jumping from Hong Kong, Vientiane, and Bangkok to Singapore to eliminate the bogus offers. None of them turned up anything credible, even for us neophytes.

When we came back, I told Ross there were noted Mafia-type gangs in Hong Kong who must have contacts with gangs in Vietnam. Ross said go back over and check it out.

I initially flew to Hong Kong and contacted a former police official in Hong Kong I had met on an earlier trip. I briefed him and asked if he could put the word out that we were a group willing to pay for information on American POWs held in Hanoi.

I then rented a hotel room and spent two days meeting with small-time smugglers, the former police official's contacts. None of them, however, had any knowledge of how to get to North Vietnam, let alone get prisoners out. This was a bust. I tried the same things in Singapore with a former judge and it was also a bust.

Through the publicity, we found an individual who had sent a letter to Dallas saying that he could facilitate a trade through India with medical supplies. At this time, Tom Marquez and I were in Bangkok following up on some other things and flew to Singapore to meet with him. It was an interesting flight as we chartered an old C-47 from Air America (the CIA-contracted airline in Laos and South Vietnam). It was a six-hour flight at eight thousand feet. We were the only passengers in the plane's empty cargo bay. We wore tropical suits and it was so cold at that elevation that I would walk in circles and put my hands over a small light that gave some illumination in the dark to try to keep warm. Marquez snuggled around his hanging bag suitcase.

We then met our contact in a hotel room in Singapore. His name was Henry

Hang Bartholomew, and he had brought with him a lawyer and prominent Singaporean judge by the name of Subrimanian. They had seen the news reports that Perot had offered to trade medical supplies for American POWs. They presented us with a plan utilizing India to help with this endeavor.

An election was coming up in India and the politics were such that a contribution to a major party's candidate for state governor could influence the prime minister, Indira Gandhi, to intercede with the North Vietnamese. India had a relationship with North Vietnam and we were told that if anyone could do it, she could. A contribution to the party would not be expected unless there was actual success in getting the POWs released.

We were skeptical but felt there was no financial risk if POWs weren't released. Thus, we began three days of negotiations for individual POWs using a dollar figure amount to equate to medical supplies for each man. The details were unbelievable and we would coordinate with Ross and lawyers at night. We had an interesting contract until we realized they were negotiating not for the prisoners but for a contract they could peddle for a fee. We then broke it off.

Henry would not give up. He had another idea he thought we should try and told me I should go to Djakarta. He was friends with the wife of Adam Malik, the foreign minister of Indonesia. He said that country had relations and an embassy in Hanoi, North Vietnam, and maybe could do something. It was worth a try to meet with him.

After some checking with Dallas, I agreed and met Henry in Singapore, who eased me through the visa line to get an Indonesian visa. Upon arrival in Djakarta, I had an evening meeting with Mrs. Malik. She spoke English and I spent about two hours in conversation with her describing the plight of the American POWs and their families. She was a good listener and stated she would pass this on to her husband and would let Henry know if there would be a next meeting. I got back to Singapore and called Marquez in Saigon to let him know I thought this was worth his coming to Singapore and joining me to meet Malik. He came the next afternoon.

While we waited for word from Henry, we needed to understand how to buy gold (since we felt this would be the best medium for our purposes) and how to transport it. Ross set up an account in a Hong Kong bank for initially a million dollars in case we needed it. We visited a couple of banks and found one that would sell us gold, but we would have four hours to get it out of Singapore. Now we had something to deal with if we needed it. (At that time in 1970, it was illegal for a US citizen to own gold in any form other than jewelry). Thus, we would have been breaking the law unless we did a simultaneous transaction ... however it was not against the law in Singapore. If we needed to trade gold for POWs or information, we had it. We would have not used it, however, without clearing it with Ross.

The next morning, we got a call from Henry informing us that Malik would meet us at 10:00 p.m. that evening. We got the visas and flew to Djakarta and checked into a hotel. At 9:15 p.m., a car and military officer met us at the hotel. Henry was not there.

We drove to Adam Malik's house and were escorted into a large room where we waited until Malik entered and sat down. We had an hour-long meeting in English. He was very cordial and said he would see what he could do.

Tom and I felt good about the meeting, but while riding back, the military officer turned to us and said that it would be fifty thousand for the meeting, which blew my mind. I told him that we did not have that amount and that I needed to check with our people in Dallas first. Someone had told Malik that we would pay fifty thousand for that meeting—probably Henry.

They let us off at the hotel, where Tom and I immediately went to our room, packed, and called the airline to get on the next plane back to Singapore. We basically fled the country and were back in Singapore before the morning. I have not been back to Djakarta since.

As a result of the growing publicity after the Christmas trips, United We Stand received a lot of mail that led us to some interesting characters.

Murphy Martin and Merv Stauffer worked the leads in Europe. Jay Holman followed one in Romania and, later the famous actor Audie Murphy called and said he had some contacts in Morocco that could help. Jay set up the trip and, on the way, Audie Murphy got sick and they canceled it. Later on, he asked if Perot could loan him two hundred thousand to get him out of a bad business deal. I had to call him and turn down his request. It was tough because he was one of my favorite Western actors.

We spent a lot of time in 1970 following up various leads, escorting wives to embassies, and meeting individuals with questionable credentials. Nothing substantial came out of any of this. We even spent time in various countries going through foreign newspaper morgues to check on communist reporters who had been in Hanoi taking pictures of the POWs being paraded around as war criminals. We had a little luck here. A POW was identified in pictures but was not on the NVA list of prisoners. It became an issue because that POW, Ron Dodge, never returned and we were able to presume he was dead. It was embarrassing to the North Vietnamese, however.

Marquez, McKinley, and I worked Southeast Asia (Vietnam, Cambodia, Thailand, Laos, Singapore, and Hong Kong). At the time, Chuck McKinley was a "rock star" since he was the 1963 Wimbledon Champion and 1964 runner up. Most of the Asian leaders liked tennis so Chuck was great for getting us meetings with high officials. I spent considerable time with Chuck in Saigon and Vientiane in the early 1970s. In Saigon, the Vietnamese made him an honorary member of the French Vietnamese Tennis Club, Central Sportife (by 1970, few Americans were allowed to be members). It was here I saw many Vietnamese leaders and was surprised how big the former general leader, Big Minh, was. General Minh became the last president of South Vietnam in 1975 as the North Vietnamese

Army was overrunning the country. He then called for a cease-fire as the North Vietnamese army was storming Saigon. They then soon changed that city's name to Ho Chi Minh City.

Often, we would have a meeting set up and it would take a day or two to materialize, so Chuck would take me over to the tennis club and teach me tennis. This is where I began to develop my lifelong love of the game.

On one occasion in Laos, Tom, Chuck, and I flew up to the Plain of Jars with Air America (the CIA airline in Laos) to visit Meo refugees in Sam Thong, a small refugee camp. We spent the day interviewing refugees and asking about American POWs with our priest friend, Father Matt Menger, who spoke Lao and Meo (Hmong). Unfortunately, everyone looked like a white man to them and it was difficult to correlate information. The Meo (Hmong) were a mountain minority in Laos who were fighting North Vietnam invaders in their area of Laos with the help of the CIA (the invasion created a lot of refugees).

On another occasion, Tom, Chuck, and I were invited to fly up to a village in the mountains in a Pilatus Porter, a Swiss turboprop designed to fly around mountain terrain in Switzerland, which was similar to the mountains in Laos. We hoped to question the local village headman. It was a sixty-minute flight and we landed on a six-hundred-foot rock strip on the side of the mountain where the village was. The three of us got out and were escorted by our CIA host to a spot where we met the village headman (chief). After a tour of the village, he led us into a thatched house, and we all sat down on some mats. In front of us sat a large clay crock filled with fermented rice. A young woman brought a bucket of water from a nearby stream and the headman poured it into the crock and began mixing it up. He then pulled out three bamboo straws, gave each of us one and proceeded to show us how to drink from the crock with the straw. I tried it. It tasted like a weak white wine but looked like a liquid with ashes in it. It definitely was alcohol. We sat there until we finished the whole crock. Unfortunately, the headman had no information on captured pilots.

By that time, we were feeling the rice wine but needed to get back to Vientiane because Chuck had agreed to a friendly tennis match with the top player of Laos that afternoon.

Chuck was still feeling the effects of the wine and the Lao champion narrowly beat him in the first set (Chuck may have let him). Chuck handily took the second set and it was diplomatically decided that they would stop at a draw. The Lao fans loved it and this event endeared us with many of the top Lao officials. We never had a problem getting a meeting when we needed them.

The CIA had a station in Vientiane and a compound. We spent some time flying with them in their Air America or Continental Air Services, contract airlines consisting of World War II cargo planes (C47 or C54 and the Pilatius Porter). I flew in all of them but preferred the Porter for its versatility.

The CIA compound also had a tennis court and a number of reasonable tennis players. One night they invited Chuck and me to come and play. We played doubles and they had one aggressive player who tried to intimidate me while I played the net by hitting the return ball directly at me as hard as he could. After a while, it became apparent that was his strategy. Chuck had had enough, so on his next two forehands, he drilled the ball directly into the guy's solar plexus. Both were dead on. The guy got the message and the game got better. (When you are a Wimbledon champion, you have the skill to place the ball wherever you are aiming at, at whatever speed you want.)

Later on in the 1980s, when I was playing a lot of tennis at Bent Tree Country Club and Chuck had moved to Dallas, I would bring Chuck as a partner and introduce him as my friend "Chuck Smith." He had gained some weight then so people did not recognize him and we had a lot of fun spoofing around on the court. We always won. It was sad when Chuck died of brain cancer in the mid-80s. I was with him to the end.

On the Christmas trip in 1969, Marquez and McKinley left Vientiane for Saigon to see if they could get some letters from NVA POWs that we could then deliver to their families. Perot had been exchanging brief communications with Pham Van Dong, the North Vietnamese leader. During this period, Perot offered to deliver letters to NVN POW families and offer financial support to NVN families to send packages to their men.

Actually, this really confused the NVN since NVA soldiers were expected to die rather than be captured. Being a POW brought shame to a family. It was great publicity, however, and angered the NVN leadership. We now began to see negative articles in NVN papers on Perot over the coming months.

My next project was to fly to Saigon with Murphy and work with Marquez and McKinley on the letters, reviewing the POW camps in South Vietnam and Laos, and preparing for another massive trip by Ross.

McKinley and I paired up and went to Laos to collect some letters from the NVA POWs in the prison camp outside of Vientiane that I had visited while I was in Vientiane at Christmas. Murphy and Marquez went to Singapore to follow up on a lead. Murphy then contracted malaria and returned to the States.

In February Tom, Chuck, and I traveled to Saigon and went through the bureaucratic process to receive authorization for Ross, staff, and eighty representatives of the world press to visit Saigon with another big Braniff plane and tour four South Vietnamese POW camps holding North Vietnamese and VC prisoners of war. We had to visit these camps first. This was a trying time, with a lot of down time waiting for meetings. We convinced the US embassy we needed to see some of the troops and went by helicopter to some of the fire bases around the area. Because of Perot's name, we got VIP treatment from the embassy and they agreed to everything we asked for and gave us a helicopter and military escorts.

At one time, Chuck had to be back in New York and Tom and I stayed to finish the advance work. Ross wanted us to call every night, but, because of the curfew in Saigon (and it was the middle of the night in Saigon when they had office hours in Dallas), the Caravelle Hotel shut its doors at 10 p.m. Therefore, we would sneak under the steel curtain closure, run through the dark to the embassy about five blocks away, make our calls on the embassy phone, and then return the same way.

After about ten days, we got a tentative agreement to bring in the plane, but what the Vietnamese wanted and what Ross expected were not the same. Thus, when I went back to Saigon by myself on March 24 to advance the April 1 trip, I had new instructions from Perot.

This time I had Army Colonel Kruger from the embassy (who set up our previous trips and accompanied us in the field in February) helping me. (The embassy and Ambassador Bruce were supporting us on this trip, so it made it easier for me to set up meetings with Vietnamese officials).

It was still a difficult process. They only were going to let us bring twenty press representatives into the camps, even though eighty were coming with Perot. Ross wanted to give the Christmas packages destined for Hanoi, which we still had, to the NVA POWs. However, the general in charge would not let us because he told me that this would make it seem to the South Vietnamese people that the government could not take care of the POWs and he was afraid the NVN would use this as propaganda. (It was a good argument that I could not refute.)

At one point, I met General Throng, head of the Political Warfare Department (propaganda) and spent several meetings trying to convince him that having the world press witness how well the SVN was treating the NVA POWs would be a propaganda coup since it was well known that the NVN treated the American and SVN POWs badly. (He gave me a book and film on the Battle of Hue and Tet in 1968, which I have in my library).

There were a number of letters exchanged by Marquez and later me with the South Vietnamese officials in February on these subjects and later when I came back in March to set everything up. I opened the discussions again to try to persuade General Throng. Interestingly, I did not get permission for the eighty members of the press until the plane was approaching Saigon. (The situation was particularly stressful because I did not want to tell Ross that I had failed).

The large press party toured four prison camps: Phu Quoc Corp 4, Pleiku Corp 3, Bin Hua Corp 2 and DaNang Corp 1 (either Tom, Chuck, or I had visited them in February to check them out as we had wanted to make sure the Viet Cong and NVA POWs were treated well). We had previously gathered the letters from prisoners, although few wrote. But the number did not count … the thought of letters being delivered to families did. (We controlled the letters and did not let anyone copy the names, and since they were not delivered as I figured they would not, I had them translated to put in the file in Dallas.) It was a great tour for the press as most had not been to Vietnam and this allowed them to see the good side of South Vietnam (which General Throng promoted).

It was a great tour in Saigon and that much press drove the NVN leadership nuts. We then went on to Laos and took them through the Laotian POW camp, saw Vientiane, and visited with Laos officials and cultural sites.

After Laos, we flew to Paris to try to deliver the letters to the NVN at the Paris Peace talks. We spent a couple of days flaunting publicity around the fact that the NVA were even cruel to their own soldiers while the SVN took good care of the NVN and VC POWs.

After a couple of days of again trying the NVN in the "court of world opinion," we flew back to Dallas, since (as expected) the NVN had rejected our requests.

CHAPTER SEVEN

OTHER UNITED
WE STAND ACTIVITIES

Our April 1970 "Round the World" trip, in which we toured around with the world press actually visiting "the POW camps in South Vietnam and Laos," was a great opportunity for the world to see how differently the two warring sides treated captured soldiers. By the spring of 1970, the North Vietnamese really began to hate Perot because he had turned the bad publicity on them and they were losing "face." Numerous articles in their papers condemned him as a propaganda lackey for Nixon. This enraged Ross and just encouraged him all the more to come up with a bunch of new projects to keep the issue alive in the media.

It apparently reached a stage that year where the FBI called Ross and informed him that they had sources telling them the Black Panther leader Eldridge Cleaver had been in Hanoi and the North Vietnamese intelligence service had put a contract on Perot. The FBI had no conclusive proof that Cleaver accepted a contract but felt that Perot should be on guard anyway.

EDS, being a company with a lot of ex-military officers, decided to set up a "killing field" in the office so that, if a dangerous person made their way to the thirteenth floor, we had a defense line set up where there was always a shot at them. Each of us on the staff in Perot's area who knew how to handle a gun was assigned a 9 mm pistol. (There was not a lot of security in those days in that multitenant building, so we wanted to make sure the thirteenth floor was prepared).

We would have periodic shooting practice. I would take all of them out to Perot's cabin on about forty acres on Lake Grapevine where we would practice. Since we all owned other weapons besides pistols, we would often take some of these weapons along too. On one occasion, one of the guys brought tracer shells he had smuggled back from Vietnam. There was a cardboard box on the side of a hill about three hundred yards away. He shot at it, and you could follow the tracer bullets with their red tail as they hit around the box. Unfortunately, we also set the hillside on fire and spent a frantic amount of time putting out the fire and leaving several acres of blackened earth. Fortunately, the grass grew back before Ross came out there again.

Fortunately, too, we never had to use the weapons against the Black Panthers or anyone else. Still, I always had the loaded pistol in my desk drawer while I worked for Ross. Merv did too.

The 1969 Christmas trips created a lot of interest in the POW issue among the American public. The message going forward was that the North Vietnamese and Viet Cong were "barbarians" who starved, tortured, beat, and kept American prisoners of war chained in solitary confinement for years. Further, up until 1969, the North Vietnamese had not identified who had been allowed or denied adequate communication with their families.

For the first few months of his campaign, Perot tried to reason with the North Vietnamese leadership, through some communication by cable reinforced with press backup. Nothing worked, so Perot began a phase that within five months created an outcry that would reach the White House and Congress.

He began by going on TV and radio talk shows talking about the issue and what people could do. Further, around the country near military bases, there were some organizations of wives of the POWs and the missing servicemen. Since United We Stand's mission linked up with many of their objectives, Ross traveled to visit with a number of them in the winter and spring of 1970. Another project involved collecting thousands and thousands of letters from American citizens and delivering them to NVN embassies around the world.

Additionally, Ross assisted the wives' organizations to coalesce into the National League of Families of Prisoners and Missing in Southeast Asia. This grew into a forceful and influential organization with chapters around the country under the initial leadership of Syble Stockage, a smart and effective leader. It was a great organization, which UWS and Perot worked closely with as the issue became more prominent in the media. They were extremely effective. I cannot overstate the hard work and successes the wives' organizations had in this campaign. I worked and traveled with many of them and had the highest respect for how they handled themselves under very trying conditions.

During this same period (1970), Perot was funding more trips to Paris and other capitals where there were NVN embassies, as this was where the NVN could personally feel the growing wrath of the American people. Also, he was spending more time speaking around the country (I, too, went on a speaking circuit whenever I was back in the country, especially after the April trip to the SVN and Lao POW camps … I would speak to military groups, churches, civic clubs and, in most cases, I filled in or was a surrogate for Ross as his schedule was so hectic).

When I filled in for him, my standard introduction was, "I know you were expecting Ross, but he, unfortunately, had to cancel and sent me." In those days, the most beautiful movie star was Raquel Welch and the ugliest was Phyllis Diller, a brilliant comedienne, whose persona was dressing like a hag-like wife. So I would begin my speech by saying, "I know it must be disappointing to come here expecting Ross Perot and then I show up. It's kind of like having a date with Raquel Welch, and when you show up, Phyllis Diller is at the door." This always brought down the house. My speech was basically background about POW mistreatment, our objective and activities, and how you too could help. (I would also talk about the Christmas trip and trying to deliver gifts to the POWs in Hanoi, which made for a great story).

During this time also (with all the publicity), we still had a lot of letters and calls from individuals who said they had information and could help. Murphy and Jay were still spending much of their time in Europe following up on these leads. Again, there was no success nor any confirmation that these characters were credible sources, but it often took time to determine this. There were some volunteers, including religious leaders and college professors whom Perot financed to go overseas, presumably to meet with NVA or politically aligned officials. They wrote great memos back, and in most cases, they asked for more money. I do believe that the majority of them were not dishonest and wanted to help and maybe thought that they could. My sense is that they were dealing with a determined and focused totalitarian government (NVN) and they had no clue how to deal with a culture like that, leaving them vulnerable to all sorts of chicanery.

By the end of April in 1970, Perot, UWS, and the new National League of Families had fanned the flames of the POW issue. After the publicity of Perot's second round-the-world trip to publicize the excellent treatment of North Vietnamese Army and Viet Cong prisoners in South Vietnam and Laos, a good many Americans already knew that the US servicemen kept in Hanoi and caged in jungle camps were being brutally tortured.

Ross then came up with the idea that thousands of citizens would be visiting the US Capitol every day, and that setting up replicas of the cages used by the VC and the cells used by the NVA in Hanoi in that vicinity would show the public the conditions in which our men were being kept. They could see it firsthand from three feet away. This morphed into a campaign driven by four points:

1. Permit replicas of the cages and cells used to hold American POWs to be put in the Capitol.

2. Hold a joint session of Congress where a noted specialist would brief the body of Congress on the issue of POW treatment.

3. Include a prayer for the POWs and Missing in the daily congressional prayer.

4. Include the POW issue in the 1970 congressional election platforms.

Even when we were told that by tradition display items were not allowed in the hallowed halls of the US Congress, Ross would not be deterred.

By now, the US Congress was attuned to the plight of the POWs as a result of the generated UWS publicity, letters the legislators received from constituents, and the many visits and notes they received from the wives of the POWs from their various districts.

In April, Ross went before the House Foreign Affairs Committee and argued for the above mentioned four points. Interestingly, Ross did not have a written statement and his whole speech was simply jotted down on a single hotel notepad paper.

I had been in the room with him when he was preparing for the hearing. I think he added some points while talking, since I kept the notepad on which he outlined his points. I was with him in the hearing, at which he received an enthusiastic response to his presentation ... I should point out that before I left Ross, I compiled and edited a thick two-volume book called *United We Stand* that was a commentary and collection of primary source material on his efforts and how one man had such an impact on national policy (memos, letters, clippings, photos, and government documents. It is in my library and you should read it in conjunction with this book, as it will enrich your reading and understanding of the POW issue at that time).

Eventually, Congress and Speaker John McCormack approved the request to have the two replicas of cages in the Capitol during the 1970 summer tourist season. Now that we had permission, we had to create something.

Ross and I immediately flew back to Dallas to get on it. I contacted Peter Wolf, a well-known designer in Dallas, to explain what we wanted. We got Nick Rowe, a POW held by the Viet Cong in the Nu Minh Forest south of Saigon for five years, to help design the cage with Wolf. (Nick was the only American POW to have escaped. He spent five years in the cage and escaped in 1968 during a bombing raid. He became a good friend, but, unfortunately, was killed by communist insurgents on April 21, 1989, in the Philippines where he was the military attaché to the US embassy. I have his book, *Five Years to Freedom*, in my library, and it is a great read on how he survived).

In 1969 three POWs had been released by the NVA as a gesture to the antiwar groups in the United States (Noam Chomsky, Cora Weiss, and other antiwar individuals who did a lot of damage to the personal health and welfare of the imprisoned POWs in Hanoi).

We contacted two of the released POWs to ask them to help with the design of the cell. Doug Hegdahl was a Navy seaman who had fallen off a destroyer and been captured by the North Vietnamese. An incredibly smart young man, he played the role of a "dunce" in the POW camps so he could move around and collect POW names. He was selected for release because they thought he was dumb since he was a seaman who fell off a ship. Before being released, Doug memorized the names of all the POWs held in Hanoi, many of whom our military did not know were alive or a prisoner. The second was Bob Frishman, who was so badly wounded they decided to release him because he was unlikely to survive in prison.

With Rowe, Hegdahl, and Frishman, we now had three experts to provide the details for two incredibly shocking, realistic, exact-size replicas of a VC cage and an NVN cell with life-size POW mannequins inside. The display went into the

US Capitol on June 1 with Speaker McCormack and Ross giving the speeches. Both cages had plaques attached telling the reader what they could do to help bring awareness to further the cause. Peter Wolf was very proud of his work as it was so realistic and millions of people came to Washington that summer felt the agony of our POWs. The NVN hated this move, which could be one of the reasons they began to move POWs into larger groups. Also, I think it was the beginning to be part of the political conversation and affect the thinking of the policy makers in Washington. By fall, the issue was intensifying.

The displays were a big hit and generated a lot more publicity on the issue … (The NVA were going nuts on this guy Perot, as he was disrupting their propaganda war).

Further, as a result of Ross pushing the Committee hearing, we got all of our points, plus an extra one:

1.   the replicas in the Capitol;

2.   the daily prayer included POWs and MIAs;

3.   the Joint Session of Congress speech on September 21, 1970, brought all the lawmakers up to speed on the issue;

4.   the issue was included by candidates in the 1970 congressional elections;

5.   a letter was signed by eighty-nine members of the Senate and sent to NVN, demanding better treatment of the prisoners.

The last point was another idea Ross had, so I spent a week in Washington working with Senator Bob Dole (R), Senator Birch Bayh (D), and their staffs, drafting the letter and convincing other senators to sign it. I worked with Ross as we went around and met with individual senators. It was a real high for me to sit down with some of the lions of the Senate (Kennedy, Fulbright, Mansfield, etc.), and be able to talk with them. We got the resolution signed and sent it to Hanoi.

During this period, we did another big project, which was a POW MIA convention at the DAR Convention Hall. Senator Dole spearheaded this event, which was a real success and generated even more publicity. I got to know Senator Dole during this period and would see him on occasion when I was advancing for the White House.

During the summer, UWS launched letter campaigns to start chapters around the country, generating much publicity and concern.

As I mentioned earlier, one group in California came up with the brilliant idea of selling bracelets with a POW or MIA name and their shoot-down or capture date. These bracelets captured the imagination of the American public and gave the POW issue another boost (and also more funding to further the cause). They had a powerful impact, especially on keeping the conversations about the POWs alive.

In June 1970, I organized and escorted three POW wives, Cathy Plowman, Janie Tshudy, and Cathy Parish, to New York for a week of planned interviews with major media. They were a real hit, and we got a tremendous amount of publicity across the nation. During this time, there were also many spontaneous activities designed by local groups that kept the issue in the press and the minds of the public. Billboards were popular and easy to rent in communities. One strategy that had a lot of success was using announcements at football half-times that could be viewed on national television.

All this created a froth of activity that even foreign politicians and countries saw as valuable opportunities to score points with whatever public they were addressing. The Swedish PM offered to hold the American POWs in Sweden until the war ended; the NVN increased the number and length of the letters the POWs could write and increased the package size to five kilograms. The Pathet Lao now called the men POWs; American politicians were passing resolutions and assigning certain days for the cause.

The antiwar groups were protesting the cage and cell replicas displayed in the Rotunda of Congress (because the latter meant that they were now sharing their war narrative with the POW/MIA families and losing some of their momentum).

We found out from the POWs who returned that their treatment changed radically in 1970 ... I believe this was a direct result of Ross Perot's continuing efforts. Further, the men found out about Perot while in prison, because as pilots were shot down and captured, they would pass on that there was a crazy Texas millionaire who tried to bring them gifts and further was trying to ransom them out. Later they got word about UWS pressure and the family activities.

One of the direct results of the effort was a raid in November 1970 in NVN, at a camp called Son Tay. The raid was led by Army Colonel Arthur D. (Bull) Simons and about fifty very brave Special Forces. Unfortunately, the NVN had already moved the POWs out of that camp, located northwest of Hanoi, in the summer. So, the team came back empty-handed, only winning a firefight with some Chinese soldiers in the wrong place and a few staff in the vacated camp. (I traveled with Bull into Laos in 1973 and he told me a lot about the raid and some good stories surrounding it. Heather David has a great book called *Operation Rescue* if you want to learn more about it.)

Unfortunately, the CIA had shut down our government satellite coverage of the camp that summer, as they did not want to make the Russians suspicious. The timing could not have been worse. Consequently, we did not know the prisoners had been moved from the area. (Bull told me that, while training for the raid, they would assemble the camp replica after dark and take it down before daylight to avoid Russian satellites).

This elaborate attempt on a raid did, however, have a big impact on the POWs' living conditions as the NVN now moved them into large groups so as to better defend against another attempted raid. The real success of the failed Son Tay raid was better treatment for our men, who could now visit and have church services.

The Son Tay raiders were real heroes as when they departed in the helicopters into the heart of NVN, they knew they might not return alive and yet volunteered for this mission.

More needs to be said about the anti war movement tactics and the pain and suffering they caused to POW's and their families. I will let another book cover it because the data is now there.

A good example, however, is Nick Rowe. Captured by the VC in 1963, he was held for five years before he escaped in 1968 from his captivity in the U Minh Forest. Once captured, he went through intensive interrogation and, rather than give them important military data, he made up some to throw them off. Also, he gave them false info that helped save some lives on his former base. Three months before his escape, a top official from the Viet Cong headquarters came to visit the camp where he was now the only POW, as the others had died or been killed.

For years, they tried to get him to make a political statement in favor of communist causes. Since he had been held for five years, it would be a political coup if he would intellectually denounce the war, and they worked over two years to get him to do it by providing or denying food and medicine that would save his life. It was a cat and mouse game, but a major priority for the top ranked VC in the area. Actually, Nick told me playing the game kept his sanity.

Then this top VC officer came to the camp with a file on Nick that showed that he had lied in 1963 and now would probably be executed. The file was provided by an antiwar group with detailed background information on Lt. Nick Rowe. He could not believe that the antiwar group would stoop that low, to do research on the American POWs and provide this information to the enemy. Fortunately, a B-52 raid and helicopter cleanup allowed Nick to make a miraculous escape a few months later, or he may have been executed.

In 1971 we still continued some clandestine activities. Tom Marquez and I traveled to Asia with Anna Chenault (wife of General Chenault of the Flying Tigers of World War II) and Tommy (the Cork) Corcoran (aide to President Roosevelt). Anna offered to open some doors in Asia for Ross, so he took her up on it. Anna was an incredible woman and a person of influence in Washington. We went to Taiwan, Hong Kong, Singapore, and Saigon. We met a lot of leaders and influential people and explained our issue. It was a great trip and I felt once again the plight of the men was getting more understood in Asia too.

In one interesting episode in June, an individual called and asked for money for himself and six other students to go to Moscow and on to Hanoi. He stated that they would be given three POWs to bring back with them as part of a student exchange program for socialist organizations. We decided that, if it were true, I could go along as an additional student. They agreed.

To test it out, I was supposed to meet them in a basement floor of a building in Washington, DC (which, interestingly enough, was about four blocks from the White House).

I put on "my-best-look-like-a-student-sweater" and flew to DC for the time and date of the meeting. I found the building and, at the precise time, went down to the basement floor and into a large room that was set up with informative books and pamphlets on communism laid out on tables. It was right out of central casting; I did not realize that it was apparently legal for the communists to recruit students.

I did not find this individual who was supposed to meet me, but, as I was reviewing some of the pamphlets on the table, a young man in a sweater came over and introduced himself as Ivan Bulbolski and wanted to know who I was. I told him that I was to meet someone. We chatted a little. I "shopped" around for an hour, but no one other than Ivan ever approached me. He may have been the guy and gotten cold feet or realized I was not a far-left student. Anyway, we heard nothing more about these students or from their leader. What is also interesting is that, in a matter of a few blocks, I went from there to a meeting in the White House with some officials on POW matters.

Henry Kissinger and Le Duc Tho (the NVN negotiator) began negotiating a peace treaty in Paris. If nothing else, the NVN now knew how important the POWs were to this process as many movements on their behalf were forming. The NVN embassies were getting a lot of letters and visits during 1971.

The men were still suffering. They were malnourished. They had badly healing wounds. They were still being interrogated and tortured. But they had heard of the efforts on their behalf, so they had hope.

CHAPTER EIGHT

PEACE AND POWS
RELEASED ... WORLD TRIPS

In late fall 1972, the NVN agreed to a peace treaty. At the last moment, they reneged and Nixon was furious. Finally realizing that only force would bring the North Vietnamese to heel, Nixon decided to bomb Hanoi that December and sent in the B-52 bombers. Bombs "rained down on Hanoi," as many of the POWs there later testified. Much damage was done and the world screamed for the United States to stop, but Nixon kept it up until the NVN finally had enough and agreed to terms. After ten years, US involvement in Vietnam was finally over.

One provision of the treaty was the return of all of the POWs and accounting for any MIAs (if possible). During January and February 1973, nearly sixteen hundred men were released—by order of the date they were shot down and captured, starting with those in 1964.

Each planeload of released POWs was flown to the Philippines, where the men were taken to a hospital to get medically checked and debriefed, after which they were sent on to the States to be reunited with friends and family. It was a joyous occasion, covered by the press.

The returnees renewed friendships, wrote books, and went back to their careers; some ran for political office. Several became congressmen. Two, John McCain and Jerry Denton, became senators. James Stockdale ran for vice president on the Perot ticket in 1992. Sam Johnson became our congressman in Dallas and he and his wife, Shirley, became close friends.

Soon after the men were released, many of the senior officers flew down for a visit with Ross to thank him for all he did. During the conversation, they also mentioned how they wanted to thank the Son Tay Raiders for their failed effort. Ross suggested they might want to throw a party somewhere on some weekend to thank them and, if so, he would pay for it.

A couple weeks later, Colonel Sam Johnson came back to Ross and suggested San Francisco for a party. Ross loved it and told Merv Stauffer and me to go out and organize it. Merv flew out and met with officials of San Francisco to explain what we wanted to do while I set to planning the detailed events. Initially, I worked on this in Dallas and then moved to the San Francisco Fairmont Hotel, which we set up as our weekend planning office. One of the events Ross wanted was an old-fashioned ticker tape parade. As I wrote earlier, I had some experience with this in San Francisco during the Nixon campaign in 1968, when we did a parade for Nixon. Actually, the city is really set up for that, so you can work with their professional staff, although at the time I added some balloons bursting out of the street elevators as they opened from the sidewalks. They were very effective. (I had to add a little Nixon advance man touch).

There was a lot of work to do and our staff in Dallas was great with the details. Sally Bell was the glue that held it together. Still, we faced a number of challenges.

First was to get a contact list for the invitees, which included the fifty-nine Army Green Berets led by Bull Simon and the sixty-six POWs held in the Son Tay Camp led by Render Crayton. Additionally, Ross wanted the senior POW officers, as well as all their wives. Not all of the invitees made it, but we had over two hundred eighty people.

Fortunately, Bill Clements, a good friend of Ross's, was deputy secretary of defense. Ross called him, explained what we were going to do, and asked him to give us the contact information of the Raiders, Son Tay Camp POWs, and the senior officers. Of course, the Defense Department had all the names and addresses. Clements opened up the Pentagon for us and I sent each individual on the list an invitation letter on behalf of Ross. If they would respond to a phone number, our staff would make all the travel and hotel arrangements for them, as guests of Ross Perot.

Bull Simons, the leader of the Raiders, thought it was a publicity trick and turned it down. So I called him (not knowing then that I would be spending a lot of travel time in Laos with him that year) and convinced him that Perot was a good man who was trying to thank Bull and his men in a tangible way.

We booked the rooms at the Fairmont Hotel. Ross's instruction to me was the lower the rank, the better the room. Thus, the senior officers got regular rooms and the lower-ranked enlisted got the suites. Some of the Raiders were taken off mountain tops in Laos or Thailand just for the weekend and flown to San Francisco … and their wives, whom they had not seen for months, were flown in from Fort Bragg, North Carolina. Most arrived on Wednesday or Thursday.

Ross wanted the major events on Friday, followed by a luncheon at the Hilton and a dinner that evening. He wanted movie stars at the tables, so he called his friend Taft Schribner (head of Universal Studios) to see if he could get some to attend. Schribner's assistant, Herb Steinburg, helped me arrange it. We had Ernest Borgnine, John Wayne, Clint Eastwood, Red Skelton, and the Andrews Sisters. Wayne spoke at the luncheon, with Borgnine as the MC. Eastwood, Skelton, and the Andrews Sisters attended the dinner. After the luncheon, Wayne approached me and asked if he could come to the dinner too, and I, of course, said yes (yes, yes, yes). At that time, John Wayne was one of the biggest stars in Hollywood.

The big thrill for me was when I first met John Wayne—and what a meeting! I am in the lobby of the Fairmont Hotel, waiting. He walks in about 10 a.m. that

Friday morning. I see him and go over and introduce myself as Mr. Perot's assistant, charged with working with him on the luncheon at the Hilton where he was to speak. We already had a suite for him. When I shook his hand, I noticed it was among the biggest hands I had ever shaken.

He told me to come up to his suite with him. So, Herb and I followed him up. Upon entering, he asked me if I wanted a drink and I said no thanks, but he asked me to pour him one and pointed to a tall water glass. I opened the bottle of scotch and filled the glass. He then sat down on the table and said he was going to jot down what he was going to say. I went to the other end of the table and quietly sat there while he worked.

Suddenly, there was a knock at the door and Wayne asked me to get it. I did so, and suddenly Red Skelton was standing in front of me. Now Skelton in 1973 was the most famous comedian in the United States, with his own TV show. I grew up with his humor. He was my dad's favorite, and mine too.

He came in and went over to Wayne and asked if he could get a picture. He also asked for him to speak into a recorder. As it happened, John Ford, one of Hollywood's most acclaimed directors and the man who made John Wayne famous, had recently passed away. Red was putting together a recording including Wayne, Henry Fonda, Gary Cooper, and a couple of others who were in a photo taken on a fishing trip in Mexico back in the '40s with Ford. The picture and voice recordings were to be given to his family.

Wayne told him to wait until he had finished his draft of the luncheon talk. Skelton came down to my end of the large dining table. Here he proceeded to tell me jokes, all of which were off-color (dirty). This somewhat clouded the former great impression I had of Red Skelton.

Wayne finished and Skelton got the picture and recording he wanted and left the suite.

Wayne said he was ready and made a couple of comments on what he was going to say. I then mentioned that he may not want to say anything that was too incendiary, since we were hauling the POWs and Raiders in open-sided wheeled cable cars from the parades and there were no ropes so they could just jump off. Further, we had word that there may be protestors at the Hilton during and after the luncheon. (This was still during the war and San Francisco was the hotbed of protests). I was concerned that his comments might prompt the Green Berets to leap into the protestors if his comments so incited them.

Wayne looked at me and, in typical John Wayne fashion, said "F—K 'EM." I now really became a John Wayne fan. Fortunately, there was no incident resulting from the luncheon speech.

What is really neat about Wayne is that he went to the dinner that night, not as an entertainer, but as a guest, and we placed him at a table with some senior NCO raiders, who had just come over from Thailand and Laos for that weekend. It was a great thrill and he took several of them out on the town drinking, after which he came back to the hotel and made the kitchen open up for some bacon and eggs.

When I came down at 6:00 a.m. the next morning, there were four of them at the table, looking well-worn and liquefied. Wayne had gone back to his suite.

I often think about how these guys flew back on Monday to their military installations in Laos and Thailand, and how when friends asked what they did over the weekend, they must have responded, "I got drunk with John Wayne." (And I am so pleased that we took the pictures and sent it to them to prove it).

I also had a brief experience with Clint Eastwood, who like Wayne, was among my favorite actors. After the dinner that evening, he came over and asked if we could talk a minute, which, of course, thrilled me. He said he was making another "Dirty Harry" movie and needed an aircraft carrier as a prop. (Eastwood's "Dirty Harry" movies were very popular movies in the 1970s). He was not having much luck with the Navy and wanted to know if Mr. Perot could help him. I told him I would pass the request on and, if he could, Ross would probably try to help. (This is one of the things I liked about working with Ross—I could meet these bigwigs, but I also knew they saw me as a tool to get to Ross so I did not think of myself as a big shot).

Thanks to Ross, Eastwood got the carrier for his movie *Magnum Force*, which came out that year highlighting a motorcycle chase throughout a mothballed aircraft carrier. To this day, I love that movie.

The weekend turned out to be a success, and the dinner was outstanding. We did a photo op so everyone could have a picture with the movie stars and Governor and Mrs. Reagan. Wayne made sure he got in a picture with each raider and POW.

Perot ended up spending well over a quarter million dollars (in 1973 dollars) on this event, but he was very pleased with it. I too liked it, and not just because he gave me a handsome bonus for the job I did.

Two other events during this period involved round-the-world trips. Two years earlier, in the summer of 1971, Ross had asked me to set up a thirty-day trip to see the "great civilizations." He wanted Ross Jr. (fourteen) and Nancy (twelve) to experience these places. Originally, it was going to be a six-person trip, including Sharon, Ross, and Margot. However, Sharon's mother was diagnosed with brain cancer and Sharon, six-month-old Gar, and three-year-old Tanya went to Spokane to be with her. So I ended up going alone with the four Perots.

I planned the trip and contracted with friends and business acquaintances or professional tour guides. We started in Hawaii and then went on to Japan, seeing Nikko, Tokyo, and Kyoto. Then on to Hong Kong and Macao. From there, we flew to Bangkok, using that city as a base to go to Laos (a war zone). Later, Ross and Ross Jr. flew out onto a US aircraft carrier to watch jets fly off to bomb North Vietnam.

From there, we flew to Israel. We were met by the mayor of Jerusalem, Teddy Kollek, who arranged for three days of incredible tours and meetings with top officials. The highlight was when Ross, Ross Jr., and I flew from the West Bank to the Sinai Peninsula and landed at a secret airbase in the desert. We were in a small German plane and did not recognize anything when we landed, as even the runway was desert camouflage. The plane went down an incline into an underground hangar. We were picked up and taken by vehicle to the vacant town of Kantara on the Suez Canal, where we went into a firebase along the canal. The construction using RR rails and ties along with dirt and rock was impressive. I had been in a firebase in Vietnam, but this was far superior.

We were then driven back to the base and taken into a briefing room, where we met General Ariel Sharon, who briefed us on the Egyptian/Russian front, which we had just seen a part of. (Sharon went on to become the prime minister of Israel). I remember asking General Sharon after the briefing if they had contingency plans. He responded that they had "contingency plans from Baghdad to Khartoum."

I was very impressed with Israel and the people there. We had interesting dinners and lunches, where we met a good cross-section of Israelis. There was a strong sense of pride and patriotism wherever we went. They were still carrying the glow of the June 1967 war, in which they defeated three Arab armies in six days.

We then flew to Greece (as we could not go directly from Israel to Egypt because of the politics). We saw the grandeur of Greece, and our transportation was punctual and comfortable; however, our tour guide (Spiro) lacked knowledge. I brought a number of history books along with me on the trip and studied them each night for the areas covered the next day. Thus, in some cases, I often knew as much as our guides. (In Spiro's case, I knew more).

On the last day, Ross asked me to rent a large yacht so we could cruise the Greek islands nearby. This was early on a Sunday, so I called the US ambassador and told him who I was with and wondered if his office could help us rent a yacht. He came through, and we had a hundred-footer for the day that came with a crew of seven and even a speed boat for water skiing.

From Greece, we went to Egypt and the highlights of that great civilization. Visiting the museums, Souk, temples, and Pyramids was a great thrill. Two funny incidents happened here.

At an area near the Pyramids, you could rent a camel ride that would take you down to the Sphinx. It was about a two-hundred-yard ride. Ross Jr. and I each got on a camel and rode down the hill. At the bottom, in front of the Sphinx, were a large number of beggars. They aggressively asked for money when we dismounted the camel. We could see that Ross Sr. was now getting on a camel and coming down to meet us, so I told the men that the man coming was a very rich American. When Ross arrived, he was mobbed as he tried to dismount. At this point, I took a great picture of him kicking at these men while trying to get off the camel.

Later, Ross saw a beautiful white horse and asked me to see if I could get it for him to ride. (He was an excellent rider.) I went over to the owner and explained that Mr. Perot was a famous Texan who loved horses and that he was an excellent rider. I offered him a handsome sum to ride his horse, and he agreed. It was beautiful to see Ross take off on this horse at a gallop into the desert. At one point, about a half mile away, he went up on a mesa and reared up with the horse. All those watching were impressed. He then disappeared for a while and the owner was getting nervous. All of a sudden, Ross and the horse broke out into the open and then trotted back to the owner. It was impressive to see him ride that white Arabian stallion.

From Cairo, we flew in a huge Russian Aeroflot plane to Rome, spending three wonderful days there and then on to Florence.

It was a great trip, during which a funny thing happened that manifested itself about fifteen years later. While we were in Egypt, we went into a souk (market) and Ross wandered into a shop that had oil from flowers grown on an island in the Nile. Further, this oil was used as a base for fine perfumes in France.

The owner pointed out to Ross a case of twelve beautiful ornate cut glass bottles with oil in them, which he said had belonged to King Farouk who was ruler of Egypt in the 1950s. We did not believe him, but Ross wanted the case and told me to get it. I spent a long time negotiating with the owner and finally got a price that would not make me ashamed. I also arranged for it to be mailed to Dallas.

A little later, we were in Florence, Italy. Ross and Margo had been out shopping for artwork. Ross came into my room and handed me a painting by an artist named F. Zanato. He said, "It is a gift because of your talent in negotiating with the Arabs." The picture was of two Arabs sitting in front of a mosque. (A very detailed watercolor, dated 1906).

Now, fast forward fifteen years later. I am with Hunt Oil doing business in Aman, Jordan. We are guests of the government and are on a tour. One place we stop is Jordan's National Art Museum. There was one wing of paintings by European artists who painted in the Middle East at the turn of the twentieth century. At one point, we came to a section of nothing but F. Zanato paintings. I told the guide, oh my gosh, I have one of his paintings in my home. He said, "Keep it, as it is very valuable."

When I returned to Dallas, I set up lunch with Ross. I asked if he remembered buying me that painting and then told him the story of its value. His response in typical Perot fashion was, "Remember Meurer, I just loaned you that painting." Of course, he was kidding.

In the summer of 1973, Ross had another round-the-world trip he wanted me to set up. This time, Margot was invited by C. Y. Tung, the famous Hong Kong shipowner, to launch a very large crude oil carrier, VLCC, in Osaka, Japan. At a meeting in New York, he had told her that he would invite her to launch his next ship. The plan was to fly to Osaka and then on to Hong Kong for some launching parties and then on to London. On this trip, Sharon joined us. A couple of funny incidents happened on this trip.

Ross wanted to have a really nice gift for our host, C. Y. Tung, and for it to be given on the last night in Hong Kong. For this purpose, he bought a beautiful, but extremely fragile, Boehm Porcelain bird called the Arctic Tern. It was packed in a good shipping box and, as long as it was not opened, the integrity of the careful packaging should have held. One of my jobs was to get it there safely.

In Hawaii, when we were ready to board our Pan Am flight to Japan, a Pan Am security official asked me what was in the box. I explained to them what it was and that I wanted it with me in first class. They refused and said I would have to open it. I knew that if I opened the box, we would have a problem, so I asked to see the Pan Am manager.

He came over and I told him who I was and pointed out Ross Perot to him. I explained what was in the box and who it was for. I told him that if I had to open it up, it would make both my life and his miserable. I told him that before the box would be open, that man over there would make two calls: one to the White House, since he was on a White House mission, and the other to Najib Halaby, the president of Pan Am, who is a friend. The manager understood and gave me a first-class seat to strap it in.

Margot and I did play a joke on Ross with that porcelain bird, however. Ross was paranoid about the box, and he was always nervous when I was carrying it. On the evening of the dinner when Ross was to present the bird to C. Y., I took it out of the box and prepared it for presentation (cleaned it up). I then took the empty box with flaps open and walked into Ross and Margot's suite. Ross was standing in the living room and rose when I walked in with the box, which he thought still had the bird in it. As I approached, I faked a trip, and the box soared through the air toward Ross and hit the ground before his outstretched arms. There was a moment of panic until he realized it was just another practical joke. We laughed, but his laugh was shallow.

We had a great dinner that evening, but little did I know this would be the end of my part of the trip. (Sharon went on with Ross and Margo to London on an incredibly long flight via the Middle East. In fact, Sharon said Margo was reading the book *Winds of War* and was halfway through it by the time they reached Saudi Arabia. Ross ran out of work and reading material so he tore off the part of the book which Margo had finished. Ross is a fast reader, and by the time they were over France he had already finished the torn portion and would take a page as soon as Margo finished it. I imagine they really did not enjoy that fine novel).

At the dinner that last night in Hong Kong, I was seated next to the head of C. Y. Tung's security, John Tuan Mu. Formerly he had headed up security for Chiang Kai-shek and the Nationalist Chinese in Taiwan. He was a tough cookie, and I enjoyed conversing with him. At one point, I explained about the POWs and mentioned that now that they were released, we were wondering if all of them were out.

He said that he knew nothing about the American POW issue, but he knew the Asian communist mind. He said that if there was value, they would keep some and that we would never know about it. Further, if they had no further use for them, they would kill them, and, again, we would never know about it. This haunted me and I told Ross about it that evening.

The very next morning, Ross told me to book a flight for Laos and go in and sniff around to see if I could find out anything. I caught the next flight. For a week or more, I spent time with my many contacts and making even more, especially in the mountain people (Meo) community. None, however, could provide any information if there were remaining POWs. I did remember that Bull Simons had organized the Ka (in the panhandle of Laos) to fight the Vietnamese. Maybe he might have contacts that we could pursue. I called Ross, who agreed and told me to get in touch with Bull. I did and encouraged him to join our team since he was now retired, running a pig farm in Florida. I met him in Bangkok and this led me to another great adventure with an incredible man.

CHAPTER NINE

THE SEARCH FOR
ANY REMAINING POWS OR MIAS

I spent a lot of time between December 1969 and the fall of 1973 on the POW issue. The trip itineraries would vary, but one was very unusual. I needed to get out of the country fast. This particular route would take me, via various means, from Vientiane, Laos, to Dallas, Texas.

I left Vientiane in a black government car that took me south about eight miles, to a Mekong River crossing. I hopped into a river canoe, with a long crankshaft outboard motor, on the Laos side, crossed the wide river, and docked in Thailand. I cleared customs at the river town and hailed a rickshaw bicycle driver, pulling a two-wheeled seat behind him. I climbed in. The driver, with calves bigger than his thighs, carried me to a train station about five kilometers away, where I bought a first-class cabin compartment ticket and boarded a train. It was evening, and the train was to arrive at Bangkok International Airport in the early morning.

The train was a piece of art from the last century. It was a wooden, narrow-gauge train, a left-over from the British and unique to Thailand. My compartment was small, with a fold-down, wooden bed on one side and a wooden fold-down bowl holder for washing on the other side. The large window to the outside consisted of wooden slats (no glass or screen). They opened and closed, and I could shut them tight. It was really unique to travel in such a relic.

When the conductor came around, I ordered a dinner of Thai sausage and beer. Afterward, I washed up in the sink and decided to climb in bed to read. I turned on the reading light, leaving the window slats open. I soon fell asleep but neglected to turn off the light or shut the slats.

I awoke to a pounding on the door and my chest covered with a variety of insects, some as long as four inches. The conductor came in and admonished me that I was not to open the slats at night with the lights on, as the illumination attracts insects. It took us a while to clean up and clear out the interesting assortment of bugs that one can pick up while traveling across Thailand at night.

We crossed Thailand diagonally and arrived the next morning at the airport, as the train has a terminal stop there. I disembarked and made a very long walk over a pedestrian bridge, hauling my luggage to the terminal and eventually to the

Thai Airways counter. I bought a ticket to Dallas via Tokyo and flew out a couple of hours later. When I arrived in Dallas, Sharon met me and took me home. This journey was a record for me, a nonstop journey back to Dallas that had included walking, limo car, exotic river boat, bicycle rickshaw, train, jet plane, and Sharon's car to home. It had lasted over thirty hours.

Now to continue. Once the NVN released all of the men they said that they had as POWs and the hoopla over the returnees started to die down, many with ties to the issue felt that the VC and NVN had not kept their word and still held some men captive.

It was a fact that there were still hundreds of men listed as missing in action (especially in Laos) and their families wanted more answers. As a result, a new organization grew out of the old, one that was more aggressive and stressed taking action to obtain more information and put pressure on the communists.

Our government did a review and eventually came out with an actuarial number that was close to the number that had been released after adjustment. This is to say how many pilots may have been killed in the air when a plane was hit, how many would survive bailing out and then landing uninjured, how many died on the ground from wounds or were killed by tigers or snakes. The government eventually came out with a statement that basically said all the captured men had been released.

The conclusion was not accepted by many, especially Ross, as there were over three hundred pilots shot down in Laos who had not been accounted for. As a result, he sent Bull and me back to Laos in July of 1973 to look for clues and information about these men. Bull had worked and lived with the mountain peoples (Ka and Meo) in the early '60s in the panhandle of Laos and the heart of the Ho Chi Minh Trail, so I felt he had native contacts that I had no access to. Further, Bull still had old military and CIA contacts and associates in both Laos and Thailand.

Bull was an incredible leader, and I learned so much from him. He had a logical, no-nonsense mind. At the age of fifty-two he had a thirty-two-inch waist and could do fifteen hundred sit-ups. In Vientiane, we would spend the evenings in the Lang Xang Hotel bar and he would tell me stories about his war experiences in World War II, Korea, and Vietnam. The Lang Xang bar was the spy center for Vientiane. This was not a war zone, so the NVN, VC, and Pathet Lao had embassies there, as did the Americans, South Vietnamese, Russians, Chinese, French, and all the other countries messing around in the war in Vietnam. Thus, in my four years going to the bar in the evenings, I met a lot of interesting people. I also learned how to keep my mouth shut and listen.

Bull told me a lot about the Son Tay raid, much of which was classified. How they got into a fire fight and shot up some Chinese soldiers and how he killed the camp commander and his wife in bed. (It sounded horrible, but they were in the way of the mission, and soldiers die).

Unfortunately, Bull told me the raid was not successful because the NVN had moved the POWs from the Son Tay camp in July 1970 (the raid was in November). Further, he told me that our military had decided not to fly any more satellites over the camp area in June since they were concerned the Russians would pick up the intelligence that the United States was looking in that area. He said they would assemble a camp replica each evening and dissemble it each morning to avoid the Russian satellite cameras for the entire six months of planning. When they did launch the raid in November, the camp was empty of POWs. Ironically, it may have been the Perot factor that caused the North Vietnamese to move them.

Unfortunately, Bull had a heart problem six years later, right after he led the 1979 raid in Iran to get two EDS managers out of jail. He died on the operating table when they tried to correct the issue. It was a sad day for me.

Interestingly, we talked the night he returned to Dallas from the 1979 raid in Iran. Ross called and said that Bull wanted to meet me for dinner, so we had a four-hour dinner at my favorite Chinese restaurant, during which he told me the whole story of the Iran raid. Bull told me about hiding in an attic for many weeks in Tehran with only five-pound cans of Spam and cheese to eat. (This may have been the cause of the heart problem). You can read about this in Ken Follet's book, *The Wings of Eagles*, which talks about the EDS raid into Iran led by Bull Simons. There was also a TV movie made about it.

Now back to 1973 and our effort to find info on any POWs/MIAs still left behind. Upon arrival in Vientiane from Bangkok, I proceeded to introduce Bull to some of my contacts.

The information we received was discouraging because those who were in the flow of information generally felt there were no more POWs in Laos and that the ones who had been shot down had either been killed in the crashes or died in the jungle. If any did remain, they probably wanted to be there voluntarily. We also got information from other individuals with questionable credibility that they had special information about men being held or moved in certain areas. They made interesting stories if you really wanted to believe them and caused one to spend money to follow up. At the end of the day, we concluded that there was no hard information here that indicated there were men left behind.

However, there were four individuals (one I knew and three were friends of Bull's) who we felt had credibility so we decided to see if they could help. None knew if any men were left behind, but they all had organizations that could possibly do some thorough checking. Thus, we set up four different plans to search for men in Laos and named the teams, Alpha, Beta, Charlie, and Delta. We (Ross) provided funding where needed. We asked that they determine (1) if any of the men were alive; (2) if so, where they were; (3) if they were dead; and (4) if so, how did they die.

Further, if they should find any evidence of men alive, they should make no attempt to rescue them or announce the discovery since it could put the men's lives in danger. They should simply notify us so a plan could be set up. Bull stressed this to them emphatically and then again. The four teams were as follows:

ALPHA TEAM

Doctor Jiggs Weldon was a doctor attached to the embassy in Laos. I came to know and admire Jiggs and his associate, Pop Buell. (During the war, a mountain tribe called the Hmong were fighting the NVN on our behalf. The CIA supplied them with advisors, weapons, and fire support. There was a massive refugee camp for those displaced by the NVN in an area called Sam Thong. Pop managed this effort).

Jiggs's job allowed him to travel around Laos. By 1973, he told me he felt that there were no men left behind. We would have long arguments on the subject, and he felt that, even if there were men left behind, our activities could jeopardize them. I tried to convince him otherwise.

When I introduced him to Bull, he then realized how serious Ross was about trying to bring comfort to the families of the missing. As a result, he approached me with an idea he felt could possibly provide some information. Essentially, he said he had a close relationship with high government officials in Laos. According to him, if you did a big favor for a Lao, they would often feel obligated to reciprocate if they could.

His plan was to provide some needed medical or educational services in the United States for children of selected Lao officials. The money would be seen to have come from Jiggs's personal savings. He would hope that once this was accomplished (especially the medical services) and following a delayed point in time, then he could go back to them to ask a favor in the form of a question—"Are there men left behind?"—using the family issue as a justification. He would explain how the families of these men needed closure. He did not know if it would work, but he felt that it was worth a try as if any of the high Lao officials had any information on missing men, they might tell Jiggs.

We agreed, and Jiggs told us he would need $50,000 to set it up. Jiggs did it and several Laotian kids were helped over a four-year period. Unfortunately, these officials had no knowledge. (In my two-volume book on United We Stand, there are copious notes and letters on the plan in detail). We dealt with Jiggs for two years on this, but then the US pulled out of Vietnam in 1975, after which Laos fell to the Pathet Lao, closing down any contact we had in the area as the Lao government officials were all replaced by the communists.

Further, I moved on to work for Hunt Oil so no one was left to monitor Alpha Group. It was a great plan, but the changing political landscape wrecked it. I always felt if the NVN had not taken over SVN that Jiggs's plan may have worked, if there were men still there.

BETA TEAM

The second person was Suzanne (the name Bull used for her, anyway). Suzanne had been Miss Hanoi in 1952 and now owned a bar and brothel in Vientiane. Bull felt that she was also involved in the opium trade. He knew her from the '60s, as she had a company that supplied his troops with food while they worked in the mountains. She had advanced in her business since he had known her. We went into the bar and brothel that she owned, and she treated him like an old, lost friend. After a while, he explained why we were there and asked for her help. Since she had men traveling in some areas of Laos in the drug trade, could she see if they could inquire about any American being held in the mountains of Laos. She agreed and asked for some money to set her lines out. Bull gave her $200 in Kip and she felt that was adequate. Bull checked back in September, but Suzanne had nothing, unfortunately.

CHARLIE TEAM

Vang Pao was a Meo (Hmong) general who led his CIA-supported mountain troops against the NVN in Laos, and he was a real thorn in the side of the North Vietnamese. He was also made a general in the Royal Lao Army (as opposed to the communist Pathet Lao). He was based in the secret CIA base called Long Tieng, which was on a mountain side northeast of Vientiane, but also had a big house in Vientiane for his many wives. (Long Tieng itself was used for controlling the "Secret War" in Laos by the United States and was off limits to anyone and especially the press).

I should point out that we had an interesting experience on the other side of that mountain. Here was Sam Thong, which was the Meo refugee camp operated by Pop Buell. Tom Marquez, Chuck McKinley, and I flew in there in spring 1970 to interview refugees to see if they had seen any American pilots. Our friend and local Catholic priest, Father Matt Menger, interpreted for us. Unfortunately, we had no success getting information on missing men.

We spent most of the day there in Sam Thong, and, then in the late afternoon, we could see NVN troops on a distant hill, moving towards us and so we got out of there. During dinner at the embassy in Vientiane later that evening, I got into a conversation with the Army Attaché. He told me that the NVN would never overrun Sam Thong. I told him he was wrong and that I had just seen them coming over the hill that very afternoon. By the following day, the NVN had overrun Sam Thong.

In 1970 I got to know a CIA operative and pilot named Bob Molberg who was a friend of Vang Pao. Since he would see Pao frequently, I bought a 45-caliber revolver with a black leather holster with silver bullet casings (real show piece) as a gift from Ross to Vang Pao. Molberg delivered it personally when he returned to Laos. He got into trouble with Ambassador Godley for the way he did it and was in danger of being kicked out of Laos. I returned to Laos not too long after that and met with Godley to explain that it was my idea and that I had asked Bob to do it. Godley said Bob had violated strict regulations. I don't know if I helped, but Molberg was still in Laos in 1973, and Bull and I used him to assist us, but only for information.

Anyway, back to Charlie Team. Bull, Molberg, and I went to meet Vang Pao in his house in September 1973. He remembered Bull, and Bull introduced me as an associate of Perot's. Vang Pao asked me to thank Ross for the pistol he had given him and asked us to take back a beautiful Meo flintlock rifle as a return gift for him.

Bull then explained he was there representing Perot and not the US government. He wanted to know if Vang Pao could send some of his men into the areas of the Ho Chi Minh Trail in Laos, where US pilots had been shot down to see if they could find any information on them. He explained we had just met with Pat Landry, head of the CIA in Udorn, Thailand. Bull told Vang Pao that Landry would provide some support and provisions, which could be dropped into them. Vang Pao agreed to help but wanted to wait until after the rainy season stopped (in September) because he said his men could not swim, and it was hard to cross swollen streams. Both Bull and Molberg kept in touch with Vang Pao, who had no success in finding any men alive despite some serious efforts.

Vang Pao sent men into the area and some would seek out their relatives and ask them to go into the villages to inquire about American pilots. In the end, Bull felt that the men shot down in the northern part were turned over to the NVN by the Kha peoples. The ones in the southern part that did escape the crash either died of exposure, were eaten by tigers, or, if found by villagers, were killed in order to keep the NVN away.

DELTA TEAM

When Bull was organizing the Kha tribesmen to fight the NVN in the early '60s on the Bolaven Plateau, he worked with a Eurasian named Jean Coudeux. (I spent time, eighteen years later, working on an oil exploration contract for Hunt in that same Bolaven Plateau ... It was a beautiful area, five thousand feet above the tropical jungle forest, with waterfalls and a perfect climate).

Jean was part Vietnamese, Chinese, and French. He had worked for the CIA. They had been through a lot together, and Bull felt that he could trust him. After we returned to Bangkok, we began our search for him. Bull started calling contacts and finally learned that he was living in a small fishing village, Hua Hin, in southern Thailand. The next morning, we hired a pilot and small plane and flew south, landing the plane on the beach near the village.

We grabbed a ride into town in the back of a produce truck and found where Jean's house was on the beach. We waited about four hours, sitting on some boulders as Jean was out fishing. (I got some great pictures of Bull playing a bamboo flute, which I bought from a kid on the beach.) When Jean came home, we went over to meet him and he invited us in for a wonderful meal of fresh fish.

Bull explained to him why we were there. He told Jean that he was with Perot and not the government. He asked him if he would be willing to help us get information on missing American pilots shot down over Laos. Jean said he would and that he still had his organization intact around Pakse, Laos. He would make a trip there to gain information. We gave him some traveling money.

Several months later, Bull got the report. Unfortunately, Jean found no evidence of any pilots being alive. Essentially, when a plane was hit, if the pilot was not instantly killed, he ejected. If his parachute opened, he would have floated down into a jungle canopy where the chute could be caught and the pilot would be left dangling thirty or forty feet above the jungle floor, with bamboo and other plants below him. If this pilot were to cut himself free, he would fall and further injure himself. Cuts become infected easily in the jungle. Even if he were not injured, he would have to find water and avoid tigers, snakes, and other creatures that could harm him.

There are very few major trails in the mountainous jungle and they are used by villagers. If a pilot tried to use one, he would be sighted, particularly if he were near a village.

Jean came back with the information that to avoid the NVN coming into their villages and harassing them, the villagers would simply kill the pilots with a machete and bury them in a shallow grave. This was also felt to some degree the opinion of Pat Landry, the CIA agent and friend of Bull's.

Unfortunately, none of our four teams came up with any concrete evidence of men remaining in Laos. There were a number of rumors over the years. The movie industry (*Rambo* and other POW rescue movies) further incited questions by the public; at the same time, some of the families of the missing felt that not enough was done. Ross was put on a special commission by President Reagan (in the 1980s) to investigate sightings that were reported to the government, as well as other data on the POWs. Nothing came of it, and this was supposed to have closed the story.

There was a Senate Committee hearing on POWs and MIA affairs, under the leadership of Senator McCain and Senator John Kerry (both later presidential candidates), on the post-POW/MIA war efforts in 1992. I was deposed for six hours and testified on some of my activities along with Ross, Murphy Martin, and Harry McKillop. I told the senators that I did not believe there were any more American servicemen being held there against their will. Ross did not agree with me. He felt some more men were still there. (We have a video tape of our testimony in our files … also, as of this writing in 2022, no other American has been found … other than those that had themselves decided to defect and stay behind).

I might also point out that from 1989 through 1993, I went back to Laos with Hunt Oil Company looking for oil. In the process, the communist Lao government allowed me, Jim Jennings, and Ian Maycock to travel into the southeastern part of the country by helicopter and truck into the Ho Chi Minh Trail area. If they knew American pilots were being secretly held there, I doubt they would have allowed us into the area.

Interestingly, in 1993 after we had signed an oil exploration license, I was dealing with the top Lao government officials. I never mentioned my past experience with Perot and the POWs, nor my times in Laos from 1969 to 1973.

I did get to know the foreign minister and industry minister well during this period. One day, the foreign minister flew into Dallas for a visit, and I decided to take him out to our company Circle K Ranch for an old-fashioned barbeque. While driving out, he turned to me and asked why Mr. Perot still thought there were POWs being held in Laos.

I was shocked by the question, since I did not know that they knew about my background with Perot and the POW issue and I had not told them about my past dealings in Laos. I now did so during the drive to the ranch.

I, then, asked how he knew of my connection with Perot. He said, "We saw you on CSPAN." (CSPAN broadcasted the Senate hearings and they saw my testimony).

I had Ross's number on my car phone and told the minister if he wanted to talk to Perot and ask him the question directly, I would call him now from the car. He emphatically stated that he did not want me to do it.

One other great story with Bull was when we were returning to the United States and had to go through customs. I had to hand-carry the rifle that I previously mentioned Vang Pao gave me as a gift for Perot. I had no problem getting it on the airplane. Now we had landed and were going through US Customs in Hawaii.

In front of us was a military officer who had bought several suits in Hong Kong but had not declared them, which was illegal in those days. As a result, a custom agent came up to him and pulled everything out of his suitcases and then escorted him to a side room.

We were next, and Bull was already not happy that they had made him wait twenty minutes. The customs agent was rude and still angry because of his experience with the previous passenger. He was on one side of a metal table and we were on the other. As we are now standing there, he yells across to Bull, in a rough manner, to open his bags.

The next action was so typical Bull … Bull moved around the table and put his face two inches from the agent, and in a firm, growly, loud voice said, "OKAY Goddammit. I don't care what that guy ahead of me did to you, don't yell at me like that." The agent was so shocked that he said, "Yes, sir" and let us, our bags— and me with the gun—go through.

CHAPTER TEN

MOVING ON ... ROSS PEROT
TO RAY HUNT

Working for Ross Perot for seven and a half years was an incredible experience. It was during this period that he became politically connected, a famous billionaire (at a time when a billionaire was something unusual), a darling of Wall Street, a man who spent his money on great and small causes, and a household name.

As an assistant on his staff, I was exposed to many experiences. More and more, as I would accomplish a task successfully, he would trust me more and give me greater responsibilities. This is what I loved. I interfaced with politicians in Washington and the White House (due to my campaign connections and White House advance work). I got involved in his nonbusiness activities, such as the United We Stand/POW campaign and Working Americans for Tax Reform (to correct faulty tax laws). Later, I handled some of his investments, such as real estate, and even looked at some oil deals before I left. Now that he was very wealthy and famous, I would handle the many letters and calls that came in from people who wanted to pitch a business deal, had real estate to sell or develop, sought to propose an invention to be financed, or just flat-out wanted to request a loan or gift.

I would turn over any contribution requests to his sister, Bette Perot, whose office was next to mine. Bette was one of the most amazing women I have ever worked with ... and she ran the Perot Foundation. By 1974 it was a significant foundation. Ross gave away millions each year. Like Ross, she was tough, very intelligent, and had a quick mind. She also always had a witty comeback and one would have to get up very early to get ahead of her.

I had seen many a strutting man go into what he thought was a "woman's office," anticipating "controlling" Bette, and then come out with real respect and a lot of "Yes, Ma'am."

There was a pattern to these money requests and I developed a "turn down" response letter for each type and numbered them. After I read the request and it was to be turned down, I would simply write the appropriate number on the request letter. Then my assistant would just type the standard response as it corresponded to the numbers. I would spend time meeting and analyzing the more interesting business deals or real estate proposals, and if I felt there would be no interest on Ross's part, I would turn it down verbally. If I felt there was something Ross might like, I would talk it over with Merv Stauffer and get his okay to pursue it further. Interestingly, most of the deals that came in by mail were of no interest. We would probably look at a hundred deals for every one that I would spend actual time on, and maybe there were a hundred of these before we found something to invest in. Ross was a very conservative investor who kept most of his money in Muni Bonds and Treasuries or EDS stock. I learned a lot about real estate and farm and ranch land in particular.

It was a classic lesson when Ross became fascinated with exotic game parks and decided to invest in one after being pitched by a guy in a circus who brought a dog out to entertain at one of Ross's daughter's birthday parties.

Being sold, Ross decided to invest in a drive-through exotic game park, just outside of Washington, DC. He told Merv to go out and look for property, which resulted in the purchase of some four hundred acres of land. We went out and looked at it and decided it would be perfect for exotic game. Merv hired a firm to draw up a park plan and another firm to help us with the zoning change. It was a long hard fight and process to get the land rezoned, but it finally was done and we were ready to start building.

Then one day Merv mentioned to Ross, "I hope those lions don't break out and eat someone as it would be bad headlines for the Perot name." Ross thought about it and decided not to do it and told us to sell the property. We sold it to ABC Entertainment Group for a very, very handsome profit.

What I learned from this was that one real way to create value was obtaining the permitting and zoning on a piece of land ... a lesson I saw work time and again when I went to Hunt.

Another very interesting adventure Merv and I had with Ross's wealth was moving $159 million in bearer bonds (like cash) and stock certificates from San Francisco to Dallas. Ross had invested a lot of money on Wall Street during his purchase of Dupont Glore Forgan and, later, Walston and Company. The $159 million had been used for collateral and he wanted to move it from the Bank of America in San Francisco to his vault at the new EDS office in Dallas.

Merv and I flew to San Francisco and took a cab to the bank. They were prepared for us. I had brought along my beat-up college steamer truck to carry the $159 million. The bonds were $5,000 coupons, so the counting took all morning. We completed the withdrawal and packed them in the trunk and thanked the bankers. They then escorted us out to the sidewalk, expecting an armored car to pick us up. But I just hailed a cab and, to their astonishment, Merv, the trunk, and I climbed into a common yellow cab. When we arrived at the airport, we went through the American Airlines security (this was before 9/11), but when we carried the trunk through airline security, the officer wanted us to open it and I told him no and that I would like to see the supervisor. The supervisor came over and I explained that we were aides to H. Ross Perot and that we had $159 million in the trunk and preferred not to open it for all to see. I told him we would buy the trunk a first-class ticket and he agreed. We strapped it in a seat beside me. When we landed in Dallas, the Perot security team was there to meet us.

Working with Ross was such a pleasure. Every day was exciting. Between the calls in the POW campaign, traveling with him, conversing every day that he was in town and doing things with his family, I felt I got to know him well. The office atmosphere was fun, but hard-working. Often, we worked on Saturdays, but when we did, Ross would either have a nice lunch delivered or he would take us out to Steak and Ale. He would ask for our thoughts and respected our opinions on many subjects. I learned never to try to guess or make up information. If you do not know the answer, say so, but also that you will get it. This was the most important lesson I learned working for Ross.

In a stressful working environment, I found practical jokes to be important because they helped create a balanced environment. Ross loved practical jokes and we played a lot of them. (I could write a book just about these).

A great example was a joke Ross and I played on Merv. Merv Stauffer is an outstanding manager and accountant. Ross used to say, "Merv is so organized that one can hear the relay circuits behind him as he walks." Merv also kept financial records of everything he did in a little notebook that he always carried on his body. He then transferred the numbers to a permanent record. At the end of the year, he knew how many miles he had flown (this was before airlines kept track for points), how many miles he had put on his car, his average gas mileage, etc. He even kept track of his precise gambling wins and losses and submitted them on his tax return if he was in the black.

Well, this particular year, Merv had purchased a new Ford Torino and was very proud of it. Knowing he would now start keeping a detailed mileage record for it, I went to Ross and told him we ought to play a joke on Merv. He agreed. We got the groundskeeper to add some gas to the Torino every day for four weeks, and after four weeks, suck out a little bit for four more weeks. Merv would check his mileage on fill ups (in those days for that car was about 14 mpg) and for the first month, he was bragging about what great gas mileage he was getting. After we began to take gasoline out of his tank (and he had to fill it more often), he started complaining about what a gas hog it was. He finally took it to the shop to get it checked out, but, of course, they found no problems with the engine. We fessed up and had a great laugh. We got him good, which was often difficult to do with Merv.

I really enjoyed my time with Perot, but as an assistant, I had a lot of responsibility without a lot of authority. I realized that for my long-term career goals, I would need to get back into the mainstream of corporate officers at some point. Hunt was the opportunity I needed.

Fortunately, after I did leave EDS, I was able to maintain my friendship with Ross. I really loved and admired Ross and felt a loyalty to him for all he had done for me.

And over all of the years since, I kept a close and wonderful relationship with the entire Perot family, a relationship that I really cherished. Tanya, later, also had a close relationship with Ross while working on a potential book about his POW activities. She did a tremendous job of archiving the files. Ross and Tanya's practical jokes are legendary, with me often as their brunt. The six-foot poster of my head and Arnold Schwarzenegger's body-builder body now hanging in the farm workout room is an example.

Ross was very good to me over the years after I left him. Of course, there was the occasional practical joke that made me feel loved. Additionally, he would give us Christmas gifts, and I would always give him a birthday gift. One year I gave him a fifty-thousand-year-old Mammoth tooth, telling him I finally found a gift older than him … He loved it and fossils followed, many of which are in his family museum.

One year he gave me a five-foot, beautifully mounted sword with a "Who Will Go, Send Me" message and the highlights of my career printed on the mount. (It hangs in my study). Finally, a few years ago, he commissioned an artist, John Martin, to do a large oil painting of me, which hangs in my study. A copy also hangs in his family museum as part of a collection of paintings he commissioned of the men and women who had been important to him in his career. This meant a lot to me, as did the years working for him, during which I learned a great deal from him that prepared me for Hunt Oil Company.

In 1989 Ross's lawyer and a close friend, Tom Luce, was running for governor of Texas. At the time, he was also trustee of the five Perot Trusts for Ross and Margo's five children: Ross Jr., Nancy, Suzanne, Carolyn, and Catherine. Tom had to resign and Ross asked me to assume the role of sole trustee. I agreed and did this for twenty-three years, until the family put all their assets in a Texas bank, at which point I became a director of the same bank.

One interesting story that came out of this was when Ross Jr. decided to buy the Dallas Mavericks, a professional basketball team. The trust had to put up the money, so as trustee, I had to put up my personal financials and fill out and sign the nongambler forms of the NBA. Now, I had never been to a professional basketball game and tried to talk Ross Jr. out of it since I did not know how they made their money. Further, every fan thinks he is an expert on the game and I told him that he would be pestered by those types of calls.

Still, he did purchase the team and I did now attend some games as a guest of Ross Jr. Four years later, he decided to sell to Mark Cuban. I now had another lesson in how to make money … you own a limited franchise and sell to a greater fool who has the money and wants to own a team.

In 2002 Ross asked me to go on the board of Perot Systems Corp, a public company that he had formed after he sold his GM stock. It was a great experience for me, as it was during a time when Congress was changing the way companies operate after the Enron scandal. A new law called Sarbanes/Oxley changed the operations in the boardroom and, as chairman of the governance committee, I spent a lot of time with the new rules. In 2009 we sold Perot Systems to Dell Computer for $4.3 billion. This was the second time around that Ross built a fine company and sold it for multiple billions.

I am still, even in my retirement, a director of the Petrus Trust Company. This is the family bank, which handles most of the family assets. As a result, I am considered a "Texas Bank" board member.

There is one other thing that I would like to explain, before I move on to tell you about my years with Hunt. Namely, Ross tried to get me to come back to EDS, and later the Perot Group, but I told him I could not since I really felt I was having an impact in the Hunt organization. Eventually, as I said, I became a trustee of a number of his trusts and a director of his successful public company, Perot Systems Corporation, so in some way, he got part of me back.

Of interest was a call I received from Ross in 1991. He wanted to have lunch and talk about a project. We met and he explained that he had been giving a lot of speeches around the country; often, during the Q&A, the audience would ask him why he did not run for president. He was thinking of setting up an organization that would identify a better way for the country to select presidential candidates.

I told him that the idea was intriguing, but I could not leave Ray Hunt as I was involved in too many things that I really enjoyed doing.

Not too many months later he announced he was running for president on Larry King Live. The next day after that, I called him and asked if we could have lunch. At lunch, I asked him what happened. He told me that he was in the Green Room talking with Larry King and told Larry the same thing he had told me: during his many speeches, his audiences kept asking him to run. King asked, "What would it take for you to run," and Ross said he'd do it if the American people drafted him. He then went on the live King show and King asked the question again. Ross qualified and answered the question before millions of viewers.

This was before social media, sophisticated cable channels, special interest channels and networks, Sling, Hulu, etc.; there were just three major networks and Larry King was a big draw on CNN, since he interviewed the most important people in the country. It was the show that everyone watched. (Today you would not be able to experience what we did in the late '80s and early '90s on TV because of the many options you have that divide up the viewership into smaller and often polarized or special interest options. Thus, the advertising dollars are less and the budgets are smaller so the shows cannot pay for the many stars and expensive productions that existed in the past. Technology compensates, but star power still draws viewers). What I am saying is Larry King spoke to an enormous portion of the nation each night in prime-time viewing hours. I think Ross saw this and made his move, as he was always thinking six moves ahead of everyone else.

Tom Luce (my good, lifelong friend, who became chairman of the Perot campaign) asked me to come on board, along with Mort Meyerson, another longtime friend. Both of these two individuals were among the brightest and most capable people I had ever worked with. I respected them so much that I knew Ross was in good hands. However, I did not feel I could join the team. One, I liked George Bush (but felt obligated to Ross so would help where I could) ... Two, I had a full, fun, and challenging plate at Hunt. I did not want to disrupt it. Three, Jim Oberwetter, the chairman for Bush, worked with me at Hunt and thus was in my group and a very close friend. Our offices were next to each other, and I did not want to create a problem for him. My instincts were that Ross could not win but could be a spoiler for Bush and I did not want to be part of that.

I did send a letter to Luce outlining what I had learned from my experiences on the Nixon presidential campaign, as well as from White House advancing.

At one point, Ross was going after Jim (as state chairman) and really trashing him. I immediately sent a long (somewhere in the files) letter advising him that I would suggest laying off the criticism and negative comments of Jim because he was a close friend of mine whom I had known and trusted for eighteen years; I also told him Oberwetter was someone who really understood politics and knew the press in Texas. I reminded him to not pick a fight with someone who buys paper by the ton and ink by the barrel. "You are new to politics and Jim is not," I wrote. It was very difficult for me to send that letter to Ross, but I was trying to stop damage occurring to two of my best friends.

As the renewed campaign progressed in the fall, EDS would not let their employees comment on Perot when asked by reporters, so the Perot campaign asked me to give a character reference on Ross, which I was very proud to do. Ross did a tremendous job campaigning and winning nearly 20 percent of the popular vote. I believe that if he had not pulled out in July and listened more to Tom, Mort, and some of the better political pros they hired, he might have had a better chance of possibly winning more votes, or at least, taking enough of Clinton's votes so that Bush would have won.

Again, as much as I wanted to get into the campaign, I felt I owed it to Ray (and all that was going on in Hunt Oil Company) to stay with the company. To be fair, Ray did tell me that, if I wanted to take some leave and get on the campaign, I could.

There are many stories as to why Ross disliked Bush and decided to run. While hunting elk on one of our many long weekends in 2012, Jim Baker (President Reagan's Chief of Staff) told me an interesting story. In the late '80s, Reagan appointed Ross to a board dedicated to resolving the lingering POW/MIA issue. Ross took the job seriously, and, in fact, called me at times to let me know he had information that he could not tell me. (I think he was teasing me).

Anyway, according to Baker, it appears a couple of ex-military guys came to Perot and told him they had identified an area in Laos where some POWs were held. They wanted resources and government help to go in after them. Ross notified the government and recommended helping them. Apparently, after vetting the ex-military and their story with other data, the government concluded it was not real.

Baker said he was in a meeting with Bush and Reagan when the president asked, after he was briefed, who should tell Perot. Bush said that he and Ross were close friends and he could do it. He called Ross and explained the situation, but Ross was angry and felt it was a Bush decision. Either way, this may well have been the decision that cost Bush the election. I do know personally that Ross really disliked Bush in the runup to the '92 elections. He would bring it up to me every time we were together that fall.

Here is another interesting story on George W. Bush (43) that, if true, may mean that Ross was responsible for George W. becoming our forty-third president in 2000. I did ask President Bush (43) on an elk hunt about it, but he disagrees. You decide.

Jim Nicholson, head of the Republican Party in 2000, told me this story. We were at a dinner in Mexico City for the inauguration of President Fox of Mexico. He found out that I was a good friend of Perot's. Nicholson's daughter decided to go to SMU and he took her there in September 2000. While in Dallas, having never met Perot, he decided to make a call on him and took his daughter with him. Ross was very gracious, and they had a great meeting. Ross told Jim's daughter that since she was in his town, if she had a problem, to call him. In early October, she had a horrible migraine headache and called Ross. Of course, he opened up the Presbyterian Hospital for her and even made a visit to her. She turned out okay.

In late October, Jim was in Dallas again and decided to go over to thank Ross for helping his daughter out. According to the story, they discussed the campaign and Jim told Ross he ought to come out and support W, as the voting was binary and the other choice was Gore.

Just two nights later, Ross went on Larry King Live news show, which just happened to be the same night the news broke that Bush had received a Driving While Intoxicated (DWI). Ross argued that it was thirty years ago and that it should not be held against him. He declared he was a very well-qualified candidate to become our president. He also said that he had two choices and he could not go with Gore. Ross, a former presidential candidate in 1992, still had influence with some voters.

Now, the 2000 election hinged on a few votes in Florida because of the electoral college rules. One could well argue that, because maybe two hundred thousand Florida voters watched Larry King that night, a small number may have been swayed by Ross's comment. (Just a few were needed, as Bush won by less than six hundred votes).

Thus, one could argue that, statistically, the 2000 election was determined by a migraine headache of a nineteen-year-old SMU student with a connection to Perot.

I first came to know Ray Hunt as a result of a campaign event during the election where George H. W. Bush (41) was running against Lloyd Bentsen for the US Senate seat in Texas in November 1970. Ray was the Bush Dallas Chairman for the event and I was assigned by the White House as the advance man, since Nixon was coming to the event. It turned out to be an outstanding, overflowing event, thanks to Ray and the Dallas team. Nixon was very pleased, and afterward, came over to me. He put his hand on my shoulder, thanked me, and told me to tell Ross he appreciated his continued support. I was in hog heaven, although I realized this was a good way to get his message of appreciation to Ross.

Ray and I became friends after this and we would have occasional lunches, dinners, and Ray would invite me every year to go hunting on his ranch in Wyoming. Also, he formed a group of up-and-coming businessmen and lawyers into a political/economic discussion group, which we called the Aardvark Society. We met eight or nine times a year at the Petroleum Club. As a result, Ray and I became good friends.

Ray originally offered me a job in 1973, but I told him that I was not in a position to leave EDS. Two years later, Ray's father, H. L. Hunt, passed away. Unknown to Ray, his father had made him executor of the will with the stipulation that, if any heirs protested the will, they would be left with nothing. His five half-brothers and sisters were not happy with this decision and were not cooperating or making his job as executor easy.

H. L. Hunt was a very successful oil man who became one of the wealthiest men in the United States. He had three families, for a total of fourteen kids. Ray was the youngest son. H. L. had been a very demanding father. When Ray and Nancy married in 1965, he told them to move into a nice big house near his mansion, Mount Vernon, on White Rock Lake in Dallas. They did, but in about six months, they wanted to move into a starter house in an area near their friends. So, one weekend when H. L. was out of town, they moved out. When H .L. came home from a business trip and found that they moved out, he was furious. The next day he called in the company's general counsel, George Cunyus, and told him to cut Ray out of the will.

As George told me later, George amended the will eliminating Ray and brought it back to Mr. Hunt two weeks later. He put the new will on H. L.'s desk and said, Ray Lee is cut out of the will. But then George added, "That kid sure has gumption." Mr. Hunt stared at the will for several minutes and then ripped it up, saying Ray was the only one that could hold the family together when he was gone. That's how Ray became executor.

As executor, he had a big job. One of the wealthiest men in the world had died and the IRS was "very interested." There were appraisals, lots of lawyers, and lawsuits by grandkids who were not in the will and felt they should be. On top of this, his half-brothers and sisters were making it difficult to do things with the assets since they now owned 18.5 percent of the estate, the rest of which was left to Ray's mother and Ray and his sisters, June, Helen, and Swanee. These half-siblings threatened to sue just to create a problem for Ray. This is what he faced going into 1975.

In August 1975 Murphy Martin called me and said that he had lunch with Ray, who mentioned to him that he would like to hire me. I told Murphy that Ray had spoken to me a couple of years before, when I was not in a place where I could leave EDS, but now I may have some interest. Within a week or so, I got a call from Ray, and we set up lunch. Over the next few weeks, we had a couple of other meetings and I became really interested. Finally, Sharon and I agreed that I would join Hunt.

In September 1975 Ray was to pick us up for a Sunday Cowboy game. At 1:00 p.m., he showed up at the door, and I told him then that, if the offer was still open, I would love to join his company. I asked him, however, to give me time to tell Ross, as I wanted to do it at the right time. The following Thursday was a relaxed day, and so I went into Ross's office to explain to him that I was resigning and going to join Ray at Hunt Oil Company.

His reaction was really strange. First, he said he had been in his study at 1:00 o'clock on Sunday (same time and day I told Ray) and randomly wondered why Ray had not tried to hire me. He said the word on the street was that Ray was having a tough time with his half-siblings, and he thought I would be just the person that could help him. He was not happy that I was leaving, and, as the years went by, he would often look at me and say, "I do not know how I let you get away.

CHAPTER ELEVEN

HUNT OIL COMPANY

My starting date for joining Hunt was October 15, 1975. (Actually, I went to work without pay for the week of the eighth, since I was going elk hunting in Wyoming with Ray for a week in November and I felt that it would be wrong to take a week's vacation a month after I joined.)

This was the beginning of nearly forty years of exciting and enjoyable employment working for an incredible man and being part of a team that built a big, private, international company, covering oil and gas exploration on six continents, pipelines, refining, LNG, electrical power and transmission, land and cattle, private equity investments, real estate development, hotels, and alternative energy.

I ended up being a senior officer and board director in the parent company, Hunt Consolidated, Inc., and at one time or another, was either a president, senior vice president, or director of any one of the fifty-six different companies in the Hunt family of companies, and a trustee of a number of the family trusts. I was also a trustee for the company's medical, pension, and 401K programs.

I do not intend to give you a year-by-year account of these forty years. Rather, I want to tell you about Ray and his interesting background and then highlight some of the exciting times doing business during the last fifteen years of the Cold War, a regional war in the Middle East, and a civil war in Yemen. I also have some stories about witnessing the "evolution" of the "democracies" in the '90s, the world of tribalism in the early twenty-first century, and the technology boom led by the internet and "Moore's Law."

Ray Hunt is one of the smartest, most perceptive, and effective business leaders I know. One can add to this is humility and caring for other people. He has an incredible mind for calculating odds, a trait needed in business and, particularly, in the risky process of finding oil and gas in a competitive world. Like Ross Perot, he is always thinking six moves ahead, is totally focused on an objective, is a visionary, has a good moral compass, and is a basic contrarian, traits that have made both men very successful, very popular, and billionaires. It was the luck of the stars for me and my family to be associated with them at an early age.

Like Ross, Ray also has a trait that makes him so effective … namely, persistence. There were many times when, on complicated deals where the odds were against us and the management team wanted to throw in the towel, Ray would say no and double down the effort.

In the 1980s, a beautiful towering office building called Fountain Place was built in downtown Dallas; it would be considered one of the most beautiful buildings in the United States. Its construction was accompanied by a lot of problems. By the time it was completed, the office space market was at a low, and the owners did not have enough tenants to service their debt. They went bankrupt and the building reverted to the banks. While the banks sold it at a loss, the buyer got Fountain Place at a reduced price. Still, the market was such that the new Australian owner did not have enough tenants, so he sought to lease out space. Ray had made an offer to buy it, but at too low a price. Now, however, our leases were up in our current building, and Ray wanted to lease space in Fountain Place. We, the management team, wanted to either build a new building downtown, move out of downtown to North Dallas, or strike a bargain lease with our current NY landlord (which was feasible, because they needed our 350,000-square-foot lease).

We definitely did not want to pay an exorbitant price in the very expensive, new building. Ray finally got tired of listening to us and struck out to do a deal himself. Because Hunt leased 350,000 square feet of office space, Ray had leverage. Fountain Place had about 1.2 million square feet and half of that was leased. The Australian needed to lease about a total of 750,000 square feet to make the building profitable.

Ray drove a hard bargain, but (1) he got a below market lease price; (2) he got a $35/square foot improvement allowance ($12.25 million for fixtures, etc. … the highest ever heard of in the Dallas market); (3) our Woodbine Company would manage the building for a 2 percent fee (an annual rate based on the value of the building); and (4) Hunt would receive a 25 percent imputed interest when and if the building was ever refinanced, in cash. (As it was, Hunt's 350,000 square feet allowed the new owner to refinance the building and he pulled out $32 million, of which Ray automatically got $8 million).

It was the deal of the decade. We, on the management team, were patting ourselves on the back about it, even though we had nothing to do with it. It was Ray's doing, with the help of Tony Copp.

I can cite a number of examples like this and will do so as we go forward on my experiences with Hunt.

Even though Ray is extremely wealthy (he has been on the Forbes billionaire list for years), like Ross, he does not flaunt it. He drives himself to the office and eats at his desk or in the company cafeteria with other employees (unless he has business meetings). He does not wear expensive clothes.

He does use a private jet, but that is more for efficiency and security so he can cover a number of states (often on the same day) to maximize time. I have traveled all over the world with him in the jet. Quite frankly, there were many times I would have preferred flying commercial, as Ray sees the plane as an office in the sky. We worked the whole flight, which is okay domestically when it is a three-hour flight but can be wearing on a long, overseas haul.

Unlike some wealthy people, Ray believes in good tips and using valet parking because he feels a good waiter or waitress and the car parkers work very hard in their jobs and should be supported.

Ray has an unusual management style. He carries a small notebook in his shirt pocket, with a 1950s Parker click pen (which he orders by the gross since this is the only type of pen he uses). When he has an idea, or someone mentions a project, he jots it down in the small notebook. He then will "flesh" this notation out and transfer it to a legal yellow pad. This pad has every line filled with a task and the responsible person to accomplish it. He then calls the designated individual to discuss and assign the task. He will then follow up with an email to the individual outlining their understanding. He assigns a time and then does follow-up memos if there are delays or problems. This is a very effective way of managing. The yellow pad looks like a mess on his desk to the casual observer, but it is an effective tool.

Ray's most frequently used word to his employees and friends is "thank you." After a task or project is finished, Ray will call and thank the person and then follow up with a beautiful letter of his appreciation and how important the job was. As one of the many recipients of many of these letters, it always made me feel good that he showed his appreciation this way. Even in this era of emails, he will send out personal letters.

Ray has the ability to dictate a letter or memo perfectly on the first round. This is an incredible talent, since he is extremely articulate and has a mind that sorts and thinks before he speaks. Ray is extremely bright with a high IQ. Combining this intelligence with his organized and articulate mind has allowed him to send out volumes of memos, letters, position papers, and highly crafted correspondence on the first try. To help him meet this standard, Ray has had a smart, efficient, and well-organized executive assistant, Cherry Sossamon, who has three assistants working for her. Cherry sets the gold standard for a CEO executive assistant.

The team does a great job in keeping the flow and allows Ray to do the work of at least two or three CEOs.

Ray is different from most CEOs of large companies in that he runs a private company where he is the "sole voting" stockholder. Further, it is a company that is financially and technically sound. A company that is a leader in its many fields. A company that is active in many different industries. He is not an employee or "ship passing in the night" like most public company CEOs. Thus, Hunt Consolidated Inc., as a company, can make very quick decisions and there is no board to okay a decision or stockholders to oppose it. (We had a board of which I was a member, but our meetings would be advisory, legal, and procedural in nature).

This was a great advantage for me when our team was traveling the world to meet with the senior leaders of countries where we wished to explore for oil. After we had acquired a license to explore and, hopefully, discover something, Ray would personally get involved with the top leadership of the country to ensure we met their expectations and to air any grievances that we may have had that could hinder our operations. Those leaders knew that over the course of a twenty-five-year project they would be dealing with just Ray Hunt.

Ray is a hard and extremely efficient worker. When I worked for him, he would start his day on the exercise machine while dictating or making phone calls. He would generally not leave the office before 7:30 or 8:00 in the evening. Then he'd work from his study at home making calls, dictating, or writing emails. He and I had different hours as I am an early riser (4:45 a.m.) and in bed by 10:00 p.m., where Ray might wake at 8:00 a.m. and work through to midnight. We traveled a lot together in the United States, Europe, Asia, South America, and the Middle East, and it was tough for me (as a morning person) to adapt to his evening schedule. I did adapt, however, thanks to time zones, as there was no way I was going to get him to adapt to mine.

The only exception was hunting, as we normally roomed in the same cabin each year and he was always up before daylight.

Ray is one who is always anticipating bad things that could happen in the future and how to mitigate the damage. Two examples of this are:

9/11/2001

At the time of the attack, Ray was at a meeting in Calgary, Alberta. In the immediate aftermath, the US government required all flights in the air to land at the nearest airport and shut down all the air space, airports, and flights in the country. Ray was instantly on the phone with Dallas, instructing our security director to evacuate the building and send people home. A lot of people were in shock that this could happen in the United States.

Now, however, he needed to get back to Dallas, but all planes in the United States were grounded. At that time, Ray was on the Board of the Federal Reserve Bank in Dallas. They had a board meeting the next day, so our pilots sought permission to fly him, in our private jet, to Dallas from Calgary. We got permission and control by Cheyenne Mountain (the military flight control in Colorado), and the Hunt jet was one of a handful of planes that was allowed in the air on September 12.

When Ray arrived in Dallas, he immediately set a security system in motion for our building. Hunt Consolidated, Inc. was by this point in Fountain Place, which was the signature building in Dallas. Like the Twin Towers, it would be a candidate for a terrorist attack. Also, about 20 percent of the building was leased by the US government for the Environmental Protection Agency, which could be a bonus target if someone wanted to take down the finest building in Dallas and kill some government employees.

At the same time, Ray told me to call an urgent meeting of the building managers and every tenant, large or small, in the building. We met in the early afternoon. Under Ray's direction and bank account, we set up a security checkpoint. The parking lot was under the building, and a big enough bomb could bring down the whole fifty-seven-floor structure. To prevent this from happening, Ray got everyone to agree to the checkpoint, saying that he would pay for it and we could square up later. Essentially, we hired security personnel at the entrance to set up a perimeter system. We designed and printed official stickers for people to use if they had parking places in the building. The system became more sophisticated as the War on Terror advanced. During this period, we developed effective evacuation techniques that would apply to situations where our employees needed to get out of the building safe and quickly (fire, tornados, dirty bombs, etc.) and out of Dallas, if necessary. Fortunately, there was no attack, but a few years later, the Dallas Police arrested a man who had a plan to bomb our building but never had the chance to formulate it properly.

BLACK SWANS

A Black Swan is a metaphor that describes an event that comes as a surprise, has a major effect and, later, may be seen with the benefit of hindsight. Essentially, it is an event that deviates from what is normally expected and is difficult to predict. Ray feels that a company that spans the globe, operates in countries that can be unstable, and is involved in oil and gas production, refining, liquid natural gas, pipelines, electricity transmission, wind power, real estate development, and agriculture can be adversely affected by a Black Swan.

Thus, he formed a Black Swan committee (of which I was a member) to address a Black Swan event, if one were ever to happen. We identified the worst things that could happen to our operating area and then randomly announced a Black Swan event, after which we observed how our managers would recover from it. We could not predict one, but we could and did plan for reaction, response, and recovery, in the event that one did occur. This is an example of how Ray's mind works to anticipate the future.

My fifty years of knowing and working with Ray have been the most satisfying period of my life and I am pleased that now, in retirement, I am still working with him and the Perot family on their family boards.

I will say more about this in a later chapter.

CHAPTER TWELVE

MY INITIAL EXCITING YEARS WITH HUNT OIL COMPANY

I joined Ray without knowing anything about the company. I knew and totally trusted Ray. And I knew his dad, at the time, was considered to be the richest man in the world. I did not know anything about their business, other than they were in oil and cattle. I was coming out of the nascent computer software world, where systems and efficiency were the order of the day.

In fact, there's a funny story: I met H. L. Hunt once, well before I worked for Ray. I asked Ray in the early 1970s, after we became friends, if I could meet his dad. This was in early 1974, before H. L. passed away. One day, Ray called and said we could have lunch with him, but I was not to tell his dad that I worked for either Ross Perot or for Richard Nixon. I agreed, as apparently Mr. Hunt had strong feelings about Nixon and Perot. Ray felt if he'd known about my dealings with them he might have said no to the lunch or spent the entire occasion discussing both men. (Here, again, is an example of Ray anticipating something and avoiding a problem, since he knew I wanted to listen to the wisdom of his dad).

We met in H. L.'s office, and his lunch was fruit and seeds. Ray planned to take me up to the Petroleum Club after, for a fun meal. I loved talking with Mr. Hunt, and his historical references to many current and past events were very interesting. When we were through, and Ray and I were to leave, Mr. Hunt told Ray to get me a packet of his health products and the books he had authored on life and philosophy. Ray did so and I still treasure the books as unique and a reflection of a core American ideology of Texas in the '50s and '60s. (The books are in my library.)

As we departed, I told Mr. Hunt I really was honored to meet him and that I hailed from out west in Washington State. Where I was raised, it was considered that a man's wealth was not based on how much money he had, but on the quality of his children. I told him I knew Ray and his son, Lamar, and, thus, where I came from, I would consider him a wealthy man.

He laughed and told me a friend of his from Houston referred to him as a super sire. Little did I know at the time that he had three families and fourteen children and that I would be involved in untangling them from the assets of Ray's Hunt Oil Company.

Another funny incident happened after I joined Hunt. Ross sent me this big poster of an angry, grizzly-faced cowboy with the caption saying, "I didn't know all this when I signed on with this outfit." I hung that in my office for two years; it was a big hit.

I did learn about the company and quickly saw what great potential it had. Ray, his mother, and sisters had inherited Mr. Hunt's Hunt Oil Company. It was not as big as the IRS, the newspapers, and especially J. P. Morgan, who did the evaluation, thought it was. I recall it being worth less than $75 million, which included the oil and gas production, refining, pipelines, two hundred fifty thousand acres of ranches, one hundred thousand acres of timber, and a packaging company. It was also a company that was losing its employees, since the older family was luring them away. As Mr. Hunt got older, most of the new assets were put into the trusts of the older family through their own machinations.

The older Hunt family (Margaret, Hassie, Bunker, Carolyn, Herbert, and Lamar) inherited 18.5 percent of the estate. They could not protest it by reason of a provision in the will whereby Mr. Hunt stated that anyone who protested the will would be cut out of it. In retrospect, their individual trusts were much larger than the estate. This did not stop them from trying to make Ray's life miserable after 1975.

Ray was in the process of beginning a hotel development on the west end of town, which at the time was an eyesore and mud pit (which later became Reunion Tower and the Dallas Hyatt). He had hired John Scovell to spearhead this project. Although young (twenty-six years old), John had been an all-conference quarterback at Texas Tech, a Harvard MBA, and was working at Arthur Anderson by the time Ray hired him. He was the perfect hire. (John went on to build Woodbine Development Corporation with Ray, which would become a premier real estate development company in the United States).

Anyway, Ray planned to use some of the oil company's assets to secure a loan for the hotel development. The older family protested and threatened to sue Ray. Generally, any direction Ray tried to take would be met with criticism and objections. It reached a point where one member of the family (sometimes inebriated) would call Ray's mother, Ruth Hunt, and harass her over the phone. It was a frustrating time for both Nancy and Ray.

Ray was finally fed up and concluded that the only way to get the family off his back was to buy out their 18.5 percent. They had the opportunity to cherry-pick what they thought were the best assets ... the timberland in Florida and select oil properties in North Dakota and Louisiana. These were identified and dumped into a company they created called Hunt Energy for tax reasons, and which they later spun off. As part of the deal, they moved out of the office building that was the Hunt Oil Company headquarters into another new building, where they consolidated all of their other holdings, including Placid Oil Company and Penrod Drilling Company.

Now, in 1976, Ray was free from their interference. He, now, would run the company as he pleased. This allowed him to receive the financing and start on the Reunion Hyatt hotel and tower project that was to totally change the west end of Dallas, eventually becoming the classic icon for the city as a whole. Interestingly, this was a unique deal, as it was a joint venture project with the city of Dallas. Half the land was owned by the city and the other by Hunt—probably the first time a public-private deal of this magnitude had been done in Texas.

Now that the older family was out of Ray's hair, our lawyers and tax people were dealing with the IRS to get H. L.'s estate settled. Ray focused on getting back into the oil business and began to hire outstanding people. In 1975 he hired Walt Humann, a rising star at LTV (a large aerospace firm in Dallas). Walt, too, brought a skill set to Hunt. He was a White House Fellow with business experience and a graduate in physics at MIT, a Harvard MBA, and a graduate of SMU Law School. Walt was also voted among the top ten young men in the country by the JCOC ... as a point of interest, Elvis Presley was also in this class and gave the other nine recipients a gold watch as a reminder. (Walt treasures that fact).

The first thing we did to get back into the oil business was to "farm into" a fifteen-well program promoted by another oil company. Simultaneously, we began to hire technical people and exploration managers. We set up exploration offices in Billings, Montana, Denver, Colorado, Houston, and Midland, Texas, and hired managers for these offices. I hired Jim Jennings in Houston, who later became president of Hunt Oil Company and one of my best friends.

We had some successes, but one of the big breaks came in 1976 and demonstrated how Ray thinks.

Having come out of EDS and a systems background, I felt we should set up a strategic plan reflecting Ray's vision for the future of the company. I got Walt and Ray together for lunch one day and suggested we come up with a long-term strategy plan. Essentially, we decided that the United States was good for our business and there was opportunity and no need to go international and incur the challenges and costs of working in a foreign country. Thus, I drafted up an outline of our strategic plan, which I would flesh out later and submit to them.

Before I could finalize it, we found out that Mesa Petroleum (Boone Pickens) was looking for a partner in a well they were drilling in the Moray Firth of the British sector of the North Sea. Ray looked at the deal, liked the odds, and decided to go for it.

So much for the strategic plan. We had a successful discovery, which became the Beatrice Field (named after Boone's wife), one of the important oil field discoveries in 1976. I learned from this that Ray was an opportunist and was willing to take risks as long as he did not risk more than he could afford to "bet the farm." This also now made us an international oil company with aspirations for finding elephants (giant oil fields). Little did I know at this time how it would affect my career as a globe-trotting executive.

Before I get into that, I need to tell you about a couple of other events that happened during this period. One was the completion of the Hyatt Hotel at Reunion in 1978 and the Reunion Tower, which redefined the downtown skyline of Dallas. Under Ray's direction, his real estate development company, Woodbine Development Corporation, run by John Scovell and his number two, Doc Cornutt (both in their twenties), put together a team and built the hotel under budget and under time. It became a real hallmark of Dallas and one of the finest hotels in Texas. (Also, it made all employees proud to be associated with the Hunt name).

The tower made the development unique because of the flat landscape and its location in the west end of town. Further, it cemented a relationship with the Hyatt Corporation. Hunt went on to build a number of hotels with the Hyatt flag. I did not work on this day-to-day, but as a senior officer at the corporate level I was involved when needed and to this day take great pride in the fact that I worked with John Scovell and the Woodbine team. (A book needs to be written by John Scovell).

The other major event was a trial wherein Ray defended the estate against a third family of Mr. H. L. Hunt. This was a difficult challenge for Ray as executor. He handled it deftly in spite of the many obstacles and challenges presented throughout this episode.

My job, along with our security director, retired Secret Service Agent Walt Coughlin— who is a whole book in himself—was to assist Ray's sisters, June, Helen, and Swanee, ensuring they avoided speaking to the press and were in the courtroom when needed.

I came to know and really admire all three sisters during this period and to realize what an incredible woman their mother, Ruth Ray Hunt, must have been to have produced such incredibly intelligent, well-informed, highly educated, and compassionate adults. Despite the trial situation, it was a fun moment for me since I was able to get to know them and develop a close relationship with all three. Those relationships have endured since 1978 to the present.

First there is Swanee, an independent thinker and brilliant woman, who is active in politics and the major issues concerning women, around the world. She was appointed ambassador to Austria during the Clinton administration and later became a lecturer at Harvard. Nobody's fool, Swanee knows her facts and could argue with a sign post and win. She excels as a philosopher, photographer, composer, and author. I've so loved our debates.

Then there is Helen, a very smart, compassionate and perceptive woman dedicated (with her husband Harvell) to preserving families around the world by helping couples in crisis communicate safely and effectively. A best-selling author, she (like Swanee) donates her time and money to their foundation for women's issues. Together, these sisters were once named the ninth most effective philanthropists in the world by Barron's. Helen is such a pleasant person to be with because she is always caring.

Finally, there is June, who has given her life and fortune to serving Christ. She could have made that same fortune with her inspirational singing voice and original music but she has freely dedicated those gifts to her cause. Founder and "Chief Servant Officer" of her nonprofit groups, she is also a prolific author and has two nationally syndicated radio programs (nine hundred outlets worldwide) that address the concerns of individual people seeking to better their lives. June has never met a stranger she wouldn't help, nor will she shirk from helping someone in need. I always feel so good after spending some time with her.

Like Ray, each sister has had such a powerful impact on the lives of others. And when you add Ray into the mix of these uniquely talented special siblings, you have to admire whatever it was that Ruth Ray Hunt did with her offspring. She was a tough, wise and perceptive woman. During this trial, I learned that she also had a good sense of humor.

Mrs. Hunt did not travel to Louisiana for the trial, but she did want a daily report, so I was designated to call her in the evening. Now, this was in January when in North Texas and Louisiana, we have flocks of obnoxious black birds called grackles. They are a littler smaller than a crow and they flock in large numbers at sunset to spend the night roosting in trees. They are noisy and extraordinarily messy. Their massive droppings resemble white Hershey's kisses with gray tops and the birds seem to hold them until the moment they get on a tree and then gravity takes over. The dropping cover everything—even other birds, especially those unlucky ones on the lower limbs.

In 1978 there were no cell phones. The popular way to call was on a coin operated pay phone, which was generally housed in a stand-alone booth, with windows and a door. One would enter, close the door, and put quarters in the slot to make the call.

Now, outside the courthouse, there was a pay phone but it was more open to the elements than most. Further, there was just enough of a plexiglass half-moon covering to shield a caller from moderate rain. It was also the only booth around and it happened to be under a huge tree—a live oak tree and a favorite of the grackles.

The first night of the trial, I called Mrs. Hunt at 5 o'clock and reported the news of the day. Throughout my recounting, the plastic shield was being bombarded with sheets of grackle drooping from the flock in the tree above. My body just barely fit under that plexiglass shield.

Later I mentioned it to someone—that it was a real distraction, those birds. Somehow, unknown to me, my comments got back to Mrs. Hunt and she sent word back that because of her schedule, she wanted me to call at exactly 5:00 p.m. the next night (she knowing that the grackles would be there). It was really the only pay phone around. After that I realized the joke and made my calls earlier.

On another occasion she called me to wish me a happy birthday on my thirty-ninth birthday. It went like this: The phone rings waking me from a deep sleep at

12:01 on August 10, 1980. The voice says, "Honey (she called everyone honey) I want to be the first one to wish you Happy Birthday today."

She was a great lady.

CHAPTER THIRTEEN

INTO THE WORLD
OF OIL AND CATTLE

Once the older family "cherry-picked" the best assets they wanted for their 18.5 percent and set up the new company with those assets, Hunt's remaining business consisted of oil and gas production in Texas, Oklahoma, and off the shore of the Gulf of Mexico. It included a forty-thousand-barrels-per-day refinery in Tuscaloosa, Alabama, an oil pipeline that ran across North Dakota, and about two hundred and fifty thousand acres of farms and ranches in Texas, Wyoming, and Montana. There was also a real estate development company called Woodbine Development Company that owned land around Dallas, as well as a nonprofitable drug packaging company whose real value was the real estate along a major Dallas highway. Ray soon sold this.

During the period I was there, from 1975 to 2015, we grew considerably. Our oil and gas business expanded around the world. We drilled wells in every continent except Antarctica. We were producing and selling crude oil and natural gas from the North Sea, Yemen, Peru, Columbia, Canada, Romania, Iraq, and the major basins in the United States. Additionally, we were partners in a $6 billion LNG plant in Yemen and a $4 billion LNG plant in Peru (where we were the operator).

LNG stands for liquid natural gas and is a way to transport natural gas efficiently. We built a giant plant that freezes gas, reducing it six hundred times into a liquid state. and then pours it into a large "thermo-like" tanker. The tanker then sails to a country that bought the gas. It has an onshore plant that converts the frozen liquid back into a gas form (expanded six hundred times) and then puts it into a distribution pipeline. This method has become popular since it causes less pollution than oil, gasoline, diesel, or coal. Further, it can be used in the cogeneration of electricity with wind or solar (since they have downtimes whenever there is no wind or sun). I spent time in the business as president of Yemen Hunt LNG while we were trying to sell the project and initially finance it. It is a fascinating business.

Another important part of the business has been the unconventional oil sector, which involves the fracking of shale to produce oil. Hunt has been one of the early leaders in this new technology for obtaining oil and gas out of tight rocks.

Additionally, the refinery operation expanded to eighty-four thousand barrels per day of refined products such as gasoline, diesel, aviation gas, and asphalt.

Our land and cattle operations expanded to over 550,000 acres (from 250,000) and I was proud of that as I was directly involved in the assemblage of this land. I was president of Hoodoo Land and Cattle Company (HLCC), which was the company that ran the purchase of land and ranching operations. This was one of the best jobs I ever had, even though it occupied only 25 percent of my time because of my other responsibilities. This was a business where the ranch managers ran the operations and I supported them.

Our real estate operation expanded into a number of company-owned assets and partnerships, where we built hotels, office buildings, office parks, apartments, and housing developments throughout the United States. For a brief time, I was president of this segment of the business, when Ray was wrapping it into multi-business real-estate company partnerships in the 1990s. Subsequently, Gene Sanger, a savvy real estate professional, was hired to run it.

We also added other businesses. Hunt Power became a company built by Ray's son, Hunter, and included power plants (at one time, a Hunt company produced a significant portion of the electricity for New York City) and power transmission where our company, Sharyland Utilities, transported electricity to many points around Texas and had access into Mexico.

In the mid-1990s, I added private equities to my portfolio, working with Ray's son-in-law, Chris Kleinert, to set up the company. Here we would invest in private companies or limited partnerships with general partners and try to be on the boards of the partnerships. We invested in companies in Europe, Mexico, South America, and Asia. It was a learning experience and, once again, for a brief time, I became president ... this time of Hunt Equities. This was the time of the "dot com" companies, when the proliferation of the internet and the rapid advancement of computer processing speed and storage capacity created opportunities for many bright young computer entrepreneurs to build incredible companies and become instant billionaires.

It was during this time I really got to know and work with both Hunter (Ray's son) and Chris (Ray's son-in-law). It was such a pleasure, as they both are so intelligent and articulate, and it was fun to see them develop into such great, humble, and respected leaders at Hunt. Equally impressive is that they both have a sense to also further their energies in helping others. Both have made an impact in Dallas and the world with programs that they and their wives, Stephanie and Ashlee, have set up. Additionally, Ashlee and Stephanie have both dedicated their energy and resources to good causes and are as hardworking (if not harder working!) as their husbands. With Ray and Nancy's programs, this Hunt family has had a great impact on Dallas and other areas where there is need (a book can be written on Ray and Nancy since they both give and "roll up their sleeves" for good causes. Add to this the good that Ray's sisters, June, Helen, and Swanee, have done and are doing locally and nationally and what their mother, Mrs. H. L.

Hunt, has done in Dallas, and you can see what makes me feel proud to work for this great family). It is safe to say that the Hunt women have had an equal impact on society with the Hunt men.

As a point of interest, since I am weaving both Perot and Hunt through this story, I would like to comment here on the Perot Charity. Ross and Margot have made many significant contributions to Dallas: the Perot Museum, hospital additions, the Meyerson Symphony Hall and so much, much more. Their children too, Ross Jr., Nancy, Suzanne, Carolyn, and Catherine, have been active in giving both their resources and time for the good of others.

Sadly, Ross passed away in June 2019. The country mourned him. It was a tough time for me as he was an important part of my life. However, Margot has carried on their giving in a major way.

I believe there is a book to be told on what a great impact the Perot and Hunt families have had on Dallas and Texas. Even more interesting would be a book written about what Dallas would look like without Ray Hunt or Ross Perot being born. Collectively, their personal impact is enormous and, more importantly, Ray and Ross inspired others to affect positive change as well. Having been personally involved with both Ross and Ray and their families (being a trustee for their kids for many years and knowing and traveling with most of them), I know what an incredibly great natural resource these two have been to our country. This is the reason I dedicated my working life to them. They had, and are still having, such a big and positive impact on so many people.

Now, going back to the business, as I said, Hunt expanded during my time with them and at least doubled the value of assets every five years under Ray. I was very proud of what Ray had done and being part of the team that accomplished this. Now for the story …

As I indicated, in 1975 it was important that Ray get Hunt Oil Company successfully back into the oil business. Since developing a well drilling package is very costly, companies generally find partners to share the cost and risk. It's called promoting and, if I put together some acreage for exploration on a prospective oil field, not only do I want to share the risk and cost but—since it was my idea and I spent months to acquire the acreage and geological data—I would like a partner (or partners) to put up a disproportionate share. (An example would be that I will give you 49 percent of the deal if you pay for the first two wells).

This is how we got back into the business: by either promoting or being promoted. Fortunately, we found some oil in those first years and hired more engineers, geologists, and geophysicists as we moved forward.

A big break came when our head of engineering, Gary Hurford, suggested to Ray that we drill a risky well through a salt dome. This was a legacy property that the other Hunt family had overlooked. Had they known, they would have insisted it be in the buyout. The property was called Eugene Island 69 and consisted of a five-thousand-acre block in the offshore of the Gulf of Mexico. Exxon had the "lease" and drilled a stinker well on it. Mr. Hunt came along and offered them a deal whereby, if we could have it and if we drilled and were successful, Exxon would come back in for 40 percent after payout of our costs. Essentially, there was a large salt dome shaped like a mushroom several thousand feet below the seabed. Salt is known as a perfect seal for oil structures. Here is a quick, simplified lesson in oil exploration to help explain this point:

You have three types of rock.

Igneous, which comes out of a volcano. Granite is an example.

Metamorphic, which is sedimentary but has been tormented and compressed with heat and pressure. Marble is an example.

Sedimentary, which is made up of small pieces of other rocks that have been broken down by erosion and have been transported by rivers or wind and deposited in the sea, lakes, or valley. Sandstone is an example.

The area where you generally find oil or gas is sometimes called a basin. Now, the basin needs some additional things.

It needs reservoir rocks that can hold gas, oil, or water like a sponge. Sandstone or limestone are examples of reservoir rock.

It needs a source rock, which could be shale that was formed by organic matter millions of years ago, was laid down in an ancient sea or lake, and then was filled over by the continuing deposits of erosive material into the basin.

It needs a structure to trap the oil or gas. There are many types of structure, but simply put, a four-way closure in the form of an inverted bowl best describes it. On top of this structure, you need a seal to prevent the gas or oil from escaping. Salt or a very tight rock above the structure can provide this.

Now, heat and pressure deep within the basin can become the kitchen that cooks the organic matter in the source rock (shale) to create oil or gas. Both the cooked oil and gas want to get to the surface and will follow whatever porous path that can lead them up there. (Only when they wander into a reservoir rock that has a seal above it do you have the oil or gas trapped, sometimes together). More than 90 percent of the oil or gas escapes to the surface in the form of seeps, swamp gas, etc.

The typical way to find a structure has been to use seismic testing. Here, scientists called geophysicists mechanically shoot sound waves into the ground and measure their speeds. The waves go down to the base rock granite, upon which millions and millions of years of sediment have been dumped and can be miles deep, and then return to a surface instrument.

The sound waves travel faster through soft rock and slower through hard rock. The scientist measuring these speeds can conclude the softer rock is more porous and, thus, could hold gas or liquid. They can also interpret a tighter rock (seal) and a structure.

From this data and other information, a prospect will be developed and sold to management or a potential partner. This is how oil geologists look for oil. It is not this simple, of course, but these are the basics.

It is said that oil is found in the minds of men because no one has ever seen an oil field and a geologist has to think three dimensionally in order to imagine a structure with a reservoir rock, a seal, and a source rock somewhere in the basin.

It is important to note that a new method was developed in the early 2000s, which involves going for the oil in the source rock (shales) and breaking out the oil and gas in a tight rock through the use of high-pressure water and sand by forcing the sand particles into the cracks. This is known as fracking, and I will touch on this later. It is more of a manufacturing process, however, since we know where the shales are and the best operators are the ones who are the most efficient.

Now back to the Eugene Island 69 prospect. (In fact, it is not an island but a federal geographic area of the Gulf of Mexico that had been divided into mostly five-thousand-acre blocks for oil companies to bid on for drilling rights). There are many areas like this that have different geographic names.

As I said, a tight salt dome, which is a fluid material and wants to rise to the surface, albeit very slowly over eons, can become a nice seal when it pushes up through porous rock, such as sandstone or limestone. Think of a mushroom's head on its stem and encased ten thousand feet below the sea flow. We know it is there because we can see it on the seismic, but because it is so thick, our sound measurements are useless. Only the mind of an engineer or geologist in 1980 could envision a mushroom shape (since not all salt domes are shaped like mushrooms). Hurford suggested we drill through the top of the salt and, hopefully, come out through it into some sand or limestone that was pierced by the salt and sealed by the salt overhang. This is exactly what happened, and we hit a multi-pay zone area going down and found a lot of oil that provided the financial resources to explore for more oil and "reboot" Hunt Oil Company.

This success allowed us to follow up on looking for more giant oil fields overseas. (Beatrice had been our first, in 1976). The first place we went to explore was China, in 1979. This was followed by Somalia and then a "home run" in the Yemen Arab Republic. Once we had cash flowing from Yemen, I spent many years traveling the world looking for opportunities. This was the exciting period of the 1980s and early 1990s.

During this time, I was away from Sharon, Tanya, and Gar for extended periods, traveling overseas and chasing new deals, or ensuring the deals we signed were progressing well, politically.

Not spending more time with the kids as they were growing up was difficult for me. (I would try to spend as much time with them as I could on those days when I was home). But I was also infatuated with the thrill of traveling the world and doing business in scores of countries that were changing because of the evolving status of the United States vis-à-vis the USSR and the Peoples' Republic of China. The United States was finally winning the Cold War. The USSR was falling apart. China was converting to socialized capitalism. Democratic governments were replacing totalitarian and socialist states in the Americas and, to some degree, in the Middle East and Africa.

This offered opportunities for a company in the oil and gas exploration business. Hunt saw this opportunity and aggressively pursued it.

CHAPTER FOURTEEN

PEOPLE'S REPUBLIC OF CHINA

I have always been fascinated with China. At the University of Washington, I majored in Far East Geography/Studies, which was basically courses on the history, politics, and geography of Russia, China, and the Far East. I was going into the military and wanted to understand our enemy. I loved these courses, which I thought only fit a military career. Boy, was I wrong!

In the Air Force, part of my lecture series for officer trainees was on Russia, China, and Vietnam. I was reading everything I could about China as a hobby … an avocation. In fact, I enrolled in a correspondence course in conversational Chinese at my first duty assignment in Loring AFB, Maine, before I was sent to the USAF officer training school to teach officer cadets. Further, I went on to spend a lot of time in Laos, Vietnam, Hong Kong, and Macao while working for Ross Perot in 1969 and the early 1970s, so I had a fair amount of experience with Asia.

Thus, when Ray called me into his office in early 1979 and said he'd just had a conversation with George H. W. Bush, who had recommended we look at China since they were opening up to the West and would be needing oil, I got very excited. I got even more excited when Ray said he wanted me to get involved in the project.

Further, Bush had told him that when he ran the US Legation in Beijing in 1976, he had a CIA staff member named Jim Lilley. Lilley was now retiring from the CIA and could be a good consultant for us if we did decide to go to China.

Ray immediately called our exploration people together and told them to come up with a plan. Bush had also mentioned SEDCO Drilling Company, headed by Bill Clements and run by his son, Gil. Bill was the Governor of Texas, and Gil was a friend of both Ray and myself. Ray met with Gil and they decided to form a joint venture after we determined that Hunt would provide the geological and geophysical expertise, while SEDCO would provide the drilling. We thought this would be a very competitive package for the Chinese.

I called Jim Lilley, introduced myself and Hunt, and arranged for him to come to Dallas. We really liked him, and I worked out a consulting contract for him with a success incentive. Jim turned out to be fantastic at his job, and we became good friends. He worked with us for about fourteen months and then went back into government once Reagan was elected.

He became a friend for life and continued to be of great help to me while back in government. An expert on China, Jim was born in that country at a time when his dad worked for Standard Oil, and he lived there until going off to college at Princeton. He spoke fluent Mandarin and gave us great advice. He was on Reagan's National Security Council and subsequently had the role of "ambassador" to Taiwan—in the mid-1980s, the United States did not have a rank of ambassador to the island, even though the responsibility was there. Then, in the mid-1980s, Jim became the US ambassador to South Korea, and later US ambassador to China in 1990. From there, he was selected as undersecretary of state for security, retiring in the late 1990s.

During this period, I was dealing with a lot of governments, and Lilley was particularly helpful to me in Yemen, Laos, South Korea, and, of course, China. He would set up meetings as well as host dinners for us at the new embassies in Asia. On occasion, we would stay with him at the ambassador's residence in Seoul and Beijing.

We made our first of many trips to China in 1979 and 1980 with Jim (before he went back into government). The one in November 1979 was interesting, since this was the first time our team had visited China. At that time, Beijing still had no tall buildings over three stories (except for some Soviet-style apartments near the subway).

Ray took some interesting pictures at the airport, despite the prohibition against doing so. He did not hear the official tell us not to take photos and they did not see him taking them. I will come back to this episode later.

There were revolutionary posters on the walls and around Tiananmen Square. There were relatively few cars compared to the thousands of bicycles the average citizen rode. In fact, cars could not use headlights at night because it would bother the bike riders. It was a fascinating sight to look down a major thoroughfare in such a major city in 1979 and see wall-to-wall bikers all wearing Mao jacket-style clothing.

We were put up in the Beijing Hotel near Tiananmen Square, the huge "parade ground"-like concrete pad across from the Forbidden City. I would jog there early in the mornings and would draw stares from onlookers who had never heard of the American penchant for jogging. I have a photo depicting this.

The Beijing Hotel was a giant hotel made up of Chinese, French, and Russian sections. I stayed in all three over the years before modern hotels were built in Beijing. They were comfortable and had huge rooms with lots of heavy drapes.

On those initial trips, we could be in China from four days to seventeen days at a time. They had no modern equipment, so we would bring in our own typing and copier equipment for making contracts and copies.

On one trip to an oil base near the Vietnamese border, we observed scores of Chinese draftsmen copying seismic sections by hand and then framing them. The results looked like frameable art and who knows how long it took them to copy the eight-foot sections? In the United States during the same period, we made copies on a facsimile machine. To this day, I regret I did not acquire one of those Chinese seismic sections.

Credit cards were not permitted in China yet, so I would carry around $20,000 cash in a briefcase to pay our expenses. Later, we could use travelers' cheques.

We would have meetings during the day and eat in the hotel for all of our meals. One day, our group went to Tientsin, a city on the coast, where the Chinese Emperor (prior to 1911) would confine the foreign delegations rather than let them live in Peking (the old capitalist name for Beijing). Consequently, Tientsin became populated by Europeans, Japanese, and Americans, who built buildings that represented their own cultures. Prior to World War II and the Japanese invasion, it was a beautiful city.

It experienced a bad earthquake in 1964 but was still an interesting city when I visited it. What struck me most was the number of prewar cars still being driven, especially the 1930s series type Mercedes Benz. I wish I had had the money and facility to buy them and ship them back to the States. I feel I could have made a nice profit, since many were classics.

In one of our meetings, Jim told me that when he was a boy, there was a bakery where his dad would take him for some orange pastries. (Jim was actually raised in Tientsin).

I asked him if he remembered where it was, and he thought we might be able to find it. I told him, let's sneak out at noon and go find it. At noon, we left the group and I went out in the street, waved down a car, and told Jim to ask the driver if he would take us to the bakery. I gave the man a wad of Yuan (we foreigners were only permitted to use RMB at that time) and we got in the car. The driver did in fact take us to the pastry shop. Jim commented that it would later be told that this is where the Chinese had been corrupted by Tom Meurer. In communist societies, one did not take bribes or excessive amounts for service.

Once we arrived at the pastry shop, a woman came over to us and Jim ordered two orange pastries that he remembered from childhood. She brought them, with the whole floor staring at us, probably amazed that a foreigner spoke their language fluently. I kept my mouth shut and smiled.

I might add we stayed there for a short while and then left to get back to the meeting. To tell the truth, I gagged on the pastry and even Jim said it was horrible. It tasted like a tint of orange on dough, with no sugar or seasoning, made from bean curd. It was tough swallowing that with a smile on my face. (I would later return to Tientsin for another interesting experience).

China fascinated me. Everything I did there I relished like a kid. When we flew into Beijing in 1979, I sat with Ray in a first-class seat from Japan. This was a year before they built the new Beijing airport, so we came into an old terminal that was out of the 1930s and the "Smiling Jack" stories. In the terminal was a giant, red statue of Mao. It was right out of central casting. I would have sworn it was a movie set.

As we approached the airport, the flight attendant announced to all the passengers that it was forbidden to take pictures once we landed. Now Ray, as he normally did, had his head in briefs and reports, so he did not hear this announcement. So, as I alluded to earlier, as we left the plane and walked the hundred-yard distance to the terminal, Ray took many pictures, including several of the giant red Mao statue. No one stopped him, so he just kept shooting, not knowing it was forbidden. (Ray also has a good eye for photography).

In doing so, he captured some of the best images of the early opening of China to the West, which I saw and envied. However, several years later the Hunts had a house fire that destroyed all those wonderful, historic pictures.

Those early trips to China were among the most interesting of my life, and I felt so grateful to be able to travel there during this historic period.

On one trip we played a creative, but risky practical joke. Once we decided to pursue China, we needed to hire an exploration manager. I started looking, and a resume came across my desk. Simultaneously, Ray got a call from a friend in Houston who recommended a seasoned manager named Ray Fairchild. I called Fairchild and flew his wife, Eleanor, and him to Dallas. I really liked him and brought him in to meet Ray Hunt. Ray liked him so we hired him. Now, Fairchild was older than most of the top executives we hired, but, at fifty-seven we knew he brought a lot of experience. Further, he had run some big exploration projects with AP Moeller in Denmark. He immediately dove into the China project and accompanied us on our next trip to Beijing.

I should point out that Fairchild was a very serious person and an expert on fine wines and food. He was refined, a former mayor of a Houston suburb, well-read, and had the air of a true gentleman and man of the world. I immediately realized that we were going to have to lighten him up if he was going to adapt to the Hunt culture.

In those early days, Chinese security would take your passport upon arrival and not return it until the day you left. On this particular trip with Fairchild, we were there for eight days. On the last day, they returned the passports to me at the hotel so I could return them to our seven-man delegation the next morning.

Coincidentally, I was shopping in the hotel that day and bought some postcards with images of Chinese opera stars on them. One of them was a wildly painted, passport-sized face with a Fu Manchu character. I was with Ray Hunt at the time and showed him the card, commenting that it kind of looked like Fairchild. He agreed and we decided to cut it out and paste it over his picture in his passport, which I still had in my possession.

We thought we would have a good laugh when I handed our passports back to each member of our delegation before our flight. That next morning, I passed them out, but Fairchild took his and put it in his pocket without looking at it.

We got on the bus and departed for the Beijing airport. I thought he would look at it once at the airport, but, to our surprise, the plane was a domestic flight from Beijing to Shanghai and security/customs did not ask for passports since we would exit China from Shanghai.

In Shanghai, we got off our plane to clear Chinese customs. It was here where we had to go through security and show our passports. We were in first class and Ray got off first, followed by Fairchild. I followed them with the rest of our delegation behind me and the remaining passengers following in a long line.

Ray went through customs first and positioned himself to take a photo as Fairchild was submitting his passport to the authorities.

To fully understand the impact of this situation, you need to picture the setting. The single line goes up to a wooden booth built for two security agents. It has two big windows in front, with two semicircle holes in the glass in which you place and then receive your stamped passport. The booth is raised so that your shoulders are at the level of the holes. An agent is in front of each hole.

Hunt went through first, giving the agent his passport through the hole in the glass. The first agent looked at it to decide if it's valid and then handed it to the second agent, standing next to him, who then reviewed it. He then stamps the exit visa and hands it back to Hunt through the second glass hole. It was a smooth process. Hunt then leaves and prepares for a camera shot.

Fairchild was next, and remember, he has not yet seen the Chinese opera star picture we stuck on his passport picture. He casually slipped his passport through the open portal and casually looked at the custom agent behind the glass.

The agent took Fairchild's passport, opened it, and stared at it for several seconds. (It was at this point that I wondered if we had gone too far and would end up in the Chinese part of Siberia).

The agent then hit the shoulder of his partner agent and passed him the open passport. Fairchild nonchalantly moved to the second window. The second agent looked at the passport and then stared at Fairchild (three times) and then sternly took the passport and pressed it against the window about a foot from Fairchild's face. When Fairchild saw what we had done, his eyes bulged and his neck extended, in an astonished stare (all of which Hunt got on camera). At this point, I realized we may have a problem, so I went up to the glass and acted out pulling the picture off the passport, and Hunt and I began laughing.

This was followed by our other four team members laughing (they knew the joke), and then the infectious laughter followed down the line of passengers waiting behind us, who had no idea why they were laughing.

Once the agent had seen me demonstrate the pulling off of the taped opera star picture, he took the hint and lifted the attached picture. He then began to laugh, as did his partner.

It was one of the great practical jokes Ray and I played, but it was "close to the margin of what could have been unintended consequences."

Two years later I went to Beijing to deliver our data interpretations to the president of the China Oil Company. All of the oil companies who were vying for exploration contracts were called to Beijing that weekend to deliver the interpreted results of their geological/geophysical surveys.

I rode in on the bus with the representatives of Exxon, Chevron/Texaco, and a number of other large oil companies. It was a long ride and I had time to tell everyone about the practical joke. As a group, their response was to laugh, but then they'd comment coldly that they would have been fired had they done that. I told them Ray Hunt was actually part of the joke. This made me realize how lucky I was to work for a company like Hunt and have a boss like Ray. We had a culture where we took risks, and reasonable risks were the key to success in the oil business.

Also, on this same trip, I learned a lesson on not using Texas humor when being translated into a foreign language. As I said, all of the oil companies were presenting their interpreted data to the president of China Petroleum, Chin Win Kai. He would make the final decision on which oil companies could make bids on Chinese blocks in the Pearl River Basin.

There were a large number of companies and each was given thirty minutes for an individual meeting with President Chin Wen Kai. All the companies had four to eight people in their delegation. All, but one, which was only me ... Hunt/SEDCO.

It had been decided that since this would be a ceremonial presentation instead of a scientific presentation, we only needed to send one person: me. I knew I had thirty minutes, which was less than fifteen minutes when you include the translation time, so I had prepared ten minutes of flowery comments about China and how pleased Hunt/SEDCO was to be included here today.

President Chin was ensconced on the second floor of the building in a room where he sat in the middle, with his vice presidents on either side. I knew both vice presidents since they had been to Dallas and I had met with them in Beijing. They spoke English and one would act as interpreter for President Chin. Now, all the oil company representatives were gathered in a big room on the first floor. They would wait until their company was called and then they would proceed up the stairs to the meeting room.

Around 11:00 a.m., a voice shouted for Hunt/SEDCO, which was my cue to grab the two oversized bright red cases (red was a favorite color of the Chinese) that held our data interpretations and climb the stairs.

I entered the room to see President Chin. I walked over to present the cases, shook his hand with a nice greeting, and then took a seat in front of him. He then spoke and asked the question, "Mr. Meurer, the other oil companies have many people in their delegation. Why does Hunt/SEDCO only have one?" The question caught me by surprise, but I wanted him to know that we did not need six people to deliver the required data to him. Instinctively, I responded with the Texas

Ranger motto, "One Riot, One Ranger."

I then realized I made a mistake, as he was confused with the translation, and I explained to Mr. You (the interpreter) that it was a Texas Ranger saying. Well, my whole thirty minutes was taken with Mr. You and Mr. Zhou trying to tell Chin what a Texas Ranger was. One even went through a fast draw act to relate it to cowboys. By the time they were through, my time was up and I left.

I now knew that I had to be careful when using my own culture's humor when meeting with people who do not speak English or understand basic American culture.

Our China venture with SEDCO for an exploration license lasted about three years. The Chinese were very smart in that they selected an area for exploration in the South China Sea called the Pearl River Basin, which covered millions of offshore acres. They then had twenty-three companies collectively pay for a seismic survey (wherein ships dragged cables for hundreds of miles in a grid pattern, directing sound down to and through the seafloor to detect possible anomalies that could be interpreted as a structure). Once the survey was completed, each company received a copy of the data and made their own interpretations and then, again, collectively delivered their interpretative data to the Chinese Oil Ministry. (This was where I did the One Riot, One Ranger thing).

There were a number of structures we all found, but then we had to bid against each other for the right to drill them. The Chinese carved the basin into blocks of about five thousand to ten thousand acres. There were only about four or five blocks that had any interest, and, because of the tough terms demanded by the Chinese, we decided not to bid. Also, by that time another interesting area of the world had popped up on our radar.

It was a stroke of good luck that we walked away from a potential contract, since no real big oil was found there. Of interest, there was one structure that was huge and all the companies wanted it. To give you an idea of how the Chinese operated, we thought one of the twenty-three companies would get the area over the structure since we all worked in good faith with the idea a company had to participate in the seismic interpretations in order to be eligible to bid on a contract for some area to drill.

However, the word was out on that big structure, and Armand Hammer and his company, Occidental Petroleum (which did not participate in the twenty-three-company survey) stole it away. He met top Chinese officials and offered to build a large coal electrical generation plant in exchange for the rights on that block where the structure was. He got them and when they drilled, the structure was a dry hole. Hammer lost money on that one, and I was glad.

We tried to do a lot more business in China in the '90s and beyond, and I spent time there on Hunt's other businesses: private equity investments and beef. However, I remember several stories from my times in China that I think you will like.

THE LAUNDRY BAG

On an early trip to China, Frank Totzke, our chief geophysicist, was my roommate. Now, Frank was the most honest person one would ever meet. A devout Christian, he would give you his arm if you needed it. I liked Frank, and he taught me a lot about the exploration side of the oil business, as did Ted Hole, our chief geologist, who was also on the trip.

We were staying in the Beijing Hotel, which I described earlier. One thing the hotel had were wonderful, ornate, canvas laundry bags. (They were embroidered with gold thread in both English and Chinese). They were so beautiful that you could frame them in a shadow box. Being of the mentality of a person who had traveled the world and took matches, soap, pens, stationery, and even ashtrays as souvenirs, I presumed that we could take our laundry bags, since we'd paid for our room. Frank really liked them, and I told him, "Let's just throw one in our suitcase when we leave." They would never miss them, and it was a good advertisement for the hotel. He was reluctant, but I kept telling him it was not a problem. Finally, on the last day, when I put one in my suitcase, he did too.

After our flight from Beijing to Shanghai, all the bags of our delegation came off the carrier quickly except Frank's, which was the last one. I jokingly told him it probably had something to do with the laundry bag, and he turned white.

At this point, I knew I had a practical joke here. When we got to Tokyo, once again, Frank's bag was really late and the last to appear. Again, I told Frank that I hoped it was not about the laundry bag. He again had a worried expression and told me that he sure wished he had not taken it.

Once we landed in Dallas, I immediately sought out his wife, Dorothy, and told her to tell Frank that she had a "call from a man from the State Department that morning and he wanted Frank to call him. It was something about a bag."

When Dorothy met Frank at the baggage claim, she immediately told him about the "call." Frank went bananas. He looked at me and unloaded about me talking him into stealing the laundry bag ... he was really upset until Dorothy told him it was a joke that I had set up. He did not laugh, and when he got home, he threw the laundry bag into the trash.

THE DINING ROOM

Another funny story was on our first trip to Beijing in 1979. We had seven in our group and would eat many of our meals in the dining room of the Beijing Hotel, as we could not go out on the public street. We had the choice of a government restaurant or our hotel. In fact, there were three duck restaurants where the government would take us for dinner. They were huge (multistoried) and served a lot of food to foreigners. The one we went to most often was located next to a hospital, so we referred to it as the Sick Duck Restaurant.

The first day in Beijing, we got a table in the center of the large dining room in our hotel. Now, this was an old hotel, so the wooden floor was kind of concave and the center was like the center point of the drain. In those days, they had American Coke by the can, but you had to use US currency ($1) to buy it. I ordered a can with my lunch.

Having ordered, we returned to our discussions, when the waiter accidentally dropped the can of Coke at the edge of the dining room. It then began to roll about forty feet and hit at the base of my chair. Now the dining room was full. I was in the middle of telling a story and picked up the can at my feet. Jim Lilley commented that it will spray all over because it was shaken up in the roll. While talking, I told him that if you put your finger over the opening when you pop the can, you can control the flow, and continued my story. Well, it did not work. As I was talking, I took the tab off and it exploded, and since I had my finger on the opening, it flowed out flat like a fire hose. Half the table and some neighboring tables got completely soaked with Coke. One of our group, Dillard Hammett, stood up on his chair and gave me a round of applause for the show. Most of the other 250 diners probably thought the whole thing was another stupid American prank.

In those early days (1979 to 1981), we were truly confined to the hotel and the duck restaurants for our meals. As I started going back and meeting more oilmen, I met Jerald Holder with City Services, who was also a bidder in the oil race for China. I got to know Jerald (a Texas graduate and varsity swim team athlete) and he taught me how to eat out in Beijing in the early days, when there were only local Chinese places for the local population. Jerald and a couple of his associates took me around the corner from the hotel to "a hole in the wall." We walked in and the people there stared at us since we were foreigners. The owner took us to the back in the kitchen behind a fireplace. We had a table for four. He brought menus, but it was all in Chinese. Jerald told me to simply point to three things, and I would love it. I did not know what I pointed to, but one was duck, one was chicken, and one a bovine of some sort, as I found out later. My second selection was some rice dishes and vegetables. The third was beer. The food was wonderful and that place became "my go-to place" when in Beijing. Further, I liked Jerald so much we hired him away from City Services. He became a key player in Hunt's activities in Yemen, Laos, and Niger.

Also, this experience with a simple Chinese restaurant taught me that while traveling in developing countries in Africa and the Middle East, Chinese food was the safest to eat because they used a lot of heat to cook with and hot tea or Chinese beer was always safe to drink. One might not always know what you were eating, but it helped prevent you from getting sick.

TRAIN TRIP ACROSS CHINA

On one of our trips to China, Jim Lilley, Ray Hunt, and I accompanied Gil Clements and Steve Mahood. Gil was president of SEDCO and Steve was the top legal officer. The five of us were put up in the Friendship Hotel near a People's

Liberation Army base in north Beijing. We had planned to stay one week to begin some negotiations, as it was before the Chinese had decided to do the seismic survey with twenty-three companies. (It was an interesting place where the soldiers would jog in a formation in the early morning. I used to jog in those days so I would get up and be out there when they came by and would follow them for a while, saying Ni Hao—hello—as I passed people).

On the third day, things were not going well. We had arrived with our top decision makers (Ray and Gill) and expected that the Chinese could make decisions on a deal. We had misread them and realized they were not ready to do so. Gil was upset and told the Chinese he was going back to Dallas to make money. Ray too decided to go back. I still had four days on the schedule so I told Ray I wanted to take a train across China and exit through Guangzhou (Canton) and another train to Hong Kong. Steve Mahood wanted to join me.

Now this was 1980, and in those days in China, not only did they take your passport but you had to have written permission or an escort to move between cities.

I asked Jim Lilley to check out the options as we went to the railway station. He first said we could not do it since we did not have a sponsor to go with us. I told him to keep talking to the agent or anybody who would listen and he finally convinced them that we had a sponsor (which we did not but told them it was the oil ministry).

This was going to be a three-day trip, so we wanted a sleeping compartment. The best they had was for four people, which was two bunks attached to each wall that would pull down for sleeping and set up for sitting. I told Jim that Steve and I did not want two other people in there, so could he tell the conductor that while I would buy the four-place compartment, just two of us would use it. It took a while for the conductor to understand it, as this was not the way things were done in communist China.

We finally got on our way. We were the only Americans on the train, but there were two other foreigners traveling to Canton too. One was a Chinese Canadian student and the other was a Kenyan student. We would see them as we were brought to and from the dining car to eat. Steve and I were isolated.

We were chaperoned if we came out of our cabin to go to the bathroom, which was interesting in that it was a toilet seat with a hole that opened to the passing tracks below. Also, we were chaperoned to the dining car for meals, where we were alone and fed last. When the train stopped at a city, we would get off the train but could not go more than twenty-five feet from the steps we came off of. It was enjoyable, and we spent most of the time watching the countryside go by from a big window in our compartment. I really saw how backward China was during this 1980 crossing from Beijing to Canton (Guangzhou).

On the first day into the trip, I realized we were going to have a problem getting two tickets in Canton for a train to Hong Kong because I did not speak any Chinese. So, when I ran into the Chinese Canadian girl in the dining car as she was leaving, I asked her if they were going to Hong Kong. She said yes. Fortunately, she spoke both English and Cantonese. The second day, I saw her again leaving and told her we were going to Hong Kong but did not have tickets. I offered to pay for both of their ways to Hong Kong if she would get the tickets for Steve and me when we arrived in Canton. She agreed and that took some of the worry off my shoulders since we did not have an exit visa, and Hong Kong was not a part of China (PRC) at this time.

When we arrived, it was a madhouse. Hundreds of people were crowded in this terminal train station to buy tickets. I gave the girl money and told her to buy tickets and that Steve, the Kenyan, and I would guard the luggage. I saw an old, wheeled "donkey" (simple four-wheeled baggage cart) and acquired it for our use. We could see the Hong Kong train behind security gates, with two soldiers at the gate.

Our Chinese Canadian friend finally came out with four tickets, but now we had to get to the train, which was boarding and almost ready to leave. We did not have time to wade through the mob to get to the entrance gate so I told her to get on the wagon. I was pulling the tongue, and Steve and the Kenyan were pushing from the back. I pulled that wagon up the gate and told her to tell the guards that we needed to be on the train and that we had tickets. She did but explained to me that the guards could not let us through because we did not have proper papers to go with the tickets. I told her to tell them again that we had to be on that train. And I tried, as pleasantly as possible, to explain to them that Steve and I were Americans and were expected in Hong Kong and that we had lost our papers. They, of course, did not speak English, but our friend partially translated. We did this for about four or five minutes and then they finally opened the gate, took us up to the train, and we boarded.

But these two guards came on with us and stayed as far as the border to Hong Kong. One sat with me and even though we did not speak each other's language, we traded pins. The Chinese soldiers in those days wore a lot of propaganda pins about the size of a penny or nickel. He gave me a pin and I had my officer's insignia from my Air Force Uniform hat and some Susan B. Anthony dollars. Based on this, we started trading until we came to the border and he got off the train.

We finally arrived in Hong Kong about an hour later and bid our two friends good-bye and thanked them again with some money to buy themselves a first-class dinner in Hong Kong. If not for her, we would have spent more time in China since we had neither a sponsor nor exit papers. It was a fun adventure, however, since we saw a part of China few Americans at that time had seen, even though most of it was from a big window on the train.

TRAVELING IN THE BOHAI SEA

In December 1980, I took another train from Beijing to Tiensin, this time to travel to an offshore oil production platform in the Bohai Sea. Our team consisted of Ted Hole, Frank Totske, and Dillard Hammett. Dillard was a good friend and a real jokester. I will speak more about him when I tell you about going to South China later.

We departed from the train and were driven to a dock, where the supply boat was waiting. Before we boarded, they brought us into a nearby building and fed us breakfast, which consisted of rice and either baby eels or a fish with eel-like eyes.

The weather was dark, overcast, windy, and about thirty-two degrees. We had a four-hour boat ride to the platform. I knew I would need to fill my stomach so that I would not get seasick. I looked at the eyes of the little dead creatures, poured ample soy sauce on them, and stuffed myself. It did not taste bad if I did not think about it.

Having been fed, we now boarded the supply boat, which was about seventy feet long with a large open bed in the back for supplies, a cabin, and bridge in front. Below deck, there was a big room that had a big table with seating around it. Also below deck, there were some sleeping quarters further back. We had five in our party, and there were six Chinese engineers and geologists (and probably one commissar). As we got under way, they wanted to use the time to tell us about the oil producing platform and exchange some technology. About an hour into the trip, the wind picked up and the board moved with the waves. We were on one side of the table and our Chinese counterparts on the other. They started with briefings from an easel in front of us. As they spoke, I could look past them, through the porthole, and see sky and then the sea as we rolled and pitched.

Soon, a young Chinese engineer was briefing us from the easel in front of our group. I noticed that he was losing some color in his face, and I could see neck muscles tighten. I knew what was coming next, so I got up from the table quickly as he threw up all over everyone else. I remember Totske had a big glob of predigested food on his forehead. All of a sudden, almost everyone else began to throw up too.

I immediately went outside and found a spot out of the wind behind the bridge and wrapped my big coat around me. Fortunately, I had purchased a big fur cap with flaps at the "Friendship Store" the day before and it kept me warm in the thirty-two degrees. Ted Hole joined me moments later, and we rode that way until we got to the rig about three hours later. Everyone else went to the beds in back to lie down.

When we arrived at the platform, the water was so rough we had a challenge walking up the gangplank from the boat. We almost lost Totske as he slipped and just caught himself on the railing. Had he not caught himself, he might have drowned in that cold Bohai Sea. The Chinese had nothing I could see immediately available to retrieve a person who fell off the platform.

We spent about two hours touring the rig and having a light lunch ... rather, most of our group passed on the lunch. This time it was rice with bits of chicken or pork, which I enjoyed with a glass of beer.

This rig produced about three thousand barrels a day and, in some places, used pipe made out of bamboo fitted together. They had about 260 people on the rig, of which 80 percent were students learning to operate a production rig. What was really interesting was that chickens were cantilevered off the side of the rig and hogs were cantilevered on a deck below them so that the hogs could eat the chicken droppings and parts of chicken that were not a part of the meals on the rig. Of course, the hogs had other food, but since they would eat anything, they too ate whatever was not used for human consumption. This was an interesting way of providing food for some 260 workers living on the rig (my lunch that day).

The return four-hour ride back to the base was uneventful … many slept … and I went back to the outside back of the bridge and watched a somewhat calmer sea.

SOUTH CHINA ADVENTURE

One of the most interesting trips we took was to South China, off the Leizhou Peninsula. Here the Chinese had a regional oil base, from which they explored offshore. This was a very large facility and it had an old Russian motel for guests, where Dillard, Ted, Frank, and I stayed. Dillard and I roomed together. We were there for about one week but the shower only ran rusty water. The only way to get clean was to use the thermos bottle water. (The Chinese used beautiful big colorful thermos bottles filled with hot water for their tea). I would pour it on a washcloth or towel and wash myself. Not the best in a tropical climate, but the best we had.

The beds had mosquito nets, and in each of our bedrooms was a toilet, which consisted of only a hole in the corner. Of course, the smell was overwhelming, especially in the tropics. However, the real attention getters were the giant cockroaches that came out of that same hole at night. I was so glad to have the mosquito net.

We would travel to various locations during the day to see the area right up to the Vietnamese border. The language barrier was interesting because of the various dialects of Chinese … Mandarin, Cantonese, and Hakka. In some cases, we would have three interpreters. Here we would ask a question and our interpreter (who only spoke Mandarin) would ask the question to the Cantonese interpreter (who spoke Mandarin and Cantonese), and the Cantonese would ask the questions to the Hakka interpreter (who only spoke Cantonese and Hakka). The answer would come back the same way. The information you ended up getting was kind of the same as you get playing the telephone game.

One evening, just before dark, I decided to leave the base by myself and walk down a road to a local village about a mile away. As I arrived, there was a loudspeaker in the center area with a voice coming out of it. As it broadcast, villagers gravitated to the center square, which had various seating areas and a big screen. I took a seat, and soon a movie came on. It was black and white and definitely a propaganda film.

I did not understand a word, but it lasted about thirty minutes and the essence of it was this Chinese actor dressed as a white man in a black suit coat and a top hat, sporting a fake mustache. He was portrayed as cheating the People and, especially, a young pretty Chinese girl.

A strong young man showed up, and the People told him about what this White Man was doing. With that, the young man fought the old White Man and drove him out of the village and saved the People's money. It was very primitive photography and acting, but fun to watch. A little like Uncle Tom's Cabin, in a way. Movie night was a great way to see a local village. I think the villagers were required to see it, as there was not a lot of reaction to it. (Like having to see a bad opera performance too many times).

The last night we were there, they had a banquet for us. Now, the big thing at the banquets was to drink Moutai, a 53 percent distilled alcohol that one drinks in a very small-sized cup. It is distilled from rice and is often buried for a long period to age it. The deputy minister was hosting this dinner, and he was a very large Manchurian who appeared to be a seasoned drinker. We decided to have a contest between the Americans and Chinese. Dillard Hammett was selected to represent Hunt/SEDCO and the deputy minister represented CNOCC. Dillard was on one side of the table and the deputy minister on the other.

They each would take a drink, put the empty small cup over their head and yell, "Gombei." After each round, Dillard would mark on a napkin. He got to seventeen marks, but the seventeenth mark went off the napkin as Dillard slid to the floor. I had to carry him to our room and put him to bed.

1. Sharon and me with President Nixon in 1976.

2. My USAF boss Col Frank Taylor promoting me to first lieutenant. He was a wise mentor.

**3. Our family at our condo on South Padre Island.
Gar, Sharon, Tanya and me.**

**4. Gar and me with his lion. We spent 23 days in the bush with Ray and
Hunter and our good friends Charlie and Tom Winn on a hunting
Safari in Tanzania, Africa when he was 16.**

5. Me trying to explain to the Peruvian general in charge of the earthquake disaster in the damamged valley that I was bringing Mrs. Nixon and Peru's first lady the next day to tour the area. No one had informed him and he was mad and refusing to do it. A couple of drinks in his tent and an invitation for him to ride in the presidential helicopter solved the problem.

6. A US anti personal bomblet during the Vietnam War dropped by B-52 bombers on the Ho Chi Minh trail in Laos. Most exploded but there were some that didn't that lie on the jungle floor and maimed many villagers who picked them up. We ran into many either like these with wings or ones I ran into that were round. Our Manager in Laos, Chris Stone, researched the bombs found in our concession area while we were exploring for oil and wrote a 2 volume report with pictures and researched backup. It was valuable for the Laos Government when they were trying to clear the unexploded bombs in southern Laos.

7. Me and Tom Cwikla in the Pakse area of southern Laos in a seismic camp reviewing data to determine if we should continue our exploration programon the Ho Chi Minh trail area because of the the volume of unexploded bombs our people found there. We determined we could because of our weapon ordinance team could isolate them. It was a thrill for me to go on to the Ho Chi Minh trail when we later were taken to our area to see the result of the bombing.

8. Me with Fulton Murray and Chris Kleinert while travelling to South East Asia looking for international Private Equity deals in the third world.

9. Me jogging in Tien Mien Square in 1980, Jogging was not well known
at the time and I would raise stares in some countries I where I would jog.
(Somalia, Laos, Yemen, Japan and Albania where I was arrested)

10. Ray, Hunter and me in Beijing in 1990. Jim Lilley was a US ambassador at the time and we were his guests.

11. Our negotiating team in Anadyr, Russia. L to R.. Gerhard Martin, Ian Maycovk, Jim Jennings, me, and Ray Hunt.

12. Hunt executives and our close friend Jim Oberwetter was selected by President Bush to be the US Ambassador to Saudi Arabia. He served for 3 years. Ray and I came to visit with him and his wife Anita in 2004. He was an outstanding Ambassador who did a lot for Saudi/US relations.

13. Ian Maycock and Jim Jennings inside a Russian half track preparing to cross 23 miles of frozen sea to Anadyr.

14. General Norman Schwarzkopf, Commander of Desert Storm, and me on fishing trip to Mexico… 3 months before he led our troops into Kuwait in dresser Storm.

15. Me and Jim Lilley in Japan on our way to China in 1979.

16. Ross at POW event. ... left to right, Harry Mckillop, me, Tom Marquez, Murphy Martin and former POW and our congressman, Sam Johnson.

17. Murphy Martin, Merv Stauffer and me at another POW event.

**18. Ray with Kasone, chairman of the Communist Party of Laos and president
of the People's Republic of Laos. (and a close friend of Ho Chi Minh) We
had just signed a contract to explore for oil in Laos. 1991.**

19. Ray and I with Bob Gates and Ken Pye, president of SMU.

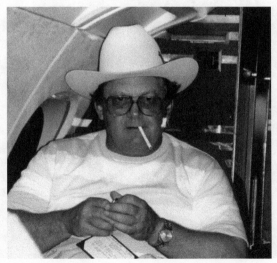

20. A picture I took of Larry Eagleburger. In 1988 on a fishing trip to Mexico. At the time he was a consultant to Hunt on Yemen. He was fun to be with him and became a good friend. Later he became Secretary of State under George H.W. Bush.

21. Me with a wild hog which I chased down and killed with a knife on the Winn ranch. Tom Winn, on the right, taught me how to do it. The two other guests were Xavier Autry and Alonzo Ancira, (two of Forbes Mexican billionaires at the time.) Later I would kid them that they were the only billionaires I knew who chased down and killed a wild hog with a knife.

22. Me with Gary Hurford with Yemeni Oil Minister Bin Housinoun during a gas agreement ceremony in 1991. He was later killed by his own guards during the Yemeni North/South civil war in 1994. He was a fine man and excellent oil minister.

**23. Beijing 1979: Ray and I saw this motorcycle outside
a shop and we could not resist climing it.**

**24. Photo in front of the $50,000 map in silver, copper and alloys that we had
designed as a gift for President Salih and Yemen to be hung in the Sanaa
Airport to trace Yemen history for tourists. Salih, instead, put it in the cadet
barracks where no one saw it. In the picture are Ray, me, Don Robillard
(deputy manager at the time but rose to be the CFO of Hunt and a key
financial advisor to the Hunt family after he retired.) Moujib al Malazi,
Bill Furr (the first Hunt Manager in yemen when it was really the Wild East)
and Gary Hurford (president fo Hunt Oil Company).**

25. Jim Jennings and me in Hanoi in 1989. We were there to discuss with Vietnamese authorities potential exploration opportunities and inform them we were in Laos and ask them if we found oil, the possibilities of exporting it through Vietnam.

26. Mujib and me chewing qat in Marib in 1981.

27. Group picture in 1985 on the rig floor of the discovery well , Alif #1.

28. Me, Abdullah Sannahani (head of Hunt Yemen Security) and
Ross Perot Jr who wanted to see Hunt's Yemen operation. Ross got
the tour from our production in the eastern desert, to the pipeline over
9000' of mountains to the giant VLCC tanker export facility in the Red Sea.
All by helicopter. Since Ross was noted as a hot shot helicopter pilot because
of his around the world trip in his helicopter, our helicopter pilot wanted
to impress Ross with his skill. That was a day of the wildest
helicopter ride I have ever taken.

**29. Anadyr, Siberia. Russia, Feb, 1990.
Our team walking in a blizzard to our meeting**

**30. Mr and Dr. Subroto in 1992. Subroto (a single name)
was the General secretary of OPEC from 1988 to 1994.**

31. Sharon and Cathy Maycock at the front door to Mouj al Malazi's 40,000 sq ft mansion on 60 acres outside Allepo, Syria in 1994. We were his guests for two weeks and travelled all over Syria at a time when Syria and the US relations were strained.

32. Ray Fairchild, Mouj al Malazi and me with the Yemen Oil Minister, Ali al Bahr signing the offshore exploration PSA.

33. Our team in Albania. We were the first American company invited to Albania to discuss oil exploration. Jim Jennings, me, and Casey Olsen (who later we on to become a top officer in Occidental Petroleum). Marku is on the left.

34. One of the many practical jokes Ross Perot would play on me. He hung this in our house depicting him as an angle.

35. Chinese delegation from one of the largest food companies in China visiting Hunt's 250,000 acre Hoodoo ranch to observe the cattle operation. Third through sixth are, Shen Shao Ming (a long time Hunt friend who works with our deals in China) me, Madam Sun (Chairwoman of Er Shang the big food company and JD Radakovich (general Manager of the Hoodoo Ranch and overall; head of Hunt ranching operations).

36. Our hunting party in Sept 2009. L to R... Secretary Baker, Ray Hunt, Mike Boswell, President Bush, me and Steve Hadley. Looking over Desolation Canyon which deeper than the Grand Canyon.

37. Me with Ray's father in law, Judge Elmo Hunter,
fishing in Mexico. Ray would celebrate Elmo's birthday by
taking guests on a fishing weekend in the Yucatan.

38. Ian Maycock in Anchorage, checking the winglet on Hunt's Challenger 601 that was damaged when it hit the runway in flight as we were departing Anadyr, Russia 4 hours earlier. Had it not been for the ice on the runway, our pilots say we would have cartwheeled with a full load of fuel. Because the winglet was not structural, we climbed back in the plane and flew another 7 hours to Dallas, …We all realized that we were very lucky that day.

39. Another Perot joke. A photoshopped picture of me with model, Anna Nicole Smith which he framed and put in the Lobby of the Hunt Offices.

40. A picture I took of President Bush with the camp cat, Killer. The two became fast friends when President Bush would join Ray Hunt on his 175000ac ranch in Utah on an elk hunt each year after he left the presidency. Later he painted a picture of Killer and presented it to Kresha and Blair Eastman who manage the ranch.

41. Tom Marquez and me over looking a megalithic stone jar on the Plain de Jars, in central Laos in 1970.

42. Ross Perot and C.Y. Tung in Hong Kong in 1973.

43. Margot Perot giving a speech for the dedication ceremony of the VLCC
(very large crude carrier) Energy Transmission in Osaka Japan in 1973.
Ship owner C.Y. Tung is on her right. At a dinner party in New York,
CY was explaining to her about these big ships that were bigger than 3
football fields. She asked so many questions that he told her that he
would invite her to launch the next one. He kept his word and we went
to Osaka in 1973. Margo was the star of the dedication ceremonies.

44. Sharon early in our seats for the Nixon Inaugural Parade in Jan 1969. Quite cold that day.

45. Col Bull Simons killing time playing the flute on a beach in Southern Thailand in 1973…we were waiting for Jean Couddeux to discuss an operation to search for shot down American pilots in Southern Laos. We rented a small plane, landed on a road going into his beach village and waited 4 hours for him to come in from fishing.

46. Chuck McKinley(1963 Wimbledon champion) and me in Sam Thong Laos,
the day before the North Vietnamese took to it 1970. Having won Wimbledon
in 1963 and runner up in 1964, Chuck was a "rock star" in Vietnam and
Laos and we leveraged this for our meeting with top officials in both countries.
In between meetings, he taught me the finer points of tennis at the old
French Tennis Club in Saigon where they made Chuck a member.

47. Ross and Pop Buell at a Meo refugee camp in central Laos in April 1970
Buell was the equivalent of a USAID director responsible for the caring
of the Meo who were driven out by the NVA in northern and central Laos.

48. Me pointing to a Russian truck on a battlefield on a battlefield near Sam Thong, Laos. (1970) The Russians stated position was they were not providing military support to the North Vietnamese.

49. Around the World to see the great civilizations….
Ross, Margo, Nancy, Ross Jr and me.

50. Ross, Ross Jr and me on the way to a meeting with Israeli General, Ariel Sharon at his base in the Sinai when Israel controlled it in 1971. I was very impressed with the Israeli military and General Sharon.

51. Me with friends on the Great Wall of China 1979.

52. Typical ferry in Laos for crossing the Mekong river.

53. Large Ferry for crossing the Mekong River…..Note the bomb casings in the trucks recovered from the Ho Chi Minh trail area. These became a "cash crop" for Laos. These are the containers dropped from aircraft which could hold up to over a thousand cluster bombs that rained down on the Ho Chi Minh trail in Laos during the Vietnam war. We had to clear the area of the unexploded bombs before we could drill our oil well in Laos.

54. My photo shot from helicopter flying over the mud flow (while advancing Mrs Nixon trip)from the massive earthquake in Peru in 1970 that killed 80,000 people.

55. Pill Box (Bunker for machine gun defense)) in Albania in 1989.. Over 170,000 were built during the rule of Enver Hoxha(5.7bunkers /sqkm) and mostly facing Yugoslavia,a perceived enemy. I was amazed when I saw them.

56. Ray Hunt and President Salih of Yemen opening the export pipeline and bringing Yemen into the family of oil exporters in the Middle East...1986.

57. Temple of Saba Queen (Sheba) near Marib I took in 1981. Today it is totally excavated and one of the more interesting ruins in all of Yemen.

58. Me with some new friends in a smugglers village in the eastern desert. I was amazed I could buy some fresh bananas in this area where I saw no real vegetation or trees. Also the Toyota Land Cruiser was replacing the camel for desert travel.

59. I took this forbidden picture in 1981 from a military helicopter although the Yemeni soldiers in big Russian helicopter did not stop me, At his time the government was concerned about Israeli spying and forbade photos from the air around cities and military installations. This picture of the old souk area shows the beauty of the Yemeni architecture.

60. Me and Mr Kim, the CEO of our partner, Yukong LTD (later became a part of SK Corp) This is at our discovery field during the flaring of a well. He became a good friend and was an outstanding executive. SK and Hunt had a close relationship and we partnered in both oil and gas exploration and LNG projects.

61. Ray Fairchild, Moujib al Malazi and me finalizing an Off Shore in the Red Sea exploration agreement with Ali al Bahr, the Oil Minister of Yemen. 1986.

62. Ross at a surprise 40th birthday party on the grounds of EDS with
employees, June 27 1972. Note the peace symbol around his neck(during the
Vietnam War),. Ross was a good sport and in the early years we would always
try to have a surprise birthday party for him. In his later years when I was with
Hunt I would still remember his birthday with some silly gift. Once he passed
65 it was fossils and old relics telling him I finally found gifts older than he was.

63. Typical boat on the Mekong river in Laos.
They were quite comfortable to travel in.

**64. Ted Hole, Frank Totske and me with Chinese
hosts in a southern China in 1980.**

**65. Ancient city of Marib. (I took from helicopter in 1981) We had our first
meeting in this 4000 yr old city in Jan 1981 with the military governor.**

66. Marku, our government host in Albania in 1989. Although short in stature, he filled a room when he walked in. One of the many individuals I met internationally who if they lived in Dallas would become very close friends.

67. Gentleman shop keeper with hisware whom I met in Lae, Papua New Guinea in Feb 1981.

68. Ian and Mujib in the old Sanaa Souk (market) during our first trip to Yemen in Jan 1981. The souk is over 4000 years old and I read that Myrrh and Frankincense originated in Yemen and I wanted to find some if that was the case. I found both and added some gold and gave it to Ross as a Christmas present.

**69. Graduation and commissioning a
2nd/Lt in the United States Air Force..1963.**

**70. Hunt team in front of the ancient Marib Dam in eastern Yemen.
(The dam is mentioned in both the Bible and Koran and originally
built in the 8th century BC).**

**71. Ray climbing into one of the 2 half tracks we used to cross 23 miles
of frozen Siberian bay to get to Anadyr from the Russian airbase
where we landed. Feb 1991.**

72. Dave Zamarippa, Chris Stone and me at a small refreshment bar on the Bolaven Plateau in Southern Laos. The Bolaven rises 4500 feet above the jungle floor. It has a perfect climate with wonderful soil and clear running water. Col. Bull Simons who spent many months in the early 1960's on it, would tell me it was the perfect place on the planet to live.

73. Our daughter, Tanya. As an author and writer, I depended on a lot on her advice and help in editing and securing an excellent publisher for this book.

74. My parents, Elbert and Dorothy Meurer.

CHAPTER FIFTEEN
THE YEMEN
ARAB REPUBLIC ... 1980

One of the most exciting adventures of my life involved the thirty years that I worked on our Yemen project. Here, we secured the government rights to explore for oil on three million acres, in the eastern desert of the Yemen Arab Republic. Against great odds, we then discovered and produced over two billion barrels of oil and gas equivalents. And this was in an area where as late as 1981 no oil or gas had ever been found.

While in college, I took a course on Southwest Asia, which focused primarily on the countries around the Persian Gulf and the Red Sea. One of these countries was Yemen, which later became two countries as a result of the Cold War: the Yemen Arab Republic (North Yemen) and the communist People's Democratic Republic of Yemen (South Yemen). The area has always fascinated me; when I first learned about it, little was known about the region because it was tribal and few travelers were allowed to traverse it freely. Luckily, my professor had traveled there and related great stories.

Eighteen years later, and now with Hunt, I looked at an exploration prospect in South Yemen that was presented to us. Unfortunately, Americans were not allowed to do business there so we had to pass on it. In 1980 US companies were not allowed to do business in certain communist countries, for various reasons. We did do business with established communist countries like China, the USSR, Laos, Somalia, and others, but they were not on the blacklist while South Yemen was, because it harbored Arab terrorists.

Still, our adventure in Yemen was about to begin, with our entry into North Yemen (the Yemen Arab Republic) about eight months later, in December 1980. We had hired Ray Fairchild as our international exploration manager in 1979 and I began working with him to set up the group. We hired an outstanding geologist, Dr. Ian Maycock, to head up our London office, which was responsible for Europe, Africa, and the Middle East. Ian was a great find, and he and his wife, Cathy, have become our very close friends.

Ian's former employer was an oil company, CONOCO, and when he left, one of his coworkers, named Mujib al Malazi, left with him. I learned a lot from both Mujib and Ian. Mujib also became a very good friend and was one of the more talented men I have done business with. He was a Syrian, a scientist diplomat, and the best negotiator I ever worked with. After leaving CONCO, he formed his own consulting firm.

One day in 1980, Mujib was in a bar in London and overheard some oil people talking about Yemen and the possibility of a previously unknown geological basin that had been revealed by a partial aeromagnetic survey in the eastern desert. As I described earlier, a geological basin, in simple terms, is a deep depression in the earth that, through eons and erosion, has been filled with eroded rock and debris; in some basins, oil or gas has been created geologically from dead plants, animals, and microscopic life. It is mostly in these basins where oil and gas are found. (An aeromagnetic survey is a tool used by oil companies to define a basin and particularly its depth by generally mapping the granite base. Here a plane files a grid pattern over the area of interest. Equipment on the plane maps the bottom of the basin so one can interpret the "bowl" from the data received. It is more complicated than this, of course, but that's the general idea).

Anyway, Mujib decided to follow up on the rumor he heard in the bar and flew to Yemen to check it out. Being Syrian, he was extremely polished, spoke Arabic, and felt at home in Yemen. There, he met with a number of officials, including the prime minister, Abdul Ghani. He also met with Ali Jabr Alwai, the deputy director of YOMENCO, the government oil and minerals company that imported oil products since there was no oil found in Yemen at this time. The closest known oil production was five hundred miles away in Saudi Arabia.

Ali Jabr showed Mujib a copy of the aeromagnetic survey that depicted the area in question as a possible ten-thousand-foot-deep basin and not just a sand fill in a depression, which was the conventional wisdom at the time.

Mujib wondered why they had only flown over half of the basin area but did not pursue it. Interestingly, I got the story later, after I got to know Ali Jabr and invited him to Dallas.

Ali trained as an engineer in Prague. He eventually became a senior executive in YOMENCO. It was his idea to conduct a seismic survey of the Marib/Jauf area of eastern Yemen to see if there was a prospective basin that could hold some oil.

In our January 1981 meetings in Sanaa on our first trip (which I will detail in chapter 17), Ali Jabr on the last day off-handedly told me that he was going to Washington to meet with the World Bank the following week. I made a mental note of the date and assumed he was going to try to get the bank to fund a seismic program. When I got back to Dallas and reported on our trip and Ian and Mujib's findings, Ray concluded that we wanted to pursue getting a PSA (Production Sharing Contract) with Yemen.

Thus, I called our head of finance, Tony Copp, who, with his experience on Wall Street, had contacts at the World Bank. I asked him to use them to find out where Ali Jabr would be. He got a number and the next week I called Ali and said I was going to be in Washington the next day and would like to invite him to dinner. Further, I also invited him to Dallas and told him I would make the arrangements. He agreed, so Tony and I flew out in our company plane to meet with him.

We had dinner at the Madison Hotel's Montpelier Room, which, at that time, was the top restaurant in Washington, DC. He brought Hassin Baker, an aide to Yemeni president Saleh, with him. Since I had already established a good relationship with Ali in Yemen, we had a really fun dinner. At one point, we got on the subject of peppers and Tony, being a relative of a famous Mexican general, bragged on his heritage and love of hot peppers. At this point, Hassin reached into his pants pocket and pulled out an exotic pepper that he'd brought from Yemen, and offered it to Tony.

Tony, a pepper eater, eagerly bit it and began chewing. It was apparent to me, since I knew Tony so well, that he'd met his match. His demeanor changed and sweat poured from his temples. After two minutes, he was finally able to talk again.

MYSTERY OF THE HALF-SURVEY

During dinner, I asked Ali about the aeromagnetic survey and why it was flown over just part of the basin.

Ali said that the Saudis were in control of that part of Yemen. So for the survey, they got permission to conduct the flyover from the Saudis, but just over the spine of the mountains since the Saudis considered the sand area their territory (which was where the supposed basin was).

They drove to Saada, a northern city in Yemen, to engage a French contractor to fly the route. Once they got in the plane, they showed a map to the French pilot and then told him that they wanted to fly over an area of the desert. The pilot said that the Saudi manager told him that they could only fly south over the mountains. At that point, Hassin pulled out his pistol and put it to the head of the pilot and Ali held up a map and pointed out on the map the route they would be taking over the desert.

They were careful to only fly out into the desert partway so it would not alert the Saudis. This is how they got the survey that showed half of the basin that bottomed to at least ten thousand feet deep. This is the data that Mujib saw and, with his experience, concluded that it could be a prospective oil area even though we only had data for half the area. This is what Ray made his decision on to pursue a contract.

Another funny incident happened at that same dinner. Ali, like many Yemenis, loved jokes. So, we would use them to bond with each other at dinner. One was a joke Hassin related about a duck. I forget the joke but remember that, in order to help interpret the English for Hassin, he had to draw a duck on the restaurant's fine linen napkin to show where exactly the duck's "asshole" was so that he had the correct terminology to tell his joke.

Now, imagine this scene. We are leaving the top restaurant in Washington, DC. It is full of the power elite in our capital city. As we get to the door, Hassin yells out, "I forgot my asshole," proceeds back to the table, and grabs the fine napkin with the duck drawing on it. He carries it out, to the astonishment of many of the diners. Tony and I tried to distance ourselves at that point.

Our trip into Sanaa during the first week of January 1981 was a real thrill for me. Here was one of the few spots of Arabia few Americans had seen. My role was to assess the government, economy, security, and business environment and then mesh that with what Ian and Mujib had found out geologically and culturally.

Remember, this was an area in which there was no known oil. In fact, later the prime minister, Abdul Kareem Eryani (who became a very close friend during my many years going to Yemen), gave me a copy of a British report written by the British ambassador, W. N. Hugh-Jones to R. C. Blackburn, Esq. of the British Foreign Office in 1952. The report was in response to London's query for the ambassador to check out Yemen as to the prospects for oil, since oil had been found in other countries around the Persian Gulf and Arabian Sea.

Here is a quote from the report of Ambassador Hugh-Jones response: "As to the possibility of a profitable concession being available near the Yemen border, I think most unlikely. It is a desperate country once away from the Asir and Yemen highlands and I should not think it likely be oil bearing. Moreover, I cannot see any company in their senses seriously considering running a pipeline through the Yemen. In any case, I do not imagine the Saudis are likely to pay much attention to Yemeni claims to the western Rub al Khali. They have quite a powerful Amirate at Najran."

What is neat is that Hunt Oil did work with the tribes, found oil, and built a pipeline from the desert to over the mountains down to the Red Sea. I took a copy of the ambassador's report, paraphrased it, and put it in a Lucite display and juxtaposed it with a picture of a Hunt worker building the pipeline across the mountains. It hung in our office.

In 1980 Yemen was divided into two countries, as I said, because of the Cold War between communism and democratic states. Of course, there were smaller, poorer, undeveloped countries that pulled into the fray, if they were politically important or had some mineral riches or significant geographic location.

The world in 1980 was divided into basically three groups: communists (led by the USSR), democracies (led by the United States), and Third World neutral countries that would play the former two against each other and hope to gain weapons and monetary resources in the process. It was a funny world between 1950 and 1990. Wars of national liberation were announced by the USSR in 1960 as policy, due to which the Soviets provided weapons and money to Third World countries to encourage them to break away from European colonial powers and create communist governments that would align against the Free World.

Unfortunately, since democracy was a strange idea to many of these countries, and our "US version" was unique and somewhat complicated in their view, we had no choice but to support the "strongmen or dictators" ruling many of them. Also, many of the Third World countries had been European colonies and they still had bad memories of colonialism and the haughty air of the British, French, Dutch, Spanish, Belgians, Portuguese, etc.

We had developed a containment policy as US security policy to put a multicountry fence around China and the USSR. It was proposed by a diplomat, George Kennan, who reasoned that if we could contain the USSR and the People's Republic of China (referred to as Red China) and some smaller communist states, their inferior economic system would eventually cause a collapse. It did in 1989. The USSR ceased to exist in 1990 and, once again, became a much smaller Russia and because of the lack of institutions and seventy years of a corrupt system, could not adapt. Today Russia is not the Russia of the past. Its economy is held up by its mineral riches ... oil, gas, gold, and hard rock minerals. Those socialist states connected to the USSR at its perimeter broke away to set up their own systems. Not all were successful initially. Meanwhile, China and Vietnam adapted their economies to become "socialist capitalists." Communist East Germany merged with West Germany and communist South Yemen merged with North Yemen. Some communist states still exist, like North Korea, Cuba, who, in their thirst for power, use their military to cruelly repress their people under an outdated revolutionary ideology.

You will read this history in many books now, but I lived through it so I want to tell you in this story how Hunt business was done during this period.

It hopefully will encourage you to read some more about the history of the Cold War as it will enrich your knowledge and help you understand how the United States worked before the 2020 pandemic, which I think may be a generational change for our country. Regardless, reading history is so important for you to understand the world in which you will live.

CHAPTER SIXTEEN

YEMEN ... STORMING OUT OF THE FOURTEENTH CENTURY

As I mentioned, Mujib had heard a rumor about a geological survey in Yemen in a bar in London and decided to follow up on it. His trip to Yemen convinced him there was information in the half a survey that few knew about or had seen. He told Ali Jabr Alawi, the deputy director of YOMENCO, that he was going to find an oil company interested in exploring for oil in the basin and would be in touch.

When Mujib returned to London, he contacted Ian Maycock, our geologist in London who also happened to be a friend of his, to explain what he had found out. Ian suggested Mujib contact Ray Fairchild, Hunt's new exploration officer in Dallas. Mujib called Fairchild and set up an appointment. They met and Fairchild was intrigued.

After Christmas and just before the New Year 1981, Fairchild and I met with Ray Hunt. Fairchild gave a briefing on international prospects, among which he had identified several potential deals. Almost as an afterthought, he mentioned his meeting with Mujib and the aeromagnetic survey in the Great Empty Quarter of Yemen. Hunt's instinct was tweaked. He liked the idea for several reasons: first, maybe no one knew about it; second, the Arabian Peninsula was the oil and gas center of the world at the time; third, for Hunt to get a concession in the Arab world would put the company in the big leagues in the world of oil (if we had a discovery); and finally the cost of entry might not be that great.

Fairchild did not know much about Mujib, but he did know it might take weeks to get a visa to go to Yemen. However, Mujib gave him assurances that if they would send someone over, he could get a visa for them in a day. Hunt turned to me and said, "Go to London and, if you can, get a quick visa to Yemen ... bring Maycock and accompany Mujib al Malazi."

I flew to London on Sunday, January 4. On Monday, Ian and I received our visas at the Yemen Embassy (just as Mujib had projected) and were on a plane to Paris that afternoon, with transfer to Yemenia Airlines that went on to Cairo, Egypt, and then Sanaa, Yemen.

We arrived on January 6 to an empty airport that looked like it was designed in the 1930s. Nothing was automated. I was told by Mujib to buy two bottles of

Scotch at the Paris airport. One would be for customs and the other for a potential encounter with a government official. Both were "used" and we breezed through customs.

We stayed at the Sheba Hotel, which was the only nice hotel in Sanaa at that time. The food was somewhat wanting, although they did offer a European breakfast with processed meat, olives, cheeses, and pastries. (A typical European breakfast).

The restaurant had a limited menu and no liquor, but Mujib arranged for us to get some wine in our room. We decided to look at other food options, since we assumed we would be there a while. The outlook wasn't encouraging, though, since we knew of no Western-type restaurants in 1981 Sanaa.

At Mujib's suggestion, we went next door to meet with a Chinese manager to see if we could eat with their senior employees in town. (The communist Chinese were building a massive road into the area in which we were interested, and thus had a crew camp for the managers and staff in Sanaa). We worked out a deal and had several meals with the Chinese, to give us some variety. The food was good and we got a nonalcoholic beer to go with it.

As I've already said, when traveling in the Third World in the 1970s, 1980s or early 1990s, I would always seek out a Chinese restaurant. I would order hot rice with some well-cooked meat, soy sauce, and hot mustard (if they had it), and a good Chinese beer to wash it down. They cook the heck out of it so one will not normally get sick from eating it.

Anyway, the day after our arrival, Mujib called Ali Jabr and set up our initial meeting with him and an appointment with the minister of YOMENCO, Ali al Bahr. It was going to take another day so we had a day to kill. I should mention that, when we flew into Sanaa, Mujib and Ian looked out the plane's window and reacted like delighted kids in a candy store when they saw all the geological structures on the ground, visible on the high desert, mostly treeless terrain.

Thus, since we had a day with nothing else to do, they wanted to go take a look at the structures and rocks we had seen from the air. So I commandeered a car and we took off out of town. Little did we realize we would run into checkpoints once we left the city.

At this time, the country was run by Ali Abdullah Saleh, who had been a mid-level military officer before helping lead a coup in 1962. In its wake, two presidents were assassinated and Saleh himself was elected president in 1979. (In an early meeting we had with representatives of the CIA, the "agency" told us Saleh would last six months, but he lasted until he was assassinated in December 2017. Also, the CIA suggested he killed his predecessor to get the job).

By 1981 Saleh only had control of the region around Sanaa and some of the coastal areas. The northern tribes ruled the rest of Yemen and he had to make a deal with their sheiks to be able to rule the country. Access to modern US and Russian weapons and facilitating our discovery of oil would allow him to do this.

About five miles out of the city, we were stopped at a checkpoint and ordered out of our car so the military could check our papers. Mujib and I had ours, but Ian had left his at the hotel. This confused the soldiers, so they argued about it for about thirty minutes and then decided to take us back to Sanaa to the jail compound.

We spent the better part of the day whiling away time while Mujib tried to speak to the jail commandant. Late in the day, the commandant came to see us, and Mujib explained that we were businessmen: a Syrian, Englishman, and American who had come to Yemen on the invitation of YOMENCO to look for oil. Mujib explained that Ian had left his papers in the hotel and we could provide them upon request. Luckily, this convinced the jail commandant that we were not Israeli spies and he released us. I was relieved because I had not told the US embassy that I was in Yemen.

An interesting sidebar to this incident came about sixteen years later, when I brought Ross Perot Jr. and Harry McKillop over to Yemen to see our operation. We were having dinner with the US DCM (Deputy Chief of Mission) at the embassy in Sanaa. He related that I did not remember him but he was a young embassy officer when I was in the Sanaa jail (I reported the incident to the embassy after being released). Two weeks after I'd left, another American was detained as a suspected spy for Israel and ended up being held for fourteen months. The DCM told us his job in the embassy was to visit the prisoner every three days throughout his detention. (I am glad we had Mujib to plead our case).

But back in 1981, as I said, I did not go to the US embassy until the next day, at which point I explained why I was in the country. The commercial officer (which in those days was often the CIA representative in the embassy) was a young man named Matt Gannon.

Matt recognized what we were doing and realized it would be in the US interest to have an American company find oil in Yemen. Consequently, he agreed to meet me first thing in the morning at the Sheba Hotel with data and information I had requested, such as names of other, non-US companies operating in Yemen (there were no US companies other than a very few contract workers); geological and hydrological maps and data in the Marib area; important families; tribal information out in the basin; and anything else he could find that might be relevant. The CIA had great data, much of which gave me confidence to recommend to Ray and the company that I saw no political or economic reason we should not pursue a contract.

Matt's information and assistance was of real help. From the names and data he provided me, I was able to meet with European and Indian country managers and learn about dealing with contract workers in Yemen. We were advised to allow 10 percent for "Baksheesh" ... bribes. We did not do it, but I will explain later how we avoided it. I even got to know a Russian hydrologist who was 6'6" and drove around in the smallest car I had ever seen.

Unfortunately, years later, I learned that Matt, who had been assigned to the

CIA station in Beirut, had the misfortune of booking the wrong flight to return to the US for the holidays. He was on the Pan Am flight blown up by Libyan terrorists over Lockerbie, Scotland, in 1989. There were 243 passengers and no survivors.

He now has a star on the Wall of Honor in the CIA Headquarters in Langley. Without his assistance, I might have concluded that the Yemen risk was too great, in line with the prevailing wisdom of most of the world's oil companies.

While I was meeting with non-oil people, Mujib and Ian were visiting YOMENCO to get data from Ali Jabr. On the second day, we also had a meeting set up with Ali al Bahr, the minerals minister of Yemen. We went into his office, and as senior representative, it was my job to give him the Hunt sales pitch, which I did with earnest conviction. Hunt was a Texas exploration and production company with a fifty-year history. I explained where we had production in the United States and the North Sea and where we were exploring (China). I also reported that we were in refining, real estate development, and had two hundred fifty thousand acres of cattle ranches in the United States. (Little did I know that this briefing may have been the reason we were awarded the exploration license, but I will relate this when I discuss the lawsuit against us in 1987).

The meeting went well and I really liked Ali Bahr. He became a friend; more than that, like Ali Jabr, he was one of the heroes responsible for bringing oil income to Yemen.

In their meeting, Ian and Mujib expressed a desire to visit Marib, in the eastern desert area, so a trip was set up for the next day. What a trip. It was like going into the Wild West in the 1800s. In fact, scholars described Yemen at that time as "storming out of the fourteenth century."

That afternoon I wanted to go to the old Souk in Sanaa, as I knew that frankincense and myrrh historically came from Yemen. A "Souk" in the Arab world is a marketplace; in Sanaa, some of the stalls are close to four thousand years old as Sanaa is considered by some scholars to be the oldest continuous city in the world. (Damascus also claims this status). Originally in ancient times, the Souk served as the site for buying and selling animals, but over the years it became a trading and buying area for all kinds of items. Each had their own special area. My favorite was the silver and gold souks. Over the thirty-one years that I visited Yemen, the Souk is where I bought jewelry, coins, and antique items. I also liked the spice souk, as this was where I found the frankincense and myrrh, the aromatic pitch from two different types of trees found in Yemen. I spent many hours in the Souk during that first trip and subsequent trips, and got to know many of the traders who helped me hone my negotiating skills. As a result, our house is full of these many treasures I brought back from Yemen.

Anyway, the next morning, we got into a Toyota Land Cruiser (which was rapidly replacing the camel in the desert) and headed east. The group included a government guide/driver, Ian, Mujib, and me. Ian was in the front seat, and Mujib and I were in the back. We drove east, out of Sanaa and toward the desert to the ancient-fortified town of Marib, which at one time was a key trading center and important stop on the Spice Trail.

Spices were important for the Roman Empire and the Arab traders would acquire them from the Malaccas and other areas, which became known later as Indonesia. They would sail their dhows with the seasonal trade winds, to and from the area to pick up the spices and then unload them in an old port that is in current Oman. They would transfer them to camel caravans, which would travel and trail between the desert and mountains in Arabia. There were cities along the route where they could be secure and get supplies. Marib was the most important of these (established somewhere around 1200 to 800 BC), known at the time as the Kingdom of Saba. At one time, it was ruled by a queen and the inhabitants were called the Sabeans: scholars argue that this is where the Queen of Sheba was from, although Ethiopia also claims her.

At Marib, there was an ancient dam (mentioned in both the Bible and Koran) that provided water for agriculture by irrigation and controlled flooding. This provided food for the city's inhabitants and food supplies for the many caravans, which would pass through on their way to Petra and the Mediterranean Sea.

We began by driving on the unfinished road that the Chinese were building, but as soon as we came out of the mountains, we started driving in the desert and soon enough, the vehicle hit a rock and damaged the oil pan. Our driver knew of a village in the mouth of a wadi (dry stream bed) where he could get it fixed. We drove for about an hour down the wadi to reach this village, which we found out later was a smugglers' town.

It was the most interesting place I have ever seen: in its architecture and varied dress of the inhabitants, it resembled the set of *Star Wars*. Our driver drove up on the side of a sand dune, got out of the vehicle, and soon came back with a man carrying a toolbox. The man proceeded to scoop out a huge indentation in the sand from under the car. Once the hole was large enough, he climbed in so that he could get to work on the oil pan.

Meanwhile, we were attracting visitors, many of whom seemed like they did not belong there. There were Saudi Bedouins, Ethiopians, and Somalis. Most interesting were the armed Yemeni tribesmen carrying curved knives called jambias in scabbards, along with AK-47s or old ancient bolt action rifles slung over their shoulders. Many were dressed in what looked like a dirty skirt, a well-worn coat, and a long bolt of cloth wrapped casually around their head.

I wanted to get out of the car and take some pictures, but Mujib said we should stay in. I told him that this might be my last day on earth, but I had to see more of this town. So I got out and he followed.

Ian followed us, and I started taking some pictures but making sure not to aim directly at our many colorful hosts. Fortunately, I could use my wide-angle lens to include them without pointing the camera at them.

An interesting incident then occurred that made us all feel better. Three of the toughest looking and heavily armed tribesmen came up to us, and one asked who we were and what we were doing there. Mujib explained that he was a geologist. Ian indicated likewise. When he came to me, I told him I was a geologist too, as I did not want to tell him I was an economist and foul something up. He laughed and then the three men broke out into what seemed like a song. I asked Mujib and he said they were singing about men who go into the desert and hit rocks with a hammer. We all laughed together, which broke the ice.

Now, I could stroll up and down the sand street looking at the wares displayed on the ground and take careful pictures. I saw parts of seismic equipment, probably smuggled in from Saudi Arabia. One could buy films, food, batteries, tools, used cars, etc. In fact, once we started the oil project, our people would occasionally buy supplies in this smugglers' town.

I actually bought some green bananas and had a picture of me taken with several tribesmen. It shows them with their guns and knives and me with the bananas. It hung on our refrigerator for years and was one of Tanya's favorites.

Now that we had the vehicle fixed, we climbed in, said our goodbyes, and headed out on a sand trail to Marib. I could see the ancient, mounded city from many miles away. Once we got closer, a paved road emerged and we passed an airstrip with a disabled C-47 parked off the runway.

A car approached us and stopped and then out stepped a man dressed in a one-piece white gown and white scarf, carrying a chrome-plated AK-47 gun. Several of his armed followers accompanied him. We were still in the car when another armed group approached. The man in white was a local sheik, and the other group represented the military governor of the region.

They began to shout, argue and point their weapons at each other. I asked Mujib what was going on. He assured me that we were in no danger. They were just trying to determine who would take us for lunch and who would take us on a tour of the ruins of the Marib Dam and Temple of Sheba. After about five minutes, things settled down, and we were told to follow the governor's men into the ancient town of Marib. (In early 1981 people were living in the ruins and the military governor had his headquarters there. By 1985 it was closed and turned into a heritage site).

It was exciting to walk into the walled city knowing that it was at least thirty-two hundred years old. We struggled to climb up to a second or third story office carved into the ruins and had a pleasant meeting with the governor. He then invited us to lunch in a tented area outside the walled city.

Inside the tent, in the center on a rug, was a whole skinned lamb on a bed of rice and seed trimming. It was soaked in the animal's fat for flavor. We were invited to sit around the meal and begin eating with soldiers sitting next to us. We all dug in with our right hands, as custom demanded.

Mujib had warned us in advance to only use the right hand, since the left hand was used for bodily functions and it would be impolite to stick it into the lamb and rice. Significantly, in Yemen it is common practice to cut off the hand of a convicted thief (I've seen it myself on Yemeni TV, broadcast as a deterrent to stealing). This is a terrible punishment, because if they cut off the right hand, it is difficult for the convicted thief to eat at a communal meal.

After observing the soldiers, I learned to stick three fingers into the rice and try to roll it with my thumb into a glob that could fit into my mouth. Alternately, I would tear off a piece of lamb and eat it separately.

As we ate, I was somewhat uncomfortable as the man next to me had set his AK-47 down on a pillow so that the muzzle was pointed at my thigh. It was a horrible feeling since I couldn't tell if there was a shell in the chamber. (However, over the years, I got used to this since it occasionally happened when riding with Yemen guards or soldiers in helicopters or vehicles).

After the meal, we were once again met at the tent by the sheik in white. He and his entourage took us to the remains of the Marib dam, about five miles away. I took a lot of pictures that day and the many times I would visit the dam in the following years. It was sad to see how each year more stone blocks had been taken from the old dam and used by local farmers for construction. The Temple of Sheba was filled with sand and only a few columns remained standing to show where it was. By the late 1980s, a new dam was built by the Turkish government above the old dam, which would remain a tourist attraction. And the government, in conjunction with a private US foundation, began working on the temple, which became an impressive archaeological site. Hunt provided them with equipment and labor to help remove the sand around it, to bring more of the ruin to the surface.

Before we left to return to Sanaa, we thanked everyone and took some pictures with the sheik and his chrome-plated weapon. I really liked him. On one of my many later trips to the desert and the operations, I inquired about him to see if I could pay my respects but was told he had recently been killed in a gunfight.

We spent about a week in Yemen on that first trip. I collected a lot of political and economic information that gave me confidence that we could do business there. Mujib and Ian liked the geology, especially after seeing a rock taken from a salt outcrop that was so rich with oil, you could light it with a match. That told Ian that there was source rock in the basin for generating oil. There still needed to be confirmation of structures and traps in the subsurface, but Mujib and Ian returned to London feeling confident we needed to go for the PSA. On returning to Dallas, I wrote a multipage report recommending we pursue a Production Sharing Agreement (PSA) with the Yemen Arab Republic.

Which we did. Unfortunately, that report was going to come back to haunt me later, during a lawsuit in which I was accused of bribing top Yemen officials in order to get the contract.

CHAPTER SEVENTEEN

EXPLORING FOR OIL IN THE "WILD, WILD EAST" OF YEMEN

After discussions with Ray Fairchild and Ian Maycock and consulting with Gary Hurford on engineering, Ray Hunt made the decision to go for an exploration contract (Production Sharing Agreement). I briefed our exploration group on our findings and explained that this was an opportunity to get a PSA on the Arabian Peninsula, which would be seen by the industry as Hunt Oil going big league (this was Ian's thought and I agreed with it).

The next step was to get Ali Jabr Alawi to come to Dallas in late January. He was in Washington that month, meeting with the World Bank. I learned of this in a conversation with him and assumed he was going to see if the bank could provide them with money that they would need for a seismic survey of the basin.

(In a seismic survey, a company lays cables on the ground in a grid-like manner and either sets off dynamite or has trucks that have a device that strikes the ground to make sound go into the earth. These cables have phones on them to record the speed of the sound waves as they travel down through the sedimentary layers of rock to generally the granite at the bottom of the basin. In this case, it turned out to be a couple of miles deep. The speed of these waves, measured as they go through the rock, gives data that geophysicists interpret. Sound travels slower through harder rock than softer rock, like sandstone that can hold oil like a sponge holds water … this is just a refresher and a bit of an expansion of what I told you earlier, in chapter 14).

Anyway, if you remember, when Ali mentioned he was going to be in DC in late January, I had made a mental note to get him to Dallas, giving us an opportunity for Hunt and Fairchild to meet him and get a better feel for a possible Yemen deal. So, Tony and I flew to Washington and picked Ali up in our plane and flew back to Dallas for a couple of days for meetings and getting to know each other better. At the end, we felt comfortable with him and told him we wanted to pursue a contract. Further, we would send a negotiating team to Sanaa.

An interesting incident happened during this period. I received a call from a World Bank officer, Tom Fitzgerald, inquiring about a rumor that we were planning to negotiate for an exploration contract in Yemen. Normally, this type of information was confidential and we would tell no one since other companies might hear about it and become competitors. I made an instant decision to violate company policy and confirmed to Tom that we were. He said he would hold off for the time and not grant Yemen the funds the Yemenis were asking for. It was a good decision, at least as far as Hunt was concerned, because if the bank had given Yemen the money, they could have conducted the seismic survey themselves and then used the data to attract other companies, potentially preventing Hunt from getting the contract.

Our negotiating team subsequently flew to Yemen, where they would be in contact with Fairchild. International PSA contracts were new to Hunt, so we hired a contract negotiator, Armand Sahakian, and attached him to our team. While we were doing this, I was negotiating with Mujib on his contract for bringing us the deal. He wanted a 3 percent override (which was the value of 3 percent of oil produced), but we did not want to do that. We settled on a contractor fee, where he would be our geophysicist on site and receive 1 percent of Hunt's net profits. This eventually turned out to be a very good deal and made him a very rich man. (In the oil industry, it is customary to pay a fee or percentage to an individual who brings you a deal that you pursue). Mujib was very important to us, as he had the relationships, knew the culture, spoke the language, and was a first-rate geophysicist. We wanted to do right by him.

That summer, our team negotiated a deal with the Yemeni government. Fairchild, Ian, Mujib, and I went over in September 1981 to sign it. We went through all the ceremonies, including pictures. Unfortunately, I had my Canon AE-1, which only I knew how to use (in the predigital days), so I was the one asked to take the pictures. Thus, I was not in the signing photo, which became the official one.

Fairchild hired a contractor, Dan Edwards, to manage the seismic phase, in which we measured the area using sound and revealed (through Mujib and Ian's talents and interpretations) that some structures did indeed exist.

During this phase, which took place in 1982 and 1983, a funny incident happened. Our exploration acreage consisted of three million acres in the Yemen portion of the desert known as the Empty Quarter, or Rub al Khali. It started just east of the old town of Marib I described earlier. Edwards and our contracting seismic company laid out a large grid pattern from which they laid their cable lines to record soundwave speed.

One day, some local tribesmen hijacked our two new Toyota Land Cruisers and drove them back to their village. We complained to the government and informed it that we could not operate if the tribes were allowed to steal our equipment. The government responded by sending in the military to the village to arrest the offenders.

After much conversation, the offending tribesmen said that they had not known these were Hunt vehicles. They said they thought they were UN vehicles. And since the UN belongs to everyone, they thought they could use them too. To make amends, they apologized and sent the two vehicles back to our camp, each with two sheep in the back, as compensation.

From then on, we put Yemen Hunt signs on the doors of all of our vehicles.

By mid-1983, Mujib and Ian had identified a number of prospects. In this case, a prospect was a subsurface structure that could trap oil, gas, and water. The only way to confirm it, however, would be to drill it.

After consultation, Ray decided to drill two wells. We felt we had some good prospects and, because of the cost ($8 million each), he decided to bring in a partner. The deal we would propose would be 49 percent for a partner who would fund the two wells.

We then went out into the industry to find a partner, but we could not find an interested oil company. They had a number of concerns.

First, the closest known oil was over five hundred miles away. Second, the area where we wanted to drill was in an unstable part of the country, where strict tribal cultures existed and every male carried a gun. Third, little was known about the stability of Yemen since the country was controlled by tribes, and even though the central government had a military, it basically controlled only the area around Sanaa and the coast. Finally, the country was at the time split into two countries, North Yemen and communist South Yemen. The early 1980s was the height of the Cold War. Our concession bordered the two states on an unstable country line.

Then one day in 1983, two Koreans walked into our office. They represented a Korean refinery company called Yukong. They also had an offshore drilling rig that they wanted to introduce to us as they were starting a drilling company. As we talked, they explained that the Korean government was allocating 10 cents of every imported barrel of oil (all oil in Korea was imported) and putting it into an exploration fund so that Korean companies could also become exploration companies. (Oil companies are simply divided into three types: [1] Companies that look for oil, generally called independents. When they find it, they sell it into a market and receive their money. [2] Companies that refine crude oil, as it is useless until it is refined into gasoline, diesel, aviation fuel, asphalt, etc., which becomes a product and sold to retail operations like gas stations. [3] An integrated company that both explores and produces oil, transports oil, refines it, and sells the products through branded names. These are large integrated oil companies, like Exxon and Chevron).

This Korean company seemed to be our last hope to share the risk in Yemen. We presented our deal at the meeting. They went back to Korea to discuss the terms and came back to us to say they were interested but only wanted to commit to one well ($8 million), which would be 24.5 percent of our deal (recall that we wanted 49 percent).

We began negotiating but told them that we needed to start drilling the well (they would reimburse us). However, if we encountered any indications that there were hydrocarbons (oil or gas) in the well, we would stop the negotiations if we did not have a deal by that point, since the proof of some type of oil would allow us to go back to the big oil companies and make a better deal with them.

We began drilling (oil term is "spudding") the well on January 24, 1984. Through most of February, the negotiations dragged on. On a Sunday in late February, Ray called us into the office. Our chief engineer Gary Hurford reported we had a tremendous "kick" in the well (a sign of tremendous pressure that normally only oil or gas can give). Gary, a very experienced but conservative engineer, was sure that we had something big down there.

Ray then asked where the Koreans were in the negotiations. John Scott, our general counsel, said that our deal was that if we had a show (kick), the deal was off. This was definitely a show. He counseled Ray to drop the Koreans, since we could get a much better deal with other companies now we could show that oil may be there. Ray asked if the Koreans were negotiating in good faith. He was told that they were so he said to keep negotiating.

Several weeks later, we did reach an agreement with Yukong. Fairchild went to Korea to sign the deal. After the signatures, he showed them the log and data and told them that we had known we had something big while we were negotiating.

They, then, knew Ray Hunt could have dropped them and gone out for a better deal, but he had not. This act created a strong relationship with Yukong (which later merged with SK Group to become one of the largest conglomerate companies in Korea). SK went on to become our partners in many deals around the world, including multibillion dollar LNG projects in both Yemen and Peru. This act showed the true color of Ray Hunt, which was now seen in Korea as someone you could trust. I have never been so proud of a company and its leader. When I would go to Korea (and it was often), I was treated with so much respect and friendship during this period.

Officially, the government of Yemen would not grant Korea a license since they did not recognize each other in 1983 (so we could not give them 24.5 percent of our license). Ray's solution was to make them an investing partner for 24.5 instead, which they accepted. During this period, I made a trip to South Korea, at the request of Ali al Bahr, to explain that the Yemeni government welcomes the Korean companies as investors. Further, I brought the Koreans' favorable response back to Yemen. It is interesting to note that soon after we signed up Yukong as our partners, the two countries recognized each other and the Korean ambassador in Saudi Arabia extended his coverage to Sanaa. It was fun playing diplomat for a brief time.

Now that the Koreans were in and paying their share, we pursued the drilling and testing of our first well, called Alif 1. On July 4, 1984, it came in and tested over 10,000 b/d of high-quality crude at about five thousand feet in a fine sandstone reservoir and incredible flow. We now knew we had something very big. We needed to prove up at least three hundred million barrels to make it "commercial" (cover costs, debt, and make a profit).

On September 27, 1985, after drilling ten more wells, the Alif 11 well proved up over 300 million barrels of reserves of oil (with each successful well, our engineers could calculate how much oil we could get from that area). We could now build a pipeline and export facility and sell the crude oil on the world market).

These were now to become really exciting times. At this time, Hunt personnel had little real experience operating overseas, let alone in a remote country like Yemen in the early 1980s. Fairchild and Maycock had worked overseas, but few of our engineers had. We had four things going for us, however. I was on the front line and could see it.

1. We had "bench strength," as we owned and operated pipelines and a refinery, handled complicated facilities, and had a seventy-year-old culture demonstrating that Hunt could get it done. Many of our employees were second- and even third-generation. Further, many were Texan, a can-do culture in itself. This was backed up with our ultra-tough men from North Dakota and the seasoned and clever men from Alabama. Our message to the Yemenis was that we were experienced oil finders, and pipeline and refinery workers from small towns in the United States.

2. Hunt had an excellent reputation in the industry. Even though it was not a major oil company like Exxon, it had the financial, technical, and political skills to match it per country. George Bush and Ray Hunt's friendship became well-known in the political world. Bush dedicated the refinery in Yemen when he was Reagan's vice president in 1987.

3. Since we weren't a major oil company, we could not dictate things to Yemen as many large companies would after such a big find. I think Saleh saw this as a plus. Further, he liked Ray, as they were the same age.

4. Finally, it was Ray Hunt that made Yemen a success for both Hunt and Yemen. His instinct led him to invest when others in the world shied away. When the massive oil field was found, he structured a deal with the largest oil company in the world (EXXON), yet told them Hunt would operate in Yemen, since our people had the relationships and would not run scared when faced with difficulties. They agreed. In very few cases did Exxon ever let a partner operate but they too trusted Ray Hunt.

Ray made four trips a year to Yemen (I accompanied him on most of these and went alone on many others) to confer with Saleh on problems our manager and technical people were having with customs, tribes, individuals, etc. Our manager compiled a list of problems and Ray would present it to Saleh and explain that these issues were costing money and time by preventing us from exporting oil. This lack of export revenue was costing Yemen. Saleh would then get on the phone and correct things. Saleh was not an educated man, so these calculations often made no impression until Ray himself explained them. This was, however, a quarterly ordeal. In the public companies, the CEO is a ship passing in the night. A CEO would not visit the head of a country where they were producing oil unless there were major problems or the CEO wanted to get more concessions. With Hunt, Saleh saw Ray four times yearly for twenty years. They became friends ... until Saleh lied to Ray and "stabbed him in the back" in an important meeting in Washington, DC, in 2005.

CHAPTER EIGHTEEN

OIL DISCOVERY AND BRINGING YEMEN INTO THE TWENTIETH CENTURY

Our discovery in the desert interior of Yemen, the Great Empty Quarter of the Arabian Peninsula, is a classic story of oil exploration in an unknown area. Once the oil was discovered in 1984, there were many tasks that had to be carried out in an unknown and untested environment.

We needed to drill more wells to prove the crude oil find. Once that was done, we needed to bring in more drilling rigs to expand our exploration of the area. Then, we would have to build a seven-hundred-mile pipeline from the desert, through tribal lands over ninety-four hundred feet of rugged mountains to the Red Sea, where we could deliver the oil.

Simultaneously, we had to build an export facility so we could take the crude oil from that pipeline, load it into tankers, and ship it to the world markets.

Initially, we needed approval of our plan by President Saleh of Yemen. Given that we would have to cross tribal lands on the pipeline route, Saleh would ensure the tribes were in agreement and would not shoot or kidnap our employees and contractors.

A little later, at the request of the Yemeni president, we would have to build a small refinery that would provide gasoline and diesel for the local area (and to operate our facilities too).

Now, none of this was free, and Hunt was going to need about a billion dollars to do it. Typically, the way to do this would be for the company to go to the bank and pledge the reserves in the ground and all the facilities to be built in exchange for a loan. This is called project financing. It works well in the United States or Europe, but in an unstable country in the Middle East, it would be a difficult sell to a bank and very complicated because of the need for insurance and maybe additional collateral.

Thus, Ray's strategy was to "farm in" (acquire) a deep pocket partner. Now that we had proof of at least three hundred million barrels through our extensive drilling, there were some big oil companies that showed some interest, as we had taken the geological risk out of the equation by finding the oil.

The true genius of Ray Hunt now emerged. He and his chief engineer, Gary

Hurford (a brilliant technical oil man, who understood the ins and outs of oil fields and developing them), enticed both Shell and Exxon into negotiations for 49 percent of Hunt's interest in the license (now 75.5 percent, since the Koreans got 24.5). Eventually, Ray decided on Exxon.

As a point of interest, Tony Copp and I were traveling the world trying to cobble up financing for the pipeline and facilities, since we did not know if we could find a partner to share the costs. We were meeting with oil companies, banks, and governments (the latter would give soft loans on good terms if we were to buy the equipment and pipe from businesses in their country).

Over the course of a year, we visited Asia, Latin America, and Europe, meeting with scores of potential prospects. One of the companies we met with was the Spanish company Hispanoil. They showed an interest and submitted a bid that included a gas field plus some cash. It was a bigger number than Exxon or Shell offered, but Ray did not want it. One thing in their bid, however, that we came away with was an "early completion" incentive. If Hunt could finish the pipeline early ahead of the projected date, Hispanoil offered to pay a $5 million bonus for every month we came in under the date. Ray selected Exxon's bid but added that "early incentive" to the deal. In the end, Hunt picked up millions because Mike Cobb and his team finished the pipeline and facilities early.

The deal between Exxon and Hunt was that Exxon would get 49 percent of Hunt's interest. (As a result, the Koreans ended up with 24.5 and Exxon with 37 percent, while we retained 38.5 percent.) The deal was initialed but before it was made official, the Exxon executives wanted to visit Yemen and have the oil minister approve the deal.

Therefore, I was sent over to Yemen on Thanksgiving 1985 to brief the prime minister, al Eryani, and the oil minister, al Mohanni. Mohanni had been the Yemeni ambassador to Saudi Arabia before taking on his ministerial portfolio and had no energy experience.

I had a two-hour meeting with them, explaining that we had initialed a deal with Exxon (the largest public energy company in the world) for 49 percent of our interest. According to the deal, they would take care of pipeline financing, allowing us to save months in time and get the project under way immediately. Hunt would remain the operator of the project. Again, this was unusual, as Exxon normally wanted to operate, but I think they realized that Hunt had the relationships with the government and several years of experience in dealing with the tribes in the desert.

I told the ministers I would be back in a couple of weeks with Ray and a couple of Exxon executives who wanted to meet them and receive the oil minister's signature on the agreement so they could be on the license officially. Although our contract allowed us to bring in a partner without government approval, Exxon wanted extra assurance since they were investing so much money. Prime Minister Eryani immediately saw the advantage of bringing Exxon in and was all for it. The oil minister, on the other hand, was quite reserved. I just assumed he had little knowledge of the business and that we needed to get him "up to speed."

In mid-December, I returned to Yemen with Ray, Gary, and two Exxon executives, Dan McGiver and Jack Crutchfield, who came over to see the country, tour our operations, meet the government officials, and get a signature from al Mohanni. Once that was done, we would fly back to Dallas to close the deal. Ray wanted it wrapped up by December 31, 1985.

We got everything done ... except the oil minister would not sign off on the contract. He wanted more time to think it over. On the last evening, three hours before our flight, Ray was very frustrated and angry, because we could not get this contract signed with Exxon until al Mohanni approved it. We were in Ray's hotel room getting ready to go to the airport, when the phone rang.

Now, here I want to go back a bit to demonstrate how things sometimes work with added creativity and great timing. Four years earlier, in October 1981, Egyptian president Anwar Sadat had been assassinated while reviewing a parade in Cairo. This obviously got the attention of most dictators in the Middle East, including Yemeni president Saleh.

Ray first met President Saleh in late 1983 and would visit with him whenever he traveled to Yemen (and usually, I would go with him). On one particular visit in early 1985, their discussion included the killing of Sadat and how Yemen had a parade stadium similar to Egypt's.

During the conversation, Ray mentioned that the US president had highly trained Secret Service Agents protecting him. In response, Saleh commented that his people were not highly trained. At this point, Ray told Saleh that Hunt had several ex-Secret Services agents on staff, led by Walt Coughlin. Further, he offered to help train some of Saleh's security if the president wanted help. Saleh said that he did. So, Ray contacted Walt and relayed the situation.

Walt worked out a deal with the Secret Service, wherein he and our two other ex-agents would bring a contingent of Saleh's protective people to Virginia for several weeks of training. Salih was very pleased with the results.

Now, back to the mid-December 1985 phone call in Ray's room. Ray picked it up and it was the president's aide calling as an interpreter for Saleh (Saleh did not speak English). He said the president just wanted to call to thank Ray for providing Mr. Coughlin's help in the training of his men. He was very appreciative. He then asked Ray how everything was going.

Ray decided to relay his frustration to Saleh. He told him about the Exxon deal and how good it would be for Yemen. He explained that with Exxon, we could immediately start building a billion dollars' worth of facilities and begin producing and selling oil by early 1986. He said he was just about to get on an airplane, but he could not get the oil minister to sign off on the contract, which Exxon required.

Five minutes after this phone call ended, President Saleh called back, telling

Ray to send the contract over to al Mohanni's house for signature. We did so, and the minister signed it. He was not happy about it, which in some ways made it a challenge for our managers to get some things done in the future.

But this incident set a pattern. If the bureaucracy gave our people problems that could affect the flow of oil, our manager would document them. Later, when Ray made his quarterly trip, he would confer with President Saleh on the major issues and resolve them. In other problematic cases, he would hold discussions with the prime minister or oil minister.

Signature in hand, Ray and the team went back to Dallas to close the Exxon deal before year's end. From Sanaa, I headed to Seoul, to brief our Korean partners on the Exxon deal, as we had not yet informed them about it. I flew from Sanaa to Frankfurt to Seoul. In those days, we could not fly over the Soviet Union, so I had to fly all the way around it. The whole flight took twenty hours. I landed in Seoul, where I was picked up at the airport and taken to the office of Mr. Kim, the Korean CEO. I met with him and his senior officers for two hours, briefing them on the deal and the activities in Sanaa. I then returned to the airport and caught a thirteen-hour flight to Dallas. I was so elated by the deal we had done that I was not even tired. (But I had set a personal record of thirty-three hours in flight over a period of thirty-eight hours ... thank goodness for first class).

The interesting thing about this was that if we had not signed the deal on December 31, Exxon might have changed their minds because of the time it took to get the minister's signature. In January, oil prices dropped to a record low, a civil war erupted in South Yemen (and our project was near the border), and Exxon lost a $2 billion lawsuit in east Texas. Any one of these events could have caused Exxon to drop the deal, or at least, amend it on less favorable terms for Hunt.

I call it the Old Hunt Luck and thank you Walt Coughlin.

Now that the deal was signed, the Hunt team went into 1986 focused on completing the production facilities, building a small refinery (requested by the government as a source of gasoline and diesel for the tribesmen in the area of the oil field), and building a seven-hundred-mile pipeline through the desert and over the mountains to a place called Ras Issa (Jesus in Arabic) on the Red Sea, where the export facilities would be built. We decided to buy an old Exxon tanker, which we renamed the *Safer*; it became a floating stationary storage unit in order to offload oil to receiving tankers. This tanker, called a very large crude carrier (VLCC), was over four football fields long (thirteen hundred feet) and could store three million barrels of oil. In order to convert it from an active tanker, we sailed it to Korea from Norway, where we had purchased it, and had it outfitted with a loading boom in the bow. It was a challenge, because a typhoon struck the area, forcing us to outfit the boom a second time. Once outfitted, the tanker sailed to the location selected offshore from Ras Issa on the coast of the Red Sea in Yemen. We had to do some additional engineering, as the typhoon in this location was seasonally very strong. Our engineers figured out a way for the tanker to feather into the wind, so loading was a little easier, but there were days they could not offload.

I was told later by a local Yemeni that, had we consulted the local fishermen about a location, we could have selected a less windy spot. This is another case in life where I feel that talking with the locals in an area where you want to invest in a project makes good sense.

Be that as it may, the tanker was a real success. We later added a pump system, wherein we could pump fifty thousand barrels per minute into a receiving oil tanker (3 million barrels an hour).

I used to visit the tanker often on our Yemen trips. The crew was Italian with a Dutch captain. The Red Sea had some wonderful tropical lobster, and initially, the Yemenis did not eat them since they looked like insects. (Later the Russians would fish them to near extinction). The Italian cook made a lobster lasagna that I would kill for (along with a lot of other wonderful seafood dishes). I always looked forward to flying out to the tanker.

The crew also used to fish off the stationary tanker. They would catch giant grouper (hundreds of pounds). Their method was a stout line and bait dropped several hundred feet off the side into the water, where the giant fish fed. Once a fish was hooked, a heavy steel sleeve with a loose line attached to a crane was slid over the taut line and allowed to free-fall into the water. The sleeve had a barb on it. As the hooked fish was played to the water's surface, the sleeve would be released and its momentum would fall hundreds of feet, impaling the barb into the fish. They would then use the crane and rod and reel to hoist the fish to the deck of the boat. The Italian cooks made great meals out of these large fish.

Once the production facilities, pipeline, and export facilities were in operation, Yemen Hunt initially exported two hundred fifty thousand barrels per day (at $16/barrel, making $4 million/day). Later, by 2004, oil was at $30/barrel, and the profits rose accordingly.

It is true that Hunt, Exxon, and our Korean partners made a lot of money in Yemen. But Hunt took a risk where no one else committed to the risk and investment. Further, until we found the oil, no oil company would invest. This is the nature of the business and why I loved it so much.

However, the big thing to remember was that a country that had been in extreme poverty was now an oil exporter. Eventually, they got 80 percent of the profit from the oil. This did wonders for Yemen, as they could now afford many services for their citizens ... schools, healthcare, sanitation, cultural activities ... And in fact, initially they did invest in many of these areas. Further, the oil wealth attracted many companies from around the world to invest in Yemen.

I noticed many improvements in sanitation, transportation, and communication technology each time I would return. Unfortunately, some (or more than some) of the money was "diverted" by President Saleh. These funds were very tempting for the president and I think he used much of it for paying off tribal sheiks and other bribes in order to keep political order in the country. Also, I think he gave big bonuses to his loyal ministers and military leaders. This was pretty obvious: you could see it in the many big mansions that were increasingly being built in a select area of Sanaa. And of course, Saleh was also adding to his personal real estate.

In the early years, we, at Hunt, were excited about the improvements to the standard of living of the Yemeni, knowing that it was a result of our efforts in finding, producing, and selling the crude oil (none of which Yemen could have done even if they had wanted to, as they did not have an oil industry or trained personnel). In those early years, Saleh and Ray became friends, which I observed in various meetings between them in which I also participated. They were the same age and could share family stories (although Ray had one wife and Salih had four). Additionally, one year, President Saleh awarded Ray the highest award in Yemen, the Order of Yemen, which Ray proudly displayed in his office (until 2005, when Saleh violated our contract and took over the oil field).

In fact, when Ray's daughter Ashlee was married, Saleh gave her an Arabian stallion as a wedding present. I remember it well, as Ray asked me to get the horse into the United States and house it at the Circle K Ranch, near Dallas. I had to get it through customs, and there were all types of health forms to fill out.

Unfortunately, the horse had some type of blood disease and would not be admitted into the country until it was cleared up. I hired a veterinarian, who flew to Yemen with a one-month plan to give the horse antibiotics to eliminate the problem. It didn't work, so after another failed attempt, we decided to keep the horse in Yemen and had an employee charged with taking care of it in a nice stable the company built. That horse lived another eighteen years before it died. I do not think Saleh ever knew we kept it in Yemen.

However, there was a related incident at a lunch hosted for us in the presidential palace. It was just Ray, me, the president, and the prime minister, Dr. Eryani (who spoke fluent English and knew the situation with the horse because I kept him informed). This was about five years after we had received the horse and stabled it in Yemen. Ray was taking a drink of camel's milk when Saleh asked how the horse was doing. When translated, the question caught Ray by total surprise, and I will always remember the white mustache that the milk left between his lips and nose. Fortunately, Dr. Eryani intervened with an answer that essentially meant "fine," and he moved quickly on to another subject while Ray cleaned his upper lip. That was the only time the horse came up.

During the early years, while we were building the facilities, we decided on other projects related to oil and gas. Yemen Hunt built four huge $400 million gas plants, where we would strip out the C-5 plus liquids from the wet gas and put it in the crude stream. Eventually, we would produce forty thousand barrels per day of these liquids and then inject the dry gas back into the formation to save it and keep it for future use.

On occasion, I would go out to the desert when they were building the plants.

When digging into the desert to put in the foundations, they often uncovered stone arrowheads, fishing points, and fossilized tree roots from Neolithic times (eleven thousand years ago). Though now a desert, the area had apparently been a land of rivers, lakes, and lush vegetation. Neolithic man fished the waters with stone fishing points and may have lived in huts on the water.

In the early days, Drs. Jim Brooks and Lou Jacobs, a geologist and paleontologist from SMU (and good friends since I was on the board of the Institute for the Study of Earth and Man at SMU) asked if they could come to Yemen and look at the rocks. Their interest was in the rocks along the Red Sea and their connection with the prehuman finds in Kenya (Lucy). We arranged for them to get visas. They spent a week and concluded the rocks were different from the ones in Kenya.

While in Yemen, they traveled to our operations in the eastern desert and spent a day in the al Jawf Valley. Few, if any, archeologists had been there and, with their trained eyes, they sighted several ancient mounds (tells). They dug into one and reasoned it may have been a Neolithic town (based on the relics). They also observed what looked like burial huts on some ridges that had stone trails leading down into the valley floor. The doors of the huts were pointing directly toward Mecca (hundreds of years before the rise of Islam).

They were supposed to return for a formal dig, but unfortunately, tribal problems erupted, and no one has been able to go into the area since then. Maybe after the civil war ceases.

Those early years while we were processing three billion cubic feet per day not only proved to be profitable but gave us experience in new technology in a growing new market for gas … LNG. In turn, this led us to Peru.

This period from 1984 to 1994 was known by Hunt as the Honeymoon Period, in which we and the government had the same interests and produced a lot of oil and gas.

CHAPTER NINETEEN

THE HONEYMOON PERIOD …
1984 TO 1994

We'd signed the Production Sharing Argument with Yemen (essentially, we get our investment dollars back with a formula and operating costs, then we split the profit with the government. They get 70 to 80 percent, and the Hunt Partners get 20 to 30 percent based on daily production figures). In the 1980s we had a fun working relationship with the government, in which we had the opportunity to get to know the important ministers very well and a couple became very good friends, especially Dr. Eryani. (We remained friends and kept in contact by email, even after we were ejected from Yemen in 2005, which I will explain later).

Many of these government ministers came to Washington, DC, and Dallas after we found the oil, and I spent many a day in lunches, dinners, or hunting with them at Hunt's Circle K Ranch, outside Dallas. (In Sanaa, I would schedule tennis games with those who played tennis. In fact, managers would leave my tennis racquet, tennis gear, and even a business suit in the manager's apartment).

When we brought the first oil drilling rig to the Red Sea port of Hodeida, the oil minister was there to meet it and led the rig convoy across the country to the eastern desert near Marib, in the Jauf basin, where we were to drill the first well. He closed down roads, removed electrical lines, and blocked commerce in towns in order for his convoy to proceed without any hindrance.

They had the same attitude when building all the production, pipeline, and export facilities. They were proud that Yemen had joined the world of Arab oil producers.

In short, after the discovery and Exxon's entry into the fray, we were fully supported by the government, since they wanted to start booking income (as we did).

We did have some "speed bumps" in the 80s. One was with customs officials wanting bribes. However, I've already explained how Ray, in a meeting with the president, handled minor Yemeni officials who wanted bribes before they would let our equipment or supplies through customs. This did make it easier for us and if we had "customs" problems, Ray would take the documentation that his managers gave him, which succinctly defined the problem and the effect it would have on completing the construction and receiving revenues for Yemen, and hand it over to the top officials. That always did it.

The other was a billion-dollar lawsuit that came out of the blue in 1987, after we'd begun producing and selling crude oil.

LAWSUIT ... ARABIAN SHIELD

Apparently in 1965, a Texas oilman named Jack Crichton (who ran for the governor of Texas and was a friend of Ray's father, H. L. Hunt) had signed a contract with the old regime in Yemen, before it was divided into North and South Yemen.

It was an exploration contract covering the whole country. It specifically required Crichton to carry out a number of seismic and geological commitments. However, he did not follow through on any of them. Then, in 1969, the country broke up and he said he could not do anything even though he ran beyond the deadline in the contract before Yemen split apart. Thus, by 1981, his contract was null and void.

Now there is an old saying in the old business, "An oil discovery has many fathers and a dry hole is a bastard." This applies to our success. We now had the biggest discovery in the heart of big oil in the Middle East in 1985. Crichton's Arabian Shield (which had a Palestinian partner and a valid US oil company partner, Dorchester Gas) filed a billion-dollar suit against Hunt for tortuous interference. This was based on a Pennzoil/Texaco case, where Pennzoil won a judgment of $9 billion. Essentially, there was a contract with a second party (Texaco), and the second party interfered with the contract of the first (Pennzoil). The court ruled in favor of Pennzoil. Arabian Shield tried to use that argument against Hunt, referring to our actions in Yemen as a tortuous interference.

I spent much of 1987 traveling the world with our Thompson Knight lawyers, Frank Finn and David Noteware, taking depositions and gathering evidence for trial. Crichton had a very flimsy case, as they did not meet any of their obligations on their concession after they signed it and waited twenty-two years (after our big discovery) before filing a lawsuit (even though we had signed our contract six years earlier, in 1981). Further, they had no real witnesses supporting their claim.

Regardless, Ray wanted to aggressively fight the lawsuit. We suspected their tactic was to get the lawsuit tried in a Texas court and force us to settle for a large amount. And so, we took depositions in Texas, London, Frankfurt, and Sanaa. For their part, Arabian Shield used a "well-endowed" female private eye, Ann Cardash, to meet our employees and consultants under false pretenses. She would contact them claiming she was with the British Museum and would be going to Yemen soon and understood they have experience in Yemen, and ask for a meeting. Once the meetings got set up (sometimes more than one), she would record the conversations with a recorder that she hid in her very large bra. During the discovery phase, we were able to get copies of the tapes and I listened to them all. This gave our lawyers a lot of ammunition when they deposed the principals in Arabian Shield.

Among other things, Arabian Shield accused me of being with the CIA and using that influence for Hunt to get the license from Yemen. They even launched a media campaign in which articles were written claiming Mujib and I illegally acquired the contract. This was all false, of course, and made me laugh when I read the articles.

However, because of our good relationship with Dr. Eryani, we were allowed to see the copies of the minutes of the ministers' meetings when Hunt had been chosen as the winner of the contract. What I did not know until I saw the minutes was that Dorchester Gas (with Arabian Shield) had also been considered for the contract.

As a point of interest, when I made our sales pitch to the minerals minister, Ali al Bahr and I told him about Hunt Oil Company. In an earlier chapter, I mentioned that during our meeting I also explained that we were working in China (as part of a group doing a seismic survey) and mentioned some of our other businesses, including land and cattle that included two hundred fifty thousand acres and thousands of head of cattle. Now, Yemeni ministers, who knew nothing about the oil business, did know about land and livestock. Two hundred fifty thousand acres was tangible wealth.

On reading the minutes of the meeting, we discovered that the reason why Hunt Oil Company was selected over Dorchester Gas was that Hunt was (in their understanding) a larger company, with interests in China and large holdings of land and cattle. Not one of the participants appeared to know that Dorchester was in fact the larger company, and one minister said he thought they were "just a gas company." This information has never come out other than what I saw in those translated minutes. It is embedded in the case document in Hunt Oil's legal department.

The reason it never came out is because the judge threw out the suit for procedural reasons. The time had lapsed for Arabian Shield to pursue the case, which was one of the tactics Frank and David had pursued. They were also prepared to go to trial that day, had the judge not ruled in our favor.

One funny incident during the deposition phase happened in London. I convinced Mujib to testify in a deposition. He did not want to but agreed, knowing what was at stake. We met in a conference room off Hyde Park, and our opponent's lawyer, named Murphy, was a very aggressive attorney. Mujib arrived smoking his pipe, which Murphy asked him not to during the deposition because it affected his breathing. Mujib agreed and put his pipe aside.

Murphy then began to drill down into the deposition, treating Mujib as if he were a liar on almost every question. Mujib held his cool, however, as I watched him. At one point, Murphy pulled out the copy of Mujib's passport and started challenging him about every page. When he got to page with the Yemen visa, he really began to fire questions. For example, when Mujib first went into the country, who did he meet with? Mujib responded with several names, including Prime Minister Abdul Ghani. Murphy then asked, how could a person of Mujib's status meet with a top leader of the country? (Mujib had in fact met with him, and even I had many meetings later with him; he became a friend, like al Eryani.) The insulting tone of the question really angered Mujib, and rather than engaging in an equally verbal response, he just grabbed his pipe, lit it, and immediately blew smoke into Murphy's face. This shortened the deposition and I was so tickled by the way Mujib handled the conflict.

Ray spent over a couple of million dollars in legal fees to defend this case. But it was less than a few days of oil income.

A funny sidebar to this is that I was called for jury duty, in Dallas, three months later. It was a case where one lady had run into a man and caused $1,400 worth of damage to his car. The damage to her car was $1,200. They were both suing each other. Additionally, her lawyer leased her the car she was driving.

The judge and the lawyers called our thirty-person jury panel into the trial room and began to tell us about the case. I sat there, furious that all this jury talent was being wasted on such an innocuous case. At the end of the briefing, the judge asked us if anyone had a question. I waited a few seconds and then raised my hand. I told the judge that all of us on the panel (from which twelve jurors would be selected) were busy people and asked, why was this frivolous case not handled in a small claims court? Others on the panel now also spoke up in support of my position, to the point that the judge pounded her gavel for order and told us to go out into the hall. Fifteen minutes later, she called us back into the courtroom and told us that we were all dismissed from jury duty and that we could leave.

I decided to go over and apologize to the judge. I told her I was sorry about the question, but I had just come off a billion-dollar frivolous lawsuit and hated to see the court being taken advantage of.

She said my question was a good one and this dispute should be in small claims court. But, she said, even with this small damage, people can opt for a jury trial. It was apparent she was not happy, and I got the feeling that those two lawyers probably stayed away from her court in the future.

CHAPTER TWENTY

THE YEMEN EXPERIENCE

By 1987 we were producing nearly two hundred and fifty thousand barrels of oil a day. We were finding new fields in the block and continued to add production. We also found a lot of non-associated gas (stand-alone) as well as associated gas (in with the oil). As mentioned earlier, our engineers recommended that we produce that gas, set up plants that would strip out the wet liquids from the gas (C5 plus), and reinject the drier gas back into the oil formation. In this way, we could inject the liquids in the pipeline, sell the gas liquids as oil, and save the drier gas for LNG. We built four plants in the desert and produced forty thousand barrels per day of liquids.

Our major trips to Yemen during this period were to clear away Yemen bureaucrats' games so our managers could continue to operate efficiently, including the four trips a year Ray would make to meet with the president and define the bottlenecks. I would be in the meetings and take notes. Some of the oil ministers did not like these trips, but they knew Ray had a purpose that was beneficial for their country.

Often a trip would coincide with the Yemen Revolutionary Day parade, September 27. It would be a big parade full of marching soldiers and assorted Russian and US tanks and personnel carriers. (The US ambassador commented to me on one occasion that he would pray that the US equipment would not break down and give the Russians a propaganda advantage during these parades). We would sit in the VIP stand close to the president and ministers. I remember that Yasser Arafat, a world-famous leader of the Palestine Liberation Organization (PLO), was a guest one year and sat two rows down from us. He looked to be about five-foot-three and had a pistol strapped to his hip; I was surprised he was so short.

The PLO was considered a terrorist organization in the '80s by the United States and Israel. It was against the law for us to deal with them. The Israelis got into a war with them and drove them into Beirut, engaging in indiscriminate slaughter. The United States stepped in (because there was so much collateral damage) to stop it and negotiate a deal whereby the PLO fighters would leave Lebanon.

They were shipped to Tunisia and some other Arab states. Some ended up in Sanaa, a phenomenon I ran into personally. One evening I went into the old Souk to do some shopping for old silver items. I took a cab from the hotel and stayed out later than I thought I would. By the time that I walked out of the old city and looked for a cab, I could not find any and decided to walk back to the hotel, which was a couple of miles away.

All of a sudden, a car pulled up with three men in it, and they asked where I was going. When I told them, they asked if I wanted a ride. For some reason, I was curious (and robbery and murder were not common things in Yemen), so I said yes. Besides, I was tired and didn't want to walk the two miles. As we were driving, they asked me what I was doing in Yemen. I answered that I was with Hunt Oil and that we were developing an oil field. Everyone knew about that and, at that time, Hunt was loved by everybody in Yemen. I then asked them (since they were not dressed like Yemenis and spoke English) where they were from. They told me they were PLO soldiers living in Yemen for a time. It was a great ride and I am glad I did it. We had an interesting short visit and then they let me off at the Sheba Hotel. They did not seem like terrorists.

New oil ministers came and went, and it was a fun challenge to develop a relationship with them. Some we trusted, and some we did not. One of my favorites was Bin Housinoon, a military officer from South Yemen.

As I mentioned, after 1969 there was a North Yemen (Yemen Arab Republic, or YAR) and a communist South Yemen. By the time we began operations in the region, they had been two separate countries for well over fourteen years.

In 1988 I made a trip with Ian and Mujib to Aden, the capital of South Yemen (People's Democratic Republic of Yemen, PDRY) to meet with the deputy oil minister, Rashed al Kalff. We were trying to get a contract to explore in South Yemen in the area that bordered our contracts' three million acres in North Yemen. We thought we had a chance to get one, although US law did not allow a US company to do business with the PDRY. (We had a Canadian subsidiary and we thought we could have them operate it).

As fate would have it, in 1989 the USSR was beginning to implode and the Russians were no longer supporting world communist regimes. Further, the Berlin Wall fell in late 1989 and now the PDRY's major sponsor, communist East Germany, also collapsed and stopped supporting communist regimes around the world.

All of a sudden, South Yemen had no support and no real revenue. Oxy Canada had found some oil in the east, but they had not established the extent of their find at that time. Thus, South Yemen was struggling by 1990.

President Saleh saw this as an opportunity and proposed a merger of North and South into a single country. They would blend the leadership so that the South was not treated unfairly. A lot of promises were made and an agreement was reached and signed. It caught the world by surprise. The South's leaders were not happy, but they had no choice. Some left Yemen to fight another day. As for the ministries, both the Southerners and the Northerners were selected to run the ministries … one as deputy and one as minister. Both were primary ministers and deputy ministers depending on the ministry.

In the Ministry of Oil and Minerals (MOMR), Bin Housinoon, a former general in the South, was selected as the new minister of oil. Now, at the time, North Yemen was very conservative. Women were veiled and not allowed to leave their house without a male relative.

At the same time, South Yemen was very progressive. Women were not veiled and could meet with male friends in a restaurant. Further, the North banned alcohol, but the South had the best German-designed brewery in the Middle East. In fact, the first real conflict after unification was because the Northerners were driving south to Aden and buying up all the beer so the Southerners were limited in how much they could purchase. I believe the new, joint government eventually closed the brewery because of Islamic law, and this really ticked the Southerners off.

The first time Ray and I met Bin Housinoon was when we were invited to his house for dinner during Ramadan (the Muslim monthly period when one abstains from food during the daylight hours. The fast is broken in the evening and one feasts until late at night).

Unlike a dinner with an official in North Yemen, where the wife would not be included, Mrs. Bin Housinoon was dressed in a beautiful dress, offered us Scotch, and joined the conversation. We would have never seen this in the North. I knew right then that there was a strong cultural divide that would be a challenge to overcome among the leaders. I believe that the South was not ideologically Marxist (communists), but they "played the game" so they could get Russian and East German financial and armament support. I also do not believe that the Russians and East Germans cared ideologically. This was the Cold War and they were countering the US moves in the world.

An interesting incident happened at one point after we started our oil production in 1987. Ray received a letter from a deputy oil minister of Saudi Arabia instructing him to stop, cease, and desist our operations because our oil field was in Saudi Arabia and not Yemen. At the time, we had contracted Dr. Henry Kissinger's firm, HKA, to advise us while we operated in Yemen. On his staff was Larry Eagleburger (a former undersecretary of state who became the secretary of state in the Bush administration) and Brent Scowcroft (who became Bush's national security advisor). He also had a number of former government people, including Paul Bremmer (a former diplomat who became the civilian administrator in Iraq in 2003) and Alan Stoga (a banker and former aide to Kissinger).

Whenever we had a ticklish political situation, we would call HKA and would meet with them either in New York or in our offices. When advised of the letter, Eagleburger said we should deliver it to President Saleh with a message that this was an issue for Yemen to handle and we are just going to ignore it. I was selected to fly to Yemen (over Thanksgiving) and deliver this message.

I flew to Sanaa and was picked up by the finance minister, who personally drove me the hundred miles to the president's palace in Hodeida, on the Red Sea. We went from about eight thousand feet to sea level on a very interesting and winding highway, in the dark.

When I arrived at the palace, I was met by Dr. Eryani, who ushered me into a big room where President Saleh was meeting with the minister of industry. There must have been a problem, as the president was shouting and berating the minister, who was shaking visibly. This concerned me a little bit as I wanted the president to be in a good mood during my presentation.

Soon, however, I went over to shake the hand of President Saleh, and Dr. Eryani explained why I had come. (He knew who I was, as I had met with him many times when with Ray).

I then placed the map that the Saudi deputy oil minister had sent Ray on the floor and explained how we had gotten it. I then said that Ray had instructed me to bring it to Saleh and tell him that we are just "oil finders from Texas" and we do not get involved in politics, that we feel this is a Yemeni issue, and that we will continue to operate as long as our people are safe. I then got on my knees and pointed to the area where the Saudi said their border was.

President Saleh then got on his knees, and with his finger, explained where the Yemen border was. It was much farther north and our oil field was definitely in Yemen. I told him I would relay our conversation to Ray. We had a nice conversation and then, as I was leaving, he told me to tell Ray that once Hunt had discovered two billion barrels, he would come to Dallas and visit Ray.

Ironically, we hit the two-billion barrel of oil equivalent in 1990, at a moment when Saleh happened to be visiting the United States.

SALEH'S VISIT TO DALLAS

President Saleh and his party of forty decided to visit Dallas for three days in 1990 and Jim Oberwetter and I spent a lot of time setting up the activities for the visit. We put his group up at the Hyatt Regency Dallas, a hotel owned by Ray. Activities included briefings on the Exxon and Hunt operation and a formal dinner at Ray's mother's lavish home on White Rock Lake (many notables were there, including General Norman Schwarzkopf, later the hero of Desert Storm, the first Gulf War, in February 1991 and my tent mate on an earlier fishing trip in Mexico).

One afternoon, I received an urgent call from the US ambassador to Yemen, Charles Dunbar, who was part of the delegation to Dallas. Apparently, the Yemeni staff and guests (Saleh had about forty in his party) were buying out most of the guns from a local gun store called Ray's Hardware. I told Charlie that there was no law in Texas to stop them if it was okay with President Saleh, and apparently it was, so let's not make an issue about it. It was not a problem, and they loaded them up on Saddam Hussein's 747, which Saleh had borrowed for the trip. I think they had a great visit.

I recall two funny incidents, however, related to this visit of Saleh's. The first was when we were in our conference room, and an Exxon executive was briefing Saleh on future technology through interpreters. There were seven of us around this thirteen-place round table. Saleh was in a chair next to me and was moving as if he was uncomfortable. His aide, Mohammed, was directly behind him near the door. All of a sudden, I heard Saleh yell Mohammed's name and then some instruction in Arabic. He then pulled his 9 mm pistol from the holster on his back and threw it up over his head to Mohammed, who caught it after it flew through the air for about six feet. Saleh never saw him but it seemed like a move he'd done before (we were lucky it did not go off in the room).

The second incident was in Sanaa. During the Dallas visit, we had set up a VIP visit to the Fort Worth Fat Stock Show, which included a rodeo and a serenade by Tanya Tucker (the famous country western singer) and cowboys carrying the Yemeni flag. Saleh loved it, and we took many pictures for his album. During the visit, we gave the Yemenis a lot of gifts, but one souvenir that we gave everyone was a small, inexpensive gold-plated key chain with the logo of the Fort Worth Fat Stock Show on it. Cost: $1.95.

Now, twelve months later, Ray and I were back in Yemen for a visit with Saleh, waiting in the lavish reception room in his palace in Sanaa. As we were waiting, I noticed a beautiful tall, glass case displaying interesting gifts Saleh had received in the course of his presidency. I walked over to view them. There were all kinds of beautiful gold bowls and plates. On the top shelf, there was a gold-plated AK-47 from Saddam Hussein. Across from it was a gold-plated automatic pistol, a gift from General Norman Schwarzkopf. But in the very center mounted above everything else, on a velvet pedestal, was that Fort Worth Fat Stock Show key chain. Unfortunately, I did not have a camera to take a picture.

There were a couple of other interesting gifts that Ray gave Saleh. Right after the discovery of oil in 1984, Ray wanted to give Saleh a gift that represented Texas, so I suggested a .45 revolver. He liked the idea so I bought a beautiful Colt revolver with a black leather holster and belt and silver (chrome) bullets to go with it.

We were scheduled to travel to Yemen the next week and I told Ray that I would go early and spend the weekend in London, meeting him at the Yemenia Air counter at London Gatwick on Monday for the flight. I decided to take the gun with me. I packed it in a briefcase, called a security friend at American Airlines, and explained that I had a gun and wanted to hand-carry it rather than check it. When I got to the airport that Friday, he escorted me through security. He then had the pilot put the briefcase with the pistol up in the cockpit.

When we landed at Gatwick in London, I retrieved the briefcase. I knew it was illegal to have a gun in London, so I was going to check it immediately at customs. When I got there, a gentleman from Nigeria had apparently been caught smuggling something, and customs was working him over.

When I finally stepped up to the head of the line, an agent (who seemingly was not in a good mood because of the previous encounter) snapped, "Do you have anything to declare?" I said, yes, I have a .45 revolver. He froze, as did other agents, and for a few seconds, no one said anything. They just looked at me. Then the agent asked if I had any ammunition and I said, "Fifty rounds, all in this briefcase." Again, he looked stunned and then responded, "Don't you know it is against the law to carry a gun in Britain?" I responded that I knew that and that is why I was declaring it. I further went on that it was a gift for the president of Yemen and I would like to leave it with them and pick it up on Monday, when Yemenia Air would assist me in getting to Sanaa.

Fortunately, there was an agent among the staff who had just retired from the British Commandos. He said he'd had to turn in his .357 revolver upon retirement and that he would personally watch the gun over the weekend and deliver it to me on Monday. I was really relieved.

To cover myself with Yemenia, I called the president's aide in Yemen and told him that Ray and I would be coming in on Monday with a gift for the president. When we landed, I gave the aide the briefcase but failed to tell him what was in it. I received a call later that night from the aide who said that he wished I would have told him what was in the case. Apparently, when they opened it, it caused a lot of commotion since the last president had been killed by a bomb in a briefcase. Things did calm down eventually and we had a nice meeting where Ray presented it to Saleh. Saleh apparently liked it, as he wore it often when he was visiting our operation in the desert.

The other gift from Hunt was a pewter three-paneled mural depicting the history of Yemen from the spice trade to exporting oil to the world. We had a first-class designer make it; our intent was to have it placed in the airport where visitors would see the history of Yemen and know they have entered the modern world. It cost $50,000 (which was a lot of money then). I spent a lot of time with Dr. Eryani before it was cast, getting the Yemeni history right.

We brought it over and had a dinner for all the ministers, prominent men in Yemen, and President Saleh. Unfortunately, Saleh gave the panel to the military academy, where few could see it since it was a classified area … It never got into the airport. I think that's the sad thing about Saleh: his focus was on power and not furthering the prosperity of Yemen.

I have so many stories from Yemen and the many friends I made over thirty years of doing business there. Because of the civil war going on now (2020), many have fled, others have adapted to the rules of one side or another. Many of the managers, ministers, and even Saleh have died. The one friend I miss is Dr. Abdul Karim Eryani. As I said earlier, we were good friends and would communicate via email when I could not visit. He believed in Ray Hunt and in what Hunt Oil was trying to do. He knew that the deal we made was a fair deal to all parties and accepted bringing in Exxon (the largest oil company in the world) and the Koreans as partners so we could export the oil and gas and bring much-needed revenue to the people of Yemen.

The time I spent with him in Sanaa, Washington, DC, and our long airplane flights was very special. Like me, he loved to read about history, politics, and economics. I would often spend time at his home discussing books. He was an unusual person ... so intelligent, so perceptive, so affable, and he could talk to anyone in perfect English. He fully understood both worlds.

As I mentioned, he was educated in the United States, a time when a few young men came out of Yemen in the 1950s to go to America. He eventually got a PhD at Yale in genetics, and he educated me a lot on that subject. I was fortunate to get to know his wife and several of his children, all of whom are impressive people.

One year, he brought his wife and four of his kids to the States for a vacation. Ray let them stay at Circle K Ranch for a few days and Sharon and I were asked to join them. We really enjoyed it. He was a wonderful husband and father. He would bring coffee to his wife in bed and include her in our conversations through translations. Further, he liked to fish. One day, his six-year-old son hooked a very large catfish, and it began to pull the boy into the water. Dr. Eryani grabbed the boy with his arms around the waist, but being only five-foot-two and less than one hundred pounds, he too was being dragged. I then grabbed both of them, and we held the fish until it broke the line. It was a wonderful, long weekend.

He died in 2014. His death was a blow to Yemen, as he was respected by most Yemenis. Had he lived, he may have avoided or negotiated an end to the current civil war. He was a man who had a lot of influence on me in my thinking about how to bring an underdeveloped country into the modern world. He was proud of being an Arab and told me that when the family vacationed in Spain one year, he found the home of a great ancestor who lived in Spain before the Muslims were ejected in 1492. He was very proud that a rusted key was still in the door.

EXPANSION

The profit that was made in Yemen allowed me to travel to other parts in the world in search of exploration licenses. Initially, the travel was with Ray Fairchild and Chris Stone (until Ray retired in 1988) and then it was with Jim Jennings and Maycock. During this period, I spent time trying to do business in over fifty countries: too many to count, but the ones that were most interesting were Laos, Cambodia, Vietnam ... Burma, Albania, the Soviet Union ... Ethiopia, Sudan, China, Somalia, Djibouti, South Yemen, East Germany, New Guinea, Guyana ... Syria, Russia (after 1989), Peru, and many, many others.

It was a fun experience to meet with senior or top leaders of many of these countries and tell them about Hunt Oil Company and what we could do. With some, we signed contracts. In other cases we did not for various reasons, most often because we realized we were competing with the major international and national oil companies that often threw money or politics into the equation.

I realized that we were special in that we were a private, seventy-year-old,

US independent oil company but yet had refining and pipeline experience. In the business in the 1980s, oil companies engaged generally in three different types of businesses:

1. Upstream … exploration and production … finding and producing the oil and gas.

2. Midstream … pipelines transporting the crude oil and products

3. Downstream … refining ... crude oil had no value unless it was refined into oil products such as gasoline, diesel, jet fuels, asphalt, etc.

We were special because: (1) we were a private company with one voting stockholder; (2) we were financially very strong (now especially with Yemen revenues); (3) we were technically very competent as evidenced by the fact that we were operating all over the world for some of the majors (Exxon, Shell, BP, etc.) who were our partners; and (4) our chairman owned the company. Thus, he could develop a relationship that many of these "ships passing in the night CEOs" could not, since oil projects lasted twenty years or more. Also, he could make an instant decision as he was the sole voting stockholder. Most other companies had directors and committees that CEOs were beholden to. Ours was an advantage when dealing with strong leaders who wanted quick decisions.

Further, we had a very low turnover in our technical employees because we were private and had incentive plans to keep them.

Ray was a close friend of George H. W. Bush, who had been either vice president or president for twelve years while we were building up our international business. In fact, as VP, George H. W. Bush came to Yemen in the late 1980s to dedicate our new refinery at Ray's request. (Ray's political connections were many; however, he did not flaunt them and told us not to … although if it came up in conversation with a foreign or oil minister, I would take advantage of it). This is why Ray was popular among many foreign leaders we dealt with. He was not a political person and many recognized that and wanted to meet with him when he visited a country. They knew that he was genuinely interested in their country and its problems. This may be why President Saleh bestowed Yemen's highest honor, the Medal of Service to Yemen, on Ray in 1989.

For the remainder of the '80s and into the 2000s, I would spend time going to Yemen with Ray and traveling the world with Jim Jennings. Sometimes both. In Yemen, I really enjoyed spending time with our employees and our Yemen friends. During this period, I was spending time in Yemen and other countries as well as doing my administrative duties. Later in the 1990s, I was also running a real estate "breakup" in the company and starting a private equity arm with Chris Kleinert (Ray's son-in-law).

By 1990 the world had changed. In 1989 the Berlin Wall fell, or rather was torn apart piece by piece by the German people. I was in the Sudan trying to get information and intelligence so we could go for an exploration contract. I was flying out of Khartoum to go directly to Toronto, Canada, for a meeting. An Air France flight had been blown out of the sky by a bomb in the country of Chad (west of Sudan) the previous week, so everyone was very nervous, especially the Sudanese official who made me strip to my shorts in a search. Eventually, I got on the plane, took my seat, and saw a copy of the *Herald Tribune* where I read about the Berlin Wall being torn down. I knew then the world would change and there would be opportunities for Hunt in the new environment.

CHAPTER TWENTY-ONE

THE PERIOD OF
LIQUID NATURAL GAS (LNG)

During the 1990s and 2000s, we discovered a lot of natural gas, either associated with the oil produced or in stand-alone fields. It took a lot of drilling and engineering to prove up seven to ten trillion cubic feet of gas in Yemen and Peru and then a lot of financing to build the plants. (Generally speaking, a trillion cubic feet is equivalent to 155 million barrels of oil and oil was selling for about $70/barrel when we went online in 2009 and 2011).

Now oil, which is fungible, is a liquid you can transport through a pipeline to export facilities where a vast world market will take it. However, natural gas is in a gaseous state, so it is difficult to transport.

When we signed the contract in Yemen in 1981, gas had no real value unless you were near a market where pipelines would deliver it. Since we were in the vast desert of Arabia and hundreds of miles from the coast, we saw no opportunity to sell gas if we found it. (This is what happened with Shell in Peru, which I will talk about later).

Our contract with Yemen stated that if we found gas, we would negotiate with the government as to our rights. Unfortunately, this caused some headaches later.

By the 1990s new technology and the demand for gas (due to environmental concerns, since it was much cleaner than coal) resulted in many countries changing from coal to natural gas for their electrical generated power. This was especially true of China, Japan, and South Korea. By now, the economics of freezing the gas into a liquid stage and reducing its volume by six hundred times allowed companies to ship the gas in giant "thermos bottle-like" tankers. Natural gas projects like this, however, required billions of dollars of investment.

First, you have to develop the gas field. Then, you have to build pipelines to transport it to a gasification plant where it can be cooled and liquified. This plant should be located at the coast, to facilitate moving the liquid gas to an export facility where it will be loaded into tankers and kept cold. From here, it will sail to a foreign market where they will offload it to a re-gasification plant on the coast, which converts the liquid gas back to a gas state (six hundred times). Now, it can once again be shipped through pipelines to power plants or for retail distribution.

Because of the vast cost, liquid natural gas (LNG) generally requires borrowing billions from a consortium of big banks so you can build all this infrastructure and facilities.

However, before the banks loan the money, they will ask for proof of a buyer for the gas. So, actually, the first thing you have to do is sell the gas to an end buyer (contingent on delivering it, according to a contract). These are big projects, involving many legal documents and contracts for loans, insurance, complicated construction, delivery, and contingencies.

It generally takes a couple of years and a team of very talented people to pull this type of deal together. In 2006 there were only six active LNG projects in the world and Hunt Oil Company was involved in two of them (Yemen and Peru). We were the "gold standard" of a wheeling-dealing Texas oil company.

In Yemen, we found a lot of associated gas with our oil. We also found separate gas fields that we capped. (In a geological trap of hydrocarbons, you can have three things ... water, oil, and gas. Sometimes all three and sometimes just two or one ... However, the gas will sit on the oil and the oil will sit on the water, so they are conveniently separated in the trap).

As I mentioned earlier, we did not want to waste the gas by flaring it (burning it off) when we produced the oil. Our engineers realized that this was a wet gas (which means it had some liquids in it), so we built some plants that would strip the liquids out of it (C-5 Plus) and add this liquid gas condensate (think like gasoline) to our crude pipeline. Then the drier gas was compressed back into the formation. By 1990 we produced forty thousand barrels of condensate a day by processing three billion cubic feet a day. (This gave us an expertise that we would apply to getting a contract in Peru later).

Ray recognized that we had potential for an LNG project in the late '80s. When we were traveling to Yemen, he would tell the president and ministers whenever he had a chance that their gas was worth something and that Yemen ought to look at an LNG project.

About that same time, we were trying to get a second contract in South Yemen. The Russians were working that area but did not have a contract. We decided to make a bold move and meet with them to discuss a joint venture with Yemen Hunt and the two Yemeni governments.

In early 1989 Frank Mytinger (our land negotiator) and I went to Moscow to meet with the two Russian state companies working across the border in South Yemen from us. This was still the Soviet Union at that time. We had good meetings, but the Russians were not familiar with risk contracts (it was a communist society and capitalism was only practiced by the Russian mob in those days). Thus, we returned empty-handed.

However, soon the two Yemens became one (1990). Now that the acreage we wanted was available, Yemen Hunt (Hunt, Exxon, and Koreans) joined up together with Total (a French company), who brought in the Russians and Kufpec (a Kuwaiti company). Hunt became the operator and we found and produced oil under the name of Jannah Hunt Oil Company (JHOC). What was interesting was from then on I could (and did) say that Hunt operated with the Russians into their first risk (capitalist) contract. (The reasons I did it is because Mobil bragged in a press release how they had one in Vietnam in the early 1990s, but this was after ours).

Let me pause here to explain what a risk contract is. As I've already indicated, in the oil business of the 1970s and '80s, oil companies dealing with countries with little or no knowledge of oil on their territory preferred to sign a production Sharing Agreement (PSA). The oil company would ask for a certain amount of acreage to explore (we had three million acres in Yemen). If the company found no oil (which was the case most of the time), they would walk away and the country did not have to invest anything. It was like a camping trip for us. We brought in all the equipment and took it out if we did not find anything.

However, if the company did find oil in commercial quantities (enough to make a profit), they would want a percent of the oil found (typically 20 to 30 percent of the oil, which they would own and could use as collateral for the banks to loan them money to build the facilities to take out the oil). This was a big risk for the company but also a great way for the country to encourage exploration without any cost from the government. Also, the value of the oil would pay for the company's operations and facilities.

As for LNG, once the countries of North and South Yemen had merged, it was easier to do business since the production of gas and the facility would now be in a single country. Here again, however, we tried to get the whole project, since we had found the gas, but the government wanted others involved in for political reasons. Meanwhile, Enron tried to "steal" it until they imploded from internal corruption (read about the Enron corruption to get the whole scope).

The French government-controlled company, Total, wanted it all, but in the end, we formed another partnership for the gas that included the government of Yemen, the Hunt Partnership (our Korean partners), and Total. Exxon pulled out because they bought Mobil and now had a lot of gas in Qatar.

Our Total-led consortium set out in the late 1990s to try to find a buyer for LNG, since we needed a gas contract before we could get financed and start to build the project. The team worked for years but could not get a substantial buyer and, thus, Yemen gave the consortium an extension on the contract to put together an LNG project.

There were about eighteen months left on this contract when Jim Jennings and Ray called me into a meeting. They informed me that I was to become the president of Yemen Hunt LNG (our company in the consortium) and my job was to make sure Total did not spend any more money uselessly, as they felt that in eighteen months the contract would run out and Hunt could then go for it and get it. Thus, I would go to board meetings in Paris, Sanaa, and Seoul with two of the greatest associates I have ever worked with: Karim Abuhamad and David

Mahmalji. Both spoke French and Arabic, among other languages, and Karim also spoke some Korean. Some of my greatest times in foreign travel were with these two great individuals. In addition to them, we had a great lawyer, Jerry Bendo, who knew the contracts backward, forward, and sideways. All had spent some time in Yemen and other areas where Hunt had operations. They were among the secret weapons that made Hunt so effective in the business of the world.

By 2004 the world of LNG was changing rapidly. The price of natural gas was beginning to rise in the world. Many countries were looking at switching over to natural gas for their power generation from the dirtier coal.

And most important, the Korean government's gas contracts were ending and they were renewing with world LNG producers. I recognized then that our partnership, YLNG, was in a position to sell our liquid natural gas. The reason for this was that our Korean partners were the only Koreans in LNG. Thus, I figured that, politically, the government would be inclined to give the Korean company a contract to buy their LNG.

Hunt's other big gas project was in Peru. In the 1990s the major oil companies Shell and Mobil found a lot of gas in an area called Camisea, located in the central Andes of Peru. By 2000 their contract had expired and President Fujimori of Peru told them to produce gas or they would not get an extension and he would open bidding to other companies. In response, Shell declared it was not economical; they decided to call the president of Peru's bluff and tell him no company would want it just to produce the gas.

Now at this point, I need to digress with a relevant story.

In South Texas, Hunt Oil had a six-thousand-acre farming operation on the Mexican border. Annually, the first of September was a big event in Texas, being the opening of the white wing dove-hunting season. Hunters from all over Texas would come to South Texas to hunt white wings (a large species of dove). For Hunt Oil Company, it was an annual event and we used it as an entertainment venue to bond with the people we would deal with throughout the year, such as our bankers, key security executives (FBI, CIA, DEA, Sherriff, etc.), and the executives of other oil companies. We would plant sunflowers and maize to attract the doves.

We had a special area set up for our guests that first and second weekend. This would include ideal shooting areas and a big tent with fans, in which we served refreshments and the best fajitas in Texas. Our guests loved it, as we would also put them up at a motel in McAllen, and on Saturday night, cross over into Mexico for a great dinner at La Cucaracha restaurant (The Cockroach), whose signature meal was frog legs.

We would fly everyone down on the company jet, making it easy for our important guests. (This form of entertainment was so successful in developing good business relationships that Ray expanded it to elk hunting in Utah and fishing in Mexico).

Eventually, some of these hunts morphed into wagering in Jim Jennings' events. Jim, one of my best friends, is the most competitive man I have ever met. His major was math, and he is very smart, with a calculating mind. He seldom loses a wager.

Harry Shimotsu, our farm manager and a decorated Japanese American veteran in World War II, had the ability to think like a plant. He had developed the hunting environment so well that hundreds of doves were always circling around the hunters to get at the maize and sunflowers. A good hunter could have shot the limit (of ten birds) within ten minutes. This was not a good thing for Jennings' guests, so I came up with an idea ... we could have a shooting contest.

We took one field and put a fruit basket in the center and made a forty-foot diameter bullseye target out of bags of flour, with four integrals.

The rules of the contest were that each hunter would put $20 in the pot, get three shotgun shells, stand at the edge of the circle, and have three minutes to shoot a circling dove. If the guest downed a dove, the dove landing closest to the basket at the center of the bullseye would win that hunter the pot. We had twenty participants (and a $400 pot).

On this day, Jennings had nineteen guests and Hunt executives. He was the first up and shot a dove that landed in the second ring. Unfortunately, none of the other eighteen guests or executives were successful in dropping a bird inside the ring. The last shooter was Steve Krowl. He stepped up and shot the first bird to come over and dropped it. It landed on the third ring outside of Jim's ... but it was not dead. Instead, it quickly came to and struggled to walk. It took a few steps and then sat down. Sensing there was now a contest, the other contestants began to move around the circle and root for the dove. Now the dove got up and began to walk for some reason toward the basket, as the shooters encouraged it with their yelling. The dove, trying to conserve what strength it had, decided to sit down one more time, just outside the area where Jennings's dove had died. The cheering of the guests must have inspired it, as it got up and struggled to walk forward. Within a few feet, it collapsed and died, just inside the location of Jennings's dove. Thus, Krowl won the $400 and became a legend.

This story floated around the oil companies, regaled by our many guests over the years who had attended the Hunt Oil Company dove hunts. The Hunt invitation was special and those invited eventually knew who the others were. The oil exploration community is not a big world, so it became a story told around the bars. Also, Jim and Steve became good business friends as a result of this incident.

Fast forward to 2000, and Steve Krowl is president of an Argentina company producing oil in Peru. Jim is president of Hunt Oil Company, which has experience in Yemen in handling vast amounts of natural gas. Steve knows Peru has vast amounts of gas discovered by Shell and that Shell would not produce because the economics of producing the gas was not there for them.

Steve called Jim and told him the situation: since Shell was "playing tough" with President Fujimori, he would open bidding for the blocks of acreage (that area where the gas had been discovered). Because Hunt was experienced in stripping liquids out of wet gas, Steve argued we could get the contract and make it a profitable venture. We took his advice, bid, and won the contract, benefitting from all the work Shell did (including a $180 million environmental study). Fortunately for us and unfortunately for Shell, they figured because of their large size they could bully Peru and found out they could not, giving us an opportunity to bid for that acreage.

Another stroke of good luck was that another bidder was Total (the giant French oil company). The bidding date was in the late summer. Like us, the Total manager in Peru submitted their bid, which was to be opened the following Monday. At the last minute, the Total manager decided to change it and up the bid and contacted Paris for permission. Unfortunately, in August, most people in France take their vacation and he could not find a Total executive to sign off on the change. So, the original bid was submitted. Ironically, we found out later that the manager's new bid would have been better than Hunt's and, thus, would probably have given Total the contract (another example of the old Hunt luck).

Now that we had the contract, we (with our partners) built the facilities in the Andes to strip out the wet gas and sell it as light crude oil (185,000 b/d). This was a very successful project.

With all this gas, Ray wanted to take it one step further and create an LNG project that would supply the world. Our key partners opposed it, so we went through much torment until we finally worked out a deal. We then began to build the second of six LNG projects going on in the world. (This was done under the leadership of Steve Suellentrop, a top ARCO executive, whom Jennings had hired to run the project. Under Steve's excellent leadership, this very complex project was completed under budget and under time). Like Jim, Steve was one of the best executives that I have worked with. I had hired Jim, and Jim then hired Steve, a great contribution to the company overall. Peru became the second successful LNG project that Hunt was in, although now we were the major partner and operator. Again, like with Yemen LNG, it was fun to go to the ceremonies for the opening of this project. These types of projects have a major impact on a country and its people. In fact, this became the single biggest single economic investment by any company in Peru. Here again, Ray and Hunt Oil employees had a major positive impact on an entire nation.

I could go on and on about the LNG projects but I now want to move on, to describe how we went after new exploration licenses once we were making money in Yemen.

CHAPTER TWENTY-TWO

STRIKING OUT INTO THE WORLD

After the discovery of the large Beatrice oil field in the North Sea in 1976, Hunt became an "elephant hunter." This is a company that is searching for giant oil fields but would not "bet the ranch" on finding them.

As I indicated earlier, we hired Ray Fairchild in 1979 to lead this effort. He was fifty-seven years of age, with decades of experience in the international area. Since we were new to international exploration and I had had other types of international experience with Perot, I was naturally drawn to assisting him in setting up the new group. Actually, I relished it and felt I could make a contribution here and Ray Hunt agreed to let me work on it.

I loved working for Fairchild. He was a seasoned executive (actually, he had been a mayor of a Houston suburb) and had worked with many international oil companies. More importantly, he taught me so much about the international oil business (the others were Ted Hole, the company's chief geologist; Frank Toksky, the chief geophysicist; Gary Hurford, the chief engineer … and later the first non-family president of Hunt Oil Company; Jim Jennings, the second non-family president; and Ian Maycock, our London manager, who was responsible for our Yemen success). All became good friends and did not mind my asking questions.

In the early days, in addition to reading everything I could on oil exploration, I spent as much time with the above-mentioned people as I could, always asking questions. I would take one or two to lunch weekly to learn from them. It was from them I learned the basics of the oil business upon which I could build my knowledge. I loved the business. I loved the people in it. I loved the excitement and working as a team in trying to discover the next big field.

I should point out here that in high school, I had concluded that I wanted to be a geologist, but my mother argued that there was no money in it and that I should go into the law instead.

So, I enrolled in prelaw at the University of Washington, but concluded quickly that the law was not what I wanted to do for the rest of my life. This resulted (to the concern of my mother) in my majoring in prelaw, communications, Asian history, geography and Far East Studies. But I did take geology and physical geology courses as electives in the process.

If you remember, since I was in ROTC for four years, I knew I had to go into the military because of the draft. I needed to graduate in four years. In my fourth year, we cobbled together my credits and I was told that I could graduate if I took my degree in Far East Geography, which was basically the geography, economics, and history of the Far East (Russia, China, and Southeast Asia). Since I was being commissioned as a Second Lieutenant in the USAF and had concluded that I wanted to be a jet fighter pilot and kill communists, this would be the perfect degree. As mentioned earlier, little did I know that it was the perfect degree that would in fact propel my career but not for the reasons I thought it would.

Again, Fairchild taught me a lot. His instinct led us initially to Yemen. But simultaneously, we were looking at other countries in the early 80s, until the Yemeni opportunity came along in 1984. Of course, China was a big one too, and I have already related some of the China stories, but I was also doing other business in China continually through 2014. I will tell more China stories later.

Among the other countries we looked at before Yemen were New Guinea and Somalia. Fairchild and I went to Papua, New Guinea, in 1981 to see if we could get a concession in the Coral Sea. We spent a week under the auspices of the government, meeting people and traveling the country. It was an amazing experience, in a country divided between lowlanders and highlanders. According to the rental car agreement, for example, if you drove into the highlands and ran over a pig, you could be killed. So, upon running over the pig, you were to immediately go to a constable's office and report it. In the New Guinea highlands of 1981, wealth was determined in pigs, land, and women—in that order.

We were invited by the prime minister to attend a meeting of parliament with him, where they were discussing and arguing whether to replace the police chief of Port Moresby. The language spoken was a blend of the native language, Dutch, and English, and I could understand every third word. It was a fascinating experience and, at that point, I realized that cultures different from ours could be just as efficient as ours in many ways.

We did not get a license in New Guinea but realized anyway that, because of the culture, history, and a new political movement that was unfriendly to oil interests, we did not want it.

In 1981 we made a deal with Quintana, an oil company out of Houston that had secured a concession in the country of Somalia but needed a partner. I was asked to fly to the capital city of Mogadishu to meet with the oil minister and sign (as an officer for Hunt Oil) the partnership agreement.

I flew to London and met with John Brannon of Vincent Elkins (the top oil and gas law firm in Texas). When I went into his office, he was in the middle of packing a large suitcase with Scotch, crackers, condiments, lots of tuna fish, and peanut butter. I asked him what he was doing, and he said finding food to eat was difficult even in the hotels in Somalia. I boasted how I had traveled the world and could always find food and would plan to meet him at the hotel. Little did I know what I would find in Somalia's capital city, Mogadishu.

I arrived at the Mogadishu airport and had to go through a long, arduous customs clearance, which included declaring all the currency I had on me. I declared the dollars and travelers' checks, but I had just come out of Kenya and had about $80 in Kenya currency, which I did not declare because it could only be used in certain African countries and, since I was going through Kenya, why bother.

I checked in at the Juba Hotel and now knew what John was talking about. I ordered breakfast and, because of the flies and flavor, could not eat it. On the second morning, I bought bananas and grapefruit at an open market and that became my basic food—along with whatever tuna, peanut butter and crackers I could mooch off John.

One night we were taken out by an embassy officer to an open field where a person came to our car, took our order, and came back with a well-cooked chicken. It was a favorite spot, as the embassy people would eat there. Basically, you tore the chicken apart and threw the bones out the window. And then watched the jackals and other predators come around the car to pick over the detritus (which probably saved money, since the owners did not have to clean up after the customers left).

We had various meetings with contractors, lawyers, our embassy, and then, on the last day, we met with the oil minister. I briefed him on Hunt Oil Company and watched him sign the government's approval of the partnership document. He wanted to make sure we were not doing business with Israel, since there was an Arab boycott of Israel and any company doing business with them. Fortunately, even though I had visited Israel, there was no Israeli stamp on my passport, since they put it on a separate sheet of paper. Otherwise I would have had trouble traveling in the Middle East. Some Arab countries would not let you enter their country if you had a stamp or visa from Israel in your passport or at a minimum create problems for you as they would assume you were a spy or doing business with Israel.

There was a moment of concern during the five days in Somalia, however. After meeting with our seismic contractors, the manager asked if I had declared all my currency and I told him I declared all the dollars but not the Kenya currency. He said that smuggling currency into Somalia is a capital offense (meaning the death penalty) and that the economy is so fragile that they monitor all the currency going in and out. This meant they would have me fill out a declaration upon leaving as to what funds I was leaving with and assume the difference was what I spent in the country. He advised that I get rid of the Kenya currency because if they found it on me, I would probably be arrested (I had already spent time in a Yemeni jail and did not want to add a Somali one to the list).

Now the trick was to get rid of the Kenya currency. It was not easy. This was one of the poorest countries in the world. I thought about ripping the banknotes up and putting them in a trash can. But there were no trash cans on the street and, even if there were, someone could see what I was discarding and report me. I thought about throwing the money down the toilet but all the water coming out of the faucets was reddish in color and they did not always work well: if it got stuck, I could also be reported.

Thus, I concluded the best way was to fold the banknotes in my handkerchief and put it in my rear right pants pocket. This I did and carried the Kenya currency around for five days.

On the last night, we had a signing ceremony dinner. Somalia was, at one time, an Italian colony, and some of the buildings, although in disrepair, were of Italian design. Our lawyer took us to a rooftop "buffet" for the celebration. They had lasagna and John and I piled it on our plate. Unfortunately, the food was cool and had been sitting out for a long period in the tropical heat. Both John and I got sick a couple of days later with an intestinal bug and he had to be flown to a hospital in Holland that specializes in tropical diseases.

The scariest part of this story happened the next day, as we were leaving Mogadishu to fly to Kenya. We arrived at 11:00 a.m. for a 2:00 p.m. flight. Again, we go through the arduous effort of filling out the currency paperwork. Of course, I decided not to declare the Kenya currency, which was still in my pocket.

We cleared security and went to the gate area to sit and wait. I observed that we were the only two whites in the airport. Two o'clock comes and goes and no plane. I asked an official and they informed us that Kenya Air had decided "not to fly" that day.

Now we had to book another flight. You could not book at the airport, only downtown at the travel office. So, John and I go through customs and I lie about my currency again. We took a cab to the travel office. We booked ourselves on a midnight flight to Abu Dhabi and then went back to the airport and went through customs, and, once again, I did not declare the Kenya currency folded in the hanky pocket of my pants.

Thinking we're finally leaving Mogadishu, we relaxed in our chairs. Not a lot of travelers go to Somalia (not then, not now), so the airport was basically empty.

Then, about 11:00 p.m., two uniformed officers approached us and said to follow them. They led us to a small room, where another officer was sitting at a table. They asked for our passports and told us to strip. Now I had to figure out my story if they found the Kenyan currency. I concluded that if they did, I would just tell them the truth. John was already stripping and I was nervously retrieving my passport, which fell on the floor.

The officer behind the table picked my passport up, looked at it, and said, "You are Americans," which I confirmed. He then said he was sorry: they had a tip that there were two Italians who were smuggling $100,000 in lira, and they had thought that we were them. He asked about our flight, and once we were tidy, escorted us to the gate of the flight going to Abu Dhabi.

Boy, was I relieved. However, the adventure was not over, because we did not have a visa to enter Abu Dhabi. Thus, the customs agent there put us in a controlled area next to a public telephone and told us we had six hours to find a flight or else they would put us on the next plane out of Abu Dhabi. Fortunately, we found a British Air flight within the time limit and flew to London. This adventure happened on my fortieth birthday, which I will always remember.

Unfortunately, we did not have a chance to really explore for oil in Somalia because when the time came for us to extend the contract two years later, the oil minister demanded a $50,000 bribe. We said no and walked away from Somalia. I read that a Swedish company was later awarded our contract area and I can only conclude that they must have paid the bribe.

To this date, no one has found oil, although politics might be the problem, since that area has separated and become Somaliland, with a parliament and currency of its own but little recognition by other countries. This makes it a high risk for a company to invest millions of dollars without knowing if they would have any legal claim to any oil, if found.

In the early '80s, US companies were at a disadvantage since Congress had passed the 1977 Foreign Corruption Act, according to which if an American executive paid a bribe to get a contract he or she could go to jail. I walked away from a couple of countries where the officials wanted bribes. The French were notorious for paying bribes, though, and we lost out on a couple of contracts in the Middle East and Laos because of the French way of doing business.

Because of our discovery of a giant oil field in Yemen and selling 49 percent of our interest for $500 million to Exxon, Hunt's financial position was strong. Further, we were on track to begin producing and selling two hundred fifty thousand barrels a day. Thus, Fairchild decided to head out into the world to find "another Yemen."

In 1986 Fairchild, Chris Stone, and I made a seventeen-day scouting trip to Southeast Asia. We were essentially meeting with oil officials to introduce Hunt Oil and tell our Yemen story in the hopes that these ministers would want to encourage us to look for oil in their countries or maybe invest with us. Burma, Thailand, and Laos were our real targets since they had little or no oil production. Thus, exploration terms would, in theory, be better (as long as the geology was good).

I thought Burma and Laos would be good politically and we needed to determine whether they were prospective geologically. Burma had an old production history but little production now. Laos had no production but was in the neighborhood. We knew Thailand was producing some oil in the Korat Basin and doing some activity offshore. Still, the country was pretty bureaucratic so we did not spend a lot of time with their ministry.

Burma was a different story. I had told Fairchild how Burma had a history of oil. Our research indicated that oil had been produced in Burma in the late 1880s:

the British used it for gun oil in India. The method of producing it was to dig a sixteen-foot hole into a shallow oil pit, send a man with a bucket down a rope, and have him fill the bucket and send it back up while he kept a rag over his mouth and nose to protect him from the fumes. Regardless, they lost a lot of native miners that way because they did not understand the danger of smelling gas fumes emitting from the oil.

Anyway, the oil was put into a British designed, rectangular five-gallon tin can and sealed with a cap. It was then tied to bamboo poles to become part of a raft (oil is lighter than water). The raft was then floated down the Mekong River to an awaiting ship in Rangoon.

Later, they devised a way to use the tin cans as a diving bell. They cut a circular hole on one side and put a sealed glass window in it and attached a hose connection at the top. The native miner would put it over his head and wrap rags around his neck to seal the hole where his head went in. Now a man at the top would pump air into the tin helmet as the miner would scoop up oil and fill the buckets lowered to him on a rope. This really increased production, but on occasion they would lose a miner when an untrained air pumper would leave on a lunch break. I told this true story to many of the Burmese officials we met and they loved it, as it showed that Burma had in fact been an early oil producer.

Our initial approach to Burma was to visit a senior official who was in Washington for the September Annual World Bank meeting. Fairchild and I met him in the Watergate Hotel in DC. He was very gracious, but after we told him that Hunt wanted to find oil in Burma and raise the standard of living through the revenues, he frankly told us that the people of Burma "have bananas and bamboo" (this is a quote) and do not need anything else. I concluded that the government had been shielding their people from the world so that the military government could control everything. Of course, with my forever optimism, if we could meet with officials in Rangoon, I felt we could convince them that oil revenue would improve their country. So, we set up a trip to Burma and Rangoon.

Fairchild and I flew into Rangoon (the name was changed to Yangon in 1989) from Bangkok. The one-hour flight was like going back in a time machine (like in China in 1979). The Rangoon airport was vintage World War II design. Burmese customs made Somalia customs look like warp speed. The agent checked everything and expected bribes to clear us. When they opened the bags, they would handle each item and ask if I needed it. Soon I figured out the game and gave them things out of the suitcase that were trivial to me but meant money to them. On future trips, I learned to go through customs very quickly with pens and finely designed Bangkok duty-free plastic bags. These were beautifully decorated and used to carry items bought at the airport. Burma had no plastic bags and no paper, so both were of value to the Burmese.

We had good meetings but still the Burmese were not ready to do a deal. We would come back another time to move it forward.

I loved Burma and the people. We would stay in the Inya Lake Hotel, which needed improvement. It was on the outskirts of the city, surrounded by many acres of beautiful grounds. I used to jog in those days and would run every morning at daybreak. On my third trip to Burma, I met a man in the hotel who told me to be careful running in the morning because cobras were along the trail in those early hours of the day. I stopped jogging at the Inya Lake Hotel after that.

In 1987 the government of Burma invited Ray Fairchild and me and our wives, Eleanor and Sharon, to Burma. We'd be traveling with Tony and Kay Copp, since we had business in Korea on the way. Also, we were going on to Frankfurt to join the Hunt party in Yemen.

We were deep into discussions with on exploration in Burma by this time. Also at this time, Ray Hunt was taking all of the Hunt managers who were to be involved in Yemen and their spouses for a tour to Yemen. Here the spouses would see the future of what their significant others would be contributing to the company. (This was the genius of Ray Hunt, to see what impact this would have on the managers of Hunt Oil in Yemen). Thus, we combined our trips with Ray's trip and went around the world to meet the team in Frankfurt.

During the stop in Burma, one morning, while Fairchild, Copp, and I met with government officials, Eleanor, Kay, and Sharon were given a government tour of the wonders and history of Rangoon. This was very special, as the government wanted to put on a special tour for the ladies. They still remember it to this day.

Then things changed. About midafternoon, an argument broke out in a video store, and the police tried to stop it. It became a major protest. Rioting broke out in the streets. Protestors were using slingshots armed with bicycle spokes to shoot at the military. The government put the entire city under martial law and we were immediately taken back to our hotel and put in our rooms. I sensed a problem or beginning of a revolution, and Bull Simons taught me in a revolution the first thing you do is stock up with water because it could be days before you know what to do, so we ordered all we could get from the kitchen.

After a while, we became curious about what was going on outside the hotel. We knew martial law was in effect for the entire city of Rangoon, and so we cautiously walked out to the barrier of the hotel and into the adjacent street. At one point, I wanted to take a picture (since I always had my trusty Canon AE-1 with me). It was really eerie since there were no moving vehicles and, thus, no real sound. Thousands of people were quietly walking to their homes from the center city (since Rangoon was totally shut down). However, when I tried to take the picture, a guard pointed his gun at me and signaled NO. In this situation, I was not going to argue.

We watched individuals, couples, and families pass by walking like zombies and not talking either from fear or just exhaustion from the walk from the city (we were located in the outskirts). It was such a weird scene.

We then snuck back to our rooms and planned our next stop while nibbling on crackers and water. Fortunately, I got a call from our embassy informing me that they had booked us out the next morning on a flight to Bangkok. Again, fortunately, the next day everything was calm and the martial law was lifted. We immediately made our way to the airport and left Burma.

That was my last trip to Rangoon. We soon realized that the terms and reluctance of Burma officials to do a deal made Burma a third-rate prospect even though the geology looked nice.

Still, it was a fun country to visit back in the 1980s, as everything looked very British but worn out. I remember they had one restaurant in the shape of a huge river boat in the water and made out of concrete. In our earlier trips, the only restaurant we would eat at (other than our one-star hotel) was a Chinese restaurant in an adjacent field. They had tables in the field and you would walk through the grass to get there. One little candle on the table.

Two of the classic stories related to Fairchild happened in Burma.

One was while we were on a plane, flying from Rangoon to Bangkok, on a Burma Airways plane. We had been in Rangoon one week and were anxious to get back to Thailand. It was a small plane with about fifty passengers. The flight was particularly full, as an entire group of Japanese tourists occupied all except for the two front seats, which Ray Fairchild and I had. Halfway into the flight, a Japanese group leader/photographer began filming the flight so the group could have a souvenir. He started at the back of the plane and then moved forward, alternating seats to get good photos of each passenger. The passengers would make funny gestures and comments. Even though I spoke only a few words of Japanese, I could tell by the smiles and laughter everyone was having a good time.

When he got to us, he made a pleasant-toned comment (which I could not understand) and Fairchild raised his right hand and extended the middle finger, smiled into the camera, and held it. The group leader assumed that it was a positive American gesture, smiled, and filmed it with a comment (which again we could not understand).

I scolded Fairchild for this but he was a World War II veteran who still carried a dislike of the Japanese. I often thought about the group leader's finished product with the finger poised and how he would have had to explain it to his clients.

The second Fairchild story in Burma stems from his love of native hats. When I traveled with him all over the world, he was always buying a native hat for his collection.

One day, while traveling in Rangoon for some government meetings, we passed a market where he saw a stack of Burmese hats (the Burmese men had a unique type of stove pipe hat and he wanted one). He immediately ordered the driver to stop in front of this hat seller and got out to meet her.

The hat seller was a short, rotund Chinese woman, who looked like she had been selling hats for years. He told her he wanted one of her hats in the pile. She selected the biggest one she could find. (Now, American heads are generally larger than the Burmese heads, and Ray was no exception). She offered it to Ray, and he put it on. It was too small, so instead of finding another larger hat in the pile, she went behind some drapes, came out with a hat, and put it on Ray. He told her that this one was a little better, but still too small. Again, she went back behind the drapes and came out with a hat. Ray once again tried it on … it was better, but it was still a little too tight.

When she went behind the drapes for the third time, I followed her. There, on a chair sat a very fat-headed Chinese boy. She had been taking the same hat and trying to stretch it by pressing it over his head, since that was the largest size she had.

I revealed this to Fairchild, and he was impressed with her ingenuity and bought the hat, wondering out loud, "why the hats always seemed sweaty." I now wish I had bought one too.

As I mentioned earlier, I spent a considerable amount of time in Laos flying around the country while working on Perot's POW effort from 1969 to 1973. (When Tanya was small, she would ask where I had been and I would tell her that I was in Bangkok where the sun would set and I could bring home the bacon … This worked … she would watch the sunset imagining that Daddy was there collecting bacon).

It was during the Vietnam War, all the way up to 1970, that we were involved in what was more or less a secret war in Laos, which was kept under the press radar since the press was concentrating on Vietnam and later Cambodia. The purpose was to stop the flow of military supplies from North Vietnam going to the Viet Cong guerillas and, later, North Vietnamese regular troops stationed in the south. The patchwork of trails, vital to the war effort of the North Vietnamese, became known as the Ho Chi Minh Trail. Due to its strategic importance, the United States bombed it continuously from 1964 to 1972. In fact, one statistic states that more energy (TNT) from bombs was dropped on the Ho Chi Minh Trail than from all the bombs dropped in all other US wars. I didn't know how true this may have been until I walked on it twenty years later.

Now that we were looking for new acreage to explore, I told Fairchild that I had been in Laos in a different life and knew a lot about the country.

Twenty thousand barrels per day of oil was being produced in the Thailand portion of the Korat Basin, which also extended into Laos. Maycock did some research and found that the French (it was an old French colony) had identified some oil seeps in the trail area.

If you look at a map, Laos has a big bulb on the long panhandle bordered by Vietnam, Cambodia, and Thailand. This panhandle was used by the North Vietnamese for their secured pathway to South Vietnam and Cambodia. Since Laos and Cambodia were supposedly neutral countries, President Johnson would not openly attack the North Vietnamese inside those countries even though they were violating the rules of war. Finally, by 1970, Nixon said enough and determined that they had violated war rules. Thus, he sent troops in to get rid of the NVA bases and storage depots. The war protesters went wild, which resulted in the student deaths at Kent State and a growing revulsion by the American people against the war. (I spent nine years of my life working in the Vietnam War in one fashion or another, which may be the inspiration for another book).

Anyway, my knowledge of the country gave me the confidence to go to Laos even though it was an old-line, Marxist society, because I felt the world was changing in the late '80s. Thus, Chris Stone and I flew into Vientiane to meet with the Lao officials in 1989. The US embassy was still there but its head had been downgraded to a chargé d'affaires instead of an ambassador.

I called Jim Lilly (now deputy secretary for security) at the State Department to facilitate a meeting with the chargé d'affaires. He said he would as long as I would not go into the jungle to look for POWs. I assured him I would not and he set me up with the chargé d'affaires, Theresa Tull, a remarkable woman who later became an ambassador. I was impressed with her; in fact, she later became ambassador to Guyana in South America and was instrumental in Hunt Oil later acquiring a PSA there, as she was the one who called me to see if we were interested.

During the Laos trip, she asked if she could sit in on my presentation to the Lao leadership. Hunt policy was, at that time, not to have any outsiders in our presentations. But she had been so good to us in setting everything up, I decided to include her, meaning she was exposed to the Hunt Oil Company sales promotion. Ironically, this gesture enabled Hunt to later get an exploration license in Guyana.

Speaking of Guyana, what is sad is we took a block in the western part of the country, which turned out to be a dry well. Fifteen years later, Exxon took an offshore block and discovered a multi-billion-barrel field offshore. Guyana, a poor country, would now be awash in oil dollars and facing the challenge of spending it for the good of the citizens, if the politics of the country would allow it.

Anyway, back to Laos: Theresa set us up with the Lao industry minister (this was as close as they had to an oil ministry, since they imported their oil products), a government aide, and the secretary of the politburo cabinet. They were interested, since no one had approached them before on exploring for oil. We returned to Dallas to report our findings.

Meanwhile, Ian was researching oil in Laos. He found a 1950 French report of an oil seep in the panhandle east of Savannakhet and in the area of the Ho Chi Minh Trail. Thus, Jennings, Ian, and I went off to Laos. This was their first trip and since I had spent a lot of time there between 1969 and 1973, it was fun for me to take them around. It was on these trips that I began to buy a lot of old silver Indochinese coins in the street markets.

The industry minister was very cooperative and provided us with the use of an old Russian helicopter and other logistics so we could visit some areas we thought might be prospective. I enjoyed standing in the back of a Russian truck driving the road to Tchepone (a battle area in 1970). We could not find the oil seep although we had some coordinates. (On occasion, a seep will stop for various geological reasons).

One activity that caught my attention was the line of dump trucks waiting for the ferry to carry their load across the Mekong to Thailand. These loads were the American B-52 bomb casings that held the bomblets and shrapnel from the Ho Chi Minh Trail area. This scrap metal was one of the largest exports from Laos to Thailand. They would collect the bomb casings and scraps and truck them to Thailand to be processed as industrial metal.

After many meetings and visits, we finally concluded that we would apply for permission to explore a large area in the center of the panhandle of Laos.

I also spent time visiting the Laotian embassy in Washington to keep the ambassador up to date on what we were doing. We developed a great relationship with the ambassador because of, among other things, Ray's sister Swanee.

Swanee is a most talented woman, as are all of Ray's sisters. One of her many talents is photography, and she had spent the previous year touring Laos and taking pictures. Her eye for composition is equal to Ansel Adams and, in Laos, she had such a palette. We enlarged sixteen of her photos of the country, framed them, and presented them to the ambassador. The Lao were delighted and spruced up the embassy walls with these large, professional photos of their country. We gained a lot of "points" for this, thanks to Swanee.

Now back to the oil. We knew where the known seep had been sited, so we applied for about three million acres as an exploration area. We were told it was ours by the minister as they liked our contract proposal.

We were feeling good when I got a call later in the week that a French company had flown into Vientiane that previous weekend and was awarded the area we had bid on. Further investigation revealed they had flown in on a private plane and distributed a lot of gifts and actually used essentially a copy of our contract to clinch their deal. They had not been visiting the area like we had. We found out later that they did not even do much exploration.

We were really upset and I took this personally, as this was the second contract where a French company had bribed a country into denying us a contract.

I knew that in two weeks the Lao foreign minister (who had become a friend of mine as I would visit him in Laos or when he came to Washington) and finance minister would be in Washington for the annual World Bank conference. I told Jim Jennings and Ian Maycock we should go to Washington and confront them with our disappointment. They agreed, so I called and made an appointment to meet them in their hotel room.

At the meeting, we made a case that we were disappointed since we had been told that the area would be awarded to us by the industry minister. I then reminded them that we were the first American company to come back into Laos and that we were a well-known oil company with a reputation for finding oil if it was there. I cited Yemen as exhibit A.

We then finished with the fact we could only conclude that the Lao government did not want to do business with American companies. We had enjoyed our relationship and wished them well ... and walked out of the room.

As we were leaving, the foreign minister said that the Lao government respected Hunt Oil Company and wanted us to find oil in Laos. He told us to submit a new contract and "assured" us we would "probably" get it.

So, Ian and Jim went back to the drawing table and concluded the Khorat Basin was also in the lower part of the Lao panhandle, so it could be prospective. Thus, after much study and research, we submitted a contract for the lower part of the panhandle ... one-tenth of the country. We sent our contract team in and reached an agreement. I felt our meeting in New York was a real success.

In the oil business, once you sign a contract to explore an unknown geographical area, a lot of things start to happen. First, you open an office in the country with a country manager to handle the administrative details. Then you have your geologist come in and do geological and maybe aero-magnetic surveys and hire a geophysical contractor to shoot seismic to get an idea what the subsurface of the area may look like. You have geologists and analysts doing research in the area of historical information that may be relevant to the region.

During the latter phase, we found a lot of "ordnance" in the area (unexploded bombs and mines), which caused us to realize that the area may not be accessible since it was on the Ho Chi Minh Trail ... the most bombed area in the history of war. A company was hired from England to do bomb clearance, headed by Paddy Rainey, an ex-British Commando. This added another $1 million to our contract.

Jennings was concerned about the security and cost so he sent Tom Cwikla, our top geologist, and me over to check it out to see if we should shut it down or continue.

Cwikla and I went to Laos, and Paddy took us into the area where the mines and unexploded bombs were. He roped off an area so we could walk through the jungle to the area we planned to drill. I was so fascinated to see the huge craters caused by the larger bombs and the fins of anti-personnel bomblets and shrapnel sticking out of the torn-up ground. Paddy set it up for us to see. I could now imagine what it must have been like for those NVA being bombed.

We spent four days there with a seismic crew and Paddy's crew. We concluded we could drill a well, but the area would have to be provided with safe lanes to the rig after it was cleared of dangerous, unexploded bombs and bomblets.

We eventually drilled the well, but unfortunately, it was dry. We could not find evidence that we should drill a second one; the French company also pulled out before even finishing their contract.

During this period of drilling, Ray, Hunter, and I visited Laos after visiting with our old friend, Jim Lilly, now the US ambassador to the People's Republic of China. Ray met with Kaysone, the communist leader of Laos and running buddy with Pol Pot (Cambodia communist leader) and Mao Tse Tung (China's communist leader).

This was an interesting meeting, as this was the first time Kaysone had met an American capitalist. It was a great occasion and I remember Kaysone telling Ray he wanted him to build a refinery immediately. Ray responded they had to find the oil first. Kaysone, an absolute dictator, was not used to someone countering his instructions, but he had a funny look on his face and then had no response.

Unfortunately, as I already said, our well in Laos was a dry hole. But an interesting side note is that technology was advancing in the early 1990s, a phenomenon very apparent in Laos. We now had a satellite phone in a suitcase that we could open up and raise a disk to the sky, allowing us to communicate with Dallas. We could send our seismic data to Dallas where geophysicists could interpret and send info back to Laos. We saved over a million dollars on our seismic contract because of this new, efficient method of communication.

However, the logistics of supplying food and equipment to our seismic camp on the Ho Chi Minh trail was not as efficient, since all of this was delivered by ox cart!

CHAPTER TWENTY-THREE

SOME STORIES FROM UNIQUE COUNTRIES AT THE TIME

ALBANIA

Albania had to be one of the strangest countries I visited. I told Fairchild and later Jennings that Albania had been producing oil offshore before World War II and maybe we should look at it. In the 1980s, it was still on the extreme end of the Communist World and "running buddies" with the Bulgarians and North Koreans. It was so bad that Albania had severed their relationship with the USSR in the 1950s (after the death of Stalin) and the People's Republic of China in 1972 (after the Nixon visit), because they felt they were not communist enough.

I spent several years trying to get an invitation for Hunt to visit the country in the 1980s. When I would go to Yemen, I would connect through Paris. On the return, I would stay overnight in order to catch the direct American flight back to Dallas. I used this time to establish a relationship with the first secretary of the Albanian embassy in Paris. His name was Mr. Shyti. Initially, my relationship was with Shyti only, but as time went on, he would add other diplomatic colleagues to our dinners.

For over two years and many expensive Paris dinners, they would hear about Hunt Oil and our interest in Albania. Then, one day in 1989, I received a letter from Mr. Shyti telling me that Albania was going to open their country to foreign oil contractors and he wanted me to know that Hunt Oil Company would be the first one invited to Albania.

We accepted and scheduled a trip in September. I was really excited because Albania was a "Stalinist" country that had been essentially closed to much of the world.

Our team included Casey Olson (a contract negotiator who later left Hunt to become a top executive at Occidental Oil Company), Jim Jennings (head of Exploration and later president of Hunt Oil Company), and Ian Maycock. We flew in from Geneva to Tirana, the capital of Albania, where we e spent about five days in meetings and traveling to parts of the country as guests of the government.

By this time in my career, I had traveled the world and seen a lot of strange and unusual places: China in 1979 when it was just opening up to the west; New

Guinea highlands in 1981; the great Empty Quarter of Arabia; a backward Burma before it changed its name; the Plain de Jars in Laos; the vast swamp areas of Tanzania; the old city of Hong Kong (the walled city of Kowloon, where in 1969 sewers flowed in the street and children were slaves to manufacturing); the Sinai desert when Israel controlled it; the ravages of war in Vietnam and Laos, etc.

However, nothing had prepared me for what I saw in Albania on that first trip. First of all, the lead government official who met us at the plane was a small man named Marco. He was about three-foot-five but seemed like six-foot-two when you dealt with him. Marco was a true diplomat. He had taught himself English when Albania had no relationships with English-speaking countries. He was a delight to converse with, as he told us all about his country, of which he was very proud. He and I developed a good relationship and I really liked him. In fact, later he sent me a bottle of Albanian Merlot that I still have as of now in the wine rack.

Our hosts were wonderful and treated us so well ... but the shock came after we checked into our hotel (which was comfortable) and had a chance to walk out into Tirana, the capital and largest city in Albania.

There were hardly any cars on the street. Occasionally, a black car (government official, I presumed) would go by and maybe a bus, but the majority of people were walking. In a way, it seemed healthy.

We had a great dinner that night in the hotel (the only place we ate while in Tirana). Basically, it was beef and wonderful vegetables, and a fine Merlot wine. It was fall, and the vegetables and fruits were being harvested. I feel they did not have the money to use chemicals in their farming (remember, by 1989, they had severed their relationship with their communist benefactors and the Bulgarians and North Koreans were not noted for their foreign aid in those days). This was 1989 and other possible benefactors like East Germany were folding up. Regardless, I felt the locally grown food was wonderful and healthy.

The next morning I went out to do my normal morning jog dressed in running shorts and a T-shirt. After about half a mile, two policemen darted out of some bushes and grabbed me. Fortunately, one spoke a very bad English and told me it was illegal to be in the streets in my underwear. They had never seen a jogger before. They took me back to the hotel but did not charge me with any crime. I thought it was very amusing and couldn't wait to tell my many jogging friends when I returned to Dallas.

We had interesting meetings in an old building that was some type of historic compound. They did a good job of relating the history of their oil production so we obtained good information that we could take back to Dallas to study and decide if we wanted to submit a bid.

On the third day, we were driven into the countryside so we could get a feel of this small country from the mountains to the sea. This is where it became surreal. There were very few cars on the roads, all of them very old ... probably other dignitaries like us. What we did pass on the road was parts of old cars that had been cut in half so they had two wheels, a backseat, and a tongue that was attached to an axle and two horses, which were pulling the contraption on the paved road. There were many of these in various forms but always pulled by horses. In fact, there were so many that after a while, it no longer seemed out of place in my mind. I never saw what happened to the front ends of the cars, but I am sure they were put to good use.

What was even more interesting was seeing the fields along the road. They were impregnated with concrete pillboxes (this is a permanent circular concrete structure that can house machine guns to defend against an invading army). They were pointed toward their northern neighbor, Serbia. I have some interesting pictures taken of them.

Farmers would have to plow around these structures, which were sprinkled as close together as every ten to fifteen acres in some fields. From this experience, I deduced much of the dynamics that led to the horrible butchery in the Balkans in the 1990s, when the communist state of Yugoslavia disintegrated into a Muslim and Christian rivalry, setting up new states.

I loved Albania, but geologically, we did not feel we could do a contract considering the noncompetition terms they demanded. Also, to this date, no big oil (elephant-size) has been found there.

CAMBODIA

Cambodia was another country we approached, and where we had meetings with high government officials. I flew into Phnom Penh from Vientiane and spent a few days with our team. On one of those days, I asked our driver about the infamous prison called Toule Soul, where the Khmer Rouge had tortured and killed prisoners. (The Khmer Rouge were communist Cambodians led by Pol Pot who killed or caused the death of nearly one-third of the population of the country during the mid-late 1970s. The book and movie *The Killing Fields* is a good place to start if you want to learn more about it).

I told the driver we would like to see the prison and he took us to this forbidding concrete building. There was nobody there so we just walked in. In one area, there was an entire wall of passport-sized photos that I assumed were a record of many of the thousands of people they executed. Most were Asians, but there were European pictures attached also. Interestingly, no one had bothered to take them down, or maybe they were preparing for a museum.

Seeing these photos and knowing that the people in them were brutally executed really affected me mentally, since I was at the very spot where this crime took place. Regaining my composure, I walked through many areas and rooms, where you could see blood-stained floors and the various tools for torture laying around, such as wire whips and electrical wires.

This was a very indelible moment and it made me very angry because I was walking through an area where so much torture and death had occurred. What really got me was the sign in the entry area where the prisoners were initially registered. Up on the wall in bold letters and bad English, it read:

THE SECURITY REGULATIONS

1. YOU MUST ANSWER ME ACCORDINGLY TO MY QUESTIONS. DON'T TURN THEM AWAY.

2. DON'T TRY TO HIDE THE FACTS BY MAKING PRETEXTS THIS AND THAT. YOU ARE STRICTLY PROHIBITED TO CONTEST ME.

3. DON'T BE A FOOL FOR YOU ARE A CHAP WHO DARE TO THWART THE REVOLUTION.

4. YOU MUST IMMEDIATELY ANSWER QUESTIONS WITHOUT WAISTING TIME TO REFLECT.

5. DON'T TELL ME EITHER ABOUT YOUR IMMORALITIES OR THE ESSENCE OF THE REVOLUTION.

6. WHILE GETTING LASHES OR ELECTRIFICATION YOU MUST NOT CRY OUT AT ALL.

7. DO NOTHING, SIT STILL AND WAIT FOR MY ORDERS. IF THERE IS NOT ORDER KEEP QUIET.

8. DON'T MAKE PRETEXTS ABOUT KAMPUCHEA KRON IN ORDER TO HIDE YOUR JAW OF A TRAITOR.

9. IF YOU DO NOT FOLLOW ALL THE ABOVE RULES YOU SHALL GET MANY LASHES OF ELECTRIC WIRE.

10. IF YOU DISOBEY ANY POINT OF MY REGULATIONS YOU WILL EITHER GET 10 LASHES OR 5 DISCHARGES OF ELECTRIC DISCHARGE.

I shuddered when I read this, knowing it was probably intended for only the middle- and upper-class Cambodians or foreigners who could read English. And these were the people the Khmer Rouge were determined to eliminate for the purity of the revolution. It was said that even anyone who wore glasses fell in this group.

On a trip in 1969, I had met and spent some time in Hong Kong with a famous American news reporter named Wells Hangen. He later went into Cambodia to cover the war. He and his crew never returned. I tried everything to see if we could find him. Basically, we found that his last known location was the "Chain of Elephants," and he had probably been captured by the Khmer Rouge. No further word was heard about him, even after the war. I thought of him and his crew while going through the prison, wondering what brutality they may have endured.

Fortunately, by 1978, even the Vietnamese felt the Khmer Rouge had gone too far and were becoming pro-Chinese and hostile toward the Socialist Republic of Vietnam. They invaded in December 1978 and removed the Khmer Rouge from power, stopping the genocide.

The other interesting tale was when we were leaving and our Lao assistant asked me if he could leave for about an hour. He took a bottle of French liquor with him. When he returned, he had two bottles, but they were now a foamy red brown color. He opened one up and asked if I wanted to taste it. I asked what it was. He gave it a Lao name, which I don't recall, but it was half fresh cobra blood and half French liquor. He had gone to a cobra farm to get enough cobra blood to half fill the two bottles. I was going to try it but then decided it was a bad idea to get sick in Cambodia, so I declined. I think he was relieved, since he could sell a shot of this liquid for $50: it was considered an aphrodisiac in Laos. To this day, I wish I had tried it, as it makes a great story.

LAOS

In southern Laos, the Mekong River above the falls was almost two miles across. The way we would cross it in our Toyota Land Cruiser was to board a makeshift "ferry" that consisted of three twenty-five-foot open boats that were strapped together, with heavy wooden planks attached cross-ways to create a deck that a car could drive upon. The middle boat had an outboard motor on it.

They would pull up along the bank and extend boards like a gang plank onto which we would drive the Toyota. The car would be secured with some ropes and we would head across the swollen Mekong with debris floating by. We would get out and walk around the car without any side rails or life preservers. The thought occurred to me that, if a log hit us, it would unravel the rope bonding, and our Toyota would go in the river.

On one trip, Linda Bigelow, Jeannie Jennings, and Sharon accompanied Jim, Lee Bigelow, Chris Stone, and me on one of these river crossings. (Lee was our manager in Vientiane, and Chris was our seismic manager in Pakse). While it was a real adventure for the ladies, it was just another day for Chris.

Speaking of Chris, one year we had meetings in Hanoi to discuss the possibilities of exploring in Vietnam. Jim, Ian, and I had made several trips there. On one trip, Chris, who was at the time our manager in Laos, accompanied us. One evening, we decided to eat at a little street restaurant in Hanoi. On the table was a platter of peppers of strange shapes that I had not seen before. Now, I like peppers, even though some are hotter than others. Casually, as we were having a beer, Chris said to me, "Tom, I will bet you $5 that I can eat more of these peppers than you can." Of course, I responded to the challenge. He said, you go first, so I bit half of the pepper and began to chew it and then swallow it. When I did so,

Chris reached into his pocket, pulled out a $5 bill, handed it to me, and said, "You win." This was the hottest pepper I have ever had. I could feel it going down my esophagus and into my stomach and intestinal tract. Never had I had such a bad culinary experience. I now creep up on a pepper before I taste one and am very wary of Chris at dinner.

I have another culinary story. One year when Jim, Ian, and I were in Vientiane, I got a call from an old Asian friend who said there were some Yunnan Chinese businessmen who wanted to meet us. I said fine, and they offered us dinner in a remote Lao home outside of the city. We drove and met with them and then had a good meeting and dinner. The food was very good and tasty (which the Chinese are noted for). It reminded me of an African antelope, called a gerenuk, that we shot and ate while hunting in Africa.

As we were leaving, I asked our host what the meat was. He said it was pangolin (which is an endangered anteater). I felt really bad about eating this poor creature because I immediately knew what it was and that it was endangered. Unfortunately, our hosts wanted to impress us and often used rare and endangered game to do so. (Glad it was not a bat, as the Covid-19 virus may have come from that).

YEMEN

On one trip to Yemen, Ray and I stopped in Paris to change planes. The second plane was Yemenia, the aviation company owned by the Yemen government. They flew an old Boeing 727 that was not as comfortable as Lufthansa or Air France. In fact, it was considerably less comfortable for the seven-hour flight, which had a brief stop in Cairo before flying onto Sanaa.

However, Ray had a policy that he would fly Yemenia whenever we could, to show support for Yemen. The government appreciated it, and that was one reason that Ray never flew our corporate jet to Yemen. (The other reason was the optics of a private jet plane, as Yemen was a very poor country).

Now this was an Arab airline, and so no alcohol was served. However, we had flown it enough that the manager sometimes had a bottle of champagne for Mr. Hunt. They would also allow us to bring some wine since they knew we were Christians and wine drinkers.

On this particular trip, we stopped in a store in the Orly Airport in Paris. I noticed wine advertised in a box, which I thought was unique and had never seen before. Also, I thought it would be less noticeable to other passengers than a bottle would be. So, I bought a liter-size box and discretely brought it onto the plane and put it under my seat. Now, keep in mind that the altitude in Paris was about five hundred above sea level while we were the equivalent of nine thousand feet in the pressurized fuselage of the 727.

About two hours into the air, our flight attendant began to serve our dinner, which was a rice plate with some pieces of meat. This was the time for the wine.

Ray and I were side by side in first-class seats. I reached between my legs, retrieved the box, and put it on my tray to open it. I looked for instructions but found none. Nor did I find an area on the top that looked like something to open.

Thus, I assumed you must rip the top off to get at the wine. With the top now ripped off, I saw a silver bag inside the box. Again, no indications as to where or how you get at the wine. Now, I was frustrated but knew the wine was inside the thin silver bladder. Thus, I took a fork and decided to pierce a small hole in the top so we could pour it out. Little did I realize the impact of the law of physics on pressure of fluid differentials. Once pierced, the wine came out with an enormous force and my immediate instinct was to shield myself and point it away from me. Well, away from me was Ray and he took the bulk between his chest and knees … and he was in a suit because when we landed, he would be met by government officials. The flight attendants sponge-mopped him as best they could, and he traveled the rest of the trip with blankets over the wet area.

It is a funny story now but it took several weeks before I dared tell it in his presence. He was really good about it other than giving me "what a dumb thing to do" look.

One of the best stories involving Ray in Yemen was when we were invited to the home to "break the fast" by Sheik Abulahum, a paramount sheik in Yemen and over the tribes where we were producing the oil.

In the Muslim world, one of the five tenets of Islam is to observe Ramadan annually for a month. The time is set astronomically and each year, the month varies. During Ramadan, a devout Muslin does not eat or drink anything during the daylight hours and is supposed to give up other pleasures also during this period.

Once darkness is determined by a senior Iman using a white string at sunset, people are notified that they may now eat and drink (no alcohol) until sunrise. Many use this time for gathering for friends and family and an evening feast to replenish the food you did not get during the day. My pious friends take it very seriously, and, by the end of the thirty days, you can tell it takes a toll on them.

Well, Sheik Abulahum was having his closest 150 male friends at his house to "break the fast" that night, when Ray and I arrived with our interpreter, Mohammed. There was this huge, long table with two lines of food laden carpets on the floor and the guests on either side. All kinds of food were aligned on the carpet, including a whole skinned and cooked young sheep about every fifteen feet. (They did not use tables but would sit on the floor to eat).

Ray, Mohammed, and I were at the front end on one side and the elder sheik was across from Ray. There were no utensils so one would eat with one's right hand. Occasionally, there was a spoon for some of the dishes. It was a fantastic array of interesting and tasty food, on that carpet. As we were eating and conversing with the sheik through Mohammed's translations, I remembered reading that in a Yemeni banquet, the guest of honor was sometimes presented the head of the sheep for the delicious brains.

I asked Mohammed to ask the sheik if this was true and was Ray the guest of honor. Mohammed relayed my questions to the sheik. The sheik's eyes lit up and he yelled something to one of the aides hovering around the food carpet. All of a sudden, the aide tore the head off the nearest cooked sheep, set it in front of Ray, and—with a cleaver—split its skull so the brains were exposed. Without missing a beat Ray grabbed one of the spoons on the carpet, scooped up a spoonful of sheep brains, and put it into his mouth. He did it a second time and the old sheik was awed by Ray and his adoption to the Arab custom. All around the carpet, the important guests were looking at Ray with a new appreciation. (Ray likes gizzards and, thus, I knew he could do it).

Then as he went for the third spoonful, I turned to Mohammed and said, "Mr. Ray really likes this. Can he get another?" Instantly, the aide again tore off the head of the next sheep in line, halved it with a cleaver in front of Ray, and set it down. Dutifully, Ray took another spoonful and then whispered to me that he was going to kill me when this was over. However, he did the second worst thing, announcing that now Mr. Meurer would have some of the brain. Of course, I could not do it, so I made a feeble excuse and lost a ton of face at the banquet.

As strange as this scene sounds, Ray made a great impression during this dinner in front of the leading sheiks in the Marib and Jauf area where Hunt operated. I think word probably went out that he was more than just a foreigner: he was a foreigner who really appreciated Yemeni food and culture.

As a result of this and the many other positive activities of the company, the Hunt name became well-respected in Yemen. This made me proud each time we returned to Sanaa.

CHAPTER TWENTY-FOUR

A FEW OF THE MOST
INTERESTING COUNTRIES

I have been asked often by friends and guests, "Of all the nearly one hundred countries you visited, and the countless cities and outlying areas in those countries, which ones are the most interesting?"

This is not easy to answer, as government structure, history, geography, culture, and the military and political adventures I encountered there were all of interest to me. Thus, I liked a number of different countries for different reasons.

Since I mentioned political/military adventures, I will address this issue first.

I have been accused of being a CIA agent by friends, foes, and even the press (especially during the Hunt Yemen lawsuit by Arabian Shield Company in 1987).

To set the record straight, other than being in the USAF for four and a half years and working off and on for the White House as an advance man for three years, I was never paid by the government for anything. I did spend a lot of time with CIA and USAID personnel in Laos during the Vietnam War (and to a lesser degree in Thailand and South Vietnam). In this case, if you remember from my discussion of my time with Ross Perot at EDS, I was seeking their help in looking for American POWs and MIAs and traveling on either Air America or Continental Air services (CIA contracted airlines) in southeast Asia.

I must acknowledge that the CIA was very helpful on my many trips to South East Asia during this time, assisting in meetings, transportation, and intelligence. And later, if you remember, when Hunt wanted to look for oil in Laos, I asked my old friend and our former consultant on China, Jim Lilley, who had spent twenty-five years with the CIA and was now undersecretary of state for security, to set up an initial meeting for me; with his help, we eventually negotiated a license to drill on the Ho Chi Minh trail in 1993. Even though it was a dry hole, I did achieve my dream to walk into the area I had studied for so many years.

In addition to my intersections with the CIA and other actors in the US government in South East Asia, we did, as a company, work with the CIA and Central Command officials on Yemen. For context, in the '80s, it was government policy for both the FBI and CIA to interview businessmen who were traveling to

China, Russia, and the Middle East at the time. This was the height of the Cold War and Russia was still considered an enemy. China was relatively unknown, particularly as Mao Zedong died and Deng Xiaoping eventually took over in the late '70s and changed government policy. Finally, in the Middle East, Yemen had had no US companies operating outside of Sanaa, but then along came Hunt, exploring for oil and finding a "bonanza" in the eastern part of the country, giving us unique insight into the country and its politics.

I was traveling to all of these countries during this time, so it is not surprising that the US government saw us as a resource, and that we were especially treated as such by the local CIA office and Langley headquarters. At the same time, our knowledge consisted of the kind of general information that any company would provide our government if asked, especially in the 1980s and 1990s, when the world was changing and Hunt was in the forefront of dealing with many communist and Mideast companies in oil exploration.

Consequently, both local FBI and CIA agents would contact me whenever I returned from China, Yemen, Russia, or other countries of interest and ask for a meeting to discuss my impressions and other information. I did this, but where possible in exchange for useful information from them: I wanted their resources to obtain data I could use for furthering Hunt's knowledge of the dangers and pitfalls of doing business abroad. Of special interest was obtaining background on the leaders and power groups and gaining awareness of cultural traits that could affect a foreigner operating in a given country.

Even though I had studied China and Russia, the information obtained via the FBI and CIA proved very valuable to us. I knew little about the current political situation in those countries and even less about their modern-day feelings toward America. Furthermore, while my undergraduate degree and teaching at the USAF officer training school allowed me to connect some of the dots on cultures, geography, and history, the CIA data was significant for us in Yemen and, to a lesser degree, in China.

For Yemen specifically, I read every book I could find on it. I joined the American Institute for Yemeni Studies, a Yemeni government-sponsored group of American and European college professors who specialized in Yemen. Their activities were supported by the Yemen government. I was made a member because Hunt was supporting some of their causes. Further, I befriended a number of top Yemen scholars with whom I could correspond on issues important to us. However, even with these resources, we found it useful to reach out to the CIA, particularly because Yemen in the 1980s was such uncharted territory.

In this case, I was able to, once again, call in the assistance of my good friend and traveling companion in China, Jim Lilley, now with the National Security Council in the Reagan White House. I explained I was flying to Yemen to "investigate" a potential deal. I asked if he could provide me some of our government intelligence and data on Yemen so that I could understand the country before meeting with some of its leaders. He sent a lot of information, which I devoured before and during the flight. Of interest was the recent history and background of Ali Abdullah Saleh, the president of the Republic of Yemen and the Yemeni relationship with Saudi Arabia. This information in particular proved very helpful.

After Ian, Mujib, and I arrived in Yemen to scope out the country, Matt Gannon, the CIA liaison, provided me with lots of information that led us to believe we could deal with the Yemeni government and the tribes in the east. It gave me the confidence I needed to recommend to Ray that we could do business in Yemen if we found oil. Thus, after Ian and Mujib concluded that the geology suggested there was oil and gas in the Marib area, I went back to Dallas and recommended we go forward with Yemen as we could live with the political and economic risk. I always credit Matt Gannon with helping me make my decision.

Once our Yemen adventure got underway, the CIA was initially very helpful. In 1984 they sent a team to Dallas to brief us on the northern tribes of Yemen and their relationship with the Yemeni president. They even left us a confidential map that listed the tribes in northern Yemen, which was useful to us when we built the pipeline.

Furthermore, in the 1980s the CIA had a mid-level executive development program, in which they toured various parts of the United States. They reached out to us and asked whether, when they came to Dallas, we would teach a class on private companies and how they operate differently from public companies. We agreed and set up a class that I taught. It took a while to prepare, but I loved it. Ray added the cream on top of the pie when he came in for the question-and-answer session. The CIA was appreciative.

Ray Hunt would occasionally meet with Bob Gates, the deputy director of the CIA, who later became director of the CIA and then secretary of defense. (Gates became a good friend, with whom we hunted and fished over the years. Ray was also instrumental in helping Bob get the job of chancellor of Texas A&M in between his tours as CIA director and secretary of defense for two presidents.) Also, in 1985, we had meetings with CIA director Bill Casey in Washington, DC, in his seventh-floor office to bring him updates on our activities in Yemen.

Initially, some of these meetings were set up by Kissinger and Associates. But eventually the government realized that Hunt was deeply ensconced in Yemen and wanted to know more about our operations and the oil, particularly as Yemen sits on the entrance to the Red Sea and is thus of immense geopolitical interest.

Finally, speaking of Casey, the only time I was personally approached by the CIA (other than an interview by a CIA recruiter when leaving the Air Force) was when Ross Perot was working with the Reagan administration on a special POW committee. Casey, then-CIA director, asked Perot if he knew of any businessmen who traveled a lot in the Mideast and who liked adventure. Ross gave him my name, and Director Casey asked him to have me call him on a private secure number. And so Perot called me when he got back to Dallas and asked that I call Casey on the secure line.

I was curious, so I called the number Ross gave me. Casey answered after one ring and said he wanted to meet me. I told him we had met in his office briefly a couple of years ago with Hunt and referenced the Grenada tourist poster in the entrance to his office that read "Closed for renovations." He laughed and wanted to know when I would next be in Washington. I told him I would get back to him. Sadly, within a few weeks, I read that he went into the hospital and was diagnosed with brain cancer, which eventually killed him.

Had he lived, though, he still may have not been able to fully sell me on some strange adventure. Several years later I was flying with Bob Gates to go hunting on our Hunt plane (just him and me). I referenced this story and Gates told me that Casey had a lot of unconventional ideas, most of which did not work.

Now, going back to the subject of countries that I liked. I have traveled in well over one hundred countries and did actual business in fifty-one. Actually, this number is debatable, since some of the countries I traveled to no longer exist, either as independent countries or colonies (the USSR, Czechoslovakia, South Vietnam, South Yemen, East Germany, the Royal Kingdom of Laos, Hong Kong, Macao, and others). Also, some of my travels took place during the last part of the Cold War, a period when many countries changed their economic or political philosophies and/or governments. Somalia, Ethiopia, Laos, Cambodia, Burma, Korea, Romania, Poland, Albania, Vietnam, and many other countries still exist but have reformed, modified, or changed their names.

Now, to describe my favorites:

1. People's Republic of China: I had studied the history and economics of China in college and the military. To fly into this land, forbidden to Americans for so long, and see in person what I had learned about in books was one of the greatest intellectual thrills of my life. And then, to follow its progress over numerous visits for the next thirty years was incredibly fascinating. China is the future competitor of the United States and will undoubtedly restore its place as a world power.

2. Albania: Another communist country that did not allow American visitors for decades and finally opened up in 1989 (in the case of Hunt I feel they did so because of my efforts for four years and my meeting with Mr. Shyti). When I first visited, I felt I was back in the early nineteenth century.

3. Yemen: This was a tribal country storming out of the fourteenth century. I had studied its physical geography in college but still knew little about it. As a result, I crammed for two weeks before I flew into the country on volumes of data and information that Jim Lilley had sent me. Never had I enjoyed myself so much as I did during that week (even though we ended up briefly incarcerated). Yemen will always be a part of my life.

4. Laos: I loved Laos. A beautiful, peaceful country whose people were bordered by more aggressive neighbors: Vietnam, Thailand, and China. I was there searching for information on American airmen shot down during the Vietnam War (1969 to 1973) and later, exploring for oil on the Ho Chi Minh trail in the area we bombed more than anyplace else in history during that war (1987 to 1993).

5. Mexico: I became president of the Hunt Mexico Company in the 1990s. We had investments there in private equity, real estate, and agriculture. Sharon and I traveled all over Mexico during this time and I was on some Mexican companies' boards so would spend a lot of time traveling on business too. I love Mexico. It is so sad that the drug cartels have destroyed this wonderful country. I do predict that one day the flow of people will go south to Mexico from the United States. The climate, people, resources and physical beauty will make it a leading country of the world if they can get the right government in place, get rid of the cartels, and improve their judicial system. Of all the world I have traveled, it is, in my opinion, the perfect geographical place to live (along with Chile and New Zealand).

6. Chile: A natural beauty unmatched. It is like someone flipped the west coasts of some of Mexico, California, Oregon, Washington, and British Columbia to create a country of unparalleled beauty. The gorgeous Andes frame it on the east, and the Pacific Ocean lines it on the west. The country is long and narrow and covers the Atacama Desert (the driest place in the world ... unfortunately, our efforts to find oil there were futile) to the forested mountain fjords in the south. If I were a young man at the time I traveled there, I would have moved there to start my life over.

7. New Zealand: Another place I would have moved to if I were a young man. It has a perfect climate, wonderful caring people, good institutions, English Common Law, and the English language. If the world goes bonkers, it could be a safe haven to live in comfort.

So, as you can see, I have reasons for preferring my favorites. In essence, I liked all the countries in which I did business or which I visited for other reasons. But only a few would I want to live or work in.

The only country I want to visit and have not is North Korea. Jim Lilley had offered to include me on one of his advisory trips there but he died of prostate cancer before we could organize it. His death was a great loss to his family, country, and me personally.

As I said earlier, there were eight countries created by the Cold War and I visited seven of them: South Vietnam, North Vietnam, North Yemen, South Yemen, West Germany, East Germany, and North and South Korea. One has to be my age to have visited those countries. South Vietnam ceased to exist in 1975. Few if any could get into South Yemen unless you were a communist ally or terrorist … The Cold War was challenging in the early '80s and North and South Yemen and West and East Germany merged in the early '90s. I bet there is hardly anyone alive today who has visited seven out of eight, like I did.

As for my favorite cities (from 1969 to 2019), I will list ten: (1) London, (2) Dubai, (3) Singapore, (4) Rome, (5) Hong Kong, (6) Bangkok, (7) Toronto, (8) Lima, (9) Frankfurt, and (10) Vientiane.

I list them all for different reasons, as cities that I visited at a time when they were among the great or most interesting cities of the world. London still has to be a favorite because of the history, language, and ease of moving around. Definitely not the British food, though. Fortunately, I found a lot of ethnic restaurants that shielded me from their bland meals of blood and internal organs.

The best food was in Paris. I did a lot of business there and French history of course is interesting. The Parisians, however, seemed to be arrogant toward English speakers, an attitude that comes through loud and clear. Somehow, this middle-sized country, with a mediocre military in the twentieth century, still wants to act like the bedrock of European civilization. I will not judge, but they really needed help … We did bail them out in World War I, World War II, and Vietnam and you would think they would be grateful. However, I do have to say that if it were not for the French, Washington would have lost the battle of Yorktown and maybe the Revolution. And when Napoleon sold us the Louisiana Territory in 1803, he made possible the Manifest Destiny of our country. So the French are not all bad.

International travel is fun and a great learning experience. If they can afford it, most parents should arrange travel for their kids in order to expose them to other cultures. We did it with our kids. We arranged trips to Mexico, Canada and Europe, with a special trip to East Germany in 1982 so Tanya and Gar could understand what communism offered. Tanya was mouthing off one day as an early testing teenager would do, saying that she could say whatever she wanted in any country. I decided to test that theory of hers.

It was such a great experience for the kids to witness a communist state. I had to apply six months in advance to get the clearances and when we got to the East German border (remember this was at the height of the Cold War and East Germany was the enemy), the East Germans were confused. Customs held us at the Eisen border for two hours because they could not understand why a US oil executive would take his family to Karl Marx Stadt for vacation. He must be a spy. At the border, they would only use German so I had to use my college German and a Cassell's German/English dictionary in order to try to communicate.

Our time in "Karl Marx Stadt" was indelible. Before the communist government had changed its name, it had been known as Chemnitz; it had been totally destroyed by Allied bombing in World War II and was now an ugly Soviet-style city. There were no common restaurants, no shopping areas, and only one major hotel. We were followed everywhere by the secret police and only ate in the hotel, where we were watched by other patrons who could not afford the steak dinner for four we ordered. The dining room was filled mostly by party people and Bulgarians, Cubans, and other allies of East Germany, who came there on the Saturday night to drink beer and have some cheap cake. They watched us as we ate our steaks.

It was a great experience for the kids to witness what life was like in a communist country if you were a common citizen. They had a "Friendship" store, where non-Germans could buy things with hard currency (dollars, marks, francs or pounds). Most of the goods were junk. I bought a candle stick engraved in medieval German, which sits now in our entertainment room. When we left the city to get out onto the East German freeway, we were stopped on the access road for not having our seat belts fastened. When the officer approached the car, I asked why he had stopped us. He said, no seat belts. I asked what the fine was and paid the officer (this must have been a bribe, as they could not possibly have seen if we had seat belts on, sitting at a roadblock a half a mile away). We did get two tickets, which I framed.

It was a great experience, especially since we left East Germany through another exit, which was illegal and I had to do a lot of explaining. The kids got a chance to see guard dogs barking around the car and soldiers pointing AK-47 machine guns at them. I only wish I had the time and resources to do more with the kids in the 1980s … as this was when they were in their formative years.

CHAPTER TWENTY-FIVE

OTHER BUSINESSES I WORKED IN HOODO LAND AND CATTLE COMPANY

Public companies normally do not own large, non–income producing land holdings unless there is a good profit off of them from agriculture operations (cattle, orchards, crops, hunting, and/or mineral royalties). The reason is that these types of earnings must equal the earnings from their main business and most agricultural operations are not very profitable and risk bringing down the value of the stock price of the company overall. Thus, most public companies do not own large, non–income producing landholdings (unless the landholdings are just a small fraction of the value of the company or they are into timber or combine mineral production with their other operations).

Private companies with the right business plan, however, can use raw land to their advantage. Private oil- and gas-producing companies that may be also in real estate development often have financial objectives based on building asset value and deferring taxes and not making quarterly profits. They are not concerned about quarterly reports to their stockholders or being reported on in the *Wall Street Journal* like public companies.

Hunt fits this model. Buy land (with available minerals) far enough outside a growing city and wait for the city to grow to you. As a family company, there is no pressure to show earnings immediately. While waiting, farm it or run cattle on the land to defer taxes and, hopefully, carry the cost of the land. (If you have the mineral rights, this can add income if you are in the right locations).

This was essentially the Hunt model when I joined the company in 1975; at the time, Hunt was ranching and farming over 225,000 acres. During my time in charge of this business, we increased those holdings twofold.

This additional acreage was possible because Ray normally preferred to buy anything that touches his properties. It was my privilege to work with great managers (George Brown, J. D. Radakovich, Blair Eastman, Jeff Hass, Johnny Frosch, and Harry Shimotsu), who easily recognized opportunities for the company. We would buy with cash, terms, or trades. We would purchase from landowners, bid in auctions, purchase directly from state or federal governments, buy companies that had land in their assets, or provide estate deals to elderly owners (where we would buy the land of an elderly couple but let them live on it as long as they lived or unless they decided to leave it).

A large portion of this property was added through the purchases of state lands in auctions, or just buying out individual ranches and companies with land. By 2015 Ray controlled 550,000 acres of farms and ranches in Montana, Wyoming, Utah, Colorado, Arizona, and Texas.

These are beautiful properties, some of which could become national parks.

The Hoodoo Ranch outside Cody, Wyoming, is the "queen of the fleet." At 275,000 acres, it is 37 percent of the size of the state of Rhode Island. It ranges from five thousand to ten thousand feet, has major rivers flowing through it, and is one of the great historical ranches of Wyoming, bordering the wilderness area next to Yellowstone Park.

The Preston Nutter Ranch is in eastern Utah and comprises 175,000 acres on the Tavaputs Plateau, running from 10,600 to 5,000 feet. Unlike the Hoodoo, it is very remote. We initially acquired it when we purchased an oil exploration company as part of our efforts to expand into US oil production. (It had over a billion barrels of tar sands on the property, but this had no commercial value in 1993. Thus, we got the ranch for a little over a million-dollar valuation in the original purchase of $370 million). The Preston Nutter borders the Green River (one the best rafting rivers in the United States) and Desolation Canyon (which is deeper than the Grand Canyon). It is a nature preserve and truly could be a national park.

At one end is an escarpment overlooking Desolation Canyon, where one can sit in a lawn chair and see 25 percent of the state of Utah. Ray used this spot for special entertaining and elk hunting for those who wanted to hunt or just observe. Guests included former president George W. Bush, former secretary of state James Baker (both many times), former CIA directors Bob Gates and Michael Hayden, and former chairman of the Joint Chiefs of Staff, General Peter Pace.

It was a Who's Who of top business and former government officials coming to the ranch for over eighteen years (also Hall of Fame quarterback, Roger Staubach). (Again, I should point out that none of these guests were in public office at the time when they were invited to the ranch.) This was a special treat for me as I was included and had opportunities to spend time with these individuals, some of whom became friends later.

A later acquisition was the HNZ Milky Ranch, which we invested in with a partner. This was seventy-five thousand acres next to the Petrified National Park in Arizona. (It also came with 360,000 acres of mineral rights on land in Arizona and New Mexico). In 2018 Hunt sold seven thousand acres ladened with fossils, Native American relics, and prime petrified wood to the National Park Service.

This ranch is leased by Traegen and Marilyn Knight, the most impressive couple I have ever met. I so wanted to hire them for our Hunt system. They are truly a ranching family living in the high desert outside of Holbrook, Arizona, in the century-old company ranch house. They homeschool their four wonderful children and still participate in kids' activities in an adjacent town.

The ranch is teeming with archeological items from early Americans and wonderful Triassic (221 million years old) petrified wood and fossils. It is an unusual property and will have some increased value some day because of the potash or solar energy potential.

In Montana, Hunt owns the thirty-thousand-acre Hoodoo 71. A great cattle ranch, it also has development potential since it includes over two miles on the Yellowstone River (where Lewis and Clark passed), with equal federal highway and rail frontage.

Of course, there are Texas ranches, Circle K and Lamar. These five-thousand-acre and nine-thousand-acre ranches are within forty minutes of downtown Dallas and within a few years of development potential (Sharyland, in south Texas, was sold in 2019).

I took over as the president of Hunt's agricultural business in 1991. Since I was raised in farming, I guess Ray thought I knew something about it.

Initially, we named the business the AgHunt Oil Company (AGHOC). Later, I suggested Ray change it to the Hoodoo Land and Cattle Company since, if you were a "land and cattle company" you were "big time" in the cattle business. By 2015 Hunt was among the largest cattle producers in the United States with about twelve to fourteen thousand head and over five hundred thousand acres.

I initially knew little about the cattle business, but fortunately, I knew that I knew little. My job was to identify and hire good managers, provide them with the resources they needed, and give them the space and support to run the business. If a manager did not cut it, I fired him and hired or promoted a new one. After a couple of years, I had assembled the team we wanted.

Fortunately, we had with us one of the top cattlemen in the United States, a legend in the business named George Brown. I relished spending time with George, who ran Hoodoo from 1967 to 2009. I would go to the ranch four times a year and also have a weekly conference call with him and the other managers. During the two or three days I would spend with him each quarter, I would either fly over the ranch with him in his Super Cub and/or drive around the property. At times, we would also go to the Montana ranches (at the time, sixty thousand acres across two ranches on the Tongue and Yellowstone Rivers) to see the managers and their operations. Sometimes he would take me to bull sales or cattle auctions. Over many years, this drive time gave me the opportunity to ask many questions and learn from the master.

George retired in 2009. The "entire state" of Wyoming turned out for his retirement party, which Ray put on at the Buffalo Bill Cody Museum. During his career, George had crashed three airplanes and walked away so one of the best lines at the retirement was from Hunt's chief pilot, George Vaeth, who stated, "George Brown was the only cowboy he knew who broke more airplanes than he did horses."

I used to have some thrilling flights with George in the Super Cub. Now, a Super Cub is a small light cloth-covered airplane that can take off and land on a road. It has a two-place cockpit with one person sitting ahead of the other. It is perfect for flying when flying with no wind, especially updrafts against mountains. Thus, the best times for flying it are the first two or three hours after daylight. If you are up after that, the sun has warmed the air and updrafts will give one's tummy a thrill.

The first time I flew with George, in 1975, I was hunting on the ranch with Ray. Ray asked me to stay up there for a week after the hunt was over and spend time with George and observe him. The thing is, Ray had received reports that George was using some ranch assets for his personal use. I found this to be a totally false rumor started by Ray's half-brother, Bunker Hunt. Bunker liked to go to the ranch and stay in a cabin that was next to George's house and the cowboys' bunkhouse. For his part, George didn't like Bunker being there and disrupting the operations, so he converted the cabin into a ranch office. Bunker took offense and started the rumor. Anyway, Ray had to follow up and so sent me to do so.

I found George to be a man with incredible character, honesty, and principles. I became a George Brown fan then in 1975 and my admiration only grew over the next thirty-four years. Ray felt the same way and commissioned a coffee table book about the Hoodoo Ranch and George Brown, titled *Two Wyoming Legends*: *George Brown and the Hoodoo Ranch*. Ray then had one thousand copies printed, which he gave to the Cody Museum so they could sell them and reap the income from the sales.

Anyway, back to that first flight. That November day in 1975 after Ray left me with George, he asked if I wanted to go up in the airplane. Having spent a lot of time in many types of aircraft, I said yes. We took off. On this trip, George was moving stranded cattle out of the coulees in the canyons. To do this, he would dive down between hills and over the cows to force them down to the open country so the cowboys could round them up.

On the first dive we went into, the stall indicator buzzer went off. I had flown enough to realize that this was the onboard instrument that buzzed when your airspeed was too low. I also knew that a stall mode in a canyon was NOT GOOD … Initially my instinct was to grab the stick, of which there was one with each seat so either one of us could control the airplane with it. I didn't do it, though, and we dove into the canyon three more times before we landed. My knuckles were white.

George asked me what I thought (I think he saw me as the snot-nosed kid from Dallas and relished the fact that the flight scared me). I told him when we dove into the canyons and the stall indicator went off, I was going to grab the stick but refrained when we came out of the dive with ease. George told me that he had the indicator set on "high," so we had plenty of lift. (He, however, took the stick out of the second seat after that flight, in case he ever took up someone else who may not have been as calm as me but knew a little bit about flying.

Knowing all this now, I suggested to George we go back up again and tour the ranch. He laughed and we went up again.

George and I became the best of friends after that. It was such a good feeling to be a good friend of a legend.

I had other great flights with George. For instance, we would chase wild mustangs, diving upon a stallion and the horse would raise up as if to fight us. (This was illegal, but what a thrill to see this magnificent animal try to fight this flying machine).

One of the best memories I have of this sort was when George crashed his third plane. He called me on his cell while walking on a ranch road and told me he came down between two giant boulders, severed his wings, and flipped what was left of the plane. He said he ended upside down and just punched the seat straps and fell out. He was now walking and calling to tell me about the crash as if it was just another event on the ranch. This is why I so admired the man.

Another story about George was when our Hunt Security department, headed by Mike Pritchard, was selected by Ray to have an R&R and quasi-meeting at the Palette Ranch that summer. This was the retreat area on the upper ranch that Ray made available for special employees or sections who had made a significant contribution to the company.

Now, remember George had crashed the plane, so we needed to get a new one. Our aviation department had found one in Florida, which we bought and had flown to Cody. It was yellow. George hated it and would always complain to me that it made him stand out in the air.

Well, I decided to play a practical joke on Mike Prichard.

At the Palette Ranch, we had grizzly bears who occasionally roamed around a ten-mile area. I called Kurt Blain, the ranch manager, and told him to tell Pritchard and his team of ten former Secret Service agents, Texas Rangers, Texas DPS, and retired senior Dallas cops that they might run into a grizzly.

Also, Kurt was to tell them that the Wyoming Parks and Wildlife (WPW) were very helpful to the ranch, and that whenever Kurt informed them there were guests at the Palette Ranch, they'd monitor the area for us. Further, the WPW would use a yellow Super Cub to repeatedly fly over the ranch if grizzlies had been reported (of course, the WPW had no yellow Super Cub airplanes; nor would they provide such a service).

So, with the above information, you are in a position to guess as to what happened.

I called George and asked him to circle the ranch house with his yellow plane early that Saturday morning. He did, and all ten members of the Hunt Security team ran out of the ranch house dwellings, locked and loaded to find the bear (which was not there). This story became part of ranch lore.

While I'm still on George Brown and my wonderful time with this man, I have to tell you about his fetish for making sure illegal hunters did not come on the ranch. Of course, he used the airplane to monitor these transgressions.

One fall, when I was there on a trip, he wanted to know if I wanted to fly in his new airplane (recently acquired after the one he had crashed). Of course, I said yes, as I really enjoyed seeing the expansive ranch from the air. As we were flying, George noticed a parked vehicle in the bottom of a canyon that he felt should not be there.

He told me he would dive down and pull above the vehicle (between the canyon walls) and asked me to get the license plate number once we were close enough. Now, with my eyes, you know we had to be pretty close to see the plate. The first dive, which was like "a new ride at the State Fair of Texas," I recorded two letters off the plate. The second dive (reminiscent of a World War II Japanese kamikaze dive), I recorded a number.

On the third dive into the narrow canyon, I looked but could not put together the remaining numbers. Thus, I yelled out a couple numbers (that I made up) to credibly fill out a license plate. I think George knew I fibbed, but he also knew that I knew he could not use the data for criminal purposes. Anyway, it was a great experience and gives you a sense as to why I so enjoyed my time with George and his wife, Donna.

Sometimes, George would take me to bull or equipment sales. During these times, I always asked questions and always learned something about the cattle business from the master.

Fortunately, we had the manager of our largest ranch (the Hoodoo) in the cattle business (and one of the biggest in the United States) and Harry Shimotsu on farming (Sharyland was one of the larger vegetable farms in the United States since we could double crop, because of the semi-tropical weather on the Mexican border).

I spent a lot of time with George and Harry. Both recognized that I wanted to understand the business and they really taught me a lot about the farming and cattle business.

George broke it down for me in simple terms. He would remind me that we were just in the grass business. The grass has little value ... thus, you use the four-legged animals (cows) to convert the grass to protein so you can sell it after it is processed by feedlots and slaughterhouses.

Thus, if your grass was cheaper to raise, you had an advantage over the other ranchers since you could add the weight to your cattle at a lower cost.

Further, the business is broken down into the simple steps of "breed and feed" .... You breed cows to produce calves. Thus, says George, you breed a cow and she gives you a calf in nine months. This mother nurses her calf for six months or so, and then the rancher weans the calves and puts them on grass to feed.

Once a calf reaches four hundred pounds, it becomes a stocker and is sold to another rancher, who uses his grass to fatten it up.

They can now put the stocker on ranch grass for another six months or so. Now, when this stocker calf reaches seven hundred pounds, it is normally sold to a feedlot, to fatten up some more. Then, generally at twelve hundred pounds, it is slaughtered and sold as beef products (hamburger, steaks, etc.).

This simply is a cow's life … two years from birth to slaughter. If a rancher can reduce that time, they will have an economic advantage. In the future, this will happen, unless the consumer evolves in the direction of wanting less meat. (Remember, we are in the grass business and not the cattle business …. The cows are a means to convert grass to protein that humans can use).

I realize this gross explanation may make you a vegan like your mother, but I personally think (in 2020) that beef will always be in our diet. (Maybe there will be some genetic alterations, but you will still want the taste of fat and the vital protein needed by your body).

Maybe the veggie diet will catch on, but these sad souls will never know the wonderful silvery fat taste of a choice NY strip steak dipped in chunky blue cheese.

Red meat has been in our genes since the Pleistocene. I have read that there is no credible evidence that states vegetarians live longer. Leonardo de Vinci was one and died at sixty-seven. All my aunts and uncles were meat eaters and all lived into their nineties. (Actually, I believe that purpose in life, moderation, healthy diet, exercise, and good friends you can laugh with are the keys to a healthy life).

The one thing I think that could change the beef business would be if government leaders would get caught up in the actual hysteria of an earth gone astray because of the methane released by cattle.

In seeking to solve this perceived problem, these leaders might adopt draconian measures. The perception that there is a problem in the first place would be driven in the United States by interest groups (PETA, VEGANS of the World Unite, turkey farmers, chicken farmers, fish farmers, Federal Land for Recreation, and other anti-cattle and sheep groups that saddle up with scared citizens who live along the coasts). There might be political pressure for legislation to limit or eliminate the grazing or feeding of livestock based on the belief that their flatulence and burping is the cause of 20 percent of the methane released into the atmosphere. (For us BBQ eaters, they might try to buy our vote with a clause where a family could keep one cow, if they still wanted beef, but could not sell or give beef to others. Or they could have some form of disincentive tax that would limit the number of cows a landowner could raise for meat or dairy products). If it comes to pass, enjoy your synthetic soy, milk, butter, yogurt, and cheese and everything that has a celery taste.

Freezing systems and processes that could hold frozen meat and dairy products for decades may be a good investment if these laws are passed. Also, I would try to buy up all the choice and prime beef I could and sell it to the people who bought the freezing systems.

I enjoyed my role as president of HLCC, most of all because of the employees I associated with. Cowboys and farmers and their families are the salt of the earth. They are honest, hardworking, clear thinking, and enjoy life. Even though it may have been 20 percent of my overall job, the time I spent working on HLCC was hands down my favorite.

Because of my role in HLCC, I had a lot of opportunities to indulge in one of my favorite hobbies, which I learned from my dad ... hunting. Additionally, hunting and fishing are a part of the oil business. It is a mostly midwestern, southern and western thing, related to those areas where early oil was produced.

I've already mentioned that it was a big part of the Hunt culture. Here, I'd like to tell you two interesting hunting stories that affected me directly.

In the eighties, Ray and I, with his guests, used to hunt near Yellowstone Park in Wyoming. Each year, we and four guests would take a week and ride a day on horseback into the wilderness to set up camp with an outfitter. Every day, we would fan out in groups of two with one of three guides. One day, Ray and I set out hunting. Just before dark, we saw a nice bull elk on a ridge line about three hundred yards away. Ray (in his polite way) told me to shoot it ... Without hesitation, I did and gave it a minor flesh wound (which we did not know until later), so I did not impede the elk's ability to move. It was dark so we decided to go back to our tents and find it at daybreak.

At daybreak, Ray, our guide and I went to look for the bull. When we got to the area where we'd been the night before, we saw a faint light blood spot and knew I had not gotten off a serious shot. It had snowed that night so we were able to easily follow the bull's tracks in the snow. We followed it for about forty-five minutes and then noticed that what looked like dinner plates with claw marks was following the bull, too. The guide told us it was a big grizzly bear.

We followed the tracks for another hour and could see where this great bull elk fought the big bear. Dirt, erratic tracks, and ripped up small trees provided the evidence. Eventually, we came to a small stream meadow overlooked by a ridge, seventy feet above it. As we approached, I saw the big bear hunched over the dead elk; the bear had killed it and was resting before tearing out his favorite part, the intestines. I yelled, "Bear" and it heard me and came running up the slope toward us. Our guide told us to immediately fire our rifles, which we did, and the grizzly veered off. We then went down to harvest the antlers and ivory (the bull elk has small ivory tusks in his mouth, which are left over from the Pleistocene when elk had tusks). The guide hacked off the antlers (the meat was spoiled) and said we had to get out of there because the bear would be down on us if we spent time carving out the ivory. It was a thrilling experience.

The other experience was in Africa in 1988. Ray, his son Hunter, Charlie Winn and his son, Tom, and Gar and I went to Africa for a twenty-seven-day "in the bush" hunting safari. We have the film and some of the mounts in the house and farm, although most of the specimens were destroyed in a fire at the Flagg Taxidermist in Dallas. We did save the lion, which is now a rug in the house.

It was one of the more thrilling events of my life. We had a license to hunt a male lion. I gave it to Gar, as I thought his killing a lion would give him bragging rights back in high school. So, we went forth one day, looking for lions. We came upon a large termite mound: a big male lion was behind it. He tore off when he saw us, and Gar (although he was not supposed to), shot him on the run and wounded him. Now we had a bad situation, with a wounded lion. He ran out into the swamp and I saw him about 250 yards away and decided to fire. I did not know if I hit him, since he ran deeper into the swamp. The guide said we could not leave a wounded lion on the loose and had to go after him. I told Gar to stay back with the trackers and the guide and I went after the lion into the swamp (with snakes and gators).

I had an iron sight 458 buffalo gun and the guide had a double barrel 500. These are big guns, which can stop a moving car. The swamp consisted of knee-deep water in grass and an occasional island of six-foot-tall grass. As I went out into the swamp, the only thing I was focused on was a wounded mad lion charging at me from one of the many grass islands I passed. Each island I approached evoked the most concentration I have ever felt. It was a feeling I had never had before. I have never felt so alive before or since.

Eventually, we traversed about four hundred yards into the swamp and I saw a mound and, as I approached, I realized that it was the lion. (We found out later that my shot was the killing shot.) Now we had a problem of getting the lion back over the length of four football fields. With a gun pointed to the trackers, the guide commandeered them to go out into the snake/croc swamp and haul the five hundred pounds of dead lion back to where we had initially seen the lion. I helped them do it. It was, again, one the most exhilarating experiences I ever had.

PRIVATE EQUITIES

Private equity is a form of investing where the investor buys private companies either directly or in partnership, instead of investing in public company stock. The theory is that the private company stock is more illiquid and investors hold it longer and, thus, the cost may be lower and returns are normally higher. Investors look for companies with some weakness that they can correct to add more value.

There is a lot more to it, but essentially, some businesses can just be an individual with little more than a business plan on paper (angel investing). Others could be entrepreneurs who have a business plan and have actually started a business and need cash to get it going (startup). Further up the food chain are existing companies in various stages of growth that need cash and will sell some shares to the investor or investors who can help the company grow and prosper.

Then, at the top, there can be a limited partnership where some hopefully smart and experienced financial executives convince wealthy individuals or corporate/institutional investors to put money into a fund that would allow them to build a portfolio of these companies. They can raise scores of millions to billions of dollars that can be invested in a broad assortment of private or public companies and, often, because of the size of the fund's investment, dictate the direction of the company.

Now, this is a simplified version, as a lot has changed between the 1980s, when private equity was an unconventional type of investing, and what it has become today. In 1990, when we started, there were about seven hundred private equity firms; by 2007, they exceeded seven thousand. They include various types, ranging from aggressive angel investing to huge, sophisticated funds that buy massive companies. I just want to give you a sense of the environment we were in during the initial "Dot Com" days (1990s).

In the early 1990s, Ray decided to invest in private equities. The company had some initial success in a private equity fund, so he decided he wanted to increase his stake. He reasoned that, if you did your research and invested right, you should be able to do better than in public stocks, since you presumably would buy private companies that had financial or managerial problems, and with your skilled staff would fix them and then sell them for a profit. The major factor was that the timeline was longer to get your return.

Chris Kleinert had recently joined the company, and with an MBA and some banking and marketing background, he was a good candidate to set this up. Ray asked me, as the old guy, to work with Chris to help set up Hunt Equities, which would be the company's investing entity for private equity. So, I acquired another title, president of Hunt Equities.

It was such a joy to work with Chris. He is smart, a fast learner, and one of the best people that I have worked with. He loves a challenge and will jump in wherever he sees an opportunity. Further, he is a people person who genuinely is concerned about and shows empathy for those he meets. (Interestingly, I see this trait in Nick).

Initially, we had a relationship with GE Capital (General Electric's Pension Group), one of the more successful investors in private equity in the early 1990s. Chris and I reasoned that this multi-billion-dollar corporation, which could hire the smartest people in this business, should be a safe place to learn from: we should invest in what they did. We did so, following them in the Philippines and Europe. The Philippines was a bust and Europe was a single digit return. I did go on the advisory board of the British/European fund, Compass, and hopefully contributed, but more importantly, learned a lot.

Chris then suggested that now that we had a feel of the international limited partnership private equity world, we should look for our own deals. We did. We had more success.

Now, finding private equity business opportunities is a slugging, block and tackle business. One has to "kiss a lot of frogs to find a princess." This was the first thing we learned. Secondly, I believe the management and the business you invest in are key to success. The management needs to have a "fire in their belly" to get the business working.

At one time, we thought we could buy into a private business ourselves and fix it up and sell it. However, when we did this in Brazil and some other areas, we found we did not have bench strength to manage it. This was a learning experience and Mike Bierman, a brilliant Hunt lawyer who joined the team (and whom we called the "Nose" because he could smell a good or bad deal), luckily got us out of some bad deals.

Our team at the time was Chris, Mike, and Fulton Murray. We picked Fulton from our Argentina office, as he wanted to come back to Dallas. He was a great balance to the team, being smart, methodical, and cautiously aggressive toward investing.

The three of them were such a joy to work with and went on to make Hunt Equities and, later, Hunt Investment, very successful for Hunt Consolidated, Inc. We had investments all over the world and, in the early period, I really enjoyed board meetings, working with an international list of board members, and looking for new investment opportunities. I learned a lot about running a business by being exposed to so many different businesses that were both failures and successes ... particularly in Mexico, Brazil, and Europe.

It's important to note that entered this arena during the "dot com" period of the mid-1990s and early 2000. This was a period when bright young entrepreneurs, who were in the right place and right time, started companies that today have become the largest companies in the world. I regret I was not smart enough to see their vision or have the opportunity to invest with them in the early stages. Even when they initially went public, I was not intuitive enough to buy their public stock. I came up in investing where, if a company did not make earnings or positive cash flow, it was a business set to fail.

However, now some successful investor philosophies followed a mantra that if a technology company had a good business plan, determined management, was growing and could get money from investors instead of earnings, they were still in the game. "Moore's Law" would redeem some of them. In other words, advances in technology may mesh with their business plan (Microsoft, Apple, Facebook, Amazon, Google, etc.). When they went public, they grew by buying up weaker companies on the cutting edge of the "internet" world.

This was a heady period, but it was mostly those born after 1955 who were influenced by the excitement and advancement of computer software, which became the holy grail of the era. This was a time when many sharp and intuitive individuals recognized the power and scope of the internet and set up companies to exploit it (Mark Cuban, Mark Zuckerberg, etc.). Many of these successful companies went public (sold their stock to the public market) and many instant billionaires were made. Also, many employees of these companies became instant millionaires.

Chris, Fulton, and Mike did invest in many early-stage companies through partnerships and did well (such as PayPal).

We have many stories from this period, but I have one in particular that I would like to tell. When Chris and I started Hunt Equities, I suggested to him that in the international area we should invest but also use our investing as a tool to get to know the country and its culture and build relationships that could be of value to our other businesses in that country.

Mexico was the classic case. Ray wanted to invest in Mexico since it was next door to the United States. In fact, he set up a company that I headed for a time, called Hunt Mexico, which was a collection of our business interests in Mexico.

Thus, we decided in Hunt Equities that we should invest in Mexico. We talked to several funds and finally settled on a company called Zypher Nexus as being one of particular interest. It was a joint venture between a New York firm headed by Tom Barry (a former Rockefeller Foundation financial executive) and a group of Mexican executives (Luis Harvey, Juan Alvarez, and Arturo Saval) who had experience with private equity in Mexico.

When Chris and I finally decided we would invest in Mexico, we let them know that we would commit to 10 percent of the fund they were raising ($75 million … so our share was $7.5 million). A few months later, Barry called and said they had not raised the $75 million and were going to close at $55 mm. He knew we had committed $7.5 million based on the $75 million at the same time, our 10 percent commitment could now, in theory, be only $5.5 million. Barry asked that we stay at the $7.5 million.

Chris and I agreed but saw an opportunity to play a practical joke on the Mexican executives, who were good golfers. I told Tom Barry we would agree to the $7.5 million but he was to call Luis, Juan, and Arturo and tell them Hunt's response was they would agree to that sum if Juan and Luis (the good golfers) could beat Tom and Chris in an eighteen-hole match. If not, we would only invest $5.5 million. We would set the date and they could pick the course.

A few days later, Luis Harvey called me and said he understood we had an expensive golf match. I said yes and told him they could select the course and we the time. They came back with a course between Tolucca and Santa Fe in Mexico City. (It was at nine thousand feet). I then gave him a time when Chris and I could come to Mexico City.

On the date, Chris and I arrived at the Mexico City airport. They picked us up and took us to the Las Ensenas Golf Course, west of Mexico City. It was a beautiful course with some homes that would make expensive Dallas golf course homes look middle class.

They took us to the locker room to change even though it was 1:00 p.m. and we hadn't had lunch. Then, immediately, we went to the first tee. Each of us had a caddy.

They had been practicing with their pros all morning. Chris and I were 18 handicappers, but our Mexican friends did not know that. They knew I lived on a golf course and that Chris was a good athlete so they assumed that we were low handicap golfers. They were determined to beat us and get the additional $2 million for the fund. Thus, no lunch, no warm-up, and directly to the first tee.

Their play was so good and ours so bad that they knew they had won by the eighth hole, at which point they realized it was a practical joke and we were always going to invest the $7.5 million.

We all had a great laugh, and Chris and I are now known at that course as the two gringos who lost $2 million.

This has been a great story we have told over and over with our Mexican friends and has gone a long way to developing good relationships with many Mexican executives. It also led us to develop a mutual trust with our Nexus partners that lasts to this day. Even though I am retired, whenever they are in Dallas, they call or email and we often have lunch or breakfast.

It was a great experience for me to work with Chris, Mike, and Fulton in the area of private equity for a few years. I learned a lot about the businesses and being on the boards and advisory boards in various countries. This also helped me in fiduciary roles at Hunt (I was trustee for the Hunt Pension and Hunt Thrift … 401K and medical plans). Also, it made me more attuned to looking at new deals in an area I was soon put in charge of at Hunt, called Non-Existing New Business.

POTASH

In 2008 Mike Boswell, a close friend of Ray's and mine, joined Hunt. Mike had a tremendous amount of experience and was our age. He was initially a lawyer with Aiken Gump, worked for Perot on Wall Street (a job I recommended him for when Ross asked me for a securities lawyer), and then went to work for Bunker and Herbert Hunt when they tried to corner the silver market in 1980. Eventually, he was CEO of Sunshine Mining for seventeen years. He then became a partner of legendary energy investor Boone Pickens, in his most successful energy funds. In 2008 Mike had a disagreement with Boone and left the partnership, at which point Ray offered him an office to work out of. We then had Mike do some consulting on alternative energy and finally hired him.

When Ray brought Mike on board, we went through a number of deals. One of these was a rough joint venture with a great partner, Bob Worsley (an entrepreneur who built a business on developing a magazine, *Skymall*, to fit in airline seat pockets so passengers could buy things online while sitting on the airplane). Our venture with him was a seventy-five-thousand-acre ranch with 375,000 acres of minerals in New Mexico and Arizona, next to the Petrified National Park in Arizona. This was the HNZ Milky that I mentioned earlier.

One of the minerals the ranch had on it was potash, a key ingredient in fertilizer (potassium) that helps plants' immune system, increases yield, and enhances water preservation. We knew from old well logs in the files on the property that there was potash. We did not know how much so we decided to invest in an exploration program of about twenty wells.

The results were good in that we proved up some fifty-five million tons of potassium salt (the price was $600/ton delivered at the time). We concluded we did not want to get into the mining business, so we now needed to look for a buyer for the potash and lease them the minerals.

For this purpose, we hired the top minerals team from J. P. Morgan on Wall Street. The Morgan people contracted the known producers and none had any interest. What we did not count on was that potash is not fungible like oil. You cannot just sell it off the street. Producers have contracts. There is a cartel that controls it (the Russians and Canadians are the biggest producers) and can set the prices; they have huge reserves that they can just increase with a smaller investment, much cheaper than some company starting a new mine.

Thus, we just put the potash knowledge, well logs, files, and data on the shelf and maybe someday, Hunt will be approached to sell it.

Potash is salt brine concentrate formed in ancient seas that were drying up: as they did so, the salt brine (potassium) was deposited along the shoreline and in the shallows. We cannot reproduce it, like some other minerals. The big deposits are thirty-five hundred to four thousand feet deep and, thus, are initially expensive to mine, but once a mine is operating in large rich deposits, marginal expansion of the tunnels is less expensive.

The advantage of the Hunt potash is that it is about seven hundred feet deep. Also, the world's agriculture depends on potash, so mines are being depleted. Potash is a common mineral, but a challenge to find in economic concentrations. Further, it cannot be made synthetically. If Hunt is patient, their time may come, as they have fifty-five million proven tons in the ground, close to the farms of Arizona and California.

There also may be other evaporite minerals on the HNZ Ranch that may become valuable as technology advances. I really learned from this experience, but not soon enough to save Hunt from the questionable investment or to realize the investment bank experts who we relied on were also clueless on the market dynamics. They too learned at our expense.

CHAPTER TWENTY-SIX

OTHER FUN JOBS

One of the more exciting projects I worked on was our Yemen Hunt LNG company (which I mentioned earlier). As it happens, we discovered a lot of natural gas in Yemen during our exploration for crude oil. This turned out to be a hugely profitable adventure, but a complicated one.

In terms of the profit potential, because of the clean burning properties of natural gas, it has become more popular than coal for the generation of electricity due to global warming concerns. Also, it can become an integral part of producing electricity with renewables (when the wind is not blowing or the sun is not shining, utilities burn natural gas to keep a peak load of electricity).

LNG technology is rather simple and I think the commercial economics of LNG emerged in the 1970s in Indonesia and Algeria (although initial attempts dated back to the 1950s). As I've already mentioned, the best way to transport natural gas is to freeze it into a liquid form and reduce its volume by six hundred times. Now a liquid, but carefully kept at a low temperature, it can be transported somewhat like crude oil. To do this, however, a company must build pipelines to transport the gas from the production field area to a plant near the coast that freezes the gas and then provides the facility to load the cold liquid gas onto a specially designed ocean-going tanker that will transport it to a foreign port (think of the tanker as a giant thermos bottle that must keep the gas cold).

Further, the foreign port receiving facility needs to have a pipeline facility to take off the liquid gas and then a plant that can turn it back into a gaseous state, which can now be transported by a gas distribution system.

By 1990 Ray realized that we discovered a lot of natural gas in Yemen. When we negotiated our contract in 1981, the conventional wisdom was that natural gas would not have any value. Even if we did find gas in the desert, it would not be commercial because the cost to move it to the coast and other countries could not make it profitable. (Commercial in this context means paying debt, recovering costs, and making a profit). If we had known then what we know now, we would have designed our contract differently and avoided the pain of putting together an LNG partnership.

Anyway, some of the gas we found was associated with oil field production. The rest of it came from individual gas fields that produce pure natural gas only.

This, fortunately, was a wet gas that had the potential of producing crude-like liquids if you had the proper separating plant to do it. It would mean an additional expense, however.

Ray wanted to separate the liquids at the surface and have the now-dry, separated gas be injected back into the formation to preserve the pressure of the fields and, more importantly, to avoid burning it off in the atmosphere, where it would be wasted and would create more problems for our environment.

As we continued to find more wet gas (which could provide us more liquids that we could mix with crude oil), we decided to build plants that could strip out the wet gas ($C5+$ ... a formula based on the carbon chain and designated to the higher ends of the hydro-carbon chain) and put this in the crude export stream and sell it as a high-quality crude. We would then r-inject the rest of the dry gas back into the formation. Thus, Hunt did not waste any of the gas by burning (flaring) it, like many of the companies did in the United States and the Middle East in order to capture early profits in oil sales.

Within four years, Hunt had built four plants at $400 million each that processed three billion MCF (million cubic feet) per day in the desert, which eventually produced forty thousand barrels a day of liquids from the gas before it, now dry, was reinjected back into the formation. These numbers made the World Oil and Gas Industry realize that Hunt Oil Company was not only a technical leader in the industry but also a leader in the new area of environmental concerns and setting the bar for new standards. But this did not happen overnight and took a lot of effort to get up and running.

Specifically, in the early '90s, Ray started suggesting to the Yemeni government that they should allow Yemen Hunt Oil to build an LNG project with the gas we found. We carried out some studies and concluded we had enough accessible gas (in excess of three trillion cubic feet) to build an export plant that could process and sell six million tons annually (with our Exxon and South Korean partners, we had the technical and financial ability to do it).

However, this was a time when LNG was becoming popular and there was an increasing demand for it across the globe, especially in China, Korea, and Japan. So, the Yemenis decided to open it to competition. It became a dog fight and the government eventually awarded the contract to Total (that large French company I've already mentioned with a reputation for under-the-table practices). However, the Yemeni government wanted Total to bring in Hunt and SK (Korea) as partners, since we were the ones who had found the gas and operated the necessary production facilities. Exxon dropped out, since they had purchased Mobil and now had a huge gas play in Qatar. Thus, our partnership consisted of Total, Hunt, SK, and the Yemeni government, and from now on we had to conduct our board meetings in English, French, Korean, and Arabic.

This partnership, led by Total as the operator, had four years to get a gas buyer. (Because of the $6 billion cost for the project, the partnership needed to have contracts from guaranteed buyers of the gas. Then they could use the contracts as collateral to the banks who loaned us the money). To pre-sell the gas was a real challenge that took a lot of time to negotiate, after which we had to complete airtight contracts that included production, delivery, and quality standards.

Our partnership was not able to sell a gas contract in the first four years so we went back to the government and negotiated a four-year extension. Two years after the extension, our joint efforts still had not been successful. At this point, Ray and Jim Jennings, president of Hunt Oil, told me they wanted me to take over as president of Yemen Hunt LNG (our company in the partnership) and just go to the board meetings and do everything to let the contract run out in two years, at which point we could just take it over. I was not to do anything subversive; rather, my mission was to make sure Total does not spend money needlessly and watch for opportunity.

I agreed and asked for three people to shore up my side since I was not an engineer and knew little about LNG. I was an avid reader, however, and engineering and geology was easy reading for me as I love the oil and gas business and had been in it long enough that I could understand the basics.

This project really energized me: it really was very exciting. My associates were Karim Abuhamad, an engineer assigned to the LNG project and an early Yemen team player who set up the training program for Yemenis and rose to become general manager in Yemen Hunt Oil and later served as a senior vice president of all of Hunt's Middle East operations. We worked well together and I learned a lot from Karim, who has multicultural experience and understood the nuances in dealing with our partners. More than that, he knew the technical aspects of LNG and was grounded in the Hunt culture. He is an impressive, multitalented executive, who is a key person in the Hunt organization to this day.

There was also Jerry Bendo, an outstanding Hunt lawyer with a quick inquisitive mind, who understood the complexity of the Yemen LNG contracts. He was extremely valuable with his advice to me in our board meetings. Finally, the team included David Mahmalji, our international accountant, who understood the financial implications of all the LNG contracts since he was a part of the initial team that represented Hunt. Additionally, he had spent a lot of time in Paris in his career, and because of his personality of "never meeting a stranger," knew a lot of people who could get "things done."

Now I had the expertise I needed around me. Karim spoke Arabic, French, and some Korean and David spoke French, Arabic, and three other languages that were, unfortunately, not necessary. Their linguistic talents were important, because the Yemenis spoke Arabic in their group meetings, the French representatives of Total spoke French in theirs, and the Koreans ... well, you get the picture. Because they spoke these languages, Karim and David could eavesdrop and provide intelligence that could at times influence our vote in the board meetings. These guys were great and I have never enjoyed working so much with any team as working with them in our meetings in Dallas, Paris, France,

Seoul, and Sanaa. Hunt was lucky to have the three of them at this critical period.

Now the interesting thing was that when Ray and Jim assigned me to this project, my job was to position ourselves to take over the contract when it expired in 2005. In 2004, when I took over the position and got to know many of our partner players, it began to develop as a team effort to get a buyer. I began to realize that the price of LNG was going up globally because of the growth of China and the conversion in many countries from coal to natural gas. Also, there was a lot of natural gas found across the planet that could not be produced economically, or so it had been believed. But now, because of rising prices and new technology, these gas fields could maybe be profitable. Essentially, I reasoned that with the right conditions, we may be able to find a buyer for Yemen gas before the YLNG contract ran out.

In 2005 I went to Korea for the twentieth-year celebration of SK in Yemen. I was seated with the Korean equivalent of US congressmen at the VIP table and, in the conversation (fortunately many top Koreans spoke good English), I realized that the Korean government was going out for bids for new gas contracts as their ten-year contracts were terminating. These politicians were very patriotic and, since SK was the only bidder that was a Korean company, they probably would be given a contract.

I returned to Dallas and told Jim and Ray that I believed that Total could put a contract together because of Korea and we should face the fact that the partnership may be able to launch the project with a contract. They had doubts.

We were both right, since the Koreans did sign a contract for a third of the offtake. But what surprised us was that the French decided to buy the other 67 percent through government-related companies so we now had enough to finance and build the project. It was indeed launched, in 2006, and Karim was designated as Hunt's partner in Paris. It was a several-year project with bank financing and engineering ensuring its success. I went to Yemen in 2009 for the ceremonial opening. By 2012, the partnership and the Yemeni government were making a good profit.

But then a civil war broke out in Yemen in 2015, driven by Iran's support of the Houthi Shiite minority and their desire to disrupt the underbelly of Saudi Arabia. This shut our sale of gas and, as of this writing (2022), the situation has not improved. Iran's interference has caused the death of thousands either through famine and disease or counterattacks by a coalition force trying to drive them out. Both sides carry the blame, but Iran more so in my opinion.

This was one of the many great projects I was privileged to work on while with Hunt. There were many others, as often Ray would throw me into areas where there was a problem or a challenge.

OTHER JOBS ... BLUE BIRDS

When I interviewed with Ray in 1975, we discussed what I was doing with

EDS and Perot. After describing my background and functions, I jokingly said that I also have Blue Bird tasks. These were jobs that Perot would randomly assign to me, since they had no home. This was kind of a joke and Ray laughingly said he may have some of those too. Little did I know that over time, he would have a lot of these and I would love doing them.

Over time, various titles would be assigned and accumulated (at one point on the corporate records, I was listed as president of five Hunt companies, officer of fifty-two, director of too many to count, trustee of many trusts, and board member of most of the family boards). This was heady stuff, but most of the titles were titular and all that was required was my signature or a name since all these were Hunt-owned companies. Some were operating titles, however, and these I enjoyed.

In other cases, I would take over a function or individual business unit. Sometimes, when we got the unit running, it would be reassigned. Others would be a project with a defined time for completion.

My original title was vice president of administration, which covered the nonfinancial departments in the company. Later, it was a catchall for anything that did not have a box in the corporation. As the years went by, functions and jobs were added to or deleted from my "box."

Thus, eventually, my role became a catchall for activities and startup businesses within Hunt that had no defined parameters or were problem areas. The key to success was to latch on to good managers who were smarter than me.

AVIATION

One of the functions that was put in my area was the aviation department. Initially, when I joined the company, we had a Lockheed JetStar, a four-engine, eight-passenger plane that H. L. Hunt had bought back in 1968.

By 1988 it was twenty years old and, because of the company's success, Ray felt we could afford a new airplane. He told me to look for one.

We bought a twelve-passenger Challenger 601, which I negotiated for and felt we got a good deal. Ray could design the interior the way he wanted. (Just the interior design cost $2 million in 1989 dollars). He approached it systematically, knowing that the plane was an airborne office that was more efficient than flying commercial (although there were times I would rather fly comfortably in first class on American Airlines and get a fun meal with wine served by a flight attendant … especially on overseas flights, where I could get some sleep).

On the Hunt plane, I would typically have to work the entire flight, since there was no outside interference. Our meals were from KFC or fruit, meat, and cheese plates. Ray designed the seating so that we had meeting areas of different configurations depending on the business and number of flyers. This was extremely efficient and I would argue that because of this we did deals that may not have been accomplished otherwise.

In 2005 Ray decided to upgrade to a new plane, so I negotiated for a twelve-place Challenger 603 and an eight-place Lear 40. By 2014 business was good and Ray decided he wanted Challenger 605s; we knew Bombardier (Challenger's manufacturer) was having some financial problems, so we made a very good deal on these. After I retired, Ray bought a couple of Falcon 2000s, which are great planes.

I really enjoyed working with the pilots and ground staff. We had some good managers who kept the passengers safe and the planes running. In my last year, we hired Jerry Aiken, who had extensive experience as an aviation manager. I enjoyed working with Jerry and seeing him bring the aviation department to a new level in both aircraft and efficiency. As of this writing, I am a member of the Hunt Aviation Committee and we have periodic meetings. In my retirement, and if doing something related to Hunt, I am still privileged to occasionally fly on the company planes.

Over the years, I have done a lot of flying, especially overseas. American started the Frequent Flyer program in 1981 and I was an initial member. (I earned over six million miles on American and a cumulative two million on other airlines during the '80s and '90s). In the following years, most airlines followed suit and then refined the programs to where today most earn more money selling miles via credit card expenditures than seat sales. After 2001 and 9/11, we started using the company planes more because it was such a pain to go through security (we do not have to do that with the private flight base operations at the airports). This could save me between two to four hours a day when I was traveling, since you needed to be at a commercial airport generally two hours before the flight. Sometimes, I could make meetings in two or three states in one generally long day. We could do business on the plane without interruptions. Also, coming to a business meeting in your private plane, I feel, added something to the meeting, especially if you were negotiating and they knew you did not need to get to the airport to catch a commercial flight.

A lot of people criticize corporate executives for having the luxury of a private jet. In some ways, I agree with them because many use it for their personal pleasure and charge it to the company. Mostly, these are executives of the company (employees like everyone else) and this is wrong.

However, many corporate executives use the plane as a tool that allows them to save time, do business with their team on the plane and, thus, create a value added for the company. I can tell you that even with a private jet, travel and time away from the family is still wearing, but it beats commercial travel.

Over the years of flying millions and millions of miles in private, commercial, government, and military aircraft, one is bound to have interesting aircraft experiences.

During this period, actually, one might have crashed, crash landed, flown into a wrong airport, flown into a forbidden area, been hit by gunfire, or spent nights in airports because of weather, terrorist threats, or airline inefficiency.

Well, I have experienced all of the above over the years but would like to relate the four most exciting incidents.

Crash Landing

As a sixteen-year-old, I had never flown in an airplane. The father of my best friend's girlfriend owned a single-engine plane in the small town where I grew up. He owned a company called Lynden Transfer and was one of my idols. One day he offered to let the three of us go up in his plane and see the country from the air. It was such a thrill for me: It was a four-place single-engine plane and I was in a back seat behind the pilot's seat. We flew for about an hour and it was then I knew I wanted to be an Air Force pilot.

As we were coming in for landing, there was a malfunction. He could not get the left landing gear to drop. Thus, we flew around dropping fuel and he told us that we were coming in on one wheel in a wet hay field. When we hit the ground, the plane turned to the right and nosed in. (My legs ended up under the pilot's seat but I only suffered scratches). However, a wing and propeller were damaged.

It was a wonderful experience and I would do it again. Several days later, the story was leaked to my mother and she got really mad at us.

Wrong Airport

As for landing in the wrong airport, I had a board meeting in Mexico City so flew down there on the company LearJet. Arriving near the Toluca Airport (outside the city), we encountered fog. We circled for about an hour but could not land, so I called the board chairman and told him that I could not make it and that we were running low on fuel.

The pilots said Acapulco was the closest airport so I told them to refuel there and, because I missed the board meeting, to return to Dallas. We landed in Acapulco.

The airport authorities had no knowledge of our coming. Mind you, this was an area for drug running and a cartel headquarters. When we landed, there were just the two pilots and me. When we taxied up to the terminal in the Lear, soldiers were there to meet us. The pilots went into the airport headquarters to explain what happened and why. The problem was that we wanted to exit Mexico, but the paperwork said we had not even entered Mexico since we did not land anywhere we were supposed to, landing in Acapulco instead.

Since I was the only passenger, they took me to a bare holding room, where they held me for about four hours. They finally concluded I was not a drug smuggler. They then wrestled with the problem of issuing me an exit visa when I did not have an entry visa in the first place (this is a rarity on a passport). So eventually, they stamped me in and out at the same time. Unfortunately, it was a real waste of time and jet fuel.

Rough Landing

On one trip in the 1990s, when Ray and I were traveling to Yemen, we picked up a Lufthansa flight from Frankfurt to Saana via Cairo.

When we landed in Cairo four hours later, Lufthansa had a crew change so a new crew was now going to fly the plane to Saana. Now in Cairo, the elevation is about five hundred feet and, in Sanaa, it is about eight thousand. For some reason during the flight, the new crew or the automatic system did not adjust the instrument for the elevation difference. (At the higher elevation, the air is lighter so a plane needs to adjust as it will have less lift).

We were now three hours late at around midnight on the approach to Sanaa International Airport. Because some adjustments were not made and the air at eight thousand feet was so light, we slowly just dropped out of the sky on the approach and hit the runway, breaking three of the tires and wheel wells on the Airbus. We hit the ground so hard I thought I had injured my jaw.

We were taken off the plane far out on the runway, and when we left three days later, it was still there waiting for repairs so they could return to Germany.

Near Crash

The near crash was in Siberia, Russia. At the end of the Cold War, Hunt was among the first companies to try to do a deal when Russia opened up to foreign investors. We had signed contracts and sent geologists to Siberia to scout prospective areas. In February 1990, we liked what we saw and decided to send a team to the town of Anadyr on the Bering Sea to sign an extension to the contract so we could do a seismic option. From there, we were to go to meetings on the Kamchatka Peninsula and Vladivostok to sign further agreements.

So, in February 1990, we took our Challenger 601 and flew to Siberia via Alaska as it was shorter than going over Europe. In the plane were Ray, Jim Jennings, Ian Maycock, our German consultant Gerhart Martin, and me. Our route was to fly directly to Anchorage, Alaska, from Dallas and then meet up with a Russian navigator who would board and guide us into Anadyr, four hours later (just south of the Arctic Circle).

The first problem we encountered was translation of speed between the Russian navigator and our pilot. We use miles/ hours and they use a different measurement. As a result, when we were approaching the Russian airbase at Anadyr, the pilots had calculated the cross winds at 10 mph when they were actually 50 mph. Fortunately, as we touched down, the plane skidded on the ice-laden Russian runway. For some reason, they did not clean all the ice chunks off, which may have saved our lives later.

When we arrived, some base personnel came out in the weather to meet us, as it was dark because of the extreme northern latitude in winter. All other planes that day had diverted (as we would have, if we had known the cross winds were

50 mph). However, because of our landing the Russian airport staff considered these Texas pilots bold heroes because they came where others feared to go. Thus, they wanted to meet them. Our three pilots stayed on the base and were wined and dined for five days, regaling their hosts with stories of life in America.

The base was on one side of an immense frozen bay and the town of Anadyr was twenty-three miles on the other side. We immediately were put into half-tracks to cross the ice-laden bay in the dark (dark comes early in February in the Arctic Circle). The Russians had two half-tracks for us since they did not have radio contact out in the bay and, if one half-track broke down, they could get the other passengers in the second before we froze to death.

Anadyr was an interesting town ... It was an ugly Soviet-style city with standard apartments where tenants hung their clothes drying outside even in the winter. We would walk everywhere and the temperature was mostly around zero. For four days, we ate reindeer cooked in various forms for three meals a day with cream whitefish, Hungarian tomatoes, and Vietnamese rice. This is all that could be brought in by ship before the bay froze in late September. There was plenty of vodka. The evening meals were fun and very filling. The reindeer was pretty good because it was sauced and seasoned. I got a little tired of it for breakfast, though.

What was really interesting was our rooms. We had a square bathtub that was on a platform three feet off the floor so you had to climb up to get into it. Everything was steam-heated and the rooms were overly warm.

Our clothing was heavy hooded parkas, snow googles, thick mittens, mukluk boots, and wools underneath. I was perfectly comfortable walking around in the early morning and evening when we were not in meetings or meals.

We had meetings during the day to brief the governor and officials on our finds and inform them we wanted to execute the next phase of our contract, which was a seismic project. One day we met with the leaders of the Chukotka Reindeer Association. They were concerned about bringing heavy equipment in and disrupting the herds and herders. We tried to reassure them.

On the fourth day, the governor called us into a meeting to tell us he received a call from Moscow and the terms of the contract had changed. Ray was not happy about this and told him that we had planned to visit an area along the east coast of Kamchatka and Vladivostok. However, since we had a signed contract with the new Russian government and they did not honor that contract, we would cancel our remaining schedule and return to Dallas since the sanctity of contract was a bedrock upon which US business rested.

Unfortunately, most of the Russian bureaucrats did not understand the principles of rule of law or risk reward. They had been conditioned under seventy years of communism and had not been exposed to capitalism.

Ironically, the only group that understood a form of capitalism was the Russian mafia since it was conducive to criminal activities in a communist state. In the following ten years, they teamed up with powerful bureaucrats to control the major natural resource industries in Russia. (We went back in 1999 for a week to see if we could now do business and concluded no, since most of these now-Russian companies in natural resources were put together by questionable means and we saw no real protection for a foreign investor).

Thus, that afternoon we were herded back into the half-tracks and returned to the air base, from which we planned to immediately return to Dallas.

There had been a blizzard the day before, but our pilots had cleared the snow drifts that covered the wings. The winds were so bad, however, they had to put fuel trucks in front of the plane to veer the snow off. By evening, they had cleared the snow, but the storm was still blowing.

Our chief pilot, Jim Wilson, said he was comfortable taking off that evening. Ray was considering it, when the copilot, George Vaeth, came up to him and said if he made the decision to fly that night regardless of the weather, he would not go and instead would get a flight to Moscow the next day and find his way back to Dallas. Ray then decided that we would spend the night.

Fortunately, one of the Russian scientists offered to let us stay with him, his wife, and child in their apartment. We took them up on it. I had brought fresh oranges and bananas with us on the plane and took a bunch to their apartment with us. They were the most gracious hosts.

All four of us shared one room … three on the floor and one would get the bed … Obviously, we would yield to Ray for the bed, but being the kind of person he was, he took a blanket and found the roughest part of the floor and gave Gerhart the bed because he was in his 60s.

Our hostess had a wonderful dinner prepared with good wine and we really enjoyed it. I gave her a bag of oranges and bananas and she was thrilled because they get no fresh fruit up there.

Their boy was about ten and had a pet monkey. Later, during dinner, our hostess left the table and then I heard her shout and scream. Apparently, the boy did not know what a banana was and was feeding them to the monkey. At least, the oranges were salvaged.

It had snowed all night and the pilots had to clear the plane the next morning, which was bright and sunny. By 9:00 a.m., we were ready to take off. The runway was still not fully plowed and packed snow pieces were lying on the runway. I gave what remaining food and produce we had on board to the customs people (a bribe to make sure we were cleared).

We taxied to the end of the runway, bumping on small ice chunks. Our pilot then turned and powered up and we began moving down the runway again with occasional bumps from pieces of ice.

I am facing the rear of the plane in my seat and am taking pictures of the Russian military equipment as we reach take-off speed. I then see the left wing going up and conclude the right wing is going down and we may crash. I go into a body fold and feel a bump where the right wing is located.

Our pilots did a full power and rudder control and we slowly came back to level wings as we climbed to altitude. Knowing we had barely escaped a crash, we opened up the wine during our four-hour flight back to Alaska.

We did not know how lucky we were until we landed in Anchorage and George Vaeth and I got out to check the wing. It was as if someone had taken a hacksaw and some sandpaper and removed a quarter inch of the winglet.

We were very lucky. Apparently, the right wing had hit the ground in the air (the slight bump we felt) but because of the ice on the runway, we slid rather than cartwheeled in that fraction of a second. I took a picture of the winglet, which is now in the Hunt Hanger.

The pilots said the last twelve inches of the wing was not structural and we could still fly, so we refueled, got back on the plane, and flew another seven hours to Dallas. We were all pretty wired and Ray instructed us to never tell his wife, Nancy, about it.

It was one of the times I cheated death and has been a great story to tell over cocktails.

CHAPTER TWENTY-SEVEN

AND MORE JOBS

As I alluded to earlier, in the mid-1990s, Chris Kleinert, Ashlee Hunt's husband, was hired by Hunt Consolidated, Inc. Chris is a very bright and personable executive who received his MBA from TCU and worked for Procter and Gamble and a major bank. Based on this training, Ray reasoned that Chris had the "moxie" to be a key executive in the family company and he was right.

The first time I met Chris he was dating Ray and Nancy's daughter, Ashlee, at SMU. We had dinner one evening in an Italian restaurant with Nancy's father and mother, Judge and Shirley Hunter. (Judge Elmo Hunter was a famous federal judge who tried a lot of the Chicago criminal cases and one of the smartest and most perceptive men I have ever met. He was a joy to be around). Now, we selected this place since Ray, unbeknown to Elmo, had a fish mounted for him on its wall. Elmo had caught the permit in Mexico the previous spring.

Let me digress here. For several years, Ray would sponsor a fishing trip in Mexico to celebrate Elmo's birthday. Each year he would invite different people … like Bob Gates, former director of the CIA and later secretary of DOD, Larry Eagleburger, former secretary of state, John Gavin, movie star and former ambassador to Mexico, General Norman Schwarzkopf, and many other notables and company CEOs. (I should point out that none of our guests were in public office at the time). It became an in-thing to be invited to Elmo's birthday party in the Yucatan. (I always felt so privileged to be a part of it). General Schwarzkopf was my tent mate for four days and three nights, so I got to know him and we became friends. Four months later, he went on to head the Invasion into Kuwait (Desert Storm, the first Gulf War in 1991). I sent him a book on terror control in Iraq, just before he led the troops into Iraq, and he wrote me a nice letter back while in his bunker (which is really a collector's item).

Now, going back to Chris, Ray brought the mounted fish to the dinner and I worked with the manager to put it on the wall above the long table where we were sitting. Everyone at the table knew that it was a fish that Elmo had caught (except Elmo and his wife, Shirley).

Throughout the dinner conversation someone would casually mention the fish on the wall … Nancy said it must be a fish from the Mediterranean Sea since it was an Italian restaurant. Shirley (not knowing it was Elmo's) said it should not have been mounted since it was so small.

Ray eventually got up and gave his talk while Chris (who was just meeting the mob here) stood up and delivered the fish to the Judge in a very classy manner. I knew right then I liked the kid and he was the one for Ashlee. The Judge was completely surprised that the fish was his.

I really enjoyed working with Chris. He had an "I never met a stranger personality" and an analytical mind that made him perfect for the new role of private equity. I enjoyed in those early years working in this area with Mike Bierman, Fulton Murray and Chris. Chris built a very successful business line for Hunt that returned a lot of capital when it was needed; he then went on to head the entire investment side of the business.

A natural athlete and former baseball player, Chris has a Bobby Jones golf swing and could be a no handicap if he played regularly. In order to spend more time with him and get to know him, we would have a tennis game at Bent Tree Country Club at 6:00 a.m. a couple of times a week. I loved tennis in those days and especially playing against Chris, who was such a challenge. Fortunately, we played before the club opened (we had a special key), as our competitive yelling and shouting may have created problems later in the day. On very rare occasions, I would beat him and that really made my day.

BUILDINGS ... FOUNTAIN PLACE AND HUNT HEADQUARTERS 1900 NORTH AKARD

Another "task" that was added to my portfolio was new buildings. In 1989 we leased and decided to move to a new building in downtown Dallas. As I briefly touched on earlier, it was called Fountain Place and was the most advanced building in Dallas in the late 1980s. Unfortunately, when it was built, the market was soft and it had some finishing problems and could not be leased up. Ray recognized an opportunity since he felt the problems were solvable and knew he could negotiate a good lease since Hunt had 380,000 square feet to trade with (35 percent of the building).

Our lease in the old headquarters was up, and we had to negotiate new terms. Personally, I was in favor of hard negotiating with the owner of the building we were in. John Scovell wanted Hunt to build a building in the Reunion property that we owned. Doc Cornutt wanted to build a building in North Dallas where many of our employees lived. But Ray wanted to stay downtown.

As I mentioned already, at that time, the office market was soft and the building Ray was looking at had some construction problems that were being cleaned up. For example, windows kept falling out because of some faulty frames. Also, the design was such that in winter, ice would form on the slanted sides and then slide off in big sheets when it warmed up. Ray knew all these were solvable issues so decided to negotiate a favorable deal. At first, he tried to buy it at a low price. A New York bank owned it and wanted to get out from under it. Ray's offer was too low, however.

The building was sold to an Australian investor. He now owned a building that was less than 50 percent leased. Ray decided to go for it, and since the rest of us felt it was a bad deal, he decided to ignore us completely and then secretly negotiated a very favorable deal with the Australian, Kerry Stokes.

The deal he and his financial chief, Tony Copp, did was unbelievable.

First, he got a well-below market lease rate for a Class A building in downtown Dallas.

Second, he got an unheard of, unbelievable $35 per square foot build-out allowance ($12,500,000).

Third, he got the management contract for his real estate arm, Woodbine Development Corporation, which was to be paid $2 million per year to manage the building.

Fourth, he got a carried interest of 25 percent if Stokes ever refinanced the building. Interestingly, because of Hunt's added square footage, Stokes now had the building leased at 85 percent. Now he refinanced the building and pulled out $32 million. When he did, Hunt got $8 million out of it.

Fifth, Hunt got the two top floors, which was the peak of the building (floors 57 and 58), and a total of about two thousand square feet. The space was all glass with a 360-degree view. We made a conference room on 58 and a dining area on 57 and it was the place to be invited to in the 1990s. It had some railings for window washers around it. I remember the time when we put on a very fancy lunch for some top Mexican officials with whom we were meeting. All of a sudden, four buzzards landed on those railings and intensely stared down at us from about fifteen feet, while we were eating. It made such a great lunch conversation.

When we would meet with those Mexican officials in Mexico City, they would always open the meeting with the story about the buzzards. That facility was essentially in the sky overlooking Dallas and was a wonderful sales tool for our various businesses.

By 2004 I reminded Ray that our leases were coming up again and we could extend or look elsewhere. We could not beat the building we were in, since it was on the "Park Avenue" of Dallas.

By now, Ray felt he wanted to make (I think) a statement to show he was committed to downtown. The mayor was Laura Miller, a liberal journalist who did not understand how the economy of Dallas worked and who wanted Dallas to be free of companies that wanted special deals to come to the city. Before becoming mayor, she was an investigative reporter for a local newspaper called the *Dallas Observer*.

She did not like some of the wealthy in Dallas, since she felt they were exploiting "someone." Once elected, with no experience in the "art of compromise" to get something done, she basically destroyed Dallas as a major sports center.

The Dallas Cowboys wanted to build a new stadium in Dallas, but she fought it when they requested some bond money to help finance it. The city council in Arlington saw an opportunity and offered to help finance it. Thus, the new stadium went to Arlington, which now has the most advanced sports and entertainment complex in Texas. That could have been in downtown Dallas and earned the city millions of dollars in tax revenues and been a future center for athletic activities in the Metroplex. By her actions, Miller and her allies deprived Dallas of millions of tax dollars.

Now, Laura Miller did not like Ray Hunt. Ray had signed a master agreement in the mid-1970s with the then-city manager, George Schrader, to develop the Reunion area. Ray had sixteen acres and the City had fourteen acres in an ugly sump area on the far west edge of downtown. The plan was to develop the area together. They negotiated a master agreement where Hunt would build the first facility and would lease the rest of Hunt land to the city for parking lots in lieu of taxes to be paid on the raw land. (I believe this was the largest deal between a private developer and a city in the nation). Ray built the Hyatt Hotel and Reunion Tower in the first phase (which is a Dallas landmark). The city then built a sports arena and parking garage. Ross Perot Jr. later bought the Mavericks and built a new stadium at Victory, thus making the old area obsolete.

Later, the old arena was torn down because the cost to maintain it was a drain and the land was traded to Hunt for Hunt land that was next to the Convention Center. While in office, Mayor Miller sought to change the master agreement. With that background, the conditions were lined up for a fight with Mayor Miller.

Our lease for Fountain Place was set to end in 2007. In 2004, I told Ray we should start negotiating for new leases. Again, John wanted to build at Reunion. Ray was leaning toward building his own building.

I called Gene Sanger who headed Hunt Realty and suggested he find some locations. He did and then we got Ray in Gene's car and drove around to see some of the listings. We initially took him to Reunion to show how bad that choice would be for our office building and then stopped by four others. The minute we saw the last one, at Akard, Ray knew it was the one. There was a contract on the property but we submitted a backup and soon got it. Pat Gibson, who later became head of Hunt Realty, successfully acquired this lot and later the one next to it.

Next, we selected a developer (our Woodbine partner), an architect, Beck, and a designer, Gensler. Now with a rough plan, we approached the city council, telling them we would build downtown if we could get a tax abatement (reminding them that Hunt had owned property in many great locations in the suburbs). Laura Miller fought it, but the council came through, especially since they had previously given a Japanese company a tax abatement for building downtown.

It took two years to build the fourteen-story, 480,000 square foot building. It was state-of-the-art construction and cutting-edge design. Ray was the assistant architect and his creativity gave it the touch that allowed it to win many national and international awards. Initially, I was spending about 30 percent of my time on the building and then 80 percent of my time in the last year of finishing out. It was a special building.

It was engineered for our people who would spend a third of their day in the building. Gensler, led by Judy Pesek, did an outstanding job with the design that Ray wanted. Beck led by Rick del Monte did a wonderful job on the design of the building. They and their staff were such a joy to work with. Woodbine's engineer, Dana Swope, was the real conductor on this project that made it "sing." It is professionals like her that made my job so enjoyable. She was smart and tough and made very tough contractors tremble if they did not meet the schedule or acquired the supply they promised.

We went with a basic standard size office for professionals, managers, and officers. All others had well-engineered cubicles. This initially eliminated the "my office is better than yours" game. Additionally, we had light from the window bleed into the corridor through three-foot glass windows on walls and partitions so that every employee had access to natural light. The shades and lighting were computer-controlled so every desk had adequate lighting in the workspace. Our furniture was selected by employee votes, as were the desk chairs. We had specifically designed desks for our geologists, engineers, and geophysicists so they could lay out maps and logs. (Within four years, these became obsolete because they could now use computer screens for this function).

Ray wanted the employees, rather than the executives, to have the best part of the building so he designated the top two floors for meeting rooms and cafeteria. We contracted with Wolfgang Puck to prepare and serve the meals to our employees at a subsidized price so that even the lowest-paid could afford a good meal. Additionally, he had them provide subsidized meals after 3:00 p.m. so single and working mothers (and fathers) could bring home a dinner and they would not have to stop to buy food or cook when they got home. Many employees took advantage of this option.

The top of the floor was incredible, because of the view. Even though we were only fourteen stories, we were on the high point in Dallas and though we were surrounded by tall buildings, Ray realized that that location would have the Arts District on one side and the old Cumberland School on the other side and the freeway (later Klyde Warren Park) in front of us. Thus, we had great unencumbered views on three sides, which probably made it the most expensive piece of real estate in Dallas at the time. And even then, Ray went further to make it an indelible experience for anyone who visited it.

The ceiling was a replica of the night sky as it had been when Hunt Oil Company was formed in 1930 ... and of course the view around Dallas was such that the food service workers who normally worked in the lower bowels of a building were excited to work on that floor.

The food was outstanding ... Puck hired Michelle Millwood as manager, and her creativity made the Commons a wonderful place in the company.

It had a practical side too, as now employees could get wholesome tasty food without leaving the building. Additionally, if you were trading calls with someone, you could normally find them up there for lunch.

We built a master coffee bar on each floor where coffee, water, and soft drinks were available to employees free of charge. Also, the bars had refrigerators and microwaves if someone wanted to bring their own lunch. We designed long stand-up tables so people could converse while having coffee. These and the Commons did a lot for internal communications, which is essential in business.

We took our two required fire stairwells and widened them and made them user-friendly with color and sage sayings on the walls. Additionally, we built a see-through circular stairway that connected the seventh to the twelfth floor out of stone and decorated each floor stop with an attractive fossil display at the elevator lobby and at the entrance to the restrooms.

The displays were all interesting and unique. On the seventh floor the display was five mammoth tusks of various sizes that I bought from some Russians in a hotel room in Tucson, Arizona in 2005. I paid $300 per tusk and wrote a check since they did not take a credit card and I had no cash. I had read Russian gangs had a business going because of global warming. They had people looking at the melting glaciers in Siberia for frozen mammoths that were twenty-five thousand to fifty thousand years old. We discovered they would hack off some tusk and sell them at fossil shows. They had nine on the bed in that hotel room and we bought six of them.

By 2006 the Chinese had found this market and were buying up everything since the tusks were ivory and the Chinese would use them for intricate carvings. The sale of elephant ivory is illegal, globally, so this was the only legal ivory they could get. The price really went up the next year and, by 2007, these Russians were no longer traveling to Tucson as the Russian government was aggressively trying to stop the smuggling mammoth and mastodon tusks trade. I went back to the show in 2017 and the price of mammoth tusks was in the thousands, if you could find any. Also, on that first trip, I could have bought some mammoth body hair (it was reddish and coarse) but did not and have always regretted it (although it could have been fake).

Another fossil (although a replica) was the Utahraptor head on the thirteenth-floor restroom. I wanted this item because of the story behind it and its adjacency to our Preston Nutter Ranch.

The movie *Jurassic Park* came out while we were building the headquarters. In the movie, if you saw it, these small dinosaurs called raptors were portrayed as predators, about six or seven feet in height. At that time, the largest raptor that had ever been found was about three feet high.

Paleontologists (scientists that study dinosaurs) kind of laughed at the movie since they felt Steve Spielberg had taken a "Hollywood license" to create something that was not known to exist.

However, after the movie had been out for about six months, a seven-foot raptor was discovered in Utah not too far from the Preston Nutter Ranch. It was named the Utahraptor and the bones and skull were taken to the Natural History Museum in Price, Utah (near our ranch). I asked our manager at Preston Nutter (Blair and Kresha Eastland were "big dogs" in that part of Utah) to see if we could get a cast made. Somehow, they got it done and it's on the thirteenth floor of the Hunt Headquarters. Interestingly, the finders named the fossil after Spielberg as he was going to make a contribution to the museum. We wanted this replica as I felt this was a story that all employees and guests could relate to since most had seen the original *Jurassic Park*.

Another unique thing about the building is that we designed the elevator lobbies in concave form so you feel you are walking into a slightly enclosed space.

Then we added different unique rock slabs on the walls that either were from a country where we were doing business or from one we had targeted. Every lobby on every floor is unique and beautiful.

The lobby at the entrance is the best one, as this is where the guests first meet the company. It is glass on three sides and can be seen from the road. Many people come in thinking it is an extension of the Dallas Museum of Art next door since we had an incredible mineral display that people could see from the street. There are water gardens on all sides and inside the lobby (some are so subtle that we eventually had to put stanchions around because guests talking on cell phones would occasionally fall in). Often, we would have people come in off the street thinking it was a fancy hotel (the Fairmont next door).

One of the great displays is the Life in the Day of Hunt, which are large photos of the company activities that are changed quarterly, and also a plinth of flags of the many countries Hunt is doing business in.

However, the best is the Foucault Pendulum. In the front center of the lobby, Ray wanted a signature piece that could be seen from all three sides. I wanted to put a cave there that had stalactites and stalagmites from caves in China, which we could get because of the Three Gorges Dam being built that would flood those caves. I envisioned guests walking through this impressive cave.

Ray rejected the idea because he wanted something that could be seen from the road.

I then mentioned a Foucault Pendulum I had seen in the Smithsonian Museum in Washington, DC. It was an experiment that demonstrated the earth's rotation. The pendulum would swing to-and-fro while the earth rotated beneath it. Pegs were mounted on the rim and the arm of the pendulum would slowly knock down the pegs as the earth turned.

Ray liked the idea and chose to have our design team build an original one out of colored rock that was cut and shaped with high pressure water and then assembled into an elaborate tile-like carved display that clearly demonstrated the rotation of the earth and was also a piece of art. It became an instant success and immediately attracted guests when they first went into the building. Most thought it was a type of clock until they read the plaque.

Actually, it became a challenge after Klyde Warren Park opened next door because visitors to the Arts District, after seeing the elaborate display, assumed it was just another building in the Arts District and would walk in to check it out. We eventually had to put guards at the entrance to explain that this was an office building.

Ray and I liked practical jokes, and, with the pendulum, we saw an opportunity. The Woodbine Real Estate offices were on the third floor and John Scovell's office was directly above the swinging pendulum. In fact, his large antique conference table was directly over it. Thus, we wanted to make John think he was hearing the tick/tock of the pendulum.

After we moved in, we had a small metronome put in the big leg of his conference table. We turned it on to the slowest cadence and it was "tick/tock" all day long. He thought it was the pendulum and was very upset that we did not figure it out before we built the thing (he would call me four times a day). I sent our building manager, Ben Tyner, up to see how he could mitigate it (Ben was in on the joke). He told John we could put egg carton insulation on the floor (raising it two inches) and cut the sound by 50 percent. John was furious.

John never figured out the cadence difference between the metronome and the pendulum but a young engineer who worked on the building and worked for John told him the truth on the third day (because it was Christmas bonus time). I had wanted to let it go on for a week.

This was one of the best practical jokes we have ever played and the whole town eventually knew about it.

We played another good joke on Gene Sanger, the head of Hunt Realty. The seventh floor was designed for our real estate operations and Gene's office was a large corner office that "winged out." Now, the first seven floors of the building had a southwest corner that was curved. The eighth through the fourteenth floors were changed to a rectangle shape.

Because of the change we made, an outdoor deck attached to the eighth floor, which was actually the roof of the "winged out" seventh floor. Thus, a big portion of this deck was over Gene's office. It was very elaborate, with several large planters spaced around. It was to be used for entertainment.

When the deck was being completed, I invited Gene to come up and see it. At that time, we were putting yards of dirt into the huge planter over Gene's to-be office. Because of the irrigation and weight, he was convinced that it would eventually leak and would flow down into his office after a huge rain. He grumbled about this for the next week.

I made a mental note and then called Ben Tyner and told him we wanted to play a joke on Sanger and explained Gene's paranoia over the huge planter above his office. I then asked Ben to wait until we had a major rainstorm after we moved in, and then set up a huge rain damage mess in Gene's office to simulate a bad leak.

Ben did the job just right. A couple of months later, there was a three-inch rain one Sunday afternoon. Ben came in very early that Monday morning and replaced two beautiful ceiling tiles with two he had made wet and stained. He then put a bucket of water up there with a small pin hole that would drip through the stained tiles into a large black plastic garbage can. To this, he added yellow tape lines to show it was a damaged area encompassing half of Gene's office.

Gene came in that morning, called me, and asked me to come down to his office as he wanted to show me something. I acted surprised when I saw the mess. He then harped that he had warned us that this would happen and he was not happy.

He left to go into a meeting with Ray and told me he was going to bring Ray around to see the damage. (Ray, of course, was in on the joke).

When he left, I called Ben and he and his team carted all the props away and replaced the two ugly stained tiles with the two clean ones.

About twenty minutes later, Gene returned with Ray explaining the problem and then walked into the office to show him. Of course by now things were back to normal.

For a moment he was confused, trying to find the damage and the props. He then saw my smile and knew he had been had. Everyone had a good laugh.

Another good joke we played was in the old Fountain Place building. This is one of the most unusual and beautiful buildings in Dallas because of its shape, which also created a lot of columns and posts errantly in the offices on one side. One year, Jim Jennings (before he became president) was in charge of all oil and gas exploration for Hunt. He had a big office, but it had 4x4 buttress support going through it. It actually made the office more interesting but theoretically took sixteen square feet out of it. That year, Jim promoted Ian Maycock to chief geologist and moved him from London to Dallas. When he came over for the review, I showed him an office next to Jim's, which was open and did not have a buttress, telling him that this would be his office. He was very pleased at having such a big, impressive office.

Now, the joke that Jim and I played on him was this. Again, we had our then-building manager, Bob Todd, build a cheap 5x5 sheet rock structure and place it in the center of the office (a false buttress bigger than Jennings's).

When Ian returned to the US and was moving into his office, he was shocked to see this clunky structure, bigger than Jim's, in the middle of the office and which of course he had not seen when he looked at the office earlier in the year. I told him that the company had a policy that a subordinate could not have an office larger than his boss's so we had to take twenty-five square feet out of his. I told him not to worry because he could now hang more pictures, maps, etc. He was confused and was certainly ready to give his Scottish opinion, when the group in on the joke burst into the office and Todd tore down the structures. Ian had a good laugh.

Over the years, I have played a lot of practical jokes ... too many to mention here. I inherited this tendency from my Dad and his family. My Dad had an incredible mind for practical jokes. Also, he had his six sisters and a brother who were flowing with them. Most people at Christmas bond and refresh. My Dad's family played practical jokes on each other at our Christmas Day dinners.

I loved it and learned the technique of how to be funny but not to do harm or have anyone be embarrassed or lose face. In fact, I learned that a truly good practical joke is one where the recipient enjoys telling it to him or herself.

That has been one of the real joys of working for Ray and Ross, as this was their philosophy too.

REAL ESTATE

In 1991 Ray asked me to take over some of the real estate operations (another addition to my existing duties). Up to then, Hunt had a real estate subsidiary called Woodbine, which was run by John Scovell, who reported to Walt Humann. Also, our CFO, a brilliant accountant named Doc Cornutt, was forming some real estate limited partnerships with partners who had great ideas and the "fire in the belly" to build a business but needed capital to execute.

By 1991 much of Hunt's real estate was not doing well and Ray had paid millions in interest payments to hold everything together. The real estate market had gone through a "negative" tax change and the "savings and loan" scandals of the late '80s. As a result, the real estate industry was on its knees.

So, that year, Ray decided to break up the real estate properties and make our executives our partners and set them up in joint venture companies with the real estate assets he owned. Essentially, he fired Walt and John and made them partners so they had their "hind ends" hung out on the deals they would now do. We took the real estate assets and broke them up so they could manage them for a fee and then try to build the partnership.

Walt did not want to build a big business (but just operate a profitable project or two) with this opportunity, since he was also involved in many Dallas community activities that had a great impact on the growth of Dallas. Walt was later recognized with many prominent awards for these endeavors. He is an incredible person who I am honored to call my colleague and friend.

John went on to build an incredible company in the partnership, one that has left its mark on properties all over the country. Initially, he did not want to do this and I spent three months negotiating with him on the breakup to make him happy. John is another good friend with a brilliant mind and a nose for quality real estate.

Ray asked me to take over the real estate operation in order to get it running. Essentially, we now had a number of different limited partners with business from apartments, hotels, office buildings, lot developments, and industrial and commercial warehouses spanning the United States.

I was the coordinator of this until it was up and running and then turned it over to Gene Sanger, who was a true real estate professional who began to build Hunt's real estate division. We then put the family real holdings (separate from in the company) into a company called Hunt Resources, which I ran with the sole purpose of selling or liquidating. It took a couple of years but eventually we were successful (another part time title and job).

I could not have done any of this without having great people who worked for me in the area.

I found out in my career that the trick to being a successful executive was to hire people smarter and more competent than you; don't take credit for anything but pass it on to your associates; and make sure you recognize and reward them.

This has been the key to my success. I have always had a saying on my office wall that stresses this point:

"THERE IS NO LIMIT TO WHAT A MAN CAN DO OR WHERE HE CAN GO IF HE DOESN'T MIND WHO GETS THE CREDIT."

CHAPTER TWENTY-EIGHT

MY FORTUNATE CONNECTION WITH THE PEROT AND HUNT FAMILIES

I was very fortunate to have been able to link my career to the families of two of the great leaders our country produced in the last half of the twentieth century: H. Ross Perot and Ray L. Hunt.

For over fifty years, I have been privileged to know, work for, and become close friends to both men and their immediate families. How did this happen?

I often think the path of life is like a forked tree. One makes decisions as one goes forward along the path, at every fork that comes along. The key, I believe, is to be prepared for opportunity when it strikes.

Some people are prepared to take a risk, some are somewhat apprehensive to do so, and some are happy with a risk-free and secure environment. I for one have always been willing to take a risk if I feel it will move me forward and help my family.

This may have been driven by a simple event that happened when I was ten years old. My mother was moving furniture into a room and I was helping her. She was convinced a bed would not fit in the tight space she wanted it to fit into. I told her it would and she doubted me (I was not sure but I knew it would be close). I still argued with her and told her to trust me. She agreed and I moved it: it fit perfectly, with half an inch to spare.

I think this simple event led me to believe nothing was impossible and that feeling became a baseline for the confidence I had in myself. I think high school sports and activities re enforced this too.

Now, during this journey, in retrospect, I realize there were many friends or strangers who, by their actions, influenced me directly or indirectly to take these forks.

It is kind of like the great 1930s Jimmy Stewart/Donna Reed movie, *It's a Wonderful Life* shown every Christmas. However, instead of me not being there, if these individuals had not been there, I know that my life would have been different.

At this stage in my life, I now relish reflecting on the people who influenced my course in life … and there are many.

Obviously, a key influence is your parents and friends while growing up. There are many people in your formative years that influence your decisions. We all should, when we get to that reflective period in life, try to recall those people, as they are the ones you are beholden to (or wish you'd never met). Remember that these folks can come from all walks of life.

As for me, I will list the major ones in my formative years and then the few specific ones later who caused me to take "the forks."

First is my mother. She was extremely intelligent and today would be a great leader, if not president of the United States. She was an outlier and, by her actions, gave me the confidence to take risks. She encouraged me to always be polite and engage in conversation and would challenge me at the dinner table to discuss the news of the day. As a teacher, she would take additional college courses during the summer to work for a PhD credit. She would take me with her (under age seven) and put me in the college day care while she was in class. (I got kicked out of one for being an outlier ... arguing with the teacher). When I turned seven (no child labor laws then), I was farmed out into the fields to pick strawberries and raspberries so I would learn the "life of farming," which I did for the next nine years. This made me want to go to college so I would not have to in fact live life as a farmer. (Ironically, all I want to do now is farm and experiment with my automated greenhouse on our farm outside Dallas).

She instilled this attitude toward life in my sister, your aunt and great-aunt Connie. Now you know why she takes charge no matter how large the group.

My dad never met a stranger and he taught me how to meet and listen to people. I got my love of telling stories from him. He had a great way to hold a listener captivated by his varied life experiences. He was one of the best storytellers I knew until I met James A. Baker III.

My father did not go to college. He could have done so on a baseball scholarship but he needed to work to make ends meet since he lost both his mom and dad before he graduated from high school.

Where I lived in northern Washington State, hunting and fishing were not only a sport, they were a source of good fresh food. My dad spent many weekends teaching me hunting, fishing, clamming, crabbing and picking fruit and nuts from wild trees. He taught me a lot about animal behavior.

As a very good athlete, he would work with me constantly on football, basketball, and baseball (all of which he played). As a result, I became a good athlete in all three sports in high school and in baseball for a year in college (football ... quarterback was my best but at 5' 9.5," I was too short and light for college so I opted for baseball). And because of my mom's encouragement, I became class president of three classes, the student body president, and president of the all-county high school confederation. Additionally I engaged in a whole slew of other student activities during my high school years (the nice thing about a small high school is that one could participate in many activities and build self-esteem and a skill set).

High school teachers had great influence … coaches on leadership and character … others on learning and culture. Later, some college teachers had a little more influence on me. But, because of the small size of the high school, I had teachers who were my parents' friends, and, in essence, were embedded in the Lynden community and made sure all their kids had the best they could give them.

Thus, as Hillary Clinton wrote, "we had a village that raised us." Later, in the 2000s, I was selected as an outstanding alumnus of Lynden High School and was asked to speak to the student body during their homecoming weekend. My topic was on the advantage of being raised in and attending a school in a small town. I stressed the personal skills necessary in dealing with people who knew your parents. If you forgot to say hi on the downtown street to a friend of your mom's, you got chewed out when you got home, as Mrs. So and So called her and told her Tommy did not say "hi" (got a great laugh from the student body).

The other thing I stressed was the ability to build one's self-esteem in life. Since there were so many athletic, cultural, academic, and leadership roles available in the smaller school, more students could partake in them and gain confidence and guidance (my talk must have scored, since a large number of teachers came up to me and asked for my written presentation).

Now, as to the forks of life and those who influenced me, I will now lay down the trail for you to follow.

The first is Franz Michel, professor of Far East History at the University of Washington. He got me interested in China and Russia. Thus, I took my geography degree in this area.

Another, Professor Peterson, taught a course on Southwest Asia and sparked my interest in a country called Yemen, which was little known then. She had spent time there and really piqued my interest. It might be argued that, because of that, Hunt ventured into Yemen in 1981. When the Yemen deal was brought to us, I was excited about it because of what I had studied and what we did not know about Yemen. This is why I felt we should go look at the deal and went with Mujib and Ian to visit the country. We discovered oil and gas in great quantities, changing the country and our company, too.

I was in the Fiji fraternity (Phi Gamma Delta), which was among the top fraternity houses on campus. One of my fraternity brothers, Steve Duzan, was very bright and we bonded quickly (as my mom always told me to learn from those smarter than me). He was ambitious and a risk taker (after college, he started a drug company and made a "zillion dollars").

In his junior year, he became homecoming chairman and talked me into becoming the sign chairman. This was a big deal at our university. I was apprehensive but Steve convinced me to do it. The next year, he talked me into throwing my hat into the group applying for homecoming chairman. I did and was selected. It was a great learning experience for me, and when I applied to the AFROTC, I was a candidate with leadership skills. Score one for Steve Duzan, as that was a fork in my road (to become important later).

Because of the homecoming chairmanship, baseball, and several other campus activities and participation in honor organizations, I was awarded Distinguished Military Graduate in Air Force Reserves Officer Training (an honor given to just 10 percent of graduates). This was very important in the 1960s and gave me special status as a Regular Officer in the USAF and eventually, I think, got me assigned to the USAF officer training school in San Antonio, Texas. Here I did well and loved my job of lecturing to the officer trainees on foreign affairs and war.

But I knew my long-term future was not in the Air Force. I decided to take a risk and resign my commission (and reject a comfortable life in the USAF) in order to go to the Thunderbird School in Arizona (even though Sharon was pregnant) to obtain an advanced degree in international banking with a future job in mind.

The fork here was Doug Collins, a close friend and fellow officer at the USAF officer training school, who gave my name to Jim Just, a recruiter for a small software company called Electronic Data Systems in Dallas. It was owned by a guy named Ross Perot.

Jim Just called me and came to San Antonio to interview Sharon and me for a couple of evenings. The interview would not be legal now, since we had to tell him everything we had done since age six and take a battery of tests. Apparently, I passed the tests, since he invited me to Dallas to visit the company. After meeting Ross Perot and getting a feeling for the EDS, when I got back to San Antonio, I told Sharon that this was the future and that I wanted to join EDS. She agreed and I called Mitch and told him I accepted. We shifted from Arizona to Texas for our future. Thanks to Doug Collins.

Another fork was in the spring of 1968. I described it a bit previously but want to pause on it a little here, with more detail to illustrate this "fork in the road" concept. Now, with EDS, we lived in an apartment in Richardson, Texas, and one Sunday afternoon at the pool, we met some neighbors, Ron and Ann Walker, who told us they had gotten our mail by mistake. They were from Arizona and Ron worked for Hudson Pharmaceuticals. He was telling me that he had been approached by a friend to work for Richard Nixon's upcoming 1968 presidential campaign as an advance man. I had never heard of an advance man and Ron's detailed description made it seem like a job from heaven on a campaign. I told him how lucky he was.

Interestingly, I was called into Perot's office a couple of weeks later and asked by him to come up with a plan on how computers could be used in the 1968 campaign. I think I was selected because I was the only liberal arts major in the training program and knew something about foreign affairs. Another trainee and I drafted up a plan (in those days, computers were bulldozers of information and did not have today's magic algorithms) and brought it back to Perot. He took it to New York to present the concepts to Nixon. Nixon liked it and wanted Perot's support. Perot said he could give money but he could also handpick some of his people to work on the campaign. Nixon liked the latter idea.

Ross came back to Dallas and called me to see if I would like to work for Nixon. I said I was a Reagan man but would love the opportunity and would give it all I had. He said a man named John Ehrlichman was coming in the next few days to interview individuals for the campaign. I told Ross I was really interested and knew what they were looking for (thanks to Ron Walker).

A few days later, I met with Ehrlichman. He was a real estate lawyer from Seattle. One of his biggest clients was the father of my pledge class fraternity brother Kemper Freeman. We had a great conversation and he really drilled down on my activities in college. I really liked John and got to know him better during the course of the campaign.

The next week, Ross called me and said Ehrlichman wanted me on the team and asked me to report to a room at the Statler Hotel in downtown Dallas the following week. Here I would meet John Nidecker, an old, experienced advance man, as well as another advance man trainee like myself. Nixon was coming to Dallas and we would set up an airport rally at Love Field.

On the appointed day, I showed up at the room, and when I walked in, I met Rally John Nidecker, a legend in the campaign world who, over the next few months, would teach me a lot. The other trainee, who was very surprised to see me, was Ron Walker. (As I mentioned earlier, to this day, I think he figured I maneuvered into the position after talking with him at the pool).

Ron became a great friend and went on after the campaign to join the White House Staff, rising to become head of the presidential advance staff and, later, head of the National Park Service. He served as a top executive at Korn Ferry and became a key person in Republican circles (including a role as director of the 1984 Republican Convention in Dallas).

So as you can see, my work on Ross's staff was another fork that opened up a lot of opportunities. Ross by this time was a known personality with vast wealth and was getting involved in both national and international activities. He threw me into the middle of many of them, where my advance man training and White House contacts were helpful.

There were many other forks I took in the business world that led to an interesting and enjoyable business career. Of course, the biggest fork of all was going with Ray Hunt, which was prompted by Murphy Martin.

Murphy had a tremendous influence on my life. He was a successful nationally known newsman who operated out of New York and traveled the world as a top ABC reporter covering the major events overseas and in the United States in the late 1950s and 1960s. Later he was the anchor on ABC in New York on the evening news (this was when there were only three networks for the entire country).

As a result, he had many famous friends (names you will now need to google but were world famous then, like Howard Cosell, Mickey Mantle, and many, many others). When I would travel to New York on business with him, we often went to a bar in the late afternoon to have a drink with these friends. It was a different world for me.

Murphy also had the most perfect vocal cords and a distinctive ability to frame words into pictures or on a canvas. I used to love to hear him just talk. He taught me many useful tricks, as I was giving a lot of talks on the POW activities during that period and needed to be able to convey a convincing message. He and his wife Joyce were very close friends of ours.

At some point, they decided to leave the high life of New York and move back to Dallas. Murphy was hired by ABC's Channel 8 and became a local newscaster and had a weekly special interest program, which is where he met Perot and which led to his being hired by Ross to run his POW program.

Actually, we had a group I called the M5S that worked with Ross on the POW issue and all had great influence on me.

M-1 was Chuck McKinley, the 1963 Wimbledon Champion in Tennis and the 1964 runner-up. I have told you of my experiences with Chuck in Vietnam and Laos. He imparted to me his love of tennis. We became good friends and he opened me up to his world on Wall Street when I would go to New York.

M-2 was Murphy Martin. I have explained above some things about him and earlier mentioned his POW activities. He was a key leader and inspiration for all involved.

M-3 was Tom Marquez. Tom was the first person that Ross hired when he started EDS and was a very close confidante. He was very bright and perceptive.

I traveled all over southeast Asia in 1970 and 1971 with Tom, following up on the many leads we had after the Christmas Trip and Ross's subsequent appearances. We spent many months in Asia following leads that were not productive but made us more cautious. I learned a lot from Tom. He and his family are true and close friends to ours. He was an extremely talented individual who was instrumental in the growth of EDS.

M-4 is Harry McKillop. Harry was a VP of Braniff Airlines when Ross rented the three planes in December 1969. He became a legend on that and the later trips as he could always get the problem solved. I relished nothing more than working with Harry on a project, as I would know that we could always get it done. Harry was a living legend and went on to work for Ross doing the impossible in his China and Russia ventures in the 1980s and 1990s.

M-5 was me. It was so fun to work and learn from the above-mentioned people and befriend friends with these incredible individuals and Stauffer. The true brilliance of Ross Perot was to find and put together a team like this to get things done on this particular problem.

S-1 was Merv Stauffer, Ross Perot's chief of staff. Merv was a machine. As Ross would tell it, he was so organized he was like a circuit board: you could hear the circuits close as he walked by (this was the greatest compliment I ever heard from Ross).

Merv ran the day-to-day activities for Ross and was also involved in the POW efforts. He did the Paris wives' trip and, initially, set up the San Francisco POW parade before he turned it over to me to plan and operate, because he needed to be in Dallas. He was key to keeping all of our POW activities on track.

Now, going back to Murphy and why I went to work for Ray. Murphy had a chance lunch with Ray in September 1975. Ray told him he wanted to meet with me on a subject. Murphy passed the message on and I called Ray. It was here that Ray wanted to talk to me about a job. He had approached me a couple years earlier, but I told him I could not leave Ross because of what he was going through with the Wall Street problems and I would not leave him.

However, now that Ray's dad had died and he was executor of the will and president of Hunt Oil Company, he said he really would like me to come onboard. This time the time was right, because my work with Ross had become routine, although I loved working with him. Also, Ray and I had become good friends over the past five years and I trusted him. I knew nothing about Hunt Oil or the dynamics of the families. I was ready for a new challenge and was willing to take the risk. Thus, I resigned from EDS and joined Ray on October 8, 1975.

There were many other people who had a great influence on me but were not "career fork decision" makers. Hunt was the last big career fork until I decided to retire. Yet, life is also full of minor "tree forks," which can be a decision that can change your life forever.

A good example of this was when I decided to resign my commission and leave the Air Force. Prior to meeting the EDS recruiter, I had looked at other options. I interviewed with CIA and State Department recruiters. In those days, they had career tests and my results came back that I had an ear for language and would make a good diplomat. I became kind of excited about the Foreign Service.

Thus, I decided to take the Foreign Service exam that was given twice a year. I was to take it in San Antonio on a Saturday in the early fall. Two days before the test, I was invited on a very special hunt by my former boss, who now headed up Special Services for the Air Force. The hunt was to be on a special USAF hunting preserve on Matagorda Island in Texas. Only senior officers and their guests were allowed, but since I was a guest, I was allowed on the island with the generals even though I was a lowly captain. This was a chance of a lifetime and I decided that maybe being a foreign service officer was not my lot. Thus, I canceled my test and went hunting. Had I not done that, I might have landed in the State Department.

I then decided I wanted to get into international banking and enrolled in the Thunderbird School in Phoenix. I was accepted and flew out to check out the school and apartments. We would have taken that route had not Doug Collins caused a fork to point to EDS.

By this example, you can see that there are many opportunities that will come along in your life. I think the key is to prepare yourself so you can take advantage of them.

You will find that you will meet many people in your life's work. I say pick the smart, ambitious, and morally straight ones to associate with. But, again, try not to say a bad thing about someone and always give the credit to someone else. (People will know how smart you are).

RAY AND ROSS

I know this is rambling and want to circle back one last time to share some thoughts on working with Ross and Ray.

First, having known and worked with them for over fifty years, I feel I came to really know, admire, respect, and, most importantly, revere them. Over time, I came to understand their strengths.

Second, because of who they were and what they had accomplished, they rose to the top of the businessman side of the political food chain. Anyone in the upper leadership in the United States would "always return their phone call." This was because of their reputation in the business community as well as of their overall accomplishments (Ross being older was a little earlier, but Ray came along at an accelerated pace). This unlimited access in the United States (and in many other parts of the world) gave them an influence that few had. To this was added the fact that they were not intimidated by anyone and believed in their cause when they made those calls.

Further, unlike a corporate CEO or Wall Street bankers, they were not "ships passing in the night." Those are often executives that are also employees to be retired by sixty-five to clear the field for younger executives. Some, unfortunately, do not act like the employees they are.

Ray and Ross were private owners who had no one telling them what to do (both were majority stockholders: Ross could control EDS and later Perot Systems, while Ray controlled 100 percent of his business). They could use their wealth to try to do good as well as build a great company for their family and employees. Essentially, both had one stockholder controlling the company.

Fortunately, this was the business environment I grew up in. Also, fortunately, I got to work closely with both of them during this period and observe the genius of both.

Further, during this period, I was exposed to and became acquainted with many famous people. My point is that having seen Ross and Ray interact with so many of these leaders, I realized that often Ross and Ray displayed more intelligence, perception and, more importantly, vision, than the ostensible elites they spent time with.

Also, I understood while sitting in the conversations that these strategic visions came through if the conversations allowed for it.

It was an eye-opener for me to see the difference between these two men and those they were meeting with (and this was over fifty years of history). Both Ross and Ray did business in turbulent times and both faced challenges (Ross with Vietnam and Iran and Ray with Yemen and Iraq).

Again, trying to keep my focus on the personalities, I want to first highlight Ross's great qualities as I saw them and then will list Ray's.

Ross

1. Ross had the ability to think six moves ahead on anything he planned. His brain worked like a time machine, which became the key to the success of his first business, EDS. No one thought that far ahead. Ross was a true visionary.

2. Ross was one of the best speakers I ever observed (a master communicator like no other I have heard ... this includes President Reagan). He kept his sentences short and succinct and would paint a canvas that a three-year-old idiot could follow. It reminded me of when I taught at the officer training school ... In my lectures on Simplicity in War, I told the cadets that Napoleon would have an idiot on the general staff. When the generals brought in the "order of battle" plan, Napoleon would ask the idiot to read and explain it. If he could not, then he would then instruct the generals to rewrite it ... it was important that all the troops understand the order of battle. I think Ross instinctively felt this to be important in political America, as evidenced by his simple charts during the 1992 presidential campaign.

3. Ross was persistent. Giving up was not an option, and if he really believed he was right, he had the ability and resources to convince others that he was. If he thought he was right, it was better to get out of his way, as he would make things unpleasant for you if you tried to change his mind.

4. Ross enjoyed the "common hard-working, middle-class people." These were his roots and, although he made billions, he never forgot them. He would always argue for the rights of hard-working people.

5. Ross enjoyed being around the military. He felt our country owed these men and women and their families a debt. This eventually became one of his many causes.

6. Because of his empathy, personality, and vision, he was able to attract great and talented people to help him build a great company. These were

in turn able to attract others who had the same values, culture, persistence, and drive that built EDS and later Perot Systems.

7.   Ross's most brilliant move was to marry Margot Birmingham. This wonderful woman, in my opinion, controlled and inspired him so he could do what he did. I traveled around the world for thirty days with them in 1971 and again for fifteen days in 1973 and saw what an influence she had on him and how much he loved her. They were a team that accomplished a lot and had such a great impact on America. Further, they raised five outstanding children (Ross Jr., Nancy, Suzanne, Carolyn, and Katherine). I witnessed the two older ones growing up and saw the remarkable attention the parents paid to their kids. I was witness on occasion to Ross's raising of Ross Jr. and exposing him to quality education, important personages, impactful national events, and all the unusual training activities he could absorb. Jr. indeed absorbed a lot.

Ross would have me spend time with Ross Jr. when he was in high school and help him with subjects of an international nature. He did not need help, but I could and did more discussion because of my recent experience teaching international affairs to bachelor and master's degree officer trainees at the USAF officer training school. He absorbed this like a sponge.

Further, I helped him with some of the projects that earned him an Eagle Scout Award (which in the mid-to-late twentieth century was among the top honors for a high school student and is still an indicator on how a young woman or man may do in life). I really enjoyed those early years with young Ross, as he really loved and admired his dad and did everything he could to please him. Perot also did something else that really developed young Ross and made him comfortable around famous people.

Ross and Margot would have dinner parties at their estate on Strait Lane for the accomplished and famous when they came through. As a teenager, young Ross would be invited to these dinners and often sat next to the guest of honor, be it a famous banker, CEO of a major company, movie star, or royalty from overseas. On a very, very rare occasion, I would be invited to some of these dinners and I always remember when Ross hosted Lord Mountbatten (later Viceroy of India). Ross Jr. had a very engaging conversation with him, some of which was about the history of World War II. This exposure had to build the young man's self-esteem and, equally important, perception of history.

I often thought about Ross Jr. going into his Saint Mark's history class and correcting his teacher by saying, "I was with Lord Mountbatten the other night and he told me that this was the way the World War II India campaign was conducted." Maybe it did not happen, but I do know that over those years he learned a lot from the Wall Street bankers like David Rockefeller, etc., CEOs, and celebrities that gave him a "degree of confidence and more importantly first-hand knowledge." To this day, Ross Jr. impresses me with his vast knowledge in so many areas and the energy he has to pursue all of his interests. His wife, Sarah, has been a key factor in this too, as she is well educated, smart, beautiful, and an important partner to his success.

Ross Sr. also exposed Jr. to physical training by using his influence with the military to get him into some elite training. Helicopter training was another interest, which prompted young Ross to tell his dad he wanted to be the first to fly in a chopper around the world, which he did, and that helicopter is still in the Smithsonian Museum.

Sorry to get off track here, there is an incredible background of stories to tell about Ross Jr. But I will leave that to Darcy Anderson, Russell Freeman, Mike Berry, Peter Altabef, Dell Williams, Todd Platt, and others. I can assure you it will be rich.

I didn't mean to leave out the daughters, but my exposure to them was limited mostly to Nancy and Carolyn.

I went on the thirty-day world trip I mentioned before with Nancy and have interacted with her over the years in our board meetings and events. She is one of the most composed and controlled women I know and nothing can shake her. She is extremely smart and makes everyone she meets feel like they are the most important person she is talking to for the moment. On the world trip I organized, she was eleven or twelve. Definitely old enough to absorb the thirty days of real time world history, but too young for the dose a malarial medicine I gave her. In those days, we used the weekly dose, which was called Aralen. For adults, it was a pill a week, but for twelve or under, it was half a pill. It took two weeks to figure out, and for those first two weeks, she was always sick the day after the medicine. Once we figured out how I screwed up, she was okay the next day. She was very gracious and this incident became a joke.

When I moved to Hunt and was traveling the world in the oil business, I would take the comfort bag (barf) from an unknown and unique regional airline, fold it up into an envelope form, put a stamp on it, and send it to her. To this day, we laugh about my screw-up.

Carolyn is another Perot daughter I have come to know because of her incredible leadership in developing the Perot Museum of Nature and Science.

I had been a board member of the Dallas Museum of Nature since the mid-1990s. I decided that keeping the museum in the allegedly crime-ridden Fair Park area was a lost cause. I decided to resign from the board, but we had just recently hired a business consultant to become the new director, Nicole Small. We had hired the consulting firm to tell us what we needed to make a great museum and her report set out her vision like a road map. I decided to stay on the board as long as we could get out of Fair Park. Nicole encouraged me and made some bold moves to consolidate the Science Museum and Children's Museum to give the DMNH some bulk. We built the board with visionary people. The top among them was Forrest Hoagland, who was key to building the Houston Museum and graciously led us on how to build a great museum. He gave us the experience and Nicole gave us the leadership. I decided to stay (and to the point, we made a $100,000 contribution) and be on the team.

One of the early things Nicole and I did was to take her dad (who was the doctor who had delivered the five Perot children) with us out to see Ross Sr. We gave a good presentation but at that time, Ross was not into brick and mortar. He was gracious but turned us down.

Nicole and Forrest Hoagland continued to lead us in raising the money and finalizing the design (this is a story in itself). But at one point, Nicole and Carolyn became connected when the Perot children and Margot decided to make a $50 million contribution that opened the floodgates as others in Dallas jumped on the bandwagon to be a part of the fundraising effort. (This is a story about the museum that has not yet been written).

It was during this period I began to see the genius of Carolyn Rathjen. Her leadership as board chairman developed a board and executive team that made the PMNS one of the top sciences and nature museums in the country. She gave Nicole the room and, more importantly, the encouragement to really build a first-class facility. It was her incredible ability to interact with all the players as a conductor would an orchestra that gave Nicole the confidence to make it such a success.

Turning now to the other Perot daughters, both Suzanne and Katherine are accomplished in their own right and are active in Dallas philanthropic activities. Suzanne is the serious one and has her dad's business savvy. When she speaks, the board listens.

Since Katherine was the youngest, I did not get to know her at all until I became a trustee of her trust. However, I first heard of Katherine during the 1992 presidential campaign. A good lawyer friend of mine was volunteering on Ross's presidential campaign and working in the Dallas campaign office. One day he told me that Ross's youngest daughter was working there and was one of the most beautiful girls he had ever seen. If I recall, he increased his volunteer time so he would work there.

Ray

Without a doubt, Ray Hunt and Ross Perot are the individuals who have had the most influence on my life. I was lucky to take those forks and to meet them early. Of course, there were forks during my time working in their areas but my fortunate success was joining them while they were in the early stage of building their respective businesses and knowing that they knew and had respect for each other.

There was an interesting result of this, which I did not see until later. Sharon and I had come to Dallas from towns in Washington State. Sharon was from Spokane and I was from Lynden. We went to the University of Washington and developed relationships with our fraternities, sororities, civic and athletic activity classmates. If I had returned to Seattle, we would have had a network to build on to find a job and UW was the "education gorilla" in the state when it comes to the alumni association.

Because of a chance meeting with Perot, I decided to change my life and convinced Sharon, who was two months, pregnant to follow me to Dallas, knowing we would have to pay for the baby with our $700 of savings. However, we both had confidence in ourselves and I knew we could find jobs somewhere to make ends meet.

The chance meeting with Ross in 1967 and the chance meeting with Ray in 1970 changed our whole life and created a magnificent career for me to work with the two great families of Dallas, if not the United States.

I think the key for me was to get to know all the key players and family members in both families. My first instinct was to cut back on my relationship with Ross after I joined Ray in 1975. (He tried to hire me back on a couple of occasions, even to the point of offering me a company in Florida to run if I would come back. Later, as he got older and even to the last, he would tell Sharon that he did not know how he let me get away).

But I felt I owed him so much, because he gave me the opportunity and then taught me an incredible amount during the seven years that I was with him as an assistant. Thus, I wanted to keep the relationship and would reach out to have lunch on occasion and always try to find an unusual birthday present for him on June 27. (When he turned sixty, I gave him a fossilized tooth from a twenty-five-thousand-year-old mammoth with the note, "Ross, Took a while but I finally found something older than you. Happy Birthday, Tom").

This opened a number of years of old rocks, mammoth tusks, Neanderthal tools, and various other fossil gifts with appropriate comments and sometimes pictures. A few of these are in the Ross Perot Museum. When visiting Perot Group Headquarters, I always looked forward to planning the next gift for his birthday.

Then, during the 1979 Iran revolution, two EDS employees were detained in Iran (a story later documented in Ken Follett's *Wings of Eagles*). Ross called me for my input, as he said the State Department was useless. I gave him my thoughts and then later, Tom Marquez called me on behalf of Ross to ask where Bull Simons was (Bull was the Army colonel I spent time with looking for POWs in Laos in 1973 and 1974).

Because Ray had one hundred thousand acres of timber in north Florida and it was in my area of responsibility, I had kept up a relationship with Bull, who had retired and lived within thirty miles of the timber farm. I gave Tom Marquez Bull's number and, later when he called again, the nearest airstrip.

I then concluded that Ross was going in after his guys ... hell or highwater. This bonded me to him even more, knowing that he would risk later potential lawsuits if any of his volunteers were injured or killed. Also, he was playing with the Logan Act, which he also did with his POW efforts and interfering with US policy.

Now, working with Ray, I realized I could not keep the friendship with Ross a secret. I decided to let him know that Ross was now a close friend and I would not betray anything confidential I had learned from him, and, likewise, that this would apply to my Hunt activities. (Additionally, Ray had called Ross and told him if he needed me Ray would make me available to finish up on projects I had been working on. I think Ross really appreciated this gesture ... a quality of Ray's).

In the business world, this would normally have been instant death but I felt I had a loyalty to both men, although my paycheck came from Ray. My mother had taught me that loyalty to one's friends and their trust were the most important assets you could have. If you lose their trust, you might as well become a crook, a bum, or both.

We have discussed how I joined Ray, so I will not review it other than saying it was absolutely the best decision I ever made. It was based on total trust of Ray, as I did not know anything about Hunt other than what I had read in the papers. Ross told me about the turmoil with the younger and older family when I was leaving, but that did not dissuade me.

Again, sorry for the slow segue to my long, fruitful, and most enjoyable relationship with Ray Hunt and his family. It's just important for me to emphasize that I was so lucky to be at the right place at the right time with the right skills.

As I indicated, I started working with Ray on a US Senate political campaign when Richard Nixon came into Dallas to campaign for George Bush (41) against Lloyd Bentsen. I was the Nixon advance man assigned by the White House and Ray was the Dallas campaign coordinator for Bush's campaign. We met here in November 1970. I also met Jim Oberwetter, Bush's key aide ... Ray later hired both of us, which has become a good story.

The chance encounter in 1970 (caused by Ross agreeing with John Ehrlichman to have me become a Nixon advance man) allowed me to get to know and become friends with Ray over the next five years. During this period, Sharon and Nancy also became close friends.

I devour books and journals to learn and assimilate. Ray is generally not a book reader but he gleaned his data from industry and intelligence reports, broadcasts, newspapers, significant magazines, and meetings with knowledgeable people ... and then could effectively take and massage this data and see six steps ahead (just like Ross).

This made me want to be part of an organization with him. I knew I could give him 100 percent of my talents and would go on the learning curve to give more. That is why I said yes without knowing what was in store in those most exciting forty years from 1975 to 2015. I trusted Ray's instincts and loved being a part of building the new Hunt Oil Company with such great employees. It was a period in the oil and gas business, influenced by politics, when the fluctuation of crude oil and natural gas prices allowed the companies who were willing to take risks to make great amounts of money, if they were not debt-ridden and idle dreamers. Hunt Oil was one of those, through Ray's insight.

Thus, I entered the "oil business" as a friend of the owner and one who had administrative and organizational skills. I knew little about the oil business (I looked at a few deals for Ross before I left but did not fully understand the geology). However, I was not initially hired to make oil and gas decisions.

True, the business fascinated me and I enjoyed the geology courses I took in college. However, petroleum geology became an avocation for me after I joined Hunt. I read anything I could find on the subject and saddled up with our top geologists, geophysicists, engineers, and landmen, taking them to lunch and asking questions. They were always willing to talk to me.

Later, I went out and sat on a well when it was going to be tested so I could understand some of the process. We sat around all night waiting and eating chili out of a can (this was exciting because it was a success and later became the first well in the Crow Field near Grand Saline, Texas).

In my role as administrative officer and overseer of human resources and the non-financial departments, Ray would have me travel with him to all the field offices, where I came to know our people. I would sit in the exploration meetings and sop up the elaborate presentations and arguments on why Ray should put up millions and drill a well. I concluded that geologists are more artists than scientists and have to put a lot of promotion into their presentations. The reason is that in exploration, often they were working with limited data. Nowadays with big and fast computers, the business is different, but back then you had rocks, maybe some nearby well data, 2D seismic, and rumors from other operators. All that may give you a 10 to 20 percent chance of finding commercial oil or gas (making a profit if you did).

One day in my quest for knowledge, I asked four people who they felt would be the most knowledgeable oil finder in Dallas. Charlie Dodge was a name given me so I called him and invited him to lunch at the Dallas Petroleum Club. We had a great lunch and he further enlightened me, but I came away with one interesting comment. When I asked Charlie what makes a great oil finder, his response was that the individual has to "think three dimensionally." As Ray would say, no one ever saw an oil field, since they are deep in the earth, but we all look for them. The oil field is in the mind of geologists.

It has been such a great honor and privilege to be associated with these two great individuals and their Dallas families. Their great abilities to focus on building a great business, concern for their partners, customers, employees, and concern for their community and country made Ross and Ray's businesses both great places to work.

In the early years, after I joined Hunt Oil Company (1975), Ray had just taken over as the president of the company. It was a difficult time as he was trying to stabilize and build the company while at the same time trying to fight off older family members who rejected his role as executor and wanted to hinder him and his plans.

Here was a thirty-one-year-old with a vision and a company with less than a $100 million valuation going against an older half-family that sat on billions by the time Mr. H. L. Hunt passed away. In Mr. Hunt's will, they received 18.5 percent of the collective estate, but they wanted to harass Ray (and Nancy) and ensure he did not use the assets to finance his vision of a new hotel and tower in the rundown west end of Dallas. (This became the very successful Hyatt Regency and Reunion Tower and eventually a transportation center in Dallas and sparked future successful development such as the basketball arena in the rundown area of town).

In fact, it was interesting, as I indicated earlier, that Ross told me when I informed him I was leaving EDS to go with Ray that he was not surprised since he had heard "on the street" that the "brothers" were going after Ray to stop him from doing his strange hotel project at the end of town and using Hunt Oil as collateral. Further, he told me that he was not surprised that Ray tried to hire me, because Ross knew that I would be one that could help him. (Still, Ross was not happy I left).

As I alluded to earlier, Ray eventually took care of this issue by offering to buy out the older family's 18.5 percent interest which became Hunt Energy and a tax exchange. The interesting thing was that because Ray wanted them out of his hair, they felt they could cherry pick the best assets in the company. They took one hundred thousand acres of timber in Florida and oil properties in North Dakota that became valuable thirty-five years later in the oil shale plays but missed a valuable five-thousand-acre property in the Gulf of Mexico (Eugene Island 69) that became the cash flow bedrock for the rebirth of Hunt Oil Company as a major independent. The oil field found here gave Ray the capital to expand the company and eventually, to find 2 billion BOE (barrels of oil equivalent) in Yemen and put Hunt on the board as a player in the world of major oil finders.

Now, there were a lot of investments that built Hunt Consolidated, Inc. (HCI became the holding company for Hunt Oil Company and Ray's other six companies defined by their businesses) over the period from 1975 to 2015 (my time as executive board member). Later, there were other significant successes, but I feel Yemen was of such magnitude of cash flow that it gave Ray the confidence to invest in other areas of business. (Hunt expanded into LNG, electrical power, alternative energy investments, ranch and land investments, private equity, and new real estate development partnerships).

Further, the success in Yemen gave Hunt Oil Company and Ray a reputation as a world oil finder. One party most interested was the US government. Both the Central Intelligence Agency and the US Central Command—the joint military command responsible for the Middle East countries and located at MacDill AFB in Florida—contacted us for information as Hunt operated with employees throughout Yemen, still relatively little known even though the country controlled the access to the Red Sea and the Gulf of Arabia.

Further, we were one of the first US companies to go to Communist China (starting in 1979) and our government wanted to debrief us on our many return trips. In the 1980s, I was traveling a lot to Yemen and China and later to the USSR, Albania, Laos, Somalia, Sudan, and a number of other countries that our intelligence agencies were interested in. It was during this period that local agents with the CIA would want to debrief us on our thoughts and observations (particularly after my many China trips). Also, I would meet with the intelligence officials of Central Command, speaking to them about Yemen and other Arab countries where we traveled.

Central Command was most interesting, as I would arrange for Ray to fly to McDill every time they had a change of command to meet the new general in charge and spend the day with him and his staff to discuss our experiences. (It was a great learning experience for us and for them too). The first one was General Norman Schwarzkopf. Also, during this period, I was invited to several symposiums they put on concerning what was going on in the Middle East.

I do not mean to go through a diatribe on the growth of the business because this is not a history of Hunt Oil/Consolidated, but I would like to point out my observations about Ray.

Ray is one of those rare multidimensional thinkers. He weighs the economic, political, community, employee, and international impact of the decisions he makes. I still enjoy observing his mind working on a problem or question. It is like watching an electrical circuit as he goes through the process.

Ray is an oil finder first and loves that role. He has his dad's gene to effectively calculate odds. He would try to maximize the use of other people's money, but followed the maxim that if you had a gut feeling, keep a larger portion for yourself. But in the last few decades of the twentieth century, finding commercial oil and gas was a risk if you were putting your own money into it. Dry holes and multi-million-dollar losses were common. However, Ray had some big finds during that period and the cash flow allowed him to expand and build Hunt into a multi-billion-dollar company.

In the nonbusiness realm, architecture and design was, I believe, a second love for Ray. I helped him do internal design in one building headquarters (1989) and a total building design for a new headquarters (2007). He was very actively involved in every facet of these buildings. He had a great design executive, Judy Pesek (with Gensler, which was the top design firm in the country) with whom he worked. It was like music to see them work together.

Ray has an uncanny ability to understand geology, engineering, and the geopolitics of a prospect and yet keep the risk in mind. In our many exploration meetings in the company, he would calculate the odds based on the data presented and make the decision to commit money to drill or not. Again, I think this was a risk gene he inherited from his dad that allowed him to calculate odds.

A case in point ... we used to have business hunting weekends with our partners, bankers, and customers, etc. on some of the ranches and farms he owned around the country. When Ray would attend, we would sometimes play poker after the meals and discussions.

On one occasion, we flew the top Dallas security officials down to South Texas for a white wing dove hunting weekend (the head of our security, Walt Coughlin, invited the top executives of the local FBI, CIA, ATF, and county sheriff and police officials, etc.).

As a group, they loved poker (and it was my experience that they were better at it than the bankers). On this occasion, we had a wild poker game and, by the end of the evening, Ray had cleaned everyone off the table.

Before I went to bed, he called me and told me to return each and everyone's losses, because he considered it a friendly game (and did not want to deprive our top Dallas security leaders of their hard-earned money). I divided it up since I did not know who had lost what. It blew their minds, but they took it and many gained a new respect for Ray as a person.

Ray is a tremendous people person. With employees and partners, he would take time to visit and thank them for what they did. He would always act like he was not in a hurry and would apologize if he would have to leave.

Ray's standard comment when he would call someone was, "I hope I'm not interrupting anything ... pause ... and if so, I will be brief, or I can call you back." Doing so made the person on the other end feel important.

In the early days before email emerged in the '90s, Ray would send a signed thank you memo to anyone who had done something important or significant. He had three assistants, one of whom was dedicated to this function. His mind is such that he can dictate the perfect letter as if he sees the whole thing in his head before he begins dictation.

Once emails entered the scene, they became "the thank you coin of the realm," but his were always expressed like a formal letter. Later Ray would type his own emails but they would be dedicated to brief instructions or acknowledgements that did not warrant a formal thank you.

Following are some of Ray's admirable traits I have observed over fifty-plus years:

1.   I worked for Ray for forty years (and knew him for fifty-plus and ongoing). As time went on, many knew I was associated with him. In all those years, I have never heard one bad word spoken about Ray (and if I did, I probably would have punched the person in the nose). Consistently, people would say how they admired him and how lucky I was to be associated with him and his company.

2. As I mentioned earlier, I think his brain works at a different level and speed. It would fascinate me in our meetings to observe how his mind would work on a problem. Often, we would reach the same conclusions but his conclusion seemed more "polished."

3. Ray and Nancy are a very giving couple who have done so much for Dallas … They have made a mark on the city without any desire for recognition. Ray's willingness to roll up his sleeves and take on and lead projects sets him apart when working on charitable, political, or "solve the problem" campaigns in Dallas. Ross was the same way.

4. One example is when Ray dug into the problems of his beloved university, SMU, when there were alumni problems in the early 1980s after the football scandal. He led the board to find a first-rate new president (Ken Pye), who began to bring the school back on track. Later, he was responsible for recruiting R. Gerald Turner, who has brought SMU to a new level. His influence on and behind the board has helped make the school a first-rate college in the United States.

5. In 2009 he was asked to lead a fundraising campaign to get the George W. Bush Library at SMU. He did and, as a result, they raised $500 million to make it the best presidential library center in the United States.

6. In the early 1990s, he was asked to come up with ideas and lead a group of Dallas leaders to develop the city to become a top medical center in the country. He did this, and today, Dallas is one of the top areas for people to come for medical treatment.

7. On political campaigns, he was a key fundraiser for the Bush families as well as some other candidates who either won local or state elections or lost out in the national election. Ray would take an active role in supporting candidates if he felt it would be good for the city, state, or nation.

8. As I mentioned, Ray is a very humble person and does not want people (who will defer to his station) to fawn over him. He will carry his own bags and help others when there is a problem. If he sees someone that seemingly has a problem in a public place, he will be there first to offer physical assistance or direct the effort to help. He and Nancy are the most gracious people we know. They see their role as being to help and serve and not take.

9. Ray does not have any real hobbies. Running his vast businesses and knowing what's going on in the national and international arena is his hobby. I think he needs a hobby … maybe invest in an inexpensive orchestra on the condition he becomes the conductor.

10. He has hunted and fished, but often these outings were in the mode to promote our business. I was on all of these trips and our guests, as I commented earlier, included three secretaries of state, one US president, two CIA directors, one secretary of defense, a chairman of the Joint Chiefs of Staff, a leader of Desert Storm in 1991, US senators, a prominent movie star, NFL athletes, and many top corporation CEOs. While Ray really enjoyed these trips, hunting or fishing was a byproduct. For me, it was a way to see some of these leaders and learn in the many discussions we would have around tables or campfire about the roles they played and decisions they made or, more importantly, the opinions they expressed. I think that these annual long weekends between 1980 and 2015 really helped further expose me to this level of people and their thinking. (I had dealt with people like them on the campaigns and while advancing also, but that was a different generation). It also allowed me to match readings, business travel, and knowledge to the conversations over the campfires. Ironically, on rare occasions, I felt I knew more on some given subjects than some of them did, which made me be more careful in some of the conversations.

11. Ray is a very caring husband and father. He dotes on Nancy and will do anything for her. They are very much in love and he always kisses her when he greets her. They love their kids and prioritize them. Sharon and I love being around them and the family. We occasionally have Thanksgiving with them. Ray has a special way of doing his turkey, by putting the twenty-pound bird in the BBQ smoker and wrapping five pounds of bacon around it. As the turkey cooks, he will remove strips of the cooked bacon and add new strips. The turkey is always so good and moist.

A good example of Ray and Nancy's commitment to a project was at South Padre Island. They have a property down there, as do we and our good friends, Mike and Sandy Boswell. In about 2007 Ray and Nancy and the Boswells were concerned about the antics of the city government, where it seemed elected officials favored local people in the tax rolls and were doing some questionable city sales transactions. Ray decided to address this, and his lawyers set up an organization called Property Owners Who Care (POWC) and put Mike and me on the board. Initially, the intent was to be an advocate group for the many thousands of property owners who did not live on the island and, thus, could not vote on issues that affected their property. Ray set up a Political Action Committee (PAC) headed by Mike and which Ray funded that could be used for campaign contributions for city candidates. He then funded the POWC and hired staff and provided a budget to operate.

It took a while to get it up and running with credibility (as some of the islanders who opposed this were living off some of the graft instilled by the existing city government).

The first thing Ray and his new organization did was tackle a purchase agreement that the city made to buy seven acres of land from a prominent developer for $5 million. We looked at the transaction and knew something was wrong since three acres of the land was tidal floodplain. Ray hired two different appraisal firms, who came up with $2.1 million and $2.4 million respectively, on the value of the parcel …. not the $5 million the city officials agreed to pay. He then publicized the results and very soon the offer was withdrawn. Later, we found out that two of the city officials were partners with the developer.

These actions and others now gave POWC some credibility and the organization grew to become an influence on South Padre Island, where we would hold quarterly meetings. Here, members (now four hundred strong) could discuss issues and hear their elected represented officials comment on their campaign pledges.

Now, because of their love and history with the island community, Ray and Nancy decided to invest more in the island and commit to making it more of a family-friendly place. They bought five acres in the heart of the entertainment district and began developing it for family-style activities. Nancy took two acres and made an incredible park out of it where families can come down and watch the sunsets and have picnic dinners, dinner at the Painted Marlin, or ice cream across the street. She also set up an incubator facility for SPI artists who could have space to work and show their art. Working with local experts, she created a business course for artists to train them how to live off and sell their art.

Additionally, Ray and Nancy purchased two giant, sixteen-foot diameter propellers from the USS *Independence*, which was a postwar Navy aircraft carrier that participated in US battles from Vietnam to conflicts in the 1990s (as it was being cut up nearby for junk). These magnificent tons of brass were placed in the park (at a cost of over $300,000) so visitors and, especially winter Texans (many of whom are veterans), could see that some dignity was left of this once great ship.

I could go on and on about the great things that Ray and Nancy and Ross and Margot have done to better our society but I will leave that to another writer as these are stories in themselves.

NOTES IN 2020

As I write this in 2020, we are in a mandated stay at home mode because of a world pandemic caused by a new, very infectious flu virus sourced in China and rapidly spreading throughout the world. Tanya is confined to an apartment in Quebec City, Nick in an apartment in Eugene, Oregon, and Amanda in her apartment in Dallas. Distancing, frequently washing your hands, and wearing masks were the rules if you want to go out.

We have been very lucky during this period. We are basically staying at the farm in College Mound, Texas. Farm life is wonderful and we are not confined to our farm. We do come into our Dallas home for a couple of days a week to pick up our Amazon-ordered supplies and replenish our food. Amanda is our caregiver, ensuring that we have what we need. Our farm manager, Chris Rotan, gets us our farm supplies.

We were very fortunate to have a comfortable place to hole up. We bought the farm fourteen years ago and added improvements over the years. My thinking was to create a property that would be easy to sell to a "survivalist" from Dallas who would want an escape where he could survive off the grid and live off the land if chaos came to Dallas.

Thus, we built a house, an art studio, a barn with a shop, a work out studio, and an equipment shed for the two tractors, bobcat, two gators, mower, chipper, and accessories. For food, we have pecan trees and fruit trees (pear, peach, plum, fig, and apricot) and installed an automated greenhouse with five separate raised gardens for our tomatoes, onions, peppers, and summer squash. Also, we have a lake and two ponds teeming with fish. We have engineered the property for wildlife that can be used for food. For power, we have the grid, diesel backup, and solar backup. Also, we use geothermal for heat and air.

For recreation, we have a shooting range, a hand ax–throwing range, a golf driving range, miles of trails, a celestial telescope, a fire pit, beautiful woods to explore, and a drone (plus the art studio and wood-working tools). Also, we have Netflix, farm chores and projects.

Thus, there is never a want for something to do.

NOTES TO NICK AND AMANDA

I believe you are entering a new world. When I grew up in the 1950s and early 1960s, the work philosophy was that if you put in more productive time than the next person, you would get ahead just because you had more learning exposure in the profession. (In the words of Ben Franklin: Early to bed, early to rise will make a young person strong, wealthy, and wise).

Throughout my career, I would get into the office at 7 a.m. (after working out at the Cooper gym from 5:15 to 6:30) and get home by 7 p.m. if I was not traveling, which was a good percentage of the time. I now know this was selfish of me, since I did not spend a lot of mealtimes other than weekends with Tanya and Gar. Because of travel, I did not become a coach for the kids' teams. I did drop golf and took up tennis at 7:30 a.m. on Saturdays so I could be back home by 9:30 a.m. when all were awake so I could spend more weekend time with the family, although there were many Saturday mornings when I worked.

This did permit me to advance my career so we could afford to send our kids to great colleges and allow them to travel the world and buy them anything they needed.

Nick and Amanda, I feel the world you are entering is so different and the general desire to become rich should not be a driver of your lives. Where you live, quality of life, friends, and adequate income to take care of your needs and maybe some surplus to buy something special or travel is important. But on top of this, I believe your generation will have unemployment, medical care, and retirement income to be taken care of by the government. Ironically, this is what we had when I was in the United States Air Force and, if I had made it a career, we would have been very comfortable, but I wanted more so I resigned my commission.

To me, the key is for you to be happy in whatever you do. Do not let money or what you think your friends think of your job versus theirs influence your choices. Do something fun that will make you want to go to work each day. It is important to give to those less fortunate and to the earth that is being ravaged. Life is shorter than you think.

Take care of your family.

EPILOGUE

TO NICK AND AMANDA SOME THOUGHTS ON LIFE

This final chapter is intended to leave you with some of my thoughts on life, the important ones that I have learned in over eighty years. There are scores of books out there, and it seems that a lot of successful people have their little book of recommendations for leadership, happiness, or success. These are just my thoughts to my grandchildren as they start their careers in life.

Obviously, the people who have the most influence on a person in the early and formative years are their parents, grandparents, uncles and aunts, selected teachers, neighbors and some fellow students. There are others but I will not dwell on this other than to say my mom was one of the smartest people I have known and my dad one of the most perceptive. From them, I got the basics of my personality, yearning for knowledge, and the "trust but verify" attitude.

While in the military, one of my bosses was a wily old colonel, Frank Taylor. I really admired and liked him. He would give me sage advice that would stick with me, such as "you only need math and English. Math that develops your thinking and English to be able to explain what you thought to others."

My mother, when I was growing up, would caution me that if I did not have something good to say about someone, I should say nothing at all. Colonel Taylor's take was that if you say something bad, it will probably get back to the person you talked about. So, don't.

I realized, thus, at an early age that if you want to make trusting friends, do not say ugly things about others. I think what I learned was to try to be friends with everyone even though there may be differences. Learn to compromise. Good friends will be important to you all through life.

The following are the seven traits that I deem important and that have helped me in my career:

1. PEOPLE PERSON. A trait that helped me through my life and business career. This also included treating everyone as an equal, no matter the occasion; recognizing individuals for accomplishments that are important to them; knowing that making people feel important and worthwhile can pay great dividends (as long as you are sincere). It is

important to take time to talk and listen to people. (Nancy Hunt is the master of this and could write a book on it).

Essentially, you need to show that you really like people and, if true, this will come out. Almost everything I have ever done has been through or with other people. Thus, my philosophy of being a "people person" is the most important trait you can have. But it has to be genuine. You must show true empathy to others who are hurting. Your Mimi is a master at this. A byproduct of this is that you will find true friends and this is one of the most important things a person can have and gather through life.

2. PERSISTENCE. If you have a conviction, don't give up. Most people give up if the going gets too tough. I have learned that if you keep focused and want the objective badly enough, you will probably succeed. Ray Hunt and Ross Perot were overflowing with this trait and I think it was one reason why they were so successful.

3. HUMOR. One of the smartest and wittiest guys I know is Doug Stewart. Doug is Canadian and we met him and his delightful wife, Huguette, on a cruise. He was a successful businessman who sold his business for a zillion dollars. They have homes and a ranch in Arizona and British Columbia and travel the world. Doug has set himself the goal to make someone laugh each day. And he is a master at it.

A case in point: We were in a ship elevator (while sailing around West Africa) with Doug and Huguette. On the elevator with us was a tall, elderly gentleman with his wife. The door opened up and a couple gets off and the gentleman's wife mistakenly follows them. She catches herself and comes back on the elevator and the old guy comments, "She will follow anyone off an elevator." Doug immediately responds with "Is that how you found her?" The comment brought everyone in the large elevator to their knees, even the couple.

My point is to try to use humor in your everyday life, as long as it is not crude and does not hurt someone. Humor with stories is very effective in building relationships. Jim Baker (our former secretary of state, treasury, and chief of staff for two) is one of the best storytellers I have ever heard. Because he has become a friend and I have hunted with him for over sixteen years, I have grown to appreciate his talent to tell a funny story. Actually, over the years, I have heard him tell the same story many times and I actually laugh harder each time he tells it because of how he has mastered the art of storytelling. I would try to learn these skills.

4. KEEP YOURSELF WELL INFORMED. (Reading and watching to acquire knowledge and current information.) Obviously, the internet can give you the news headlines but I still believe in reading the major publications like the *Economist*, the *New York Times*, *Wall Street*

Journal, and other leading print that can give you a more balanced version (even their own versions). I think most TV talking heads are now biased as they have become politically divided like the country. This may change as your generation tires of the biased reporting and the public does not adapt its appetite for news to headlines and short comments. An informed citizen is the key to a successful democracy. And a good educational system for all is the key to informed citizens.

Social media, in my opinion, is not, generally, comprised of truly informed sources and Twitter has become a way for one to blast out an opinion without substantiation. It is tough to put a good thought or analysis in a limited space.

There are many sources and they may evolve into more efficient service, but remember, current events often have no real pattern and so the pundits that give you your information are often news readers who read information pulled together by TV analysts who often do not have all the facts and are working on a tight schedule. Don't always believe 100 percent of what you see on TV or Google. Question in your mind what you see.

In essence, keep yourself informed. I think the best way to do so in the international arena is to read good books on history, cultures, and economics. This is a lot of reading of selected books but, eventually, this will provide you the canvas that will allow you to place the events of today in a current and historical perspective.

I have done this reading for over fifty years in the areas of Europe, Africa, Latin America, Asia, and the Middle East (additionally, I have traveled to most of these places). Thus, when I read about events in the papers or hear something on TV or the internet, I have a lot of "dots" that I can connect to get a clearer picture of what may be happening even though the facts are still out there.

It is really an avocation for me since I feel with my background in current reading, education, experience, and travel, I have a general feel of what is happening. I also know I do not know the cultures involved well enough to have a real valid opinion. Again, you need to keep yourself informed if you have an interest in what is going on in your country or culture. And do not think we can take our Jeffersonian Democracy and overlay it into cultures in other countries.

This is what I learned in nine years during the Vietnam War and working over thirty years in the Middle East. In both cases, our political leaders did not understand the language or the culture of the enemy or how to deal with the needs of people in those countries.

5. ENJOY WHAT YOU DO. Do not be concerned about what others think (unless it is immoral, illegal, or illogical). Thus, select a job that is fun but pays enough to take care of your needs. If the job is fun, you will do well. I have been fortunate in that I do not recall a day that I did not enjoy going to work in the USAF, EDS, or Hunt. Although, obviously, some days were more fun than others, all were inside the fun needle.

    Life is shorter than you think and you should decide where you want to be in that tunnel of life. Ross had a Thoreau saying on the wall of his office that really affected me … It read, "The majority of men lead lives of quiet desperation." Think about this and do not be trapped in a job you will hate for thirty years.

6. HOBBIES AND HEALTHY LIFESTYLE. These will round out your life. There are a lot to choose from and it makes one's life more balanced. You should establish a good exercise program that becomes an integral part of your life. Find some hobbies that test your skills and knowledge. Do something outside your comfort zone to charge your batteries. Follow a healthy eating habit. Tanya is a good teacher for how to do this. (A good filet twice a month won't hurt you).

7. FAITH should be a part of your life. There are various religions and sects of each. Find one that works for you. Faith will give you comfort in times of need to enrich your life and give you confidence in times of stress. I talk to God daily. I have found it to be a very important part of my life.

Now there are many other pieces of advice I can give you but there are any number of books that elaborate on them. It is your choice.

To me, the key is for you to be happy in whatever you do. Again, do not let money or what you think your friends think about your job versus theirs influence your choices. Do something fun that will make you want to go to work each day. You will excel if you enjoy it.

It is also important to give to those less fortunate and "take care of our earth."

And again, take care of your family.

INDEX

Currency collected by the author in over 50 years of travel.